Rulin waishi

and Cultural Transformation

in Late Imperial China

HARVARD-YENCHING INSTITUTE

MONOGRAPH SERIES 59

Rulin waishi

and Cultural Transformation

in Late Imperial China

Shang Wei

Published by the Harvard University Asia Center
for the Harvard-Yenching Institute and
distributed by Harvard University Press
Cambridge (Massachusetts) and London, 2003

Printed in the United States of America

The Harvard-Yenching Institute, founded in 1928 and headquartered at Harvard University, is a foundation dedicated to the advancement of higher education in the humanities and social sciences in East and Southeast Asia. The Institute supports advanced research at Harvard by faculty members of certain Asian universities and doctoral studies at Harvard and other universities by junior faculty at the same universities. It also supports East Asian studies at Harvard through contributions to the Harvard-Yenching Library and publication of the *Harvard Journal of Asiatic Studies* and books on premodern East Asian history and literature.

Shang, Wei.
    Rulin waishi and cultural transformation in late imperial China / Shang Wei.
      p. cm. -- (Harvard-Yenching Institute Monograph series ; 59)
    Includes bibliographic references and index.
    ISBN 0-674-01095-7 (cloth : alk. paper)
      1. Wu, Jingzi, 1701–1754. Ru lin wai shi. 2. Confucianism in literature. 3. Confucianism--Rituals. 4. China--Intellectual life--1644–1912. I. Title. II. Series.

    PL2732.U22R837 2003
    895.1'348--dc21   2003044972

Index by the author

♾ Printed on acid-free paper

Last number below indicates year of this printing
13 12 11 10 09 08 07 06 05 04 03

To Xin

Acknowledgments

This book has gradually grown into its present shape. It was intended to be a comprehensive study of *Rulin waishi* (The unofficial history of the scholars), an eighteenth-century landmark of the literati novel, but since the novel is deeply embedded in the intellectual and literary discourses of its time, I have had to grapple with the mid-Qing debates over ritual and ritualism, the construction of history, narrative, and lyricism. My research reveals *Rulin waishi* as both a product and a powerful response by a Confucian intellectual to cultural transformation in late imperial China—transformation that eventually brought to an end the Confucian world order. As such, Wu Jingzi's (1701–54) ironic portrait of literati and their predicaments provides a unique perspective on a number of issues essential to the contemporary academic disputes over eighteenth-century culture and intellectual discourse: Why did ritual itself become a problem in a Confucian society presumably guided by ritualistic norms? Why did Confucian reformers conceive of evidential scholarship as the most effective means for reversing the discursive trend of Song and Ming Neo-Confucian orthodoxy and restoring the textual integrity of the Confucian classics? Simply put, why did the problem of "history" become such a fundamental concern for Chinese intellectuals of the time? And why and how did the vernacular novel become an important medium for them to voice social criticism and moral consciousness? In my study of *Rulin waishi*, I seek to answer these questions through intensive historical research on the intellectual and literary trends of the mid-eighteenth century as well as through a close reading of the novel itself. I will argue that Wu Jingzi's search for alternatives from within the Confucian tradition and his relentless self-questioning in *Rulin waishi* represent a new height of moral imagination in late imperial China.

I am indebted to many people for aid in the research and writing of this book. First of all, I thank Patrick Hanan for his support and guidance throughout various stages of research and writing, and Stephen Owen for his insights and inspirations. My thanks are also due Ellen Widmer, Joanna Handlin Smith, Robert Ashmore, Sophie Volpp, Roger Hart, Rania Huntington, Feng Xiang, and Wang Yuejin, who read part of the earlier version of this book and suggested many useful changes. I am especially grateful to David Der-wei Wang for his insightful comments on the manuscript, and to Haruo Shirane and Tomi Suzuki for their consistent support. Paul Anderer went through the manuscript with care and offered suggestions for several major changes; Robert Hymes and Dorothy Ko made thoughtful comments on the Introduction, which helped to clarify my presentation of Confucian ritual. During the final stages, the manuscript received a careful reading from David Rolston, whose expert comments have strengthened it in both argument and presentation. Judith Zeitlin sent me comments on Part IV. Anthony Yu generously shared with me his ideas on this and my other projects. Theodore Huters, Wilt Idema, and two anonymous readers of the Harvard University Asian Center offered many suggestions for expanding the scope of the manuscript. I thank them for all their generous help.

For fellowship and sabbatical support in the early stage of research for this book, as well as in the later stages of writing it, I thank the Harvard-Yenching Institute and the Chiang Ching-kuo Foundation. Parts of this study have been presented at the University of Washington in Seattle, the University of Pennsylvania, Columbia University, Harvard University, Beijing University, Yangzhou Normal University, and the Annual Meeting of the Association for Asian Studies in Washington, D.C. I appreciate the support of David Knechtges, C. T. Hsia, Victor Mair, Lydia Liu, Qianshen Bai, Stephen West, Wai-yee Li, Peter Bol, Kang-i Sun Chang, Madeleine Zelin, and Keith McMahon, with whom I have discussed this project. Chen Meilin and Li Hanqiu have been very responsive to my letters concerning *Rulin waishi* and other related subjects. My appreciation also goes to Wu Ge of Fudan University Library, who sent me a photocopy of the title page of the 1803 edition of *Rulin waishi*, and to Zhou Weipei and Li Zhongming, who went an extra mile to provide me with photographs of Nanjing local gazetteers. I thank Ko Ch'ing-ming and Chang Shu-hsiang for conversations on lyricism, which led me to write the Epilogue. Wang Hui deserves a special acknowledgment for sharing with me his studies of the intellectual history of the late imperial era. As always, I am greatly indebted to Yuan Xing-pei and Lin Geng, my teachers at Beijing University, for nurturing my interest in Chinese literature and providing guidance for my studies of medieval Chinese poetry. Their encouragement has long been a source of inspiration for me.

My thanks also go to Leslie Kriesel for a careful editing of the manuscript; John Ziemer has done more than expected of an editor by providing comments on both the presentation and the contents of the manuscript. Their editing has spared me of many errors and improved the manuscript in various ways. My special thanks are due Chen Weigang, with whom I have discussed this and other projects. I was inspired by his vision and insights at every stage of writing, and his friendship and encouragement have been a major factor in the completion of this book. Finally, and most deeply, I am indebted to my wife, Xin, for her understanding and unfailing support. To her this book is dedicated.

A portion of Part I, "Ritual and the Crisis of the Confucian World," first appeared as "Ritual, Ritual Manuals, and the Crisis of the Confucian World: An Interpretation of *Rulin Waishi*," *Harvard Journal of Asiatic Studies* 58, no. 2 (1998): 373–424, and is reprinted here with permission of the editors.

S.W.

Contents

Reference Matter

Rulin waishi

and Cultural Transformation

in Late Imperial China

Introduction

Rulin waishi (The unofficial history of the scholars) is a familiar work to readers of the premodern Chinese novel. Composed by Wu Jingzi (1701–54) during the last two decades of his life, it is, in the estimation of many commentators, one of the highest achievements of the Chinese novel, on the same level as the contemporary *Honglou meng* (Dream of the red chamber *or* The story of the stone).[1] An ironic portrait of literati life, *Rulin waishi* was unprecedented in offering a comprehensive display of the degeneration of literati mores, the predicament of official institutions, and the Confucian elite's futile struggle to reassert moral and cultural authority. As a refined piece of artistic elaboration and narrative innovation, it also introduced a model of the novel that has inspired and intrigued many since its publication in 1803.

Rulin waishi's prominent place in premodern Chinese literature is attributable largely to its status as the culmination of the literati novel. From the sixteenth century, as the literati experienced increasing division and fragmentation as a social group, they became more interested in the vernacular

---

1. For an English translation, see *The Scholars*, trans. Yang Hsien-yi and Gladys Yang. I use this translation with certain modifications. For the Chinese edition of *Rulin waishi*, I use Li Hanqiu, ed., *"Rulin waishi" huijiao huiping ben*. Following other scholars of premodern Chinese literature, I use the word "novel" to describe long narrative stories, primarily fictional and in most cases written in the vernacular of the time and divided into multiple chapters. The Chinese term *xiaoshuo* covers a wider range of narrative genres than does "novel."

novel, despite its non-elite status and popular stance; their editing of inherited narrative materials, as well as commentaries on them, provided the elite with a medium for social comment and self-expression. Critics have long noted that literati authors and commentators of the sixteenth and seventeenth centuries played a crucial role in the transformation of the vernacular novel. However, it was not until the eighteenth century that this process reached a new stage, as can be seen in an array of works: Lü Xiong's (ca. 1642–1723) Nüxian waishi (The unofficial history of the female immortal), Wu Jingzi's Rulin waishi, Cao Xueqin's (1715?–63) The Story of the Stone, Li Baichuan's (ca. 1721–71) Lüye xianzong (Tracks of an immortal on the green field), Xia Jingqu's (1705–87) Yesou puyan (Humble words of an old rustic), Li Lüyuan's (1707–90) Qilu deng (Warning light at the crossroads), and Tu Shen's (1744–1801) Yinshi (The history of the bookworm).[2]

These novels do not form a subgenre or conform to a single narrative mode, but they do share certain features that indicate the emergence of a new kind of social perception and a new mode of literary production. All were written by individual literati authors for a literati audience, and all deal with literati concerns, more often than not with an exquisite display of the autobiographical.[3] Following the lead of a handful of predecessors in the seventeenth century, the eighteenth-century literati novelists greatly changed the way the vernacular novel was created, circulated, and received. Rather than taking advantage of commercial publishing, they often allowed their works to be transmitted in manuscript form and so generated a sense of communality through interaction with their immediate readers.[4] As a

---

2. Unlike the other novels in this list, Yinshi is written primarily in classical Chinese. To this list one might well add Li Ruzhen's (1763–1830?) Jinghua yuan (Flowers in the mirror), a work Li began writing in the last decade of the eighteenth century but did not complete until 1815.

3. Unlike such earlier novels as San'guo yanyi (The romance of the Three Kingdoms) and Shuihu zhuan (The water margin), which are derived from both history and folk literature and have undergone revision by more than one hand, each of these eighteenth-century novels is the product of an individual author. Rather than relying on oral or written sources of history and folk literature about historical personages and heroic adventures, each novel draws on its author's own erudition, experience, and imagination. Although in the previous two centuries, literati authors and editors had found various ways of addressing their concerns through the form of the vernacular novel, it was only during the eighteenth century that the literati asserted themselves as both authors and subjects; their novels of self-representation demonstrate an elite learning and sensibility that tend to preclude readership by the less-educated classes.

4. As shown in the cases of Rulin waishi and The Story of the Stone, composing such a novel required a long-term, even a lifelong, devotion; it hardly brought the literati novelist any fi-

result, each novelist formed around himself a small circle of readers, which might overlap with other circles. Scattered and limited as these groups were, they did produce a discourse in the forms of a vernacular novel and fiction commentaries on it that were closely engaged with the intellectual concerns of the time and often drew on the repository of literati learning, especially ritualism and the evidential scholarship of ancient texts and institutions.[5]

The literati novels helped to shape the literary and intellectual landscape of late imperial China. Among the questions this development raises are

---

nancial gain or advanced his official career, if he had one. Generally speaking, these literati novels were written and circulated outside the official world and the marketplace. They do not constitute part of official writing, nor are they commercial productions. It should be noted that in earlier periods, such literati as Feng Menglong (1574–1646) and Li Yu (1611–80) did become what might be called professional writers or editors. They wrote and edited literary texts for the market and were even involved in commercial publishing. But this was no longer true of most of the eighteenth-century literati novelists, whose works were often published posthumously, as in the case of *Rulin waishi*, *The Story of the Stone*, *Humble Words of an Old Rustic*, and *Warning Light at the Crossroads*. Although the vernacular novel as a genre was still not commonly held in high esteem during the eighteenth century, literati novels often generated great enthusiasm among specific literati groups. They were usually transmitted among a small circle of the author's friends and acquaintances in handwritten form, and they often elicited immediate responses and comments, some of which were in turn reflected in the author's revised version. Although published in 1711, *The Unofficial History of the Female Immortal*, which was probably the first vernacular novel entitled a *waishi*, was never truly popular. But Lü Xiong, a man of letters who drifted from one secretarial job to another in provincial and district government, managed to assemble comments on his manuscript (and prefaces to it as well) from more than sixty literati of the time, including such leading intellectuals, playwrights, and artists as Wang Shizhen (1634–1711), Hong Sheng (1645–1704), and Zhu Da (1624–1705). Although these commentators came from different regions and may not have known one another, the earliest printed edition of the novel brought them together and conjured up an imagined community of literati readers. Wu Jingzi did not go as far as Lü Xiong in promoting his novel, but he found his own way of engaging his circle of literati friends in Nanjing: not only did he re-create himself in the novel and model some major characters on his friends, he also shared his manuscript with those friends. Like *Rulin waishi*, Cao Xueqin's *The Story of the Stone* drew on his own experience. He also circulated his manuscript among his relatives and intimate friends, who were familiar with its references. Occasionally, he had to revise his manuscript to accommodate their objections.

5. Several eighteenth-century novels, as scholars have noticed, are the products of interaction with the intellectual ethos of the regions in which they were written; see Roddy, *Literati Identity and Its Fictional Representation*; and Wang Qiongling, *Qingdai si da caixue xiaoshuo*. Adopting Lu Xun's characterization of some Qing dynasty literati novelists as using the *xiaoshuo* form to show off their learning, scholars have often used the term "scholarly novel" to designate these works; see Lu Xun, *Zhongguo xiaoshuo shilüe*, pp. 294–96.

What accounts for the literati's increasing enthusiasm for writing and reading these novels? Does this enthusiasm indicate a conscious effort by literati to evoke an imagined community of critical discourse outside the official world? If so, why did the literati novelists forgo commercial publication? What constitutes the bases and sources of their social and cultural criticism, and how far does their critical discourse go, given their alleged loyalty to Confucian tenets? If literati authors were interested merely in recovering their moral and cultural hegemony, how can we explain the ironic stance that often characterizes their works?

My aim is to contribute to our understanding of these issues through a close reading of *Rulin waishi*. To put my analysis into perspective, I begin with recent discussions of the cultural transformation of late imperial China.

Iconoclasm or Ritualism

Eighteenth-century China was sandwiched between two momentous ages: the Manchu conquest and the western impact. The latter took place amid internal turmoil—the crumbling of the Confucian elite and the disintegration of local society—that signaled the decline of the Qing empire (1644–1911) and the beginning of the modern era. Although the Manchu conquest is of less historical consequence, the fall of the Ming (1368–1644) was the cause of much soul-searching by the Chinese literati in the second half of the seventeenth century, and it continued to stimulate critical reflection throughout the rest of the dynasty. Such reflection led the literati to confront what they perceived as the main threat to Chinese society—the decline of the Confucian world order. Although the intellectual discourse and practice of the eighteenth century can be seen, in various ways, as reactions to the late Ming crisis, they set the stage for an even greater crisis in the nineteenth century. Historians remind us that the eighteenth century should not be approached in isolation; we must ask whether the eighteenth century witnessed any social and cultural changes with significant consequences. If so, what were those consequences, and did they indicate any potential crises?

During the eighteenth century, the literati as a social group experienced an unprecedented degree of division and fragmentation, much of it due to the increasing competition for positions in the bureaucracy, the continuous growth of the merchant class and urban mobility, and what Benjamin Elman has called the professionalization of academics. According to Elman, in the early and high Qing periods, this resulted in the formation of an academic community in the Lower Yangtze region (that is, Jiangnan, with its cultural and political center in Nanjing, where Wu Jingzi lived and wrote *Rulin waishi*). With financial support from merchants and others, scholars devoted themselves to philological studies rather than to the established career paths of government service or moral education. Their nonofficial status allowed them to develop empirical methods of exact scholarship—a new scholarly discourse that raised doubts about the empirically unverifiable ideas that had pervaded Song (960–1279) and Ming dynasty interpretations of classical Confucianism. In an extensive survey of the eighteenth-century academic community of the Jiangnan region and its discourse of evidential scholarship, Elman provides new insights into the professionalization of the academy and the revolutionary nature of evidential discourse. He has argued that even before Chinese society was subject to fundamental crisis and the western impact, "the drama of literati disenchantment with the imperial orthodoxy had already climaxed in the eighteenth century."[6]

Elman's approach illuminates certain aspects of the changes in eighteenth-century literati culture, but beneath his analytical paradigm lie Weberian concepts of modern knowledge and scholarship. What Elman describes as the professionalization of academia in eighteenth-century China seems to echo Weber's account of the social and cultural transition of the West into the modern era.[7] In fact, at the beginning of *From Philosophy to Philology*, Elman reveals his modernist agenda by comparing the eighteenth-century evidential scholars to humanists of the European Renaissance such as Valla and Erasmus. "Like their European counterparts," he says, "Qing dynasty philologists favored linguistic clarity, simplicity, and purity. This endeavor led them to expose inconsistencies in contemporary beliefs and forms of expression." In this sense, both the European and the Chinese philologists were "scholarly iconoclasts."[8] And the predominance of philology in eighteenth-century intellectual discourse should be regarded as a movement that shook the foundation of the Confucian belief system.

Although not all modern scholars who acknowledge the revolutionary nature of evidential studies adopt a comparative approach, their implicit application of western models to eighteenth-century China brings us to the all-

---

6. Elman, *From Philosophy to Philology*, p. xix.
7. Max Weber, "Science as a Vocation."
8. Elman, *From Philosophy to Philology*, p. 3.

too-familiar debate over modernity.[9] The problem with the modernist account of Chinese intellectual life in the late imperial era is its tendency to overstate the case of eighteenth-century evidential scholarship, which prevents us from recognizing one of the most striking and significant aspects of literati discourse of that period—its paradoxical combination of cultural iconoclasm with Confucian revivalism.

This is where Kai-wing Chow's *The Rise of Confucian Ritualism in Late Imperial China* seems especially relevant. Like Elman, Chow concentrates on eighteenth-century intellectual discourse and practice, but his conclusions are starkly different. Whereas Elman sees eighteenth-century evidential scholarship as posing a challenge to the authority of the Confucian classics, Chow regards it primarily as a revival and a fresh development of the Confucian tradition in general and Song Neo-Confucianism in particular. Focusing on what he calls the Confucian ritualism of the eighteenth century, he calls attention to the literati's commitment to a specific Confucian vision of society based on ancient ritual and institutions. According to him, the philological studies of the Confucian texts, which gathered momentum in the mid-eighteenth century, were aimed at rediscovering the authentic rituals and institutions of the ancient sages. In his analysis, Confucian ritualism and evidential scholarship were interconnected, driven by a common vision. Their actual impact on society was manifested in the local gentry's effort to strengthen the lineage system and re-establish themselves as intellectual, moral, and social leaders of local society.

Chow's argument brings into focus a phenomenon of vital importance to our understanding of eighteenth-century intellectual life: philologists and ritualists belonged, by and large, to the same literati group. This is puzzling because it reveals a seemingly paradoxical correlation between philological iconoclasm and Confucian fundamentalism. Apparently the more effectively

---

9. Liang Qichao (1873–1927) once went so far as to claim that the evidential studies of the Qianlong (1736–95) and Jiaqing (1796–1820) reigns bore such a striking resemblance to the methodologies of modern western science that they should be appropriately called "scientific classicism" (*kexue de gudian xuepai*); see Liang Qichao, *Zhongguo jin sanbai nian xueshu shi*, p. 22. The questions that need to be asked are Why should the pattern of knowledge and science in the modern West serve as a pattern for our account of Chinese learning and scholarship? Did China have to follow the route charted by the West in order to be "modern"? To quote Craig Clunas in his study of Chinese print culture, our concern should be to "cast doubt on the unilinear and exclusionary nature of the arguments deployed for the single destination of modernity" (*Pictures and Visuality in Early Modern China*, p. 32).

the scholars undermined the integrity and authenticity of the Confucian texts, the more devoted they became to the ritualistic order those texts prescribed.

Chow is well aware of this paradox, which he attempts to resolve by describing the eighteenth-century philologists as Confucian purists committed to recovering the original shape of the ancient texts and validating that basis for Confucianism. However, even if this is accurate, the results of their evidential studies often pointed in the opposite direction. Indeed, whatever their intentions might have been, the eighteenth-century philologists often ended up revealing the complex textual history of the ancient documents and casting doubt on the authenticity of texts endorsed by the Song Neo-Confucians as Confucian classics.[10] Chow's study raises an unavoidable question: If the scholastic goal of the early and mid-Qing was to revive Song Neo-Confucianism, how could scholars have hoped to accomplish this by challenging the historical authenticity and textual integrity of the very classics upon which the moral authority of Confucianism and, in particular, of Neo-Confucianism had been built? In addition, we may question Chow's view of early and mid-Qing intellectual tendencies as a return to Song Neo-Confucianism, because many ritualists and scholars of evidential studies of the time were known for their opposition to Neo-Confucianism, and the orientations and practices of eighteenth-century evidential scholarship and those of Song Neo-Confucian philosophical discourse were unmistakably different.

The Paradox of the Literati Novel

Scholarship has revealed the tension present in the novels and short stories of the Ming and Qing, a tension that also appears in the intellectual discourse of the periods. Critics have chosen to emphasize either the ironic or

---

10. The best example of intellectual skepticism is to be found in Yan Ruoju's (1636–1704) questioning of the authenticity of the Old Text chapters of the *Documents* (*Guwen shangshu*), which had long been considered one of the Confucian classics. Yan's work, completed in the late seventeenth century, generated a heated debate among the scholars of the time and started a new trend in scholarly criticism. As Elman points out, "The movement to retrieve the past during the Ch'ing period was not a conscious current of skepticism. In the long run, however, the *k'ao-cheng* (evidential studies) identity that developed won breathing space for both skeptical and pious Confucians. In this way, evidential scholars advanced the front of objectivity and the cause of unbelief" (*From Philosophy to Philology*, p. 32). See also Yu Yingshi, "Some Preliminary Observations on the Rise of Ch'ing Confucian Intellectualism." On the continuation and development of evidential studies in twentieth-century China, see Schneider, *Ku Chieh-kang and China's New History*, pp. 195–200.

the moralistic veins in fiction—or the uneasy blend of both within the same work. The coexistence (and paradoxical combination) of iconoclasm with Confucian moralization translated into a pattern of narrative representation in which the parody or ironic portrayal of Confucian society became inseparable from irrepressible aspirations for moral norms and a Confucian order.

In emphasizing the role of the literati in revising narrative materials from an earlier popular tradition, Andrew Plaks has characterized the four great Ming novels—*Xiyou ji* (Journey to the west), *San'guo yanyi* (The romance of Three Kingdoms), *Suihu zhuan* (The water margin), and *Jin Ping Mei* (The plum in the golden vase)—as literati novels. Focusing on the sixteenth-century editions of these works, he identifies two characteristics as essential to the genre: an ironic devaluation of the surface meaning of the text and a deep melding of ideas based on Neo-Confucianism.

In any event, the point here is not to deny or diminish the serious dimension of Buddhist and Taoist thought in these books, only to restore the centrality of bedrock Confucian concepts within the constellation of ideas at the heart of late Ming literati culture, despite the fashion at the time of professing distaste for stodgy Confucian moralizing and the free use of un-Confucian terms of discourse appropriated from the other "schools."[11]

However, whether and to what extent these four works can be treated as literati novels and connected to Neo-Confucianism remains debatable. Plaks's statement seems only to confirm the paradox of late Ming literati culture: it highlights the tension between the conflicting impulses toward irony and Neo-Confucian moralizing that he discerns in these novels. If irony tended to devalue explicit didactic pronouncements, why would it stop short of undercutting the concepts of Neo-Confucianism, however deeply embedded they might have been?

Patrick Hanan, in his studies of seventeenth-century short stories, captures this tension by depicting the contrast between "the puritanical moralist and the bohemian man of letters, each of whom satirized the other unmercifully."[12] And indeed, each type of writer drove the other to the extreme. Late Ming and early Qing bohemians went to unprecedented lengths in debunk-

---

11. Plaks, *Four Masterworks of the Ming Novel*, p. 501.

12. By "puritanical moralists," Patrick Hanan (*Chinese Vernacular Story*, p. 164) refers to writers such as Langxian, Zhou Ji (the author of *Xihu erji*), and Master Gukuang (the author of *Zui xing shi*), whereas the bohemian men of letters include Aina (the author of *Doupeng xianhua*), Li Yu, and others.

ing cultural heroes, attacking old virtues, and blaspheming, whereas the puritanical moralists of the time single-mindedly advocated moral fanaticism and self-abnegation. There was no ground for reconciliation or negotiation.

The literati novels of the eighteenth century attempt to absorb these conflicting forces into their narrative dynamics. Although these novels do not share a common mode of representation, their depiction of the literati world and of society at large is often characterized by a serious, conservative Confucian tone. And yet irony constantly creeps in, with the free play of intellectual fancy, wit, and humorous observation that produces caricature. In an effort to understand the orientations of these novels, critics have usually turned to works of intellectual history for guidance. But as shown above, the intellectual history of the early and mid-Qing often points in two opposite directions. Some critics tend to detect the conservative vein in these novels; others see signs of a crisis of literati identity, a lack of epistemological certainty, a dwindling of interest in Song and Ming Neo-Confucian ideas of sagehood and self-cultivation, and a decline of the Neo-Confucian mode of thinking. In *Literati Identity and Its Fictional Representations in Late Imperial China*, Stephen Roddy, basing himself partly on Elman's arguments, explains:

Compared to the confidence that Song thought manifests in the power of humans to comprehend cosmic truths, then, a very profound sense of epistemological uncertainty pervades the literature and thought of the eighteenth century. No longer was a knowledge of ethical principle believed to provide a constant and secure touchstone for the multifarious occupations in which the literati engaged. . . . Hence, the unity and synthetic homogeneity of the Song view of humanity gave way to views that acknowledged the plurality and diversity of all-under-heaven, both human and natural, and indeed manifested an acute awareness of anomaly, division, and limits.[13]

In analyses such as this, the eighteenth-century scholarly discourse of evidential studies, as understood by Elman and others, offers a prism through which to perceive the intellectual orientation of the literati novels of the time.

Rulin waishi seems to crystallize the internal tension of the literati novels by combining an ironic edge with a moralizing vigor, going much further in both respects than most contemporary novels. Following either tendency results in a different approach to the novel. However, even those who recognize in *Rulin waishi* the conservative brand of Confucianism can hardly miss the irony. As C. T. Hsia has noted, "*The Scholars* was the first satiric novel

---

13. Roddy, *Literati Identity and Its Fictional Representations*, p. 20.

consciously written from the Confucian point of view. But unlike the kind of Confucian heroism endorsed in historical novels, its Confucianism is tinged with melancholy over the futility of government action or social reform."[14] Stressing the novel's ironic anatomy of the Confucian elite, May Fourth and Marxist scholars, however, have identified *Rulin waishi* as a broad attack on Confucian ideology, the literati ethos, and official institutions, of which the civil service examination system was a key part.[15] In this reading, the Taibo ceremony, the only accomplishment of the literati characters in the novel, fails to convey a positive message, since it is so ineffectual (and so ineffectually presented) as to suggest a parody. These scholars admit that Wu Jingzi still seemed to adhere to what they call an out-of-date Confucian ideal, but they attribute the novel's success to the triumph of realism, which they believe to be its main impetus.[16] Wu Jingzi's worldview is undeniably backward if judged by Marxist standards. Thus, it is realism that enabled *Rulin waishi* to yield ironic, critical insights beyond the limits of Wu's own conscious thought.[17] And these insights, May Fourth and Marxist critics argue, anticipated to some extent such modern concepts as humanism (*rendao zhuyi*). In this way, they manage to incorporate *Rulin waishi* into their teleological account of Chinese modernity. Marston Anderson, well aware of the pitfalls of either of these approaches, argues that it is impossible to pin down

---

14. C. T. Hsia, *The Classic Chinese Novel*, p. 209.

15. Hu Shi, "Wu Jingzi zhuan," in idem, *Hu Shi gudian wenxue yanjiu lunji*, 2: 1060–64; Qian Xuantong, "*Rulin waishi* xinxu"; Chen Duxiu, "*Rulin waishi* xinxu."

16. See He Qifang, "Wu Jingzi de xiaoshuo *Rulin waishi*," pp. 90, 97; and Bai Dun, "Wu Jingzi chuangzuo sixiang chutan," pp. 342–43.

17. This approach derives from Frederick Engels's remarks about Balzac. In a letter to Margaret Harkness written in 1888, Engels said: "Balzac was politically a Legitimist; his great work is a constant elegy on the irretrievable decay of good society; his sympathies are all with the class doomed to extinction. But for all that his satyre is never keener, his irony never [more] bitter than when he sets in motion the very men and women with whom he sympathises most deeply—the nobles. . . . That Balzac thus was compelled to go against his own class sympathies and political prejudices, that he *saw* the necessity of the downfall of his favorite nobles, and described them as people deserving no better fate; and that he *saw* the real men of the future where, for the time being, they alone were to be found—that I consider one of the greatest triumphs of Realism, and one of the grandest features in old Balzac" (Baxandall and Morawski, *Karl Marx and Frederick Engels on Literature and Art*, pp. 116–17). However, scholars who apply Engels's comments in their interpretation of *Rulin waishi* seem to make no effort to be more specific. Since Marxism regards "realism" as its favorite method of novelistic creation, the argument seems to be applicable to every novelist of the past, and hence inapplicable to any particular one.

Rulin waishi's organizing ideology, because, as is apparent in its episodes about filial piety, it "both reaffirms the value of a fundamental Confucian virtue and questions the social consequences of its reification as an abstract ideal."[18] For Anderson, "this is why seekers of ideological consistency in the novel will inevitably be disappointed."[19] Rather than offering an answer, this reading of *Rulin waishi* returns us to the central question perplexing historians; indeed, it forces us to re-examine the relationship between the ironic and the moralizing tendencies in the intellectual culture of the eighteenth century.

Self-Interpretation and Cultural Codes

At the heart of the cultural and intellectual transformation of eighteenth-century China lies the rivalry between Confucian ritualism and Song Neo-Confucianism. It is a commonplace that when ritualism came to dominate the Chinese intellectual landscape in the early and mid-Qing, Confucian ritualists, such as Yan Yuan (1635–1704) and Li Gong (1659–1733), openly challenged the authority of Song and Ming Neo-Confucianism—the so-called Learning of Principle (*lixue*) and Learning of Mind (*xinxue*)—and attributed the deepening crisis of the Confucian social and moral order to "empty talk" and "introspective meditation." They styled themselves Confucian fundamentalists, because they demanded nothing less than an immediate return to the ancient Confucian teaching of ritual (*li*), which they believed had long since been lost to Song and Ming Neo-Confucianism.

It is crucial to note that the two major approaches to the Ming-Qing cultural transformation—the modernist and the traditionalist—reveal an insufficient understanding of the conflict between ritualism and Neo-Confucianism. Both approaches are based on the common assumption that there is one and only one Confucianism. Their major difference lies in their explanations of its status in the intellectual life of late imperial China (and, by implication, in the literati novels of the period). For the modernists, Confucianism is the target of both evidential scholarship and parodic narrative. The traditionalists, however, insist that Confucianism is precisely the hidden objective behind the philology and the literati novels and is therefore what makes their social criticism possible. Neither approach pays enough attention to the increasing internal divisions within Confucianism during the

---

18. Marston Anderson, "The Scorpion in the Scholar's Cap," p. 275.
19. Ibid.

eighteenth century and the emergence of a Confucian consciousness capable of reflecting on its own inherent limits and dilemmas.

Such a monistic conception of Confucianism is justifiable from one point of view, for there is, as Chow has convincingly demonstrated, a notable paradox in the ritual discourse of the late seventeenth and eighteenth centuries. On the one hand, the literati tended to identify the late Ming crisis as a crisis of the Confucian social and ritualistic order; on the other, they insisted that the only effective solution lay in Confucian ritual. Working within the existing framework of concepts and generalizations, these self-styled ritualists were unable to develop a vocabulary with which to grasp what was at stake in their own experience and thought. Ironically, for all their stubborn opposition to Neo-Confucianism, they were so deeply immersed in a traditional rhetoric about ritual that they often seem to actually reaffirm the symbolic order that they so loudly rejected.

Nonetheless, the ritualists' failure to conceptualize their opposition to Neo-Confucianism does not mean that their efforts to distinguish between it and their ritualism reflected merely philosophical pretensions. We need to ask Why did ritual become such a central issue in the literati's discussion of the crisis of the Confucian world? How did they distinguish their ritual from the old ritual, which was presumably in great disorder, supposing the two types were indeed different? And what, after all, was ritual?

It is here that the relationship between literary studies and intellectual history becomes of vital importance. The impact of Confucian ritualism on the making of the literati novels has long been noted, but the prevailing perspective is not without its own blind spot. Critics often look to intellectual history for answers to questions arising from literary studies and sometimes even for the questions themselves. The core of their interpretive exercise consists of two implicit assumptions: first, that philosophical arguments hold the key to the explication of the basic issues of Confucian ritual; and second, that narrative production occupied only a peripheral role in contemporary thought, that it was a mere footnote to formal, philosophical discourse.

Both assumptions are methodologically flawed, for the simple reason that they display little sensitivity to the limits of the history of ideas; because the history of ideas focuses mainly on the participants' self-interpretation, it risks losing a sense of the larger system of values and meanings in which they partake. The intellectual shifts of late imperial China, I argue, provide a compelling case for the fruitfulness of cultural analysis as proposed by Clifford Geertz and others,[20] for a "thick description" of the literati novels tells us more about the predicament of Confucian discourse and ritualists' struggle than does the theoretical discourse of the day.[21]

It is in this respect that we can better appreciate the values of *Rulin waishi*. Of all the eighteenth-century novelists, Wu Jingzi was the one most engaged with issues of contemporary intellectual discourse. As an active member of a literati circle in Nanjing, he participated in the ongoing discussion of Confucian classics and rituals. His novel traverses a broad range of subjects: the functions of the civil service examination and the lineage system of local society, the rise of the merchant class, the decline of the literati's moral prestige and personal integrity (degraded by hypocrisy, bad faith, unrestrained competition for fame and status), and the permanent discrepancy between word and deed, name and reality, appearance and substance in the literati's sociopolitical lives. It was Wu Jingzi's ambition to integrate all these issues into a dynamic critical reflection on the predicament of Confucian ritual or *li*. And *Rulin waishi* is proof that he triumphed.

With Confucian ritual as its central concern, *Rulin waishi* is the focal point at which intellectual and literary undertakings converge. This is not to say that it can be read as a literary work advocating ritualism. Rather, its capacity for critical reflection comes to define the virtue of vernacular narrative. In his novel, Wu Jingzi suggested a subtler vision of human existence and social practice than most ritualists were prepared to accept. Delving into literati's everyday lives, he mapped out a broad discursive horizon against which to interpret and examine the ritualists' agendas. More specifically, his narrative exposes the crisis of the Confucian world at a much deeper level than that known to ritualists like Yan Yuan. It also offers a vantage from which to see both the redeeming values of Confucian ritual, which the ritualists might or might not see and conceptualize for themselves, and the limits and contradictions of their conceptualization, which they themselves certainly failed to recognize and articulate. These were profound insights, and Wu Jingzi came to them with an originality of perspective and intuition that eluded almost all of his contemporaries. In exploring alternatives from within the Confucian tradition, he illuminated how far an insider's critique of Confucianism could go even before China was exposed to the western challenge.

---

20. See Geertz, *The Interpretation of Cultures*.
21. For an explanation of the term "thick description," see ibid., pp. 6–10.

Ascetic Versus Dualistic Ritual: The Confucian
Imagination in Rulin waishi

Wu's most original contribution to the cultural and intellectual transformation of the time is his construction of two types of Confucian ritual. "Dualistic ritual" claims to be the source of ultimate value and significance, as well as the legitimate means of enforcing sociopolitical order in terms of hierarchy, status, and authority. In contrast, "ascetic ritual" regards severing ritual's link with the political world as a necessary stage in achieving its own autonomy and leaves no room for negotiation in ritualistic practice.

The first thirty chapters of *Rulin waishi* portray the literati's pursuit of career, fame, riches, and rank (*gong ming fu gui*) as reaching the point of insanity. Ironically, the Confucian rituals become a legitimate and hence convenient instrument for this pursuit. In the name of upholding the codes of Confucian ethics, the literati stage endless Confucian family rituals, but only to secure their own advantage in the struggle for power and property. Here Wu Jingzi depicted the crisis of what can be called the dualistic system of the Confucian ritual. Dualistic ritual finds the sacred in the mundane world and serves both symbolic and practical functions. The world of ritual is a normative order within which social hierarchy is described in terms of duties, responsibilities, moral obligations, and ultimately the cosmic order of heaven and earth. But this normative order is also the source of political power and the status quo, and its operation is closely bound up with social exchange, negotiation, and political maneuvering. Confucian family ritual, for example, constitutes the core of the Confucian symbolic order, but at the same time it fulfills mundane functions in determining the control and distribution of socioeconomic resources.

How does dualistic ritual cope with, if not resolve, its internal tensions? Such a system inevitably generates ambiguities in the perception of specific ritualistic behavior, for whether such behavior accords with the norms of ritual depends to a large extent on who perceives it and how it is perceived. The Confucian practitioners of dualistic ritual try to envision a world in which the cosmic/moral order expresses itself directly in the political/social order. They do not think that they live in such a world, but they attempt to create it through discourse. Dualistic ritual is thus inseparable from Confucian discourse: it is, by nature, narrative or discursive; it has to rely on the privileged narrator, who is none other than the Confucian sage himself, to secure its semantic certainty, to ensure the sincerity and purity of its agents' intentions, and, finally, to reduce if not eliminate the possibility of alternative interpretations. The success of Confucian narrative discourse depends on its ability to translate its moral vision into concrete practice and transform reality according to its self-interpretation. Ideally, if one perceives the world through the model of Confucian discourse or represents that discourse through action, it will appear as a sacred Confucian community in perfect harmony with the order of heaven and earth.

In the first thirty chapters of *Rulin waishi*, Wu Jingzi depicts a world in which the ideological function of Confucian discourse is exposed and moral rhetoric loses the enchanting power of persuasion needed to sustain dualistic ritual. Despite their verbal commitment to the moral vision of a Confucian community, the ritual organizers and participants are shown to be capable of calculating gains and losses through the manipulation of Confucian ritual. Confucian rhetoric never succeeds in persuading them to commit to any common values or common interests, nor does it help them perceive their relationship in terms of mutual respect and reciprocal obligation. The dualistic system of *li* falls apart; it is sacred in word but mundane in practice.

The institutionalized discrepancy between word and deed and between name and reality constitutes the main source of irony in this part of the novel. Wu Jingzi shows that the contemporary literati's lack of faith in Confucian rhetoric did not prevent them from taking advantage of it through the deliberate manipulation of Confucian language. Acting in a drama of impersonation, they claimed to be the spokesmen for Confucian sages and monopolize the role of the privileged narrator in declaring the purity of their intentions as they proceed to tell stories about their own ritualistic commitments. A master of irony, Wu Jingzi elucidates the ways in which the literati used Confucian rhetoric to justify their worldly gains and bargain for their own best interests: they compromised the ritual codes for their own desires and represented themselves as spokesmen of Confucian principle in order to claim a moral authority, which could easily be converted to their own political and economic benefit. As such, Wu Jingzi brought into view the worst aspects of dualistic ritual, for it was the unification of the sacred and the mundane within it that facilitated constant verbal negotiation with, and consequently the compromise of, the ritualistic obligations.

Wu's representation of the Taibo ceremony in Chapter 37 evokes a vision of the ascetic ritual of action, which is consequent upon the dualistic, narrative ritual in producing a different way of conceiving virtue, value, and the Confucian world. The episode of the Taibo ceremony consists of two major motifs: first, withdrawal from the mundane sociopolitical order to escape a dualistic world of *li* that is hopelessly caught up in irony; and second, the replacement of discourse with practice, since discourse, as seen in the first thirty chapters of the novel, not only produces endless compromises in Confucian ritual obligations but also becomes itself a legitimate tool to negotiate for political benefits and moral rewards.

Based on Confucian family ethics, the ascetic ritual goes much further both in conceptualization and in practice. Its underlying logic accounts for the series of fanatical attempts in the second half of the novel to fulfill Confucian family obligations at the cost of sociopolitical duties. This extreme behavior is meant to correct the situational ethics of the dualistic, narrative ritual, in which ritual codes are reduced to empty rhetoric or freely interpreted. In seeking a way out of the predicament of narrative *li*, Wu Jingzi seems, however, to have deliberately pushed Confucianism to its limits by making its core ethical values into absolute ritual imperatives. Within the context of premodern intellectual discourse, this absolutist urge indicates the extent to which a Confucianist could travel in seeking alternatives from within the Confucian legacies. It also produces its own dilemmas, which Wu Jingzi had to deal with in the second half of the novel.

In Search of a Normative Order Beyond Normative History: Cultural Transformation Reinterpreted

Wu's account of dualistic and ascetic rituals sheds new light on one of the fundamental divisions between Confucian ritualism and orthodox Neo-Confucianism: the latter seeks to establish and reinforce the Confucian norm through interpretation and discourse, whereas the former insists on the central role of ritualistic practice in the making of Confucianism. The issue of history, I shall argue, is essential to such divisions.

It has long been recognized that official historiography played a decisive role in the construction and reproduction of the orthodox Confucian world order. The dualistic system of *li* is, by its nature, narrative. It provides a model by which to perceive and measure the world of reality. It also demands to be translated into reality through simulated practice. This is where history comes in. Narrative ritual is history-oriented; it draws on the Confucian historical texts and the words of the ancient sages as the ultimate source of significance and also as normative models for reproduction. It was through historical accounts of the exemplary deeds of sages and cultural heroes that the Neo-Confucian moral imagination found a way to inspire common discourse and penetrate the world of daily life.

From the ritualists' perspective, however, the Neo-Confucians' heavy investment in discourse and history paved the way for their ultimate downfall. Wu Jingzi, in his critical response to what he saw as the deflation of Neo-Confucian discourse, conjured up ascetic ritual as an alternative vision. Similarly, the ritualists of the early and mid-Qing period became so disenchanted with the textual construction of Confucian history that they felt compelled to define a new ground for the practice of Confucianism. And philological evidential scholarship offered a convenient tool with which to undercut the textual bases of Neo-Confucian discourse and question the truth-claims of normative history. At the intersection of ritualism and evidential study lies the iconoclastic Confucianism that loomed so large in the cultural and intellectual transformation of eighteenth-century China.

In Search of Moral Imagination Beyond Authoritative Narrative: The Literati Novel Redefined

As a literary genre, the vernacular novel has a close affinity with official history; it draws so often on that authoritative narrative that it becomes, so to speak, an extension and transformation of official history in the popular imagination. However, its folklore origin and vernacular form relegated it to permanent unofficial or nonofficial status, as shown by such appellations as *waishi* (literally, "outer" or "other history") or *yeshi* and *baishi* ("unofficial history" or "informal history"). Wu Jingzi and his contemporary literati novelists often took the nonofficial position of the vernacular novel as the starting point of their own narrative. By calling his novel a *waishi*, Wu defined for himself an outsider's position from which to examine the motifs, concepts, and narrative models derived from normative history. In this sense, his concept of *waishi* is fundamental to the tradition of the literati novel he helped establish. It was through a critical reflection on historical narrative and its ramifications in the vernacular novel that Wu Jingzi developed his own novel as an alternative mode of moral imagination.

Rulin waishi's deconstruction of the normative narrative of official history can be taken literally. Although it is by no means a historical novel, it follows the Ming chronology from its founding in 1368 to the Wanli reign (1573–

1620), the period of its ultimate decline. Rather than confirming the narrative found in the official *Mingshi* (History of the Ming), Wu Jingzi offered a retrospective account of the corruption of the literati ethos and the resulting destruction of the empire, and his novel becomes itself an ahistorical attempt to redress the literati's failure to redeem the lost tradition and vanished empire. A similar tendency can be seen in *The Unofficial History of the Female Immortal* of the early eighteenth century, which presents a counterfactual account of how the Yongle usurpation might have been put right and the legitimacy of the Ming empire restored. Unlike earlier historical novels, which often provide an extended or supplementary version of *zhengshi* (official or orthodox history), the two *waishi* opened up a critical space outside or beyond official history.

However, in the case of *Rulin waishi*, the quality of *waishi* runs even deeper into the text and its narrative mode. Wu Jingzi sought to challenge not so much the accuracy and credibility of official history as its authoritative mode of narrative and its prescribed normative function. Essential to official history are its recurrent motifs, its highly regulated biographical form, and the way it valorizes the past and shapes reality. These features deeply affect the vernacular novel by furnishing a standardized mode of perception and conceptualization and form an integral part of its generic conventions.

Wu Jingzi was not the first to tamper with the established narrative forms of history and the vernacular novel, but he certainly went much further than his predecessors in questioning their validity. In *Rulin waishi*, the inherited mode of historical narrative and biographical form are shown to be inadequate for making sense of the world; the textual models of the past become either irrelevant or misleading, and the words of historical figures and cultural heroes are relegated to the level of mere text, deprived of their putative function in the reproduction of the Confucian norms and the transformation of reality. By demonstrating a rupture in the discursive world of historical representation, *Rulin waishi* seems to recapitulate the potential orientation of the philological studies of the time, albeit on its own terms and in its own fashion.

Wu Jingzi's questioning of the authority of historical narrative does not lead to cynicism and nihilism; instead, it constitutes an integral part of his effort to reconstruct Confucian norms. This helps to distinguish *Rulin waishi* and perhaps other eighteenth-century literati novels from the works of the seventeenth-century iconoclasts, who celebrated the breakdown of the Neo-

Confucian symbolic order. The eighteenth-century literati novelists, by contrast, sought to build their moral imagination on the ruins of the savaged narrative and discursive world. And Wu Jingzi went further than any of his contemporaries by suggesting a new Confucian vision of the ritualized world based on the absolute norms of ascetic practice.

Nor did this moralistic impulse lead Wu close to the puritanical moralists of the seventeenth century. Not only was he much more innovative and imaginative than most of them, but also his moralizing unfolded in a dynamic process of critical inquiry inseparable from skepticism and self-questioning. Indeed, he was more keenly aware than anyone else of the limitations of his own vision of ascetic Confucian ritualism. Instead of locking himself into a dogmatic position, he subjected ritualism to testing from alternative perspectives. In so doing, he did more than explore the critical function of vernacular narrative; he turned *Rulin waishi* into a critical medium that relies on relentless self-scrutiny to sustain its moral imagination.

This study of *Rulin waishi* consists of five parts. Part I focuses on the subject of ritual. *Rulin waishi* engages in a dynamic process of reflection on the dilemma of Confucian ritual; it proceeds from discrediting the dualistic ritual of narrative (Chapters 2–30) to exposing the problematic of the ascetic ritual of action (Chapters 31–55). An examination of this process sheds new light on the interconnectedness of various parts of the novel by revealing the underlying logic despite some apparent disjunctions or contradictions. I begin by identifying the generic code and textual source of Wu Jingzi's representation of the Taibo ceremony in Chapter 37 for two reasons: it defines a starting point for my interpretation of *Rulin waishi*, and it links the novel to the contemporary discourse and practice of Confucian ritualism.

Tracing the dynamic process by which *Rulin waishi* explores the theme of Confucian *li*, Part I divides roughly into two sections. The first section examines dualistic ritual and its relation to narrative discourse. My purpose is to show that rather than denouncing dualistic ritual in general and abstract terms, Wu Jingzi disclosed the secrets of its working as well as its ultimate disintegration. Dualistic ritual facilitates an exchange between symbolic and political resources and thus enables the literati characters to disguise their self-interested motivation with Confucian rhetoric or their gains by their exercise of moral discourse. This section shows the danger of Confucian ritual receding into unending verbal articulation, interpretation, and negotiation, becoming nothing more than pure fiction contingent on sociopolitical forces and utilitarian demands. The second section shifts the focus to *Rulin waishi*'s construction of the ascetic ritual of action. Through a close reading of a se-ries of stories in the second half of the novel, I illustrate Wu Jingzi's attempt to test the limits of ascetic ritual in asserting its absolute imperative. I argue that Wu's construction of ascetic ritual displays a profound insight into an alternative vision of Confucian *li* and its potential problematic, while giving the novel a critical edge and narrative dynamic rarely seen in any earlier and contemporary novels.

Part II turns to the issue of history. *Rulin waishi* claims to be *waishi* or outer/other history as opposed to a *zhengshi*; it tells a story about the end of of-ficial history by presenting a secular world of temporalities and contingencies that defies the normative mode of historical narrative. The failure of sacred history to shape or make sense of reality is best manifested in Wu Jingzi's rep-resentation of Kuang Chaoren as an officially recognized filial son in Chapters 15 through 20. The narrative breaks with the biographical tradition of using timeless character types to mirror unchanging moral verities. It evokes the im-age of Kuang from the repository of biographical narrative only to demon-strate his subsequent transformation and ultimate degradation over time. He becomes a character who has fallen from static, eternal history into the stream of mundane occurrences that shape and reshape his character and destiny. In a way, Wu Jingzi's story takes on the attributes of secular time by presenting an alternative narrative characterized by what I call "narrative perspectivism." Rather than assuming a fixed view, he conducted his narrative from interrela-tional (either interpersonal or intertextual) perspectives by exposing his char-acters to often changing, if not always conflicting, evaluations. Instead of im-posing a judgment from above, he constantly engaged in the flux of human and textual interactions and mutual responses, which in turn constitutes the inescapable condition for his own narrative.

Part III examines *Rulin waishi*'s narrative innovations by placing it within the history of the vernacular novel. The emergence of *Rulin waishi* in the mid-eighteenth century marks a new phase in the transformation of the ver-nacular novel as a literary genre. The main tradition of this genre arose from historiography and folk literature. Accompanying this tradition are two de-fining characteristics of the vernacular novel: its preoccupation with such subjects as dynastic cycles, military adventures, and religious journeys, and its simulated rhetoric of storytelling. For the literati novelists of the seventeenth and eighteenth centuries, however, the question was how to use the form of the vernacular novel to address their own need for self-representation while accommodating its inherited narrative mode. Wu Jingzi proved to be one of the most innovative writers. He reshaped the mode of vernacular fiction by diminishing, if not demolishing altogether, the simulated rhetoric of storytelling. Following some of his seventeenth-century predecessors, he also undertook a critical reflection on the inherited paradigm of the vernacular novel by parodying its standard motifs and recurrent references. In this world of parodies, the practice of translating the texts of the valorized past into reality is suspended, and the canonical discourse loses its relevance and becomes permanently hollow. In the end, *Rulin waishi* positions itself not only outside official history but also outside the lineage of vernacular fiction.

Part IV elucidates the main characteristics of *Rulin waishi* by focusing on such issues as moral imagination, self-reflexivity, and narrative. Wu Jingzi's questioning of authoritative narrative helped to redefine narrative as a critical medium. So defined, it is effective in undercutting the normative functions that orthodox history and other related genres assume for themselves. But as Wu Jingzi moved on to reconstruct the Confucian symbolic order, he was left without a third option: he had either to return to authoritative narrative or to find a way to minimize his reliance on narrative, if not dispense with it altogether. This helps to explain the dilemma seen in the section of the novel on the Taibo ceremony. In an apparent attempt to evoke the vision of ascetic ritual, Wu Jingzi briefly referred to the Taibo myth, subscribing to a faith in the core Confucian values without the support of concrete narrative. He also made use of the form of the Confucian ritual manual to emphasize the external form of ceremony and describe ritual activity in the way it is prescribed. But mythical assertion and ritual programs can hardly sustain the novel; narrative is still needed to specify and substantiate them within the concrete context of human drama. In the second half of the novel, Wu Jingzi thus occasionally slipped into the canonical forms of authoritative narrative (including historical biography), whose credibility he had already savaged.

This part illuminates the ways in which *Rulin waishi*'s creation is inexorably linked to a critique of its own choice of narrative mode and sources. It describes two defining features of *Rulin waishi* as a literati novel. First, *Rulin waishi* exhibits a compelling sense of self-consciousness as it confronts its own limitations and even contradictions in revoking the ascetic practice meant to transcend verbal representation and interpretation. Second, self-reflexivity is built into the narrative pattern of *Rulin waishi*. In making choices for his literati characters (including his fictional alter ego), Wu Jingzi almost always immediately revealed their least favorable side and then juxtaposed these choices with other equally problematic ones. This habit of always seeing something else and always alerting us to alternative perspectives is the corollary of Wu Jingzi's vocation as an intellectual novelist. My discussion in this part thus emphasizes *Rulin waishi*'s relentless self-reflexivity—a critical impulse against its own grain—that drives its narrative and defines its own existence as a new kind of vernacular novel and, indeed, as a new mode of thinking.

The epilogue examines an important aspect of the *Rulin waishi* narrative: lyricism and its broken vision. Wu Jingzi resorted to the lyrical ideal where the ascetic ritual failed—a tentative poetic solution to problems left unsolved by the institutionalized practice of *li*. However, despite his personal appeal to the lyricism essential to the tradition of literati culture, Wu Jingzi did not celebrate its triumph over the prosaic world and the eroding power of secular time. Rather than absorbing the fragmented mundane realm into a homogeneous vision, lyricism belongs only to the moment of self-absorption. It is incapable of enduring. Moreover, with it comes a nostalgic longing for authentic ritual that is not devoid of irony, for it merely highlights the absence and inaccessibility of the lofty ideal. The epilogue reveals Wu Jingzi's oscillation and struggle between lyricism and irony and his shattered faith in the totality of the lyrical vision of the world.

PART I

Ritual and the

Crisis of the Confucian World

Among the fifty-six chapters of *Rulin waishi*, Chapter 37 stands out. It describes in great detail how a group of literati, assembling in Nanjing from all quarters, build a temple and perform a ceremony dedicated to a Confucian sage of antiquity, Wu Taibo. As Qing commentators and modern scholars alike have noted, these events constitute the high point of the novel.[1]

Chapters 33 through 36 build up to the Taibo ceremony. After the project is announced in Chapter 33, readers are regularly kept informed of its progress until the ceremony takes place. All the literati characters in Chapters 34 through 36 live in expectation of the ceremony; but once it is over, they fade from the focus of the narrative, and in Chapter 46 they finally disperse. However, like Wu Taibo, whom they have commemorated, they reemerge in the memories of those who follow them. In the last chapter of the novel (Chapter 56), memory again takes the form of a ceremony, just as it did in Chapter 37: the men who participated in the Taibo ceremony are officially commemorated and celebrated. As Marston Anderson observes:

Contextually, the ritual (the Taibo ceremony) itself becomes a primary object of both desire (on the part of its organizers in the preceding chapters) and of memory

---

1. This point is articulated by Shuen-fu Lin in his "Ritual and Narrative Structure in *Ju-lin wai-shi*" and by the Woxian caotang edition commentator in his remarks on Chapter 37 (see Li Hanqiu, ed., *"Rulin waishi" huijiao huiping ben*, p. 515). For an introduction to traditional criticism of the nature of climaxes or summations in the premodern Chinese novel, see Rolston, *Reading and Writing Between the Lines*, pp. 261–64.

(on the part of the many characters in the latter part of the novel who long for it). . . . Whereas earlier incidents directed our interest forward to a long-delayed "culmination," later episodes instead fold back, returning us again and again to the still central point of the sacrifice to Taibo.[2]

Although pivotal, Chapter 37 bores and puzzles most modern readers. Even sympathetic readers find themselves frustrated, for it is, in C. T. Hsia's words, "unduly disappointing in merely giving us a bald summary of the proceedings in a solemn fashion."[3] Hsia's observations on Chapter 37 are accurate, with one exception: the chapter provides a detailed, step-by-step account of the entire ritual rather than "a bald summary."[4] Hsia's remarks do, however, capture the reaction of modern critics, who find what is supposed to be "the structural apex of the novel" anticlimactic. The novelist described each of the three consecutive sacrifices that make up the bulk of the ceremony at the same level of detail and in almost exactly the same language. The repetitive depiction of the ceremonial procedure, which occupies almost two-thirds of the chapter, seems needlessly tedious.[5] What these readers miss is an account of the ritual participants' mental states or their "psychological responses" to the ceremony.[6]

Partly as a response to such comments, other critics have tried to find new strategies of interpretation. They approach the Taibo ceremony from the viewpoint of the theoretical models elaborated in the Confucian classics, especially the *Xunzi*. Shuen-fu Lin, for example, expounds on the ethical and philosophical implications of Confucian ritual, and Marston Anderson, based on his interpretation of the *Xunzi*, explains that emotional responses

---

2. Anderson, "The Scorpion in the Scholar's Cap," pp. 271–72.

3. C. T. Hsia, *The Classic Chinese Novel*, p. 237.

4. Chapter 37 of *Rulin waishi* offers a technical account of ritual procedure that is almost unique in premodern Chinese fiction. Of Ming and Qing fiction, probably only *The Peach Blossom Fan* (*Taohua shan*), a drama by Kong Shangren (1648–1718), presents a similar case. A descendant of Confucius, Kong stages a sacrifice to Confucius in Act 3, and he presents another sacrifice dedicated to the last emperor of the Ming in Act 13. In both cases *The Peach Blossom Fan* represents the procedure of the ceremonies in much the same way as *Rulin waishi*, but its depiction of ritual is much less detailed and technical.

5. It is noteworthy that the translators Yang Hsien-yi and Gladys Yang obviously felt readers would not be interested in the repetition of the details and provided only summary statements about the last two sacrifices; see *The Scholars*, pp. 409–13.

6. In raising this issue, C. T. Hsia (*The Classic Chinese Novel*, p. 237) argues that the absence of psychological description in the ritual passage is due to a lack of appropriate narrative technique in the tradition of the premodern Chinese novel.

are not expected in the practice of Confucian ritual.[7] But questions remain: Why is the novel so preoccupied with details of ritual practice that seem to have so little literary interest? Why does it focus exclusively on the external forms of ritual action instead of other aspects of the ceremony? Action, to be sure, could conceivably speak for itself, but what it says seems obscure, if not completely incomprehensible. Late Qing commentators may not have shared modern critics' expectations of psychological description, but they had their own reservations about the representation of the ceremony. Huang Xiaotian (1795–1867), for instance, thought that Chapter 37 could not properly be called *xiaoshuo* (fiction) and thus seemed out of place.[8] But if this chapter is not *xiaoshuo*, what is it?

As I shall show below, the passage on the Taibo ceremony duplicates, or is re-created from, Confucian ritual manuals that circulated widely in late imperial times. By identifying its textual sources and generic features, I shall reveal some implicit narrative threads that help tie together seemingly unrelated episodes and scenes throughout the novel. I shall also link *Rulin waishi* with the contemporary intellectual discourse on Confucian ritual, especially the theories of Yan Yuan and Li Gong—known collectively as Yan-Li—and thus address issues of common concern to them. I do not, however, take *Rulin waishi* as merely echoing the intellectual currents of its time, nor do I try to reduce it to one statement or argument. Instead, I argue that the novel gains special significance because it addresses those common issues concretely through narrative. Wu Jingzi's narrative approach to Confucian ritual is of central importance for our understanding of the fundamental shifts in intellectual trends during the eighteenth century: it enabled him to illustrate crises in the Confucian world that lay at a much deeper level than those described by Confucian thinkers such as Yan Yuan and Li Gong; it was part of the contemporary intellectual discourse and also a critical reflection on it.

In Part I of this book, I examine *Rulin waishi* from two perspectives: as a diagnosis of the problems of the Confucian world and a recommendation of Confucian ritual as a tentative solution, and as a dynamic process of critical reflection on its own preferred solution. To be more specific, Wu Jingzi in his representation of the anomie of literati lives, like Yan Yuan and Li Gong

---

7. See Lin, "Ritual and Narrative Structure in *Ju-lin wai-shi*"; and Anderson, "The Scorpion in the Scholar's Cap."

8. Huang Xiaotian, in Li Hanqiu, ed., *Rulin waishi* (Hefei: Huangshan shushe, 1986), p. 347.

before him, emphasized the failure of Confucian discourse to sustain the order of the world. But Wu did not see that discourse itself as the problem. Through his narrative of the literati's abuse of Confucian moral rhetoric, he revealed the internal tension of the Confucian symbolic system, which both incites discourse and contributes to its dissolution. The strength of Wu Jingzi's narrative lies not merely in its concreteness but also in its power to illuminate the hidden forces that motivate individuals' words and deeds, in both their private and their public lives. Like Yan Yuan and Li Gong, Wu entertained doubts about the function of Confucian discourse that inclined him to the practice of the *li*, or Confucian ritual, as an alternative. But if Wu articulated with precision and subtlety the problems that frustrated him and his fellow literati, he was at the same time aware of his own inadequacy in coping with those problems. In his representation of the Taibo ceremony and the literati's efforts to extend the moral vision of that ceremony into concrete daily practice, Wu seems to have been trying to reconcile the need for Confucian ritual with its sheer impossibility. On the one hand, he emphasized the absolute commitment to Confucian ritualistic obligations through action; on the other, he engaged in a rigorous re-evaluation of the ritual project by exposing its practitioners to contradiction, irony, and often absurd and impossible situations. Following this line of analysis, I shall argue that *Rulin waishi* demonstrates a dynamic process of critical inquiry and self-questioning that resists any definite conclusion.

In its earliest extant form, *Rulin waishi* consists of fifty-six chapters divisible into five parts: the Prologue or Part I (Chapter 1), Part II (Chapters 2–30), Part III (Chapters 31–37), Part IV (Chapters 38–55), and the Epilogue (Chapter 56).[9] Centering around the sacrifice to Wu Taibo in Chapter 37, the main body of the novel consists of three parts. Part II offers a series of ironic tableaux of literati lives, which leads to the Confucian ritual in Part III as an alternative. Part IV then describes individual efforts to realize the ritual codes in everyday practice, all of which end in frustration and disillusion.

---

9. The last chapter of the novel is excluded from most modern editions because of suspicions that it may not be by Wu Jingzi. But there is no direct evidence to warrant its exclusion, and we have to take it into consideration in our interpretation of the novel as a whole. The first modern scholarly edition that includes Chapter 56 is *"Rulin waishi" huijiao huiping ben*, edited by Li Hanqiu and published in 1984. For more detailed information about the editions of *Rulin waishi*, see the Appendix.

Rulin waishi's moral imagination and self-scrutiny consist of three stages, marked by the construction and destruction of the Taibo temple. The rise of the temple in Part III of the novel celebrates the triumph of Confucian ritual over the mundane world as presented in Part II. But this triumph lasts only a moment. In Part IV, as individuals try to translate the norms of Confucian ritual into concrete acts in their public and private lives, they are over-whelmed by frustrations and confusions. The contrast is unmistakable: within the temple, the Confucian ceremony is a magnificent collective action that matches perfectly the description found in the ritual manuals; outside the temple, individual lives go awry. Consumed with nostalgia for the glory of the Taibo ceremony, the frustrated literati keep talking about the cere-mony and revisiting the Taibo temple, but only to confirm that they have ar-rived too late and are hopelessly adrift. In Chapter 48 of the novel, when Wang Yuhui, a dedicated compiler of Confucian ritual manuals, makes his way to the temple, he finds only an empty room with the program for the Taibo ceremony (yizhu) performed many years before, now covered with dust and almost illegible, posted on a wall. By having Wang Yuhui confront a ritual program that mirrors the text on which he himself has been working, Rulin waishi creates an internal moment of retrospective reading that reflects on Chapter 37, for the passage on the Taibo ceremony is composed precisely after the fashion of yizhu, or Confucian ritual manuals.[10] In Chapter 55, the penultimate chapter of the novel, visitors discover that the temple has been torn down and left in ruins. This study of Rulin waishi concerns, therefore, both the rise and the fall of the temple; it explores the significance of the temple's decay and addresses the question why the temple is constructed in the first place.

---

10. As a genre, yizhu refers to Confucian ritual guides or manuals. It is classified as a sub-category of shi or history. See the "Jingji zhi" section in Jiu Tangshu, juan 9, pp. 2006–9; and the "Yiwen zhi" section in Mingshi, juan 97, pp. 2396–98.

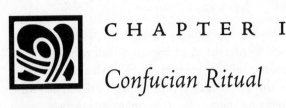

CHAPTER I

Confucian Ritual

Manuals, the Yan-Li School,

and Rulin waishi

In writing about the Taibo ceremony, Wu Jingzi relied less on observation or imagination and more on pre-existing Confucian ritual texts. He set the ceremony within a preconceived frame of reference; drew on a shared repository of ideas, rhetoric, and associations; and assumed certain responses from contemporary literati readers. In interpreting Chapter 37 of *Rulin waishi*, I begin by considering possible textual models for Wu's fictional ritual project. I then investigate his interactions with other members of the Nanjing literati circle and examine the intellectual trends of the late seventeenth and early eighteenth centuries, especially the Yan-Li school and its relationship with *Rulin waishi*. By studying Wu's circle, we can understand how he created his novel and reconstruct the context for, as well as the sources of, its creation. This line of study also helps make sense of the larger network of meaning in which both the author and his work participated. Focusing on Wu's representation of the Taibo ceremony, I examine its particular references, the milieu in which it was performed, and the conditions or contingencies that made it possible. The goal of this chapter is to delineate more clearly the critical issues to which Wu responded through narrative, as well as the vision of a Confucian ritualized world that he embraced, modified, and eventually questioned in the succeeding part of the novel.

The Taibo Ceremony and Confucian Ritual Manuals

Of the various types of texts about Confucian ritual, the most relevant to the study of Chapter 37 is the Confucian ritual manual, which offers technical prescriptions for the performance of a series of acts. Modeled on the classic *Etiquette and Ritual* (*Yili*), this genre deals exclusively with the external form of a ritual and shows almost no concern for its meaning, its function, or the participants' mental state or psychological responses. Concentrating on conventionalized ritual acts, it developed its own tradition of writing, with a schematic style of exposition, a rhetoric of repetition, and a distinctive vocabulary. Ming and Qing editions often feature diagrams that concretely illustrate ritual utensils, sites, and procedures, as well as each participant's position throughout.

Although Confucian ritual manuals date to ancient times, over the centuries, especially in the eighteenth century, they were re-edited and rewritten. As Kai-wing Chow has shown, Confucian ritual became a focus of attention in the second half of the seventeenth century, a trend later reinforced by the classicist Han learning, which, from the mid-eighteenth century on, dominated the intellectual landscape.[1] The combination of ritualism and classicism generated a torrent of discussions on the institutions of ancient ritual. Through essays, letters, prefaces, treatises, and ritual manuals, scholars engaged in detailed accounts and discussions of everything from temples to ancestral halls to clothing to ritual utensils to procedures. Even someone like Yuan Mei (1716–97), who was known for his poetry as well as his eccentric lifestyle, was interested—or at least pretended to be interested—in the design of the ancestral temples of the Western Zhou. Shi Jing (1692–1769), a member of the local elite in the Jiangnan region, evinced the same interest in his letters to Yuan Mei and claimed that scholars had long mistaken the Ming Hall (Mingtang) for the Imperial Ancestral Temple (Taimiao) of the Zhou dynasty. What interested him, however, was not the mistake as such but a formal detail: the number of gates in the Ming Hall.[2]

Among Wu Jingzi's friends in Nanjing was a well-known scholar of ritual studies, Fan Shengmo. According to a brief account of him:

---

1. Chow, *The Rise of Confucian Ritualism in Late Imperial China*, p. 8.
2. See Yuan Mei, *Suiyuan sanshi zhong, juan* 67, p. 3, 10a–b.

His scholarship was extensive yet profound. He felt ashamed to show off by producing empty words. Basing himself on careful research, he was able to duplicate the musical instruments, carriages, clothing, and utensils employed in ancient ritual. When people came to ask him for advice, he always showed them these utensils so that they could understand his instruction easily.[3]

This passage illustrates the ideal self-image of eighteenth-century Confucian scholars: they were men of few but wise words; they concentrated on the study of ancient ritual systems; and they considered it their obligation to provide a concrete model for commoners to follow in their daily practice. Confucian ritual manuals serve as precisely such a model: they are concrete, based on solid scholarship on the Confucian classics, and easy to follow.

The account of Fan Shengmo's engagement in ritual practice explains in part how studies of Confucian rituals were conducted in Nanjing, perhaps in the Jiangnan region in general.[4] During the time Wu Jingzi lived in Nanjing (1733–54) and wrote his novel, the Jiangnan region rivaled the capital as a center of ritual studies. This is reflected in the compilation and publication of ritual encyclopedias and handbooks. In 1723 or 1724, Qin Huitian (1702–64) began to work on his *Comprehensive Study of the Five Rites* (*Wuli tongkao*), which took him thirty-eight years to complete.[5] Among the eminent contributors to this monumental work were Wang Mingsheng (1722–98), Qian Daxin (1728–1804), and Dai Zhen (1724–77). Many of them also participated in compiling the dynasty's official ritual handbook, *The Comprehensive Rites of the Great Qing* (*Daqing tongli*), which was commissioned in 1736 and completed in 1756, as well as the third edition of the compendium of official regulations, *The Assembled Canon of the Great Qing* (*Daqing huidian*), which was finished in 1763. Around the middle of the eighteenth century, the compiling of Confucian ritual documents became a common pursuit of both civil officials and private scholars and for both official institutions and individuals in the capital and in Jiangnan.

As a novelist, Wu Jingzi had his own way of engaging in this intellectual endeavor. Although his anthology of poetry and *fu* provides scant justifica-

---

3. See the excerpt from *Xuzhuan Jurong xian zhi* in Li Hanqiu, ed., "*Rulin waishi*" *yanjiu ziliao*, p. 208. Chi Hengshan, a member of the local elite who initiates the Taibo project, is presumably modeled on Fan Shengmo.

4. For further discussion of the eighteenth-century Confucian scholarship on Confucian rituals in Jiangnan, see Zito, *Of Body and Brush*, pp. 69–78.

5. See Hummel, *Eminent Chinese of the Ch'ing Period*, 1: 167–68.

tion for describing him as a scholar of Confucian ritual,[6] the central scene of his novel is cast in the form of a Confucian ritual manual. Chapter 37 of *Rulin waishi* embodies almost all the features that define that generic tradition. The passage on the Taibo ceremony is preoccupied with the surface of ritual action and utilizes a rhetoric of repetition and a schematic expository style. But it does more than exemplify the format of Confucian ritual manuals in a general sense; it was probably modeled on specific types of ritual manual. Huang Xiaotian suggested that the ritual description in Chapter 37 derives from *Wengong's Family Ritual* (*Wengong jiali*), attributed to Zhu Xi (1130–1200).[7] My reading of both the novel and Confucian ritual manuals leads me to two other conclusions: first, the account of the ceremony for Wu Taibo may be an augmented version of a passage not from the *Wengong jiali* itself but from an annotated and revised version of it, namely, the *Jiali yijie* or a work modeled on the *Jiali yijie*.[8] Second, *Rulin waishi* might also be based on other ritual documents, possibly collections of Ming official ritual regulations such as *Collected Rites of the Ming* (*Daming jili*), since the ceremony in *Rulin waishi* includes both music and dance and thus apparently exceeds the family ritual in scale and presentation.[9]

---

6. See Wu Jingzi, *Chongyin Wenmu shanfang ji*.

7. See Li Hanqiu, ed., *Rulin waishi*, p. 347.

8. See Qiu Jun (1421–95), *Jiali yijie*. Qiu's edition for the most part preserved Zhu Xi's original but occasionally abridged, paraphrased, or reworked it with easier terminology. The importance of Qiu's contribution lies, however, less in his revision of Zhu Xi's text than in his additional commentary, the *Yijie*. Two things distinguish the *Yijie* from previous Confucian family ritual manuals. First, in contrast to its sources, it offers a precise description of each step of the ritual procedures as well as of the deployment of the ritual vessels. It achieves a high degree of specificity in recounting the ritual actions and thus meets the practical needs of ritual performers. Second, it introduces two directors of the rites (*tongzan* and *lizan*), who call out each step to be performed so that the participants can follow in a uniform manner. Although Qiu Jun was not the first to introduce the ritual directors, he gave them a regular role in his work on Confucian family rituals. The representation of the Taibo ceremony in Chapter 37 of *Rulin waishi* resembles Qiu Jun's *Jiali yijie* in its presentation of ritual directors, its phraseology and language patterns, and its concrete, detailed depiction of ritual procedures, which consist of chanted ceremonial injunctions and ceremonial actions and gestures. For further information, see Ebrey, *Confucianism and Family Rituals in Imperial China*, pp. 6, 173–76.

9. Official ritual guides offer canonical models primarily for rituals conducted in the official domain. The participants include the emperor, members of the imperial family, officials, and degree-holders. Official rituals differ from family rituals in various ways. Official rituals employ a large staff, including ritual directors (*zanli*) whose participation imparts a high degree of uniformity to the activities. Moreover, the music and dances that are part of official rituals create a splendid spectacle. In Wu Jingzi's time, Qing official ritual guidebooks, such

Various aspects of Chapter 37 of *Rulin waishi* betray its resemblance to these two types of ritual manual: its presentation of ritual directors (*dazan, fuzan,* and *yinzan*); its phraseology and language patterns; its concrete, detailed depiction of ritual procedures; and, finally, the format it adopts for depicting procedures that consist of chanted ceremonial injunctions and corresponding actions and gestures. One passage will suffice to show the affinities between Chapter 37 and the *Jiali yijie* and the *Daming jili*. The same pattern is repeated twice, with slight variations, in the ensuing parts of the ritual performance.

Jin Dongya [who serves as the *dazan*, or herald], followed by Lu Huashi, entered the hall. Coming to a halt, he announced: "Let all taking part attend to their duties!" The musicians picked up their instruments. "Stand in order!" cried Jin. Wu Shu with his banner led the men bearing wine, jade, and silk to the east of the courtyard. Then he instructed Zhang Tu, who was to read the prayers, to take the men bearing grain and sacrificial viands to the west of the courtyard, and took his stand below them. "Music!" cried Jin. Music sounded from the hall and the courtyard. "Invoke the spirits!" With scented candles in both hands, Chi Jun (Hengshan) and Du Yi (Shaoqing), the ushers [*yinzan*], walked outside, bowing, to greet the spirit. "Let the music cease!" cried Jin. At once it died away in both the hall and the courtyard.

"Let the votaries take their places!" cried Jin. The ushers went out to summon Zhuang Shaoguang and Ma Chunshang, who took their places to the left of the incense table in the courtyard. "Let the master of sacrifice take his place!" The ushers summoned Dr. Yu, who took his place in the middle of the courtyard. Chi and Du stood one on the right and one on the left of the incense table. "The ablution!" announced Chi. He and Du led the master of sacrifice to wash his hands and return. "The master of sacrifice approaches the incense table," announced Chi. There was an aloe wood urn holding red flags on the incense table, from which Du now took a flag bearing the word "Music." Dr. Yu went up to the incense table. "Kneel and offer incense!" cried Chi. "Pour a libation on the ground!" "Prostrate yourselves; rise. Prostrate yourselves; rise. Prostrate yourselves; rise. Prostrate yourselves; rise. Return to your places!" Du took another flag bearing the word "Silence." "Play 'The

---

as the *Daqing tongli* and the *Huangchao liqi tushi*, had not been completed. Although the *Daqing tongli* purports to be a ritual handbook, its account of ritual activity is relatively sketchy, compared with that in the *Daming jili*. The representation of the Taibo ceremony in *Rulin waishi* more closely resembles the Ming model. The *Daming jili*, of course, was not the only set of Ming official ritual regulations available to Wu Jingzi. He may have also read the *Daming huidian*, whose final edition was printed in 1588. The discussion of ritual regulations constitutes only one part of the *Daming huidian*, and it is less detailed than the account of ritual procedures in the *Daming jili*.

Air to Delight the Spirit,'" cried Jin. Jin Cifu conducted as the musicians in the hall played. Presently the music ceased.

"The first offering!" cried Jin. Lu Huashi carried out from the shrine a placard on which was written "First Offering." With Wu Shu carrying his banner before them, the ushers led the master of sacrifice forward. And as they passed down the east side of the courtyard, leading Ji Weixiao bearing wine, Qu Shenfu bearing jade, and Zhuge You bearing silk, men came out of the hall to welcome the master of sacrifice. When they came to the west, Xiao Ding bearing grain and Ji Tianyi bearing viands led the master of sacrifice down the west side of the courtyard, passing in front of the incense table and turning east. When they entered the main hall, the ushers took their places to the right and left of the table. The men bearing wine, jade, and silk stood on the left, while those bearing grain and viands stood on the right. "Take your places!" cried Chi. "Kneel!" Dr. Yu knelt before the table. "Offer wine!" Ji Weixiao knelt to pass the wine to Dr. Yu, who placed it on the table. "Offer jade!" Qu Shenfu knelt to pass the jade to Dr. Yu, who placed it on the table. "Offer silk!" Zhuge You knelt to pass the silk to Dr. Yu, who placed it on the table. "Offer grain!" Xiao Ding knelt to pass the grain to Dr. Yu, who placed it on the table. "Offer viands!" Ji Tianyi knelt to pass the viands to Dr. Yu, who placed them on the table. This sacrifice at an end, the votaries withdrew to their places, and Chi cried: "Prostrate yourselves; rise. Prostrate yourselves; rise. Prostrate yourselves; rise. Prostrate yourselves; rise."

"The first 'Song and Dance of Supreme Virtue'!" cried Jin. Clear music sounded from the upper part of the hall, and the thirty-six boys with vermilion flutes and pheasant feathers advanced to dance. The dance at an end, Jin announced: "Let all kneel below the steps as the prayer is read." Zhang Tu knelt before the prayer tablet and read the prayer. "Return to your places!" cried Chi. "Rise!" cried Chi. Wu Shu, the ushers, and those who had borne offerings conducted the master of sacrifice off to the west. Dr. Yu returned to his place, and the others to theirs. (*Rulin waishi*, hereafter *R.*, 505–7; *The Scholars*, hereafter *S.*, 409–11)

In this passage, the ritual directors orchestrate the ritual performance. Their injunctions to "prostrate yourselves" and "rise" are repeated a total of six times, each time involving four repetitions of each of the individual phrases. Here the novelist relied entirely on the rhetoric of repetition, evidently feeling no need for summary or ellipsis. A similar technique can be found in Confucian ritual manuals, particularly in the *Jiali yijie* and the *Daming jili*. In the sacrifices to ancestors formulated in the *Jiali yijie*, the usher (*yinzan*), for instance, announces a series of acts: "The ablution," "Approach the incense table," "Kneel and offer incense," "Pour a libation on the ground," "Bow. Prostrate yourselves; rise. Prostrate yourselves; rise. Prostrate yourselves; rise. Prostrate yourselves; rise. Return to your places."[10] The passage quoted above transcribes almost word for word the usher's injunctions from the *Jiali yijie* or texts modeled on it.

The injunctions are followed by actions. Here again, the representation of ritual activity in *Rulin waishi* conforms closely to the model formulated in the *Jiali yijie* and the *Daming jili*, which is characterized by its detailed coverage: nothing is too trivial to be excluded. Chapter 37 of *Rulin waishi* is in effect one of the most detailed Confucian ritual manuals of the Ming and Qing periods.

As situated in the novel, the Taibo passage is not only prescriptive but also descriptive. In representing the Taibo ceremony, Wu Jingzi created a description of ritual activity that perfectly matches the prescription: he adopted the form of the ritual manual, inserted the names of his fictional characters, and described their movements throughout the ritual procedure, just as the manuals prescribe.

Wu Jingzi not only took the Confucian ritual manual as the model for his representation of Confucian ritual but also depicted several writers or compilers of such manuals. In Chapter 48, for instance, he introduced Wang Yuhui, the holder of a licentiate degree, who dedicates his life to compiling Confucian ritual texts. Wang is given an opportunity to discourse on the content, format, and functions of ritual manuals. "The ritual book (*lishu*)," he says, "divides the three classics of ceremony into such categories as the Ceremony of Serving Parents and the Ceremony of Respecting Elders. The main text from the classics will be in large type, with quotations beneath from the classics and histories by way of illustration. Students can practice this from childhood on" (R. 647; S. 528). The response from the tutor of the local official college is encouraging: "Such a book should be recommended by the government to schools and circulated throughout the whole country" (R. 648; S. 528). Wu Jingzi may well have had himself in mind in paying this compliment to Wang Yuhui, for in composing the Taibo passage, he, too, was in the business of compiling Confucian ritual manuals. The Wang Yuhui episode thus brings us back to Chapter 37. The question to ask here is: Why should Wu Jingzi, in writing a novel about the literati's sociopolitical lives, adopt the form of a ritual manual and then give that form such a prominent position in the novel?

---

10. Qiu Jun, *Jiali yijie, juan* 7, p. 7a.

The Yan-Li School: Ritual Versus Discourse

The eighteenth-century popularity of Confucian ritual manuals has an even greater significance than might at first be apparent. Focused on the concrete, formalized, and repetitive acts of ritual, the Confucian manuals, along with other ritual texts, are indicative of the intellectual trend of the eighteenth century and can in part be traced back to Yan Yuan, an early Qing Confucian practitioner. Yan Yuan's life and thought can be found in *The Chronicle of Yan Xizhai's Life* (*Yan Xizhai xiansheng nianpu*), composed by his disciple, Li Gong, and presumably based on Yan's diary. Accenting Yan Yuan's practice of Confucian ritual, *The Chronicle* adopts the Confucian ritual manuals as a fundamental source for its narrative construction of what might be described as ritualized life.

Yan Yuan was a private scholar who lived in a small village in Hebei. Throughout his life, he was reluctant to serve the government and kept his distance from the center of power. In fact, he avoided the established routes for social advancement and cast aside almost all conventional aspects of the role of literatus. He had to farm and occasionally practiced medicine to support his family, and his emphasis on the importance for literati of having reliable skills or the means of supporting themselves was a new orientation in the literati's spiritual life.

During the second half of his life, Yan Yuan committed himself to teaching and practicing Confucian ritual. In *The Chronicle*, he is portrayed as a man whose daily life had become ritualized. At age thirty-five, Yan Yuan renamed his study Practice Studio (*Xizhai*).[11] From then on, his calendar was filled with activities ranging from the daily ritual of greeting to seasonal sacrifices to ancestors. Yan Yuan reinforced the Confucian rules for his disciples: no single moment of their lives should be without ritual. And he was no less rigid with himself. We are often told how he followed the rules of ritual in eating, dressing, walking, and interacting with others. He immediately chastised himself for carelessness if he neglected to don a hat when going out or when stepping outside to relieve himself at midnight. Even when alone, he practiced rituals such as that of greeting. And he performed this rite with as much reverence as if he were facing an honored guest (*ru lin dabin*). If a friend happened to visit him while he was performing a ritual, he

---

11. Li Gong, "Yan Xizhai xiansheng nianpu," p. 726.

would invite him to join in, for he believed that ritual was designed for practice and not for observation. Such anecdotes can be found throughout *The
Chronicle*. To modern readers, such routine ritual acts may seem trifling and
fragmentary, but *The Chronicle* organizes them in such a way as to present a
holistic expression of the ritualized life.

In the tradition of biographies of Confucian scholars, *The Chronicle of Yan
Xizhai's Life* is perhaps an exceptional case. Seldom, if ever, do we find a
biography that presents a Confucian scholar as so preoccupied with rituals
on a daily basis. What is more important to the present discussion is that in
introducing the details of Yan Yuan's daily practice, *The Chronicle* often
makes use of Confucian ritual manuals. In the section "At age thirty-seven,"
The Chronicle reads: "[Yan Yuan] practiced the ceremonies of greeting and
sacrifice."[12] What follows is a minute account of ceremonial proceedings oc-
cupying several pages. This paragraph, like the passage on the Taibo ceremony in *Rulin waishi*, is evidently re-created from ritual manuals.[13] If Yan
Yuan's life is represented as a process of ritualization, this process is, so to
speak, punctuated by performances from ritual manuals.

Something similar can be found in *Rulin waishi*: Chapter 36, which provides a biography of Yu Yude, the ritual master in the Taibo ceremony, is
followed by Chapter 37, which takes the form of a Confucian ritual manual.
Like the description of ritual practice in *The Chronicle*, the passage on the
Taibo ceremony seems deliberately to omit such verbal acts as the prayers
that were often included in ritual manuals and instead focuses exclusively on
physical actions. In both *The Chronicle* and *Rulin waishi*, Confucian ritual appears, therefore, not as a subject of contemplation and interpretation but as
concrete activities to be performed on a variety of public and private occasions. The questions I address here are: Why do the two texts emphasize
such rigid commitment to the practice of Confucian rituals? Why do they
seem to be concerned mainly with accurate execution of the rituals? Do they
offer a mere surface image or do they imply a moral vision?

In "The Structure of Chinese Funerary Rites: Elementary Forms, Ritual
Sequence, and the Primacy of Performance," James L. Watson argues for
the greater importance of performance over belief in the ritual life of late imperial times. He asserts that the proper performance of the rites mattered

---

12. Ibid., p. 734.
13. The ritual manual in *The Chronicle* was probably compiled by Yan Yuan himself. Yan
Yuan compiled many ritual texts, and his *Liwen shouchao* is based on the *Wengong jiali*.

most to everyone concerned, whereas "the internal state of the participants, their personal beliefs and predisposition, are largely irrelevant."[14] According to him, this had profound consequences for the creation of a unified cultural system in late imperial China: "By enforcing orthopraxy (correct practice) rather than orthodoxy (correct belief) state officials made it possible to incorporate people from different ethnic or regional backgrounds, with varying beliefs and attitudes, into an overarching social system we now call China."[15] Based on the observation of ritual practice, Watson offers compelling comments on Qing ritualism, emphasizing conformity to the canonical form of practice. Yet his proposed dichotomy of meaning versus performance itself needs to be historically located and defined. Furthermore, as a preconceived framework for argument, it blocks alternative views and further discussion.[16]

In a response to Watson's thesis, Evelyn S. Rawski argues in "A Historian's Approach to Chinese Death Ritual": "While many historians might agree that the Confucian state emphasized orthopraxy, they would not agree with Watson's conclusion that the state did not link orthopraxy with orthodoxy."[17] "Confucians," Rawski explains, "did not only assume that belief preceded and was the stimulus for performance; they also understood that performance could lead to inculcation of belief. Rather than making a sharp distinction between belief and practice, therefore, Chinese ruling elite tended to see belief and practice as organically linked to one another, each influencing the other."[18] As a historian, Rawski stresses, for good reasons, the role of oral and written articulations in the construction of ritual meaning. However, she seems to have skipped the crucial questions of how ritual meanings are constructed and how the Confucian scholars of different periods interpreted the meanings of ritual practice. As we will see, these are precisely the issues at the core of intellectual debate in the late seventeenth and eighteenth centuries.

---

14. In Watson and Rawski, *Death Ritual in Late Imperial and Modern China*, p. 6.

15. Ibid., p. 10.

16. In a critical, comprehensive survey of existing theories on ritual, Catherine Bell emphasizes the approach that defines ritual as action or practice. Although she admits the contributions of this approach to our understanding of ritual, Bell argues that it often succumbs to circular argument. Her own approach to ritual activities "stresses the primacy of the social act itself, how its strategies are lodged in the very doing of the act, and how 'ritualization' is a strategic way of acting in specific social situations" (*Ritual Theory, Ritual Practice*, p. 67). For her further elaboration of the term "ritualization," see Part III of ibid., pp. 171–223.

17. In Watson and Rawski, *Death Ritual in Late Imperial and Modern China*, p. 22.

18. Ibid., p. 28.

Yan Yuan, in his writings on Confucian ritual, conjured up a dichotomy of ritual as practice versus ritual as discourse or meditation. In reinforcing practice, Yan positioned himself firmly in opposition to the teaching of what he deemed to be Song and Ming Neo-Confucians, who, according to him, had replaced ritual practice with lectures (*jiangxue*) and quiet sitting (*jingzuo*). Although Confucian ritual was one subject of Neo-Confucian discourse and introspective reflection, Yan Yuan argued, it was largely confined to words and meditation. The consequences of such an intellectual tendency, as he saw it, were dangerous, for Confucian ritual propriety became isolated from action, subject only to verbal elaboration and interpretation and thus to various hypotheses and unending negotiations. Commenting on the Neo-Confucians' obsession with speech and writing, Yan Yuan wrote: "The sages' words can guide us along the road. But now no one sets his feet on the road. People just imitate the sages' words and consider it walking. Generation after generation, the words that guide us along the road become more and more numerous, but seldom are people found on the broad way (*dao*) of the Zhou."[19] Yan criticized Neo-Confucians for their exclusive focus on the verbal elaboration of human nature, inclination, ritualistic obligation, and moral principle.[20] Even more serious for him was what he saw as the ironic disjunction and discrepancy in the words, thoughts, and deeds of his contemporaries: "If even one's heart does not correspond to one's mouth, how much less would it be so of one's self, one's family, and state affairs? If one applies words to actions, there is seldom a perfect match." "By this," he concluded, "we know that without practice what we learn from the heart and what we put forth in writing and speech are simply of no use at all."[21]

Yan Yuan's critique of Neo-Confucian discourse derived from his observations and diagnoses of the late Ming crisis. He noted that in the late Ming moral education depended almost entirely on oral and written articulations. When the only thing masters teach is speech, that is all students learn. Within late Ming literati circles, talk was the order of the day. Silence occurred only at intervals, when the literati practiced quiet sitting and reflected on the words they have read, memorized, and discussed. But words, book learning, and introspective reflection seem to have led nowhere. As Yan Yuan frequently reminded his disciples and his readers, even as late Ming

---

19. Yan Yuan, "Cunxue bian," in idem, *Yan Yuan ji*, p. 86.
20. Ibid., p. 56.
21. Ibid.

literati were so deeply preoccupied with words and thoughts, the moral order they elaborated eroded and ultimately disintegrated.

Yan Yuan's distrust of discourse prompted him to explore an alternative—the Six Arts (*liuyi*, that is, ritual, music, poetry, calligraphy, charioteering, and archery). Of these, Yan stressed ritual—"the authentic Confucian teaching" of ancient times—which, according to him, had been ignored and even forgotten, because of the pernicious influence of the Neo-Confucian fondness for "empty talk." Yan Yuan insisted that only deeds can serve as the testing ground for words and thoughts. The moral order, he argued, was sustained not through writing and words but through concrete practice.[22] As any student of premodern Chinese culture knows, the meaning of *li* is not confined to ritual. In Confucian discourse *li* is so broadly defined as to designate the norms by which almost every aspect of individual behavior and sociopolitical life are regulated. For Yan, *li* is, therefore, a mediating term. It is simultaneously a synecdoche for the Confucian ritualistic order, of which ritual is the most concrete and representative part, and a metonymy for that order—the vision of a ritualized world transformed into reality through the practice of rituals designed for a variety of social occasions.

Yan Yuan's concepts of discourse, practice, and the Confucian ritualized life were further affirmed by scholars of classical learning in the eighteenth century. Of Wu Jingzi's friends in Nanjing, Cheng Tingzuo (1691–1767) was just such a scholar. In an essay entitled "On Ritual and Music" ("Li yue lun"), Cheng argued that Confucian ritual consists of two elements: art (*shu*) and

---

22. Under the influence of classicist Han learning, few scholars of the eighteenth century could avoid textual issues in their promotion of Confucian ritual, because selecting and adapting written models for practice had become very much a matter for classical scholarship. As the Yan-Li school evolved during the eighteenth century, its discourse gradually became intertwined with this new trend of Han learning. As Kai-wing Chow has noted, although Yan Yuan was known for his advocacy of Confucian ritual and the Six Arts, he gave little thought to textual problems in the classics. Preoccupied by his dispute with the Neo-Confucians, "he had always warned against excessive book learning to the neglect of practical purpose" (*The Rise of Confucian Ritualism in Late Imperial China*, p. 65). Despite his mentor's warnings, Li Gong no longer found it necessary to choose between book learning and the practice of Confucian ritual. He came to share the classicists' approach to textual studies, and his appreciation of classical scholarship was further strengthened through personal contact with Wan Sitong (1638–1702) and Mao Qiling (1623–1716), two eminent classicists from the Jiangnan region. For Li Gong, Yan Yuan's goal of restoring the Confucian world through the practice of ritual and the Six Arts could not be achieved without the help of textual studies.

meaning (*yi*).[23] *Shu* refers to the external form and other technical aspects of the ceremony (how is it designed and practiced); and *yi* to the reasons for the ceremonial system. Cheng explained: "Only when *shu* is illuminated and fully complete can *yi* be clearly manifested to the minds of all the people."[24] Since the ancient sages relied on rituals in cultivating virtue and promoting social order, to dispense with rituals would leave Confucians, whatever the good intentions behind their endeavors, with no concrete, efficient instruments. Although Cheng began with the dichotomy of *yi* versus *shu*, he ended up arguing that *yi* depended on *shu*. In his final argument, the distinction between form and meaning, between surface and substance, becomes largely irrelevant. To Cheng, as to Yan Yuan, the practice of Confucian ritual is not necessarily an expression of ideas, intentions, and emotions but a formalized rehearsal of such correct or appropriate attitudes as reverence, noncompetitiveness, and mutual respect, which are congenial to the institutions of social intercourse.[25] Thus the impact of ritual on individuals is beyond the reach of book learning, and its essence can hardly be captured through mere words. As an indispensable mode of Confucian moral teaching, Confucian ritual has significance in praxis: its moral meanings are immanent only in ritual activity.

By setting up the dichotomy of ritual and discourse, however, Yan Yuan seems to have created more problems than he solved. Although he positioned himself strongly against Neo-Confucianism, modern scholars have found it difficult to distinguish his position from that of Wang Yangming (1472–1528), who advocated "constant practice in the midst of concrete affairs." "Yan Yuan's emphasis on practice again reminds us of Wang Yangming's 'unity of knowledge and action,'" Tu Wei-ming has pointed out. "Knowledge is merely empty talk if it cannot be put to use. Genuine knowl-

---

23. Cheng Tingzuo, *Qingxi wenji, juan* 3, p. 2b.

24. Ibid., *juan* 3, p. 3b.

25. Modern theorists have developed approaches to the studies of ritual that enable us to gain a more sympathetic understanding of the view that Cheng Tingzuo suggests here. Stanley Jeyaraja Tambiah's elaboration of the performative aspect of ritual is one such example; see his "A Performative Approach to Ritual." Suzanne Langer also emphasizes that the formalization that characterizes ritual requires the adoption of conventionalized gestures as opposed to improvised action. She argues that the distinctive characteristic of ritual lies not in its evocation of feelings in an immediate psychological sense but in what she considers the "articulation of feelings." "The ultimate product of such an articulation is not a simple emotion, but a complex permanent attitude." As she puts it, ritual is not a "free expression of emotions" but a disciplined rehearsal of "right attitudes." See Langer, *Philosophy in a New Key*, pp. 123–24.

edge is simultaneously a form of acting that must make a practical difference in the world, for practicality is an essential criterion of true knowledge."[26]

It is equally difficult to see Yan Yuan as an absolute opponent of Zhu Xi in promoting the practice of Confucian rituals. According to *The Chronicle of Yan Xizhai's Life*, 1668 was a spiritual turning point for Yan Yuan. Upon the death of his step-grandmother, he took Zhu Xi's *Family Ritual* as the model for the mourning ceremony. However, his rigid adherence to the ritual codes during the mourning period ended disastrously. Not only was he physically exhausted, he also experienced tremendous frustration and confusion. Immediately after recovering from this traumatic experience, he wrote his famous treatise "On the Preservation of Human Nature" ("Cunxing bian"), in which he rejected Zhu Xi's dualistic view of human nature and returned to Mencius's view of the inborn goodness of human beings. But Yan Yuan's reflection on Zhu Xi's family ritual seems to have focused only on its technical and methodological aspects. "It should be noted," says Tu Wei-ming, "that Yan Yuan's departure from the Chengzhu school did not constitute a rejection of its ritualism. On the contrary, after his painful experience in 1668 he became even more convinced that the most authentic approach to self-cultivation was through the practice of rituals (*xili*)."[27]

We now find ourselves in a position to deal with this dilemma: Yan Yuan is hailed as an original thinker who initiated a new intellectual trend in the early Qing, but there is little evidence to confirm his originality. Did Yan Yuan deliberately distort the views of Song and Ming Neo-Confucianism in order to make his own seem more daring? Was his criticism of his intellectual rivals an empty gesture motivated by polemical rather than theoretical concerns or an act of bravado emphasizing distinctions that did not exist? In the end, we have to wrestle with the questions that remain unanswered: What, if anything, is new in Yan Yuan's thinking about Confucian ritual?

---

26. Tu, *Humanity and Self-Cultivation*, p. 200.

27. Ibid., p. 195. Stephen Roddy observes that despite Yan Yuan's critique of Zhu Xi, the two are essentially in agreement on the fundamental issues regarding Confucian ritual. But he also points out that "in the later uses of Zhu's doctrines by succeeding generations, this aspect of his thought was neglected under the increasing emphasis on principle" (*Literati Identity and Its Fictional Representations in Late Imperial China*, p. 251n8). Kai-wing Chow emphasizes that Yan Yuan continues to follow Zhu Xi's ritual texts in his daily practice even late in his life (*Rise of Confucian Ritualism*, p. 66). Patricia Ebrey notes that although Li Gong continued to criticize Zhu Xi's *Family Ritual*, he seemed to disagree with it merely on trivial details (*Confucianism and Family Rituals in Imperial China*, p. 193).

What differentiates Yan Yuan's *li* from Neo-Confucian *li*, which, according to Yan, was caught in crisis or had become a problem in itself? And what, after all, is *li*, and why had it become such a key issue in Yan-Li discourse?

Yan Yuan's writings yield almost no satisfactory answers to these questions. Instead of offering solutions, he created more problems. More precisely, his solution itself turns out to be a problem. If, as Yan observed, Confucian scholars indeed relied mainly on their studies of Confucian texts for guidance in transmitting values, cultivating virtue, and sustaining social and ritualistic order, then what prevented Confucian discourse from fulfilling its expected functions in the late Ming? Yan Yuan showed no interest in reviving words he considered to have become hollow. As if to distance himself from the Neo-Confucians, he avoided articulating in any analytical fashion his points about the nature of Confucian discourse. As a result, he was not able to reveal the causes and consequences of its failings, if indeed it had failed. Nor was he able to prove the alternative he proposed: that the Confucian social and ritualistic order will endure if and only if writing and verbal discourse are replaced by ritual action. Caught up in a sense of hopeless belatedness, he sometimes expressed doubts whether the ideal ritual of antiquity could be restored without distortion. But he was too convinced of the necessity of Confucian ritual to be able to see the fundamental problems in his own conceptualization. If, for instance, his intention was to do away with discourse, what, then, of his own discourse on the practice of *li*? For all his rhetoric and gestures against discourse, where did he distinguish his *li* from the Song and Ming Confucian discourse of *li*, if his conception of *li* is as fundamentally different as he would like us to believe?

In coping with these interpretive issues, we need to strike a balance between sympathetic understanding and critical reflection. It is inappropriate to base our interpretations of Yan Yuan simply on his own account of his difference from the Neo-Confucians.[28] Yet it would be just as wrong to regard Yan as no different from the Neo-Confucians merely because he, too, had to rely upon writing in constructing *li*. The question is whether we can find a vantage point from which to see all the complexities: both the significance *li* had for Yan and the problems arising from *li* that he himself could not see (or saw but failed to articulate). This question takes us to *Rulin waishi*.

---

28. For the studies of Yan Yuan, see Tu, "Yan Yuan: From Inner Experience to Lived Concreteness." For the Ming Confucians' emphasis on practice, see Smith, *Action in Late Ming Thought*; and de Bary and Bloom, *Principle and Practicality*.

Rulin waishi *and* Yan-Li *Discourse*

Although some fundamental problems remain either untouched or unresolved, Yan Yuan's dichotomy of ritual versus discourse found its most sophisticated and critical elaboration in Wu Jingzi's *Rulin waishi*. As literary scholars have long noted, in his struggle to cope with the crisis of literati culture, Wu Jingzi was in part inspired by Yan Yuan and Li Gong.[29] Wu's family had cross-generational connections with Li Gong, and Cheng Tingzuo, Wu Jingzi's friend in Nanjing, was one of the most enthusiastic and influential advocates of the Yan-Li school in the Jiangnan region and was in close contact with Li Gong.[30] Although Yan Yuan's activities seem to have been confined largely to the Hebei area, his books circulated in Jiangnan and other regions. Li Gong appears to have been more active in disseminating Yan Yuan's teachings than Yan himself. In 1720, Li paid a visit to Jiangnan. In Nanjing he met with Cheng Tingzuo and others and promised to move there for the rest of his life—a promise that, if fulfilled, might have changed the intellectual history of the Qing. Although Li Gong's plan was aborted because of a sequence of inconvenient accidents, the traffic of books and ideas between Hebei and Nanjing helps map out a discursive sphere in which Wu Jingzi participated through *Rulin waishi*.

A brief survey of Cheng Tingzuo's biography will tell us much about the impact of the Yan-Li discourse on *Rulin waishi*, for Cheng is regarded as Wu Jingzi's best friend (*zhiqi*) and a significant influence on Wu's views on the Confucian classics.[31] A scholar who had no official titles, Cheng Tingzuo is

---

29. See Hu Shi, "*Qingxi wenji xu*," p. 3; Wu Zuxiang, "Lun *Rulin waishi* de sixiang he yishu"; Ropp, *Dissent in Early Modern China*, pp. 75–76, 105, 270; Chen Meilin, "Yan-Li xueshuo dui Wu Jingzi de yingxiang"; Chen Meilin, *Wu Jingzi pingzhuan*, pp. 386–404; Li Hanqiu, "*Rulin waishi* Taiboci daji he rujia sixiang chutan"; Zhang Guofeng, "*Rulin waishi* jiqi shidai, pp. 13–23; Roddy, *Literati Identity and Its Fictional Representations in Late Imperial China*, pp. 63–73, 207–10.

30. When Wu Jingzi's great-grandfather Wu Guodui (1618–80) served as the chief examiner in Shuntian county in 1677, Li Gong took first place in the examination and gained his licentiate degree. Wu Guodui favored Li Gong so much that he sponsored a printing of Li's anthology. Moreover, Wu Jingzi's son Wu Lang (1719–70) once studied mathematics with Liu Zhu, Li Gong's disciple. See Chen Meilin, *Wu Jingzi yanjiu*, pp. 3–4; and idem, *Wu Jingzi pingzhuan*, pp. 388–89.

31. "Cheng Mianzhuang [Tingzuo] devoted himself to the study of the Confucian classics. Master [Wu Jingzi], too, devoted himself to the study of the Confucian classics in his old age. He said: 'This [the study of the Confucian classics] is the foundation upon which one is sup-

said to have lived in seclusion and devoted himself to studies of the Confucian classics. Not only did he align himself with the Yan-Li school in his
concept of Confucian ritual, he also lived a ritualized life much as Yan Yuan
did: "His mind was tranquil and his conduct pure. He always behaved himself in a fit and proper way."[32] Cheng left this description of the turning
point of his life—the moment he became enlightened by Yan Yuan's and Li
Gong's works.

A young man from a literati family, Cheng Tingzuo was first exposed to
Yan Yuan's and Li Gong's writings in his early twenties through Tao Yu, his
father-in-law and an acquaintance of Li Gong. One reading of Yan Yuan
and Li Gong turned Cheng immediately into a follower of the Yan-Li school.
It also prompted him to write a book. In the winter of 1714, Cheng wrote a
letter to Li Gong and sent an outline of his planned book to get his advice.
The letter begins:[33]

When I was young, I loved literary works (*cifu*) and also practiced examination essays (*zhijuwen*). Yet as for learning (*xueshu*), I was not able to tell the true from the
false and the right from the wrong. After I was twenty, I found Master Yan Xizhai
[Yan Yuan]'s *Sicun bian* (Four preservations) and your *Daxue bianye* (On the Great
Learning) in the house of Tao Zenfu [Tao Yu], my father-in-law. It was only after
that that I began to realize that among my contemporaries there were scholars in the
area of Yan and Zhao [Hebei and Henan] who still engaged in "solid learning"
(*shixue*) and thus inherited the legacy of the Duke of Zhou and of Confucius. The
learning of the sages has long been lost. During the past several hundred years,
scholars have followed either Zhu Xi or Lu Xiangshan. The two schools alternated,
each ridiculing the other. But when Master Yan Xizhai came along, he upheld the
Three Dynasties' teachings and established practices by which to correct the problems of current developments. His meritorious work of rectification and restoration
has had no match since ancient times. And you [Li Gong] came after him, just like
Mencius following Confucius. . . . Now, you—master and disciple—have obtained
the true learning of Confucianism that had been lost for two thousand years. If you
can take advantage of this moment when the trend of the past several hundred years
is about to change, then it is likely that your single call will have a tremendous response and a sweeping influence. But those who respond are still few. This is not an

---

posed to rely.'" See Cheng Jinfang, "Wenmu xiansheng zhuan," p. 12. For the study of Cheng
Tingzuo's view of Confucian ritual, see Roddy, *Literati Identity and Its Fictional Representations
in Late Imperial China*, pp. 70–73.

32. See Cheng Jinfang, "Mianzhuang xiansheng muzhi ming," p. 61.
33. See Cheng Tingzuo, *Qingxi wenji fubian, juan* 1, pp. 1a–b.

indication that the learning of Three Dynasties and Confucianism cannot be practiced in later periods. Rather, it is because nowadays scholars practice only quiet sitting and lecturing so that when successful, they can pursue official titles and salaries, and when unsuccessful, they can be at ease with themselves. What you and Master Yan teach are filial piety, brotherly love, loyalty, and faith (*xiao ti zhong xin*), along with ritual, music, military training, and farming (*li yue bing nong*). You and Master Yan practice what you both preach and thus leave no room for emptiness and unfaithfulness.

Cheng's letter to Li Gong begins with Cheng's view of the world of the literati, the choices that they face, the decisions that they have to make, and their struggles, confusions, and anxieties. Cheng listed two of his major engagements: literature and the *bagu* (eight-legged) essays that would prepare him for the civil service examinations. But, as he put it, neither of them led him to learning (*xueshu*) and enabled him to form judgments on matters of value and truth. Cheng had other choices: "Nowadays scholars practice only quiet sitting and lecturing so that when successful, they can pursue official titles and salaries, and when unsuccessful, they can be at ease with themselves." Yet the basic system and function of literati practice remained unchanged: lecturing on Confucian moral principles was merely the extension of the practice of *bagu* essays, and quiet sitting and poetry writing fell largely into the category of what might be called individual self-cultivation, albeit in different ways. As for learning, there seemed to be only two choices: Zhu Xi or Lu Xiangshan. According to Cheng, the intellectual history of the past several hundred years had been dominated by the two schools, both of which were equally misleading. To the practice of *bagu* essays and literature, which Cheng had rejected, Zhu and Lu offered no alternatives. On the contrary, Zhu Xi's philosophy had become state orthodoxy, and his exegeses of the Confucian classics had been made the standard texts for the civil service examinations.

To those familiar with the writing of Yan Yuan and Li Gong, Cheng's account of contemporary literati practice is by no means new. In fact, it draws largely on Yan and Li themselves, who were trying to present their own practice as a better alternative. Yet with Cheng as a possible mediator between the Yan-Li school and Wu Jingzi, we may be able to find an entry into the world of *Rulin waishi*. To read Wu's novel from Cheng's approach is to understand the way Wu constructed his literati world: how he divided his literati characters into different groups; defined the relations of those groups;

identified their practices, declared goals, and hidden agendas; and described the patterns of their responses to the issues at stake for Cheng Tingzuo. For instance, the world of *Rulin waishi* is organized around two poles represented, on the one hand, by the self-styled men of culture, or *mingshi*, and, on the other, by the *bagu* essayists, who are candidates for the civil service examinations. On the one side are poetry, fame, and cultural distinction; on the other are official careers, prestige, and economic and political profit. At the intersection of these two universes, at least in the second part of the novel, only one character, Du Shenqing, is able to make the transformation from a "man of refined taste" to an official. Although both groups show an equally strong interest in affiliating with those in power, they never stop deriding each other for the qualities that they find lacking: the poets brag about the respect they command for their taste and literary talent, and the examination candidates emphasize their practice of *bagu* essays as the path to glory. The verbal war between the two circles often involves a third party, represented by such characters as Zhuang Shaoguang, who lay exclusive claim to the authentic learning of Confucianism through their study and practice of the Confucian rituals. The scholars in this third party are often equipped with the rhetoric that Cheng Tingzuo used in his critique of Zhu Xi's interpretations of the Confucian classics, *bagu* essays, and the civil service examination system itself.[34] We should not forget that the novel begins by attacking the civil service examinations for providing the literati with "an easy path toward personal glory."

Cheng Tingzuo's struggles prepared him for what he described as the moment of enlightenment. Yan Yuan's and Li Gong's works raised him above the predicament of existing choices and pointed out to him a new direction that would guide his intellectual pursuits for the rest of his life. Cheng's definition of Yan-Li learning and its significance is implied by

---

34. The comments made by two characters in Chapter 49 of *Rulin waishi* are worth quoting here: "'Your mention of *The Book of Odes* reminds me of another ridiculous thing,' continued Wu Shu. 'Those who take the examinations nowadays cling blindly to Zhu Xi's interpretations, growing more confused the more they try to explain them. Four or five years ago, when Du Shaoqing compiled a commentary on *The Book of Odes* and made use of certain Han commentators, his friends were quite amazed. There is obviously no true learning today!' 'That is only partly true,' put in Chi Hengshan. 'As I see it, scholars should stick to learning without trying to become officials, and officials should stick to officialdom without trying to be scholars too. A man who wants to be both will succeed in neither!'" (R. 662; S. 540).

the way he summarized contemporary practice and the history of intellectual discourse. For the scholars caught between Song and Ming Neo-Confucianism, the only alternative is to "return to antiquity" and restore the lost knowledge of what Yan Yuan himself defined as "solid learning" (*shixue*), more specifically, ritual, music, military training, and farming (*li yue bing nong*). Here again Cheng's letter provides a guide for our reading of *Rulin waishi*. In Chapter 33 of the novel, Chi Hengshan, who later initiates the Taibo project, repeats Cheng almost word for word:

"Scholars nowadays think only of the examinations," complained Mr. Chi. "To write a couple of lines of poetry is considered the height of accomplishment, while the arts of ceremony, music, military training, and farming are completely ignored! When the first emperor of our dynasty pacified the country, his achievements were comparable to former sage-kings such as Tang and Wu, but he set up no system of ceremony and music." (R. 459; S. 369–70)

Chi Hengshan's remarks remind us not merely of Yan Yuan's criticism of the literati's obsession with rhetoric but also of Yan's theory of "solid learning." As in Cheng Tingzuo's letter to Li Gong, Chi gave that theory its standard expression in the formula "ceremony, music, military training, and farming."[35] Cheng's contact with Li Gong and his reading of Yan Yuan provide a clue to the intellectual concerns of the Nanjing literati circle. Wu Jingzi's engagement in that discussion is manifested throughout his novel. Not only did he put Yan Yuan's and Li Gong's words in the mouth of his literatus hero, but he also transformed the Yan-Li project into concrete plots. In the section after the Taibo ceremony, he presented a series of closely related episodes about individual efforts to extend the ceremony into public and private lives: the episodes of Filial Guo (Guo Xiaozi) and the Yu brothers, who devote themselves to Confucian ritualistic obligations (Chapters 37–39, 44–45); the stories of Xiao Yunxian's and Tang Zhentai's efforts to promote military training, farming, and Confucian ceremony (Chapters 39–40, 43–44); and the narrative of Wang Yuhui, a compiler of Confucian ritual manuals who struggles to match his own actions to the texts he has edited (Chapter 48).

Cheng Tingzuo's letter to Li Gong is itself an event. It was part of his effort to reach out, to search for alternatives, to establish connections with the

---

35. See Cheng Tingzuo, *Qingxi wenji fubian, juan* 1, pp. 1a–b. For further information about Wu Jingzi's circle in Nanjing and its close contact with Li Gong, see Hu Shi, "*Qingxi wenji xu*," pp. 1–4; and Chen Meilin, *Wu Jingzi pingzhuan*, pp. 386–404.

influential scholars of the time, and to frame his own engagement within the larger scene of intellectual endeavor that he represented.[36] In general, Cheng's writings suggest an illuminating approach to *Rulin waishi*; they provide an insider's view of what was happening within Wu Jingzi's circle as well as an important frame of reference for Wu's perception of the more general trend of contemporary intellectual discourse. In a sense, Wu's account of the Taibo ceremony and its practitioners can be seen as the product of his cooperation and interaction with other members of his Nanjing circle. In creating the fictional world of Confucian ritual, Wu Jingzi may even have gained knowledge and inspiration from the Confucian ritual manuals that he and his friends compiled for other occasions and purposes. From Cheng Tingzuo's two letters to Fan Shengmo, we learn that Fan and Wu Jingzi once engaged in designing mourning rituals for a family named Tan.[37] In a poem composed in 1754, Wu Jingzi gave an account of the sacrifices dedicated to Cang Jie, the legendary creator of the hexagrams, which were later considered the prototype of the Chinese script. This sacrifice, according to other sources, was organized by Fan Shengmo.[38] A scholar known for his

---

36. At the end of the letter, Cheng Tingzuo expressed his wish to go to the north to study as Li Gong's disciple, although he realized that it was impossible to fulfill the wish immediately. The effort by Cheng is only one part of the story, however. His letter was delayed and did not reach Li Gong until the winter of 1717, almost three years after it was written. In his response, Li Gong expressed no less enthusiasm than his youthful correspondent. He made his intent clear: he hoped that Cheng would be able to carry on Yan Yuan's legacy. Li Gong's letter is preserved in Li Gong, *Shugu houji, juan* 4. It reads as follows: "As I become old, other gentlemen [Yan Yuan's other disciples] are also approaching their declining years. No one except an outstanding young man is able to carry on the sagely way and pass it on to future generations. Now I have suddenly found such a man! You are young and full of talent. Your argument is brilliant like a towering torch lighting up the sky. Did heaven not bring you into being to prevent the inherited learning of Duke Zhou and Confucius from declining! If so, then Yan Yuan will be alive despite his death, and I, though declining as I am, will no longer feel so. I am so grateful deep in my heart. And my expectations for you are boundless!"

37. See Cheng Tingzuo, *Qingxi wenji fubian, juan* 4, pp. 8–12.

38. In his preface to "Rainflower Mount" in a series of poems called "Jinling jingwu tu shi," Wu Jingzi wrote: "During recent years a Cang Jie temple was constructed at the foot of Rainflower Mount. In springtime gentlemen of the prefecture offered animals and wine as sacrifices, dedicating them to Cang Jie inside the temple. The sacrifice was accompanied by ancient music and dance. Every time it was enacted, all the residents of Nanjing rushed out to watch it" (see Li Hanqiu, ed., *"Rulin waishi" yanjiu ziliao*, pp. 44–45). This series of poems was first published in *Wenxue yanjiu jikan* 4 (1956). Some scholars found in this passage a clue to the account of the Taibo ceremony in *Rulin waishi*. The similarities between the Taibo ceremony and the Cang Jie ceremony are indeed unmistakable: they were enacted at the

expertise on ancient ritual and music, Fan served as the model for Wu Jingzi's fictional hero, Chi Hengshan, who initiates and designs the Taibo ceremony. Chi discusses the plan of action and formulas for implementation with Zhuang Shaoguang, who is modeled on Cheng Tingzuo, and Du Shaoqing, who is none other than Wu Jingzi's alter ego.

The *Gazetteer of Shangyuan County* (*Shangyuan xian zhi*) compiled by Cheng Tingzuo in 1751 includes notes on ritual under the rubric of "schools" that sketch the ritual procedures from "welcoming the spirits with the Xianhe Movement of the melody" to "first offering with the Ninhe Movement of the melody" and finally to "third offering with the Chenghe Movement of the melody."[39] Each section documents the lyrics of the songs to be performed and provides the editor's notes on the question whether the ceremonial dance should be included. Cheng Tingzuo's text reveals a common engagement in editing the Confucian ritual texts among the scholars of the Nanjing circle; it also suggests a ceremonial occasion that might have involved several of Wu Jingzi's friends. Conducted in the school of Shangyuan county (whose administration was based in Nanjing) on a regular basis, the ceremony Cheng recorded was most likely guided by the school tutor. This leads to Wu Peiyuan (1688–1768), who was the tutor of Shangyuan county from 1738 to 1746 and, according to many sources, served as the model for Wu Jingzi's creation of Yu Yude, the master of the Taibo ceremony in *Rulin*

---

same location and in the same season, accompanied by ancient music and dance. Wu's report on the splendid spectacle of the Cang Jie ceremony, which attracted many from Nanjing, also reminds us of the scene we find in the representation of the Taibo ceremony. But one thing differs: the ceremony at Rainflower Mount was dedicated to Cang Jie, whereas the ceremony in the novel is dedicated to Wu Taibo. In 1748, just a few years before Wu Jingzi wrote his poems on the scenic places of Jinling, Yuan Mei, then the magistrate of Jiangning county, published *The New Gazetteer of Jiangning County* (*Jiangning xinzhi*). In *juan* 10 he listed the name of the Cang Jie temple, which was located, just as Wu Jingzi indicated in his poem, at the foot of Rainflower Mount. And he identified the organizer of the Cang Jie ceremony as Fan Shengmo, who was Wu Jingzi's friend and known especially for his knowledge of ancient rituals and music (*Jiangning xinzhi, juan* 10, pp. 134). It is thus no coincidence that Fan Shengmo served as the model for Chi Hengshan, who initiates and designs the Taibo ceremony in *Rulin waishi*. He was probably also a vital source of knowledge and inspiration for Wu Jingzi's creation of the Taibo ceremony, for the evidence shows that they often cooperated on rituals. For instance, they once engaged in designing mourning rituals, and their experiment provoked protests from their common friend Cheng Tingzuo. This debate can be inferred from Cheng Tingzuo's letter to Fan Shengmo in *Qingxi wenji fubian, juan* 4, pp. 8–12.

39. Cheng Tingzuo, *Shangyuan xian zhi, juan* 9, pp. 12–15.

waishi. In this sense, *Rulin waishi* provides an implicit dialogue not merely with Yan-Li discourse but also with the ritual praxis of Wu's literati circle in Nanjing.

Although I take Yan Yuan's theory of ritual versus discourse as the point of reference for my interpretation of *Rulin waishi,* I do not regard the novel as the narrative affirmation of Yan Yuan's theory nor as an (auto)biographical record of the ritual lives of its author and his friends. *Rulin waishi* is not a footnote to the intellectual discourse of the day but a discourse of a different order. An acute observer and incisive critic of contemporary literati lives, Wu Jingzi endowed his novel with insight, intellectual alertness, and a sense of sophistication and subtlety that cannot be summarized in an abstract formula or conclusion. His narrative says things that would otherwise be impossible to express and reveals the contemporary cultural and intellectual ethos in a way that no theoretical discourse could adequately convey. As we shall see, the novel addresses the common issues of the day in its own terms.

In fact, although Hu Shi claimed that *Rulin waishi* "is a novel that advocates the doctrine of the Yan-Li school,"[40] its narrative of ritual praxis often evokes a variety of contradictory interpretations; different moral codes, attitudes, and criteria encounter one another but cannot be reconciled. Vexed by the apparent inconsistencies both in theme and in narration, some critics have gone so far as to suggest that parts of the novel are probably forgeries.[41] But they are unable to produce any evidence for their hypothesis, and their attempt to base it on probable authorial intention begs the question. More problematic still is their assumption that authorial intention is single, coherent, and consistent and can therefore be securely grasped. These critical discussions seem to follow a common logic: if a perceived inconsistency in the novel cannot be explained as the result of a forgery, then it is a sign of self-betrayal or of thematic and narrative disorientation.[42]

To understand the implications of the Taibo ceremony, one must read the succeeding parts of the novel that concern individual practice. Although scholars have tentatively established a link between the Taibo ceremony and Yan-Li discourse, they seem unable to substantiate it with a solid interpreta-

---

40. Hu Shi, "*Qingxi wenji xu,*" p. 3.

41. For instance, Zhang Peihang argues that parts of Chapters 36, 38–40, 41–44, and 56 were written by someone other than Wu Jingzi; see his "*Rulin waishi* yuanmao chutan."

42. For further discussion of the editions and authorship of *Rulin waishi,* see the Appendix.

tion of the section of the novel under discussion. Focusing on this section, I argue instead that Wu Jingzi engaged in a dynamic process of critical inquiry and self-reflection by questioning the very values of the ceremony that he apparently affirmed in Chapter 37. Conceived of in this way, his narrative of individuals' ritualistic undertakings enabled him to reveal the problems of practice that Yan Yuan had glossed over. To elaborate his solution to these problems, Wu Jingzi drew on the conceptual and rhetorical repertory of Yan Yuan and other Confucian ritualists, but he neither concluded that his own solution was final nor spared it from scrutiny. It is this relentless self-scrutiny that gives the novel its critical edge and energy—as the novel progresses, Wu's solution becomes a problem itself.

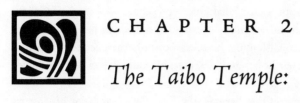

CHAPTER 2

The Taibo Temple:

Ascetic Versus Narrative Ritual

Although Wu Jingzi, like his fellow literati, was interested in Confucian ritual, he chose to compose a novel instead of treatises, essays, and ritual
manuals. The question is why. Did he achieve in fiction something more
than his contemporaries did in their essays? What does Wu Jingzi, as a novelist, tell us about Confucian ritual? And how does the novel as a sensitive
register of contemporary culture capture the symbolic system of *li* that is
embodied in ritual? I shall begin to address these questions by analyzing the
episodes that follow the Taibo ceremony.

Filial Guo: Ascetic Hero in Action

Filial Guo is introduced immediately after the Taibo ceremony is announced
in the headnote to Chapter 37: "Through sacrifice to an ancient sage, scholars revive ancient ritual in Nanjing. / A filial son is seen off by his friends to
search for his father in Sichuan." Despite his absence, Guo, through Wu
Shu's mediation, comes into contact with the members of Yu Yude's circle,
including Du Shaoqing, Chi Hengshan, and Zhuang Shaoguang, men who
establish their reputations by their practice of the Taibo ceremony and their
unfailing support of filial sons and chaste women. According to Wu Shu,
Guo, who "has traveled through the country for twenty years in search of his
father," deserves their commendation (R. 513; S. 416). In response, Du Shaoqing treats Guo with ceremonial respect, and Yu Yude and Zhuang Shao-

guang write letters of recommendation to friends in places that he will visit in his travels. Their approval of Filial Guo represents a new stage of Confucian practice, in which the ceremony is extended outside or beyond the temple. As Filial Guo leaves Nanjing, he takes not only their letters of recommendation but also their hopes and blessings; his journey has been endowed with new significance.

During the Ming and Qing periods, the filial son's search for his lost father was a common theme in literature and biography.[1] The story of Wang Yuan provided basic motifs. In history and in fiction alike, Wang Yuan's journey is portrayed as an ordeal or adventure, as he struggles with hunger, cold, and frustration, not to mention wild animals, foreign lands, and wars. It also acquires an allegorical dimension through anecdotes about dreams, omens, miracles, and the revelation of the will of spirits or gods. Although it is preoccupied with the filial son's fantastic journey, the story begins in the real world. In *juan* 3 of *Shi dian tou* (Rocks nod their heads), for example, the narrator offers a detailed account of the tribulations caused by the corvée system in rural areas. This explains the father's desertion of his wife and infant son and thus sets in motion the rest of the story. When Wang Yuan finds his father in a Buddhist temple, the moral drama takes a final twist: the father, ashamed of deserting his family, refuses to return home with his son. It is only because of the son's insistent appeals that he eventually changes his mind. As in many such tales, the story ends with a family reunion, and the government bestows an award on Wang.

The story of Filial Guo follows the established route of Wang Yuan's journey until the reunion scene. This alteration changes the nature of the narrative. Filial Guo is faithful to the model of Wang Yuan, but his father refuses to play the prescribed role. Guo's encounter with his father thus leads not to a reconciliation and reunion but to a confrontation.

Recognizing his father, Guo knelt down and sobbed. "Please get up, sir," said the monk. "I have no son. You must have taken me for someone else." "I have traveled thousands of miles to find you, Father. Why won't you recognize me?" "I told you just now, I have no son. You must look elsewhere for your father. Why come crying to me?" "Though I haven't seen you for so many years, Father, do you think I don't

---

1. The story of Wang Yuan was rewritten many times in the Ming and Qing periods. It can be found in Li Zhi, *Xu cangshu*, p. 483; and in *Mingshi*, *juan* 297, p. 7604. It also feeds on literary creation, and variants can be found in *Shi dian tou, juan* 3, pp. 45–71; Zhou Ji, *Xihu erji*, pp. 585–603; and *Bieben Erke pai'an jingqi, juan* 19, pp. 1a–28b.

know you?" The filial son knelt there and would not rise. "I took orders as a boy," protested the monk. "What son could I have?" At that Guo wept bitterly. "You may not recognize your son, Father, but your son insists on recognizing you!" His persistence made the old monk lose patience. "You scoundrel!" he shouted. "You've just come to make trouble. Get out now! I'm going to close the temple gate!" Still Guo knelt there sobbing and would not leave. "If you don't go," threatened the monk, "I'll fetch a knife and kill you!" "Kill me if you like, Father!" cried Guo, prostrate on the ground. "I cannot leave you!" In a rage, the old monk pulled Guo to his feet, seized him by the scruff of his neck, and pushed him out, locking the gate behind him. He then went back into the temple and turned a deaf ear to his son's cries. (R. 527–28; S. 425)

Guo tries everything that Wang Yuan does, but his journey goes awry. At its end, Guo is confronted with a situation beyond his control and comprehension: for all his loyalty to his prescribed role, he must now act alone, without the cooperation of others, to make his story a successful one. Wang Yuan's father fails to appear. Instead Guo encounters a distorted mirror image, Wang Hui. Like Wang Yuan's father, Wang Hui abandons his family and refuses to return home, but for completely different reasons. He is, we are told in Chapter 37, a fugitive because he once participated in a rebellion against the throne. Thus, from the very beginning, his crime shapes his identity. Recasting his identity has consumed much of his life, and when this new identity is threatened by his son's unexpected appearance, he panics and reacts with fury. He rejects Guo and threatens him with violence: the outraged father seeks to erase all traces of his own past, his son included.

The episode of Filial Guo is designed to frustrate conventional expectations. Guo's journey fails to yield the anticipated result, and his loyalty to his father comes at the expense of his loyalty to the throne. It is difficult to comprehend this story without taking into account its deviation from the canonical narrative of the filial son. But why does *Rulin waishi* create such an unconventional, peculiar image of a filial son to embody the moral vision of the Taibo ceremony?

To answer this question, we must comprehend the role the father plays in the narrative of Filial Guo. For all the ethical and narrative conflicts it provokes, the father's behavior contributes, in its own way, to the image of Guo as a filial son. That image is created, so to speak, at the expense of the father. Devotion to a legally guilty, socially unfit, and morally problematic father requires courage, determination, and willingness to sacrifice oneself. The father's misconduct prevents Filial Guo from fulfilling his ritual obligation, and his persistence, despite all the tremendous difficulties, serves to highlight his devotion and commitment. The father's rejection spurs the son to extreme actions that demonstrate the strength of his moral will. This becomes even clearer in the second half of the Filial Guo story. With no hope of winning his father's recognition, Guo does the best a son can do under these circumstances. He rents a room near the temple where his father lives and bribes a priest to take fuel and food daily to his father. After exhausting his resources, he hires himself out as a laborer to nearby families, earning a few cents a day in order to support his father until the latter's death. In his final appearance, in Chapter 39, Guo is on his way home carrying the bones of his deceased father. After hearing this story, one of Guo's friends comments, "When he has carried his father's bones home and buried them, he will have fulfilled the ambition of a lifetime" (R. 538; S. 433). Guo's lifelong effort to restore the lost family bond presents filial piety in its extreme form, as a sacred obligation. As such, it transcends mundane duties and demands absolute commitment. Filial Guo symbolizes such commitment: regardless of his father's character, behavior, and treatment, he pursues his ritualistic obligation to the exclusion of his other duties.

Subjected to frustration, virtue must bear the unbearable. Yet the narrative of Guo's loyalty to his father contains no psychological conflict or struggle. Even at the moment of crisis, when Guo is rejected by his father, there is no mention of Guo's mental state.[2] The crisis is merely part of the ordeal through which he demonstrates his moral excellence. However difficult and complicated the situations he confronts, Guo has no problems of individual choice, decision, or moral conflict: he does what he is supposed to do. His actions can be best interpreted as an extension of Confucian ritual. As described in Chapter 37, Confucian ritual consists of a series of prescribed acts; it demands conformity through action rather than through individual choice and decision. As in ritual, the rules of filiality determine Guo's behavior at each step of his journey. He does not choose to stay after having been rejected by his father; rather, he "is chosen" to do so. And his response to the ever-changing and complex outside world is predi-

---

2. Wu Jingzi's deviation from the established model of the filial son narrative becomes more evident if we read the Filial Guo episode with reference to, for instance, "Wang Liben tianya qiu fu" in Shi dian tou. Unlike the Filial Guo story, the account of Wang Liben (Wang Yuan)'s journey in search of his father is packed with supernatural revelations, dreams, and psychological struggles. See Shi dian tou, pp. 45–71.

cated on a ritualistic obligation that permits no adjustment to circumstances.

Since psychological struggles involving choice, decision, and internal moral conflict play no part in Guo's journey, there is no need for him to speak. In a novel known for its portrayal of the literati's excessive use of Confucian rhetoric, Guo stands out for his extraordinary silence. He scarcely introduces himself even on the occasions when he should do so, and he never talks about his motivations. In a sense, his silence speaks for itself: if filial piety is a sacred ritual obligation, it must be acted out as prescribed, without negotiation or compromise. His father may be a fugitive, but Guo does not use that as an excuse to avoid his obligation; nor does he find it necessary to justify his commitment to that obligation. As if he were participating in a ritual, Guo rises above the temporary flux of mundane affairs, conflicting interests, and sociopolitical forces. His ritual, though silent and enigmatic, is complete in itself and on its own terms.

In the account of Filial Guo, we once again encounter the interesting parallel between *Rulin waishi* and *The Chronicle of Yan Xizhai's Life*. In *The Chronicle*, Yan Yuan, like Filial Guo, makes several journeys in search of his father. After extraordinary efforts, Yan learns that his father has passed away long before. Although he cannot serve a living father, his journey assures him of his origins and provides an opportunity to fulfill his ritual obligations. *The Chronicle* presents Yan performing a series of ceremonies in front of his father's tomb in Manchuria and before his father's tablet, which Yan Yuan carries back to the ancestral temple in his hometown. Yan Yuan conducts himself strictly according to the requirements of the ritual manuals, even going so far as to regulate his cries—how many, where, and how loud—as if he were acting in a play. The report of his ceremonial activities concludes with his own comments on the texts of Confucian ritual: "[Yan Yuan] read 'The Death Ritual for the Shi' in the *Etiquette and Ritual* and sighed: 'The books by ancient sages mostly record activities, whereas the books by scholars of later periods mostly articulate theories; this is the difference between concreteness and abstractness.'"[3] In recommending the *Etiquette and Ritual*, Yan Yuan reveals his ideals for his own ceremonial practices. His comment applies, it would seem, not only to *The Chronicle* but also to *Rulin waishi* and its narrative of Filial Guo's ritual journey to restore a lost family bond.

---

3. Yan Yuan, *Yan Yuan ji*, p. 758.

Another link suggests that this parallel between the two texts is no coincidence. Filial Guo's father rebelled against the Ming and then spent the rest of his life in hiding; according to *The Chronicle*, Yan Yuan's father was captured by the Manchus and then died from unknown causes. Although *The Chronicle* seems to gloss over the history of Yan's father, it places Yan in a situation in which he has choices but acts as if he does not. And it is precisely his denial of choices that helps him define his ritual: in his journey he follows a path that has no crossroads. In Yan Yuan we find a prototype for Filial Guo, an ascetic Confucian hero adhering to his ritualistic obligations both in routine practice and in extraordinary circumstances.

Narrative Ritual

The story of Filial Guo is a story of extremes. Middle ground and middle conditions are excluded as options: the choices are ritual and nonritual; between right and wrong. The clash is implicit in the contrast between Guo and his father. Seldom do we encounter a story of a filial son in which the father bears so much blame for neglecting his ritualistic obligations. Seldom, if ever, does such a story end with the conflict between father and son left unresolved. In *Rulin waishi*, this conflict occurs not merely between two individuals but between two different worlds: the father inhabits the world of narrative ritual or narrative *li*; the son, through committed action, struggles to restore the ritual order. The clash between the two worlds is the key to the meaning of the Filial Guo story: since Guo's ascetic practice is a critical reaction to his father's narrative ritual, its extremism can be measured in terms of the extent of the narrative ritual.

The motive forces that govern the father's world are revealed in an anecdote about Wang Hui in Chapter 7. As if to highlight the contrast between father and son, this story, too, focuses on the subject of filial piety. Wang Hui and Xun Mei have just passed the metropolitan examination and are waiting for an official appointment when news of Xun Mei's mother's death reaches the capital. Xun Mei knows that the standard procedure calls for him to return to his hometown to observe a three-year period of mourning before assuming an official position. But Wang Hui does not want his fellow graduate (and future political ally) to lose a chance for official appointment. He suggests that they conceal the news until Xun has received an appointment. Xun Mei had decided to petition for mourning leave, but now, under Wang Hui's influence, he changes his mind and tries to find an alternative.

They invite Jin Dongya, a clerk whose job it is to keep the records in the Board of Civil Office, to discuss the matter. Jin explains that it would be inappropriate for officials to conceal the death of a parent. Exemption from or a reduction in one's ritual obligations is sometimes made, but the likelihood of a successful application is in direct proportion to one's official rank. But Xun Mei's rank is not high enough. The only way for him to obtain an exemption would be to plead with high-ranking officials for a recommendation. In the next scene, Xun Mei doffs his mourning robes and secretly visits his teachers, Director of Studies Zhou Jin and Examiner Fan Jin.

Although Confucian texts are the approved guides to sociopolitical practice, everyone tries to find an excuse for not complying with them. From Wang Hui's and Xun Mei's perspective, ritual obligation is externally imposed and thus undesirable, particularly when it conflicts with one's interests. This attitude is inscribed in the official rules—high officials can receive exemptions from their obligations, their duty to the throne serving as a legitimate excuse. The result, as shown in Chapters 2 to 30, is an endless negotiation that makes compromises between the Confucian ritual codes and the contingencies of political life.

Ironically, if Filial Guo had been in Xun Mei's position, Wang Hui, his own father, would have advised him not to fulfill his filial obligations. In Guo's case, the excuse would have been persuasive, for Wang Hui committed a crime against the throne that could legitimately exempt Guo from his filial duties. The story of Wang Hui and Xun Mei suggests the range of choices before Guo. Accordingly, each step he takes can be read as an implicit rejection of the choices his father made.

The literati characters in Chapters 2 to 30 are all well versed in Confucian rhetoric. They are, indeed, well enough educated to be able to camouflage the profits of their official chicanery, and they are equally capable, when necessary, of justifying their pursuit of self-interest with moral rhetoric. Constantly engaged in negotiation, interpretation, and self-representation, they either substitute words for deeds or pretend that words are deeds. This is evident in Chapter 5, in which Wang Ren (the name is a pun on "without benevolence") promises to help Yan Dayu establish Yan's current concubine in the place of his dying wife (Wang's own sister). Wang speaks sternly out of a sense of justice: "The great thing about us scholars is our adherence to Confucian moral obligations (*gangchang*). If we were writing a composition in which we spoke on behalf of Confucius, we would take exactly the line we are taking now" (R. 77; S. 59). Wang Ren's grand statement is juxtaposed with a behind-the-scenes exchange of favors and money that undermines its credibility. "Yan Dayu," the novel continues, "gave another fifty taels of silver to the Wang brothers, who then left, exuding righteousness from every pore" (R. 77; S. 59). With Wang Ren and his brother Wang De (a pun on "without virtue"), the fight for self-interest is above all a game of impersonation in which one "establishes words" or "speaks on behalf of the Confucian sages" (dai shengxian liyan).[4] Like candidates for the civil service examinations, who use the same expression in describing their bagu (eight-legged) examination essays, the brothers are now able to profit from Confucian rhetoric with an awe-inspiring sense of self-righteousness.

Justifying himself in terms of composing bagu essays, Wang Ren unwittingly points out the nature of his own conduct. The speech that Mr. Gao, a Reader in the Hanlin Academy, gives in Chapter 34 sheds light on Wang Ren's self-representation. Commenting on Du Shaoqing's father, an honest official, Mr. Gao says:

While in office he showed no respect for his superiors but simply tried to please the people, talking nonsense about "fostering filial piety and brotherly love, and encouraging agriculture." Such phrases are mere figures of speech to be used in composition for the sake of moral cultivation, yet he took them seriously, with the result that his superior disliked him and removed him from his post! (R. 466; S. 375)

According to Mr. Gao, Confucian teachings such as "fostering filial piety and brotherly love" are at worst "nonsense" and at best "mere figures of speech." Those who take them seriously end up being removed from office. In the domain of politics only power matters; legitimacy and morality remain important only in discourse, which is confined to its own territory, apart from action. Mr. Gao's remarks unerringly reveal the secret of the Wang brothers: equipped with a repository of "figures of speech," the brothers create their own fiction about themselves. Seldom, if ever, does their fiction come into conflict with the ritual, which, contingent upon narration, negotiation, and circumstantial interpretation, is itself a fiction that has no substance; as Mr. Gao puts it, it is merely part of the stories that literati tell about themselves and to each other.

---

4. In the Ming, candidates for the civil service examinations were required to compose the bagu essays in the voice of the Confucian sages. For a further study of these essays, see Qian Zhongshu, Tanyi lu, pp. 32–33.

Enacted on domestic or public occasions by the members of the elite, Confucian rituals, as we see again and again in *Rulin waishi*, are inseparable from narrative discourse; more often than not, they are merely the subject of discourse, isolated from the realm of practice. This is, Wu suggests, where things go astray. As ritual action is replaced by a discourse of ritual, it is denied its own role as a medium for transmitting values, promoting virtue, and constructing social reality. Just as serious to Wu Jingzi is the fact that once ritual comes to rely on discourse for meaning, it is susceptible to changing interpretations and unending negotiations and compromises.

Nowhere is narrative ritual more obviously represented than in the episode of Fan Jin's observances of the mourning period in Chapter 4. Soon after Fan passes the provincial examination, his mother, elated by her son's success, dies of apoplexy. Much to his dismay, this incident delays Fan's taking the metropolitan examination. During the period of mourning, Fan meets Zhang Jingzhai, a retired official, who persuades him to make a tour to raise some money:

"Of course," Zhang said, "the proper thing is to remain in retirement for three years. But on account of the funeral expenses, I think you would be justified in trying to raise some money. There is no need to be too scrupulous. Since your great success, you have not yet been to see your honorable patron; and Gaoyao County is extremely rich—we may be able to raise some money over there. I want to visit him too, so why don't we go together? I'll be responsible for all the expenses on the road and see that you're not troubled with them." "It is exceedingly kind of you," said Fan Jin. "But I am not sure whether this is correct in terms of ceremonial procedure." "The correct procedure varies according to circumstances," replied Mr. Zhang. "I don't see anything inappropriate here." (R. 59; S. 45)

In proposing the fund-raising trip, Zhang uses the words *qiufeng* (to solicit money or gifts with legitimate excuses), a locution that betrays the evil nature of his suggestion. Later, it is confirmed that Zhang himself tried to benefit from this trip. The death ritual for Fan Jin's mother provides them with a legitimate and convenient excuse. Instead of giving a definite answer to Zhang's suggestion, Fan Jin responds with a question that demands a further assurance rather than a rejection; he is, indeed, willing to be persuaded. Zhang's response is in itself a guide for reading Part II of the novel; it sums up the logic that governs the conduct of most individual literati. A literal translation is "Ritual is made up of principles, but it can also be adjusted according to circumstances" (*Li you jing, yi you quan*), a paraphrase of

Zhu Xi's words.[5] Zhang Wenhu (1808?–85), a Qing commentator on the novel, reveals its function in the civil service examinations: "This is an expression that can help one in composing the *bagu* examination essays." Zhang's comments reflect the fact that Zhu Xi's interpretations of the Confucian classics constituted the standard curriculum for the examinations.

Like other Neo-Confucians of the Song, Zhu Xi participated in constructing the *daotong*, the "unified succession of the Dao," a term derived from *zhengtong*, a line of legitimate dynastic succession, but it denies political institutions direct access to the moral authority of the ancient sages. Instead of confirming Zhu Xi's discourse, Wu Jingzi, however, portrayed its absorption into official institutions.[6] In so doing, he revealed Neo-Confucianism's inherent tendency toward compromise. In this scene, Zhang quotes Zhu Xi's words to justify the compromising of the ritual codes.[7]

The Dualistic System of Li

Like Yan Yuan, Wu Jingzi depicted literati discourse as an exercise in empty rhetoric, a game with words, but he also disclosed the hidden forces that shape the rules of the game and contribute to the discrepancies between word and deed. In most cases, Wu portrayed his literati characters not as transgressors of the existing sociopolitical and symbolic system but as impostors, pretenders, quacks, hypocrites, and tenacious status-seekers who play with the rules and use them to gain whatever advantages they can. Accordingly, their degeneration is not personal; it indicates how far the system allows or even encourages them to go. In his ironic account of the literati world, Wu thus went beyond exposing individuals' misappropriation of Confucian rhetoric or bemoaning the inadequacy of words to cope

---

5. Zhu Xi, *Zhuzi daquan, juan* 14, pp. 8b–9a.

6. *Rulin waishi* often targets Zhu Xi's philosophy and exegesis of the Confucian texts. For instance, in Chapter 34, Du Shaoqing criticizes his contemporaries for blindly adhering to Zhu Xi's interpretation of the Confucian classics, and in Chapter 49 Wu Shu discredits Zhu Xi's exegesis of the *Book of Odes* (*Shijing*).

7. Such criticism of *Daoxue* or *lixue* (Learning of Dao or Learning of principles), especially Zhu Xi learning or Zhu Xi discourse (Zhuzi xue), is common in the literati discourse of the Qing period. Even the Kangxi emperor (r. 1662–1722), who recognized *lixue* as the official state philosophy and promoted such *lixue* scholars as Xiong Cilü (1635–1709) and Li Guangdi (1642–1718), distrusted such scholars, because "they speak of *lixue* all day long, but what they do completely contradicts their own words" (*Donghua lu, juan* 32). For further study of this subject, see Chen Meilin, *Wu Jingzi yanjiu*, pp. 197–225.

with reality; he elucidated the irrevocable dissolution of the Confucian norm (*li*) itself.

I shall proceed with no preconceived definition of *li*, but with a range of questions about its attempt to unify the realms of social, political, and moral practice. At the core of what is called *li* lies a double assumption: first, the demarcation between the realm of mundane experience and the realm of sacredness, which is formed of the ancient texts, discourse, and myths and is thus "always the source of significance as well as the realm of being of significance";[8] and second, the possibility and necessity of representing sacredness in the mundane world through a variety of social praxes such as ritual. Thus, the Confucian ritualized world may be called, to borrow a phrase from Fingarette, "the mundane world as sacred."[9]

This concept of the sacred does not presuppose the existence of a transcendent order distinct from society; rather, it denotes the normative order that serves both as a basis for society and as the ideal against which social reality is measured. In other words, the dichotomy of the normative order and its representation in the mundane world is framed within the same structure of classification. Here we may refer to Benjamin Schwartz's characterization of the dualism of the Confucian ritualistic order.[10] On the one hand, the world of *li* is a normative order whose harmony is maintained when everyone plays his appropriate part within the larger whole. Social hierarchy, in this sense, indicates only distinctions in terms of duties, responsibilities, and moral obligations. If everyone behaved precisely in accordance with ritual prescriptions, the society would be transformed into "a sacred community" in Fingarette's sense. But on the other hand, the world of *li* is a sociopolitical order within which human beings are stratified in terms of authority, power, and wealth. Since the normative order of *li* is at the same time the source of political power and the status quo, it is in reality inseparable from social exchange, negotiation, and the struggle over the control and distribution of political and economic resources. As a result, *li* possesses two seemingly antithetical characteristics: that of a normatively ordained institution and that of an instrument of sociopolitical exchange and maneuver. In Confucian practice, there is an inevitable conflict between the normative order prescribed by *li* and its actual representation in the sociopolitical sphere.

---

8. Fingarette, *Confucius: The Secular as Sacred*, p. 66.
9. Ibid.
10. Schwartz, *The World of Thought in Ancient China*, pp. 67–69.

Since the same system of *li* functions to maintain both the normative order and the sociopolitical order, whether something is done in accordance with the prescriptions of *li* or out of instrumental calculation is a matter of perception. It may be difficult, if not impossible, to describe moral or ritualistic conduct without at the same time evoking an alternative interpretation. The question, then, is how to cope with this dilemma. In fact, neither Fingarette nor Schwartz explains if or how the dualistic system of *li* resolves its internal tensions. It is at this point that the role Confucian discourse plays in social integration comes to the fore.

In a recent study on the interaction of Confucian narrative discourse and social reality, Weigang Chen argues:

Confucian narrative indicates the system of social schemes; it represents exemplary role models and practices in such a way as to constitute a sense of reality to the members of the society. We may call this narrative reality the "narrative world" or the "text world." In contrast to this narrative world is the actual world in which strategic actions and instrumental concerns are prevalent. The crucial question is how these two worlds can be connected to one another? The answer to this question leads us to what is called *phronesis*. In the Confucian context, *phronesis* can be defined as a way of life whose practitioners consider themselves bearers of the narrative world. It is through their social practice that narrative cuts into reality and the interaction between text and reality becomes possible.[11]

The role of narrative in constituting and transforming reality can be taken in different senses.[12] In the case of Confucian narrative discourse, we may, first

---

11, Weigang Chen, "Confucian Marxism," p. 286.

12. The role of verbal articulation and narrative discourse in shaping the sociopolitical world has become the subject of scholarship in a variety of academic fields. Lynn Hunt, in *Politics, Culture, and Class in the French Revolution*, contends: "Revolutionary language did not simply reflect the realities of revolutionary changes and conflicts, but rather was itself transformed into an instrument of political and social change. In this sense, political language was not merely an expression of an ideological position that was determined by underlying social or political interests. The language itself helped shape the perception of interests and hence the development of ideologies. In other words, revolutionary political discourse was rhetorical; it was a means of persuasion, a way of reconstituting the social and political world" (p. 24). In *Language and Symbolic Power*, Pierre Bourdieu explores "the possibility of changing the social world by changing the representation of this world which contributes to its reality or, more precisely, by counterpoising a *paradoxical pre-vision*, a utopia, a project or program, to the ordinary vision which apprehends the social world as a natural world: the *performative* utterance, the political pre-vision, is in itself a pre-vision which aims to bring about what it utters. It contributes practically to the reality of what it announces by the fact of uttering it, of

of all, emphasize its ideological aspect in a Marxist sense. *Li* provides an arena for the representation and regulation of competing political and economic interests. Yet it cannot be fully legitimized unless it is infused with an ideal vision of the whole society as a "sacred community of human beings." The virtue of Confucian narrative discourse lies in its ability to describe social hierarchy, the status quo, and political relationships in ethical language. In this language, a son's loyalty to his father and commoners' obedience to the elite are imbued with moral obligations and necessity. The structure of power that underlies such ties of obedience and loyalty is either disguised or interpreted as something else. In this ethical language, its literati practitioners find both the ideal and the rhetoric that they need to conceal, from themselves as well as the public, the true interests at stake in their sociopolitical and ritualistic practices. This is what I call the ideological aspect of Confucian discourse.

But it would be inappropriate to consider Confucian discourse merely an expression of an ideological position that is determined by underlying social or political interests, for the language itself often helps shape the perception of interests and the construction of the actual world. The same is true of Confucian rhetoric, so long as it functions as a scheme of perception and conceptualization and a means of persuasion. It can be argued that Confucian discourse participates in constituting sociopolitical reality by providing a vision of a Confucian moral community that allows one to define one's relationship with others as well as oneself. One either perceives the world through the model provided by Confucian texts or comes to represent Confucian texts through action. In other words, one can cope with the internal tension of *li* through the reinforcement of *phronesis*, and the Confucian ritualized world is made possible precisely through this process of transformation from texts to reality, from the past to the present, and from the sacred to the mundane.

The dualistic *li* relies on discourse to mediate between its ideal vision and the real world; discourse plays an indispensable role both in evoking that vi-

---

pre-dicting it and making it pre-dicted, of making it conceivable and above all credible and thus creating the collective representation and will which contribute to its production. Every theory, as the word itself suggests, is a program of perception, but this is all the more true of theories about the social world. . . . Many 'intellectual debates' are less unrealistic than they seem if one is aware of the degree to which one can modify social reality by modifying the agents' representation of it" (p. 128).

sion and in transforming it into reality. But *li* also needs narrative to help secure its message and dispel alternative interpretations. Since the dualism of *li* generates inevitable ambiguities in the perception of a specific ritualistic act, we need an authoritative narrator to guarantee the purity of its agent's motives. This narrator speaks with unquestioned moral authority, and this authority is duly complemented and reinforced by the omniscient point of view from which he sees the world and illuminates the truth about it. Indeed, important to this narrative world is not merely what one does, but why and how one does it; our ability to form a moral judgment about a specific deed depends, to a large degree, on our apprehension of its agent's attitude, demeanor, and inner world. Accordingly, I shall argue that the dualistic system of *li* is inseparable from narrative representation; it is, in fact, constructed through discourse, and its moral implications are secured by the omniscient narrator, who is none other than a Confucian sage.

Rulin waishi offers a negative, mirror image of dualistic *li*, the symbolic system of the mundane as sacred. In the episodes of Fan Jin and the Wang brothers, the internal tension of *li* serves as the fundamental source of irony. Fan Jin and the Wang brothers embody the dominant codes of this dualistic world, which center on the court as the source of both moral and political authority, and identify ritual order with mundane order. They and the other major literati characters in Chapters 2 to 30 spend their lifetime struggling to get to court. The first step in this journey is to take the civil service examinations, in which they "establish words" or "speak," as they themselves put it, "on behalf of Confucius." In a sequence of farcical and scandalous scenes, Wu Jingzi showed the literati taking advantage of this dualistic system through deliberate manipulation of Confucian discourse: on the one hand, their practice of moral rhetoric provides them a legitimate "shortcut to personal glory," to use Wang Mian's words in the introductory chapter of the novel; on the other hand, their reference to Confucius also enables them to represent themselves as spokesmen for Confucian principles and thus to lay exclusive claim to moral authority, which, once obtained, can easily be converted to political and economic benefit.

These episodes suggest the need for a re-examination of the function of words in the larger symbolic world of *li* by demonstrating a consistent pattern in the way literati use Confucian rhetoric. When Wang Ren claims that "The great thing about us scholars is our adherence to Confucian moral obligations," he is making a statement that amounts to nothing more than a gesture. In fact, it is irrelevant to him whether he believes what he says or not, as is the question of "believing" itself, for he now chooses to play roles. And the success of his role playing is secured by his own definition of what he has been doing all along. Even when he finally fails, under outside pressure, to fulfill his promise through action, he does not necessarily break his word, at least from his and Mr. Gao's perspectives. For his promises are "mere figures of speech," to borrow Mr. Gao's phrase, "to be used in composition for the sake of moral cultivation." The Wang brothers episode indicates the degree to which words are separated from thoughts and deeds. Confucian discourse does little, if anything, to ease the tension between ritualistic obligations and sociopolitical demands. Nor does it fulfill its ideological function by persuading its users to believe in the moral vision it conveys. Instead, it provides the Wang brothers with a legitimate instrument for disguising their self-interested agenda and bargaining for economic and moral rewards. Those who, like Du Shaoqing's father, have faith in Confucian discourse and strive to express it in their lives are derided as dupes. In these stories, *phronesis* is represented as failure rather than success.

The Yan family ritual described in Chapter 5 of the novel is an instance of narrative ritual enacted in the domain of family life. It demonstrates how Confucian discourse, ritual obligations, and socioeconomic interests are intertwined in a complex process of negotiation and ultimately contribute to the making of an uncanny ritual—a family scandal in the form of a ceremony. The major character of the story is Yan Jiansheng (Licentiate Yan, whose name is Yan Dayu or Yan Zhihe), who has bought himself the rank of student in the Imperial College. When Lady Wang, Yan Dayu's wife, becomes seriously ill, the relationship between Wang and Zhao, Yan Dayu's concubine and the mother of his only son, becomes delicate. Yan Dayu intends to make Zhao his wife after Lady Wang's death, and that is also Zhao's wish. There is, therefore, a conspiracy of consent between them, although both seem to be principally concerned about their son. Yan is afraid that his family property will be appropriated by his nephews, who are as greedy as "starving wolves," if he fails to make his son the legitimate heir. Zhao knows, better than anyone else, that her status in the Yan family will not be secure unless her son has the right of inheritance. Thus, for different purposes, Yan and Zhao join in conducting a family ritual that provides them a legitimate ground, as well as the guise of decency, for social maneuvering.

The ceremony is prefaced by a series of negotiations. Zhao manages to win permission from Lady Wang, and Yan Dayu works hard to get Wang's two brothers to endorse Zhao as his legitimate wife. The behind-the-scenes negotiations involve rhetoric, tears, and, most important, money. Under the stress of these circumstances, Lady Wang eventually and reluctantly gives permission, and this in turn licenses Yan Dayu and Zhao to carry out their plan. They are now acting in the name of Lady Wang to fulfill her dying wish. The most important thing is to hold a ceremony legitimizing their marriage before Lady Wang dies.

Three days later, accordingly, Wang Ren and Wang De came to Lady Wang's house and wrote scores of invitations to relatives from the various branches of the family. And all of them came, with the exception of Yan's five sons [Yan Dayu's nephews] from next door. When the guests had breakfasted, they went to Lady Wang's bedside to witness her will, which her brothers drew up and signed. Meanwhile, Mr. Yan put on a scholar's cap, a blue gown, and a red silk sash, and Concubine Zhao dressed herself in crimson and put a gold chaplet on her head. As they worshipped heaven and earth and the ancestors, Wang Ren drew on his vast erudition to write a most moving announcement of this marriage directed to the Yan ancestors. Having informed the ancestors, they left the shrine. Then Wang Ren and Wang De sent for their wives, and they all kowtowed together to the new husband and wife. All the relatives congratulated them in order of seniority, after which the stewards, manservants, and maidservants did reverence to their master and mistress. The new wife went in alone to bow before the dying mistress, calling her "Elder Sister." But Lady Wang had already lost consciousness. (R. 77–78; S. 59–60)

Lady Wang is a member of the audience for whom the wedding is designed, but, paradoxically, the wedding presumes her death. At the final phase of the ceremony sanctifying her new status as Mrs. Yan, Concubine Zhao enters the inner chamber alone to bow to the dying Mrs. Yan, while the latter, as expected, collapses physically and psychologically. Although it is fully justified, the title "Elder Sister" is given to Mrs. Yan on the assumption of her death. Coming from the mouth of Concubine Zhao, it is not a blessing but a curse, or a curse in the guise of a blessing. As we know, a central concern of Confucian ritual is with "naming," and nothing is more important than rectifying names (zhengming) so that everyone occupies the prescribed position. But the relationship of the two "sisters" goes awry, because we know, as they do, that they cannot both survive under the same roof.

Their ceremonies at an end, the guests crowded into the great hall, second hall, library, and inner chambers to sit down to more than twenty tables. They feasted till midnight. Mr. Yan was acting as host in the great hall when his son's wet nurse burst in breathlessly and cried, "The mistress has passed away!" Weeping, Mr. Yan went to the bedroom and found his new wife beating her head against the bed. At his entry, she gave a cry and fainted. They helped her up, prized open her teeth, and poured hot water down her throat. Then she came to herself and rolled on the floor, tearing her hair and sobbing as if her heart would break. Not even her husband could calm her. The two sisters-in-law took advantage of the confusion to whisk away the clothes, gold, and pearls. One of them even picked up the gold chaplet that the new wife had let fall and concealed it in her clothes. Mr. Yan told the nurse to bring in his son and threw a coarse linen cloth over the child's shoulders as a sign of mourning. The coffin had been ready for some time. They placed the corpse in the coffin, which had been set in the central hall. It was now dawn. All the guests filed in, bowed before the coffin, and went home. (R. 78; S. 60)

The wedding ceremony of Yan Dayu and Zhao is followed immediately by the funeral for Lady Wang, which turns out to be a farce. Concubine Zhao, now the legitimate wife of Yan Dayu, has done everything to hasten the collapse of Lady Wang. But the recent bride has no trouble transforming herself into chief mourner. With an exaggerated performance, she tries to win a reputation for sincerity and honesty. It is noteworthy that her melodramatic act is accompanied by the farcical behavior of the other participants in the same ritual: Lady Wang's sisters-in-law sack the bedroom and whisk away all the valuables. The farce, to be sure, contrasts the wedding and the funeral, but they are really no more than an acceptable guise that gives both Concubine Zhao and the Wang brothers a legitimate excuse for seizing the Yan family's property.

Rulin waishi thus once again confronts us with the compact between moral authority and mundane power, a dangerous alliance in which domestic dissension is represented as a ritual. The problems stem from the dualistic system of *li* itself, for the Confucian ritual provides its practitioners with a legitimate arena for social maneuvering; their participation in the ceremony enables them to articulate mundane interests in terms of ritual obligations. If Confucian ritual is both sacred and mundane, then it is sacred in words and mundane in reality. And the crisis of narrative ritual is in part predicated on Confucian discourse, which seldom functions in the way that Confucians describe.

The Yan family ceremony is an occasion for words. At the climax of the wedding of Yan Dayu and Concubine Zhao, "Wang Ren drew on his vast erudition to write a most moving (*kenqie*) announcement of this marriage directed to the Yan ancestors." In defending this marriage, Wang Ren refers to the virtue of filial piety at the core of Confucian values, because Yan Dayu and Concubine Zhao best fulfill their moral obligations toward the ancestors by preserving the Yan family line. Despite their well-articulated moral commitment, however, the ritual organizers and participants prove capable of clear-headed calculations of gain or loss throughout the entire series of machinations otherwise known as the Confucian ritual. Concubine Zhao knows what she wants, although she makes her son the main subject of her ritual discourse. Whereas she is motivated by her aspirations for status, the Wang brothers care only about the money that will come with endorsing her as a replacement for Lady Wang, their dying sister. The same is true of those who oppose the wedding. In the Yan family ritual, Confucian discourse is invoked only to be deflated. It does not succeed in persuading its practitioners to commit to common values or common interests; nor does it help them perceive their relationships in terms of mutual respect and obligation. Instead, the conflict of interests becomes so evident that words can no longer bring the family together. Nevertheless, Confucian rhetoric is not irrelevant. To the brothers, it serves as a perfect instrument of social exchange, negotiation, and maneuvering, for the competition guided by self-interest is, above all, a fight for the right to speak for Confucius.

At stake in the Yan family ritual is the issue of rhetoric versus praxis or words versus deeds, and this opposition informs the narrative structure of this part of the novel. In this episode, the interrelated issues of Confucian rhetoric, authority, mundane interest, and status unfold at various levels of the text: in the Wang brothers' use of the *bagu* model to conceive and generate their self-representation; in problematizing their self-representation; and finally, in raising the overriding question of who controls Confucian rhetoric. This question becomes particularly relevant to *Rulin waishi*, because in the novel, especially in Part II, the conventional narrator, blessed with both moral and narrative authority, withdraws, allowing the characters to usurp the Confucian rhetoric customarily used in his representation and evaluation of them. This is where *Rulin waishi* deviates from the narrative model of the traditional novel—an issue to which I shall return below. For now it suffices to say that the subject matter of *Rulin waishi* is closely tied to the issue of narrative: in the novel the crisis of Confucian discourse occurs not only on the level of subject matter but also on the level of narrative structure.

As I argued above, because the implications of dualistic *li* are determined, to a certain extent, by its practitioners' motivations, we cannot decide that a specific act is "moral" unless we are informed that it is done with good intentions, sincerity (*cheng*), and a sense of reverence (*jing*). But in *Rulin waishi*, the omniscient, authoritative narrator who is supposed to provide us with this information forsakes his role. Literati characters, equipped with Confucian rhetoric, step in, making themselves the narrators of their own stories. This structural change leads only to a parody. The characters "know" their own intentions, but their narration serves only to hide those intentions from the public; more often than not, they claim for themselves the good faith that they do not have and never even think of having. Wu Jingzi often contrasted his characters' self-representations with the information he offered about them through other means; at other times, he left them suspiciously unconfirmed. As such, he repositioned himself in this changed narrative structure: by allowing the characters to appropriate the sages' words for their own purposes, he abandoned the role of the ideal narrator necessary for the operation of Confucian discourse. Even more important, he highlighted the function of Confucian discourse in the mundane system of social exchange and maneuvering. There is no impartial, disinterested, and thus perfect agent for this discourse; nor is the discourse unmediated. In these stories, the meanings of Confucian discourse are by no means transparent or self-evident; they are always conditioned by the inescapable mundane context within which they are constructed, circulated, and interpreted.

However, if narrative ritual is caught in a crisis, the crisis can be attributed not so much to the contextualization and the corruption of Confucian discourse as to the dualistic system of *li*. The unification of mundane and sacred within that system facilitates the verbal negotiation of ritualistic and official obligations and the exchange of symbolic and political resources. As the story of Wang Hui and Xun Mei illustrates, the elite characters who play with this dualistic system often cite official duty as a legitimate excuse for ignoring ritual obligations. The system allows them to use moral rhetoric to justify their official engagement, despite the benefits they receive from controlling sociopolitical and economic resources. As a result, ambiguity inevitably emerges in conceptualizing "virtue" and distinguishing "moral deeds" from self-interested acts. Out of this ambiguity arise the literati's dramas of self-representation as staged in *Rulin waishi*, dramas of moral rhetoric and deception. The novel does not offer a better alternative to narrative ritual in Chapters 2–30. An alternative is, nevertheless, implied in the way the novel diagnoses the problem of narrative ritual: if rhetoric fails to cope with the internal tension of the dualistic system of *li*, then the only solution is to get rid of dualism. The account of the Taibo ceremony in Chapter 37 represents just such an effort to redeem the Confucian world.

Ascetic Ritual

The Taibo ceremony described in Part III of the novel (Chapters 31–37) is a response to the crisis of the Confucian norm. In contrast to dualistic, narrative ritual, this new project consists of a withdrawal from the mundane world and the replacement of discourse with practice. The result is what might be called "ascetic ritual," which Filial Guo confirms through action in Chapter 37. The contrast between ascetic ritual and narrative ritual throws the meaning of the Filial Guo story (Chapters 37–39) into sharp relief.

In contrast to the depictions of the literati's struggle to get to court that fill Part II of the novel, this section begins with an account of other literati's journey in the opposite direction. It is inaugurated by the narrative of Du Shaoqing, a member of the local gentry, who, while on his way to Nanjing to seek out understanding friends, turns down an official recommendation to participate in a special examination for "distinguished" scholars. As the narrative proceeds, it becomes clear that the first motif of ascetic ritual, withdrawal from the mundane world, is oriented toward the creation of a distinct space for the literati: as they detach themselves from the court, the center of the official world, they converge on Nanjing, where they create a center for themselves by constructing the Taibo temple.[13]

The dichotomy of court and temple is highlighted in Chapters 34 and 35, in the episode in which Zhuang Shaoguang is invited to the court and consulted by the emperor about Confucian ritual and music. Although Zhuang offers advice, he immediately petitions to leave. In the next episode we are told that Zhuang, as he has promised, has returned to Nanjing in time for the Taibo ceremony organized by his fellow literati. When placed in the po-

---

13. Martin Huang, in his reading of this section of *Rulin waishi*, argues that Beijing and Nanjing represent two completely different choices in life for a literatus; see *Literati and Self-Re/Presentation*, pp. 53–54. See also Yue Hengjun, "Shiji de piaobo zhe," pp. 149–66.

sition of choosing between court and temple as the arena for promoting Confucian ritual, Zhuang, without hesitation, chooses the latter. And the temple, still to be completed, is defined not so much by what it is as by what it is not; it signals, in other words, a retreat from the mundane world.

Zhuang's confrontation with the prime minister offers a clue to his choice. Knowing that Zhuang Shaoguang is likely to win imperial favor, the prime minister delivers a message through Vice Minister Xu, who has recommended Zhuang to the court. "Why don't you bring him to see me, sir?" the prime minister asks. "I should like to have him as my pupil" (R. 481; S. 389).[14] By applying the terms "teacher" and "pupil" to his prospective relations with Zhuang Shaoguang, the prime minister is suggesting political patronage. Keenly aware of his own role as a literatus, Zhuang finds this outrageous, for in his vocabulary the term "teacher" is reserved only for Confucius. "Since there is no Confucius in our age," retorts Zhuang, "I have no desire to be any man's pupil. Besides, the prime minister has served so many times as chief examiner that he has innumerable members of the Hanlin Academy as his pupils. Why should he choose a rustic like myself? I dare not accept this honor" (R. 481; S. 389).

In light of the social and political maneuverings in the previous part of the novel, the prime minister's behavior comes as no surprise. In this episode the prime minister acts like the Wang brothers, who secretly exchanged favors and money with Yan Dayu in Chapter 5. His political deal is, above all, a game of moral rhetoric in which he speaks either for Confucius or as Confucius: he would make Zhuang his "pupil." Even when, out of frustration, anger, and personal malice, he tries to block the emperor from appointing Zhuang, he demonstrates a remarkable consistency in his command of moral rhetoric: he is opposed to Zhuang, as he puts it, because he wishes to forestall the perception that court promotion depends solely on chance; his sole concern is to discourage opportunists.

Since court politics involves behind-the-scenes exchanges disguised with moral rhetoric, the Confucian ritual promoted by the court becomes another instance of narrative or discursive ritual. From this perspective, one may argue that the novel represents its literati heroes' withdrawal from the court as a means of saving them from the dualistic world of the mundane as sacred, the world of *li* that is hopelessly mired in irony. Accordingly, the construc-

---

14. The Chinese term is *taoli* (peaches and plums), which Confucius once used when referring to his pupils in *The Analects*.

tion of a distinct and homogeneous space for those heroes serves to diminish the room for verbal negotiation between ritual engagement and sociopolitical activity; it protects their ritual practice from alternative perceptions and interpretations.

The motif of withdrawal seems to have been derived from the myth of Wu Taibo, the Confucian sage to whom the ceremony is dedicated. Although the myth is not explained in the novel, an updated version of it can be found in the story of Yu Yude, which becomes such a prominent part of the novel that it makes any direct reference to the myth itself unnecessary. Wu Taibo, the eldest son of King Tai (Taiwang) of the Zhou dynasty, was admired by Confucius as "a man of virtue in its supreme form" (zhide) for yielding the throne to his youngest brother and fleeing to the southeastern region later known as Gouwu.[15] To the Ming and Qing literati of this region, Wu Jingzi and his Nanjing friends included, Wu Taibo was the founding father of the Wu clan and of civilization in this region. His handing over power to his brother was construed as the manifestation both of his brotherly love and of his filial piety.[16] Wu became a symbol of "yielding" (rang) and was paradoxically entitled the "king of yielding" (rangwang), or more literally, the "king who became a king for having yielded the throne." This title best illustrates the unresolved tension between the Confucian sage and the king, the head of the political system. In this sense, the selection of Wu Taibo as a symbol of the ritualized world in Rulin waishi is itself an implicit assertion that the ritualized world embodies a higher order and therefore cannot arise from sociopolitical reality.

According to legend, after abdicating the throne, Wu Taibo traveled to the region of Wu, where he began to construct his own civilization. His legendary founding of this ideal kingdom has a remote echo in Rulin waishi in the collective practice of Confucian ritual, a ritual conducted in Nanjing (in the Wu region) and dedicated only to Wu Taibo. For the leading characters in this episode, including Du Shaoqing, the author's autobiographical alter ego, the Taibo ceremony is a moment of self-celebration: the participants reinforce their bond with Wu Taibo as common ancestor and try, moreover, to further identify with him by re-enacting the motifs of the Taibo myth in

---

15. See Liu Baonan, Lunyu zhengyi, p. 57.

16. In the Shiji version of the story Wu Taibo gave up his claim to the throne because his father favored his youngest brother as successor. The Taibo story undoubtedly tells us much about politics, power, and scandal. For further study of the Taibo myth, see Part IV.

their own stories. As the central event of the novel, the ceremony is also a celebration of a symbolic triumph of the local over the center, of private virtue over public duty, of family tradition over political engagement, and finally, of the ritualized world over the mundane world.

The motif of withdrawal not only defines the relationship between the ritualized and mundane worlds but also sets the tone for relationships within the ritualized community. Commenting on what he believed would be achieved by a ceremony conducted in a Taibo temple in Meili, allegedly Wu Taibo's hometown, Du Zhao, a scholar living in the Yongzheng and Qianlong reigns, claimed: "The Taibo ceremony will enable the literati-officials, countrymen, and young fellows to rise and prostrate themselves, and to yield to one another in the Taibo temple so that, without being aware of it, they will be imbued by the lingering influence of this supremely righteous man [Wu Taibo]."[17] Despite (or even because of) his wishful thinking, Du Zhao hit upon the reason for Wu Jingzi's fictional ritual. According to Du, the ceremony offers people of different ages and social classes an occasion to relate to one another through their common commitment to the patterns of human conduct and intercourse set out in the Confucian canon. This interpretation does not fit Wu Jingzi's Taibo ceremony exactly, for it is open only to literati and thus is an assertion of literati distinctiveness. Nevertheless, in creating his imagined literati community, Wu held his ground: the Taibo ceremony is neither an official ritual celebrating the status quo nor a family ritual reinforcing the family hierarchy. Despite its concrete setting and the wealth of details, it is not predicated on any specific sociopolitical occasion. Its participants, detached from mundane interests, enter a world governed by a different set of rules: once the ceremony is under way, official status, rank, and hierarchy—all essential to the sociopolitical order—seem to have been temporarily suspended; there emerges, to borrow Victor Turner's term, a relatively undifferentiated communitas.[18]

Connected to this point is Du Zhao's exclusive emphasis on the ritual act. For him, this utopian ritual is nothing but a formalized pattern of "yielding" and "prostrating." He believed that the long-lasting and profound influence of Confucian ritual is reflected not so much in their practitioners' consciousness as in their behavior. So did Wu Jingzi. In Chapter 37, Wu illustrated

---

17. Du Zhao was also the teacher of Wu Peiyuan, the model for Yu Yude in *Rulin waishi*. See Du Zhao, "Chongxiu Taibomiao beiji," in Wu Xi, ed., *Taibo Meili zhi, juan* 4, p. 14a.

18. Turner, *The Ritual Process*, p. 96.

Yan Yuan's *li* by focusing exclusively on the ritual participants' submission to the prescribed ritual patterns. Yan Yuan suggested that only through the constant repetition of formulaic patterns of ritual activity is one able to turn moral propriety into a permanent disposition, into a durable way of standing, walking, and speaking, as well as interacting with other human beings. From this perspective, Confucian moral life is nothing but the continuation or extension of ritual, and in the ideal Confucian world everyone knows his proper position and does what he is supposed to do without conscious effort. Thus, in the scene of the Taibo ceremony, all we see is a canonical pattern of ritual acts that keeps repeating itself, while the ritual performers' sentiments, mental states, and perceptions are left unmentioned. Again, as if echoing Du Zhao's assertion, a character in Chapter 47 makes a retrospective comment on Yu Yude, the ritual master and the Wu Taibo of the present day: "Dr. Yu doesn't lay down restrictions, but people are so influenced by his virtue that they naturally refrain from improper conduct" (R. 642–43; S. 524). Yu Yude does not use coercion or verbal commands or instructions. With the proper ritual gestures and comportment, he presents himself in the proper ritual setting. That is all he does, but a miracle occurs, according to this observer: those who participate in or observe his ceremony succumb to his influence like grass before the wind; "They naturally refrain from improper conduct." Of course, like other lofty statements expressed in *Rulin waishi*, this comment is inevitably subject to alternative views, but what is germane here is that it reinforces another motif in Chapters 31 to 37: the replacement of discourse with practice.

If the motif of withdrawal drives home the point that a commitment to ritual obligations must be made at the expense of mundane interests, this second motif further suggests that such obligations must be carried out through acting rather than by speaking and thinking. Through the motif of action, Wu Jingzi consciously confronts the problems he raised in his account of narrative ritual in Chapters 2 to 30: hypocrisy, insincerity, and the discrepancy between word and deed that undercut the morality that the literati claim for themselves. With the reserve of a dispassionate observer, he showed how often his literati characters contradict their own words in their actions. Despite his general lack of interest in their inner lives, he does sometimes reveal their motivations, as well as the way in which their moral instincts are corrupted by other thoughts—calculations of gain and loss, anticipation of the consequences of speech and action, and the desire for reward and fame. In Chapters 15 to 19, Kuang Chaoren, an innocent village boy who travels to the city for a better life, gradually absorbs the ethos of the various literati circles he has joined (candidates for the examination, civil officials, and self-described men of letters) and ends up becoming the worst of them all. The irony of his story is that he is corrupted by his contact with the educated elite and ultimately by his reputation as a filial son, which facilitates his entry into those circles. Another example of literati corruption can be seen in the story of Xun Mei, mentioned earlier. The first idea that crosses Xun Mei's mind on the news of his mother's death is to return home to observe the mourning period. But he is immediately contaminated by Wang Hui, who persuades him to negotiate an exemption from his obligations.

As a master of irony committed to Confucian ideals, Wu Jingzi could not tell his stories about literati corruption without proposing a better alternative for them (and himself). But what? If, as Wu believed, the original moral state has been lost, should he try to restore it by reinforcing such practices of Neo-Confucian self-cultivation as quiet sitting, self-examination, and lecturing, or should he return to the basic instruction of *The Great Learning* (*Daxue*): be sincere in your intentions? For Wu the answers to these questions are obviously no. In any event, he escaped the irony of repeating the rhetoric of his literati characters, which has been either discredited or proved ineffectual. To him it seemed clear that to do away with hypocrisy, deception, and insincerity, one must abandon efforts to work out alternatives through introspection and, at least temporarily, dispense with introspection itself. There is no way to teach anyone to be sincere: a person is either sincere or not. Nor is it possible to teach about sincerity, for the conscious effort of teaching itself endangers the state of being sincere. Note that Yu Yude lays down no rules by verbal instruction; his virtue is embodied in the ritual he enacts, and his biography in Chapter 36 is followed (and complemented) by the representation of his ritual practice in Chapter 37.

To return to the story of Filial Guo in Chapters 37 and 38, the two motifs of the ascetic ritual are intertwined in it, with new developments and variations. The Taibo ceremony provides an occasion during which the members of the literati community become temporarily sanctified participants in a sacred, ritualistic order. Although conducted in the temple, it is intended to transform the outside world. Filial Guo seeks to define for himself an autonomy of ritual in the realm of everyday practice, a realm beyond both the temple and the official world. His lifelong journey to restore his relationship with his father best illustrates the nature of this attempt. For him there is no need for justification nor room for negotiation. However complex the situation he confronts, he enacts his own ritual in a sacred realm governed by absolute moral imperatives. It becomes clear that Filial Guo's ascetic ritual is a critical response to the narrative ritual of dualistic *li*, in which the obligation of filial piety, though fully endorsed, is flexible, negotiable, and always dependent on circumstances. Whereas literati characters, including Guo's own father, use words either as a substitute for action or as an excuse for nonaction, Filial Guo pledges his filial obligation through determined action. In this Guo seems to have become an embodiment of a concept; he is less an individual human being than a ceremonial being. This impression is reinforced by a narrative that focuses mainly on surfaces and makes no visible connection between action and consciousness. As a hero of ritualistic action, Guo is reduced to a silence that does not so much prompt our curiosity about his inner life as make it largely irrelevant, for the narrative directs our attention away from his psyche to his actions. Guo may not be a convincing character, but the important thing is that he embodies the essence of the ritual he enacts, the asceticism that demands action, self-sacrifice, and absolute commitment.

Filial Guo's Final Confession: A Moment of Disillusionment

Filial Guo is, however, less blessed than Yu Yude, for his journey brings him back to the world of irony and complexity from which Yu has withdrawn. Although Guo has the narrator's unfailing approval, his story ends in frustration and leaves no model worthy of emulation. When Guo makes his final appearance in Chapter 39 with the bones of his deceased father, he shows no sign of fulfillment or relief. He confides in Xiao Yunxian, a young swordsman:

"To risk your life for the public good shows courage and gallantry. But this is not the Spring and Autumn period or the age of the Warring States [770–256 BCE], when you could win fame by such exploits. Now that the whole country is united, a modern Jing Ke or Nie Zheng would be considered lawless. With your character, looks, and talents, brother, to say nothing of your integrity and courage, you ought to serve the state in some capacity. Then with your sword you could win titles for your wife and sons on the battlefield, and make a name to be handed down in history. I tell you, brother, I studied the military arts as a boy, but to no purpose; for owing to my father's trouble, these twenty years I have led the hard life of a wanderer. I am old now and unfit for anything, but you are at the height of your youth and vigor. You mustn't throw away your opportunities. I hope you will remember an old man's words!" (R. 537; S. 432)

This is the only time that Filial Guo reveals himself. But his self-revelation leaves most readers confused. Guo is encouraging Xiao to serve the dynasty rather than be a "swordsman," which, according to him, is equivalent to being an outlaw. Advising Xiao to win honors for his wife and sons in battle on behalf of the court, he literally repeats the words of Song Jiang and other outlaws in Shuihu zhuan;[19] this reminds us of the hidden side of Guo's own image. Guo may not be an outlaw in the true sense of the word, but his loyalty to his outlaw father leaves him in a similar position. Thus it is not until the end of the episode that the repressed conflict between loyalty to the father and loyalty to the throne begins to present itself to his consciousness; his statement is part of his strategy of pre-emptive defense. And his awareness of the need for defense inevitably undermines the vision of the ritualized world as a field of moral autonomy. Although his action satisfies ritual requirements, Guo has to compromise, at least in words, with official ethics. In the ritualized world Guo sees no room for individual choice and moral conflict, for its perfect order permits no options; but in the world of reality, he remains torn between conflicting obligations, with no perfect solution in sight.

What is most damaging to his vision of the ritualized world is not Guo's struggle but his loss of certainty and moral confidence in what he has done. At the most frustrating moment, he even admits regret about his own past: "I studied the military arts as a boy to no purpose; for, owing to my father's trouble, these twenty years I have led the hard life of a wanderer." Although he has been placed in a situation over which he has little control, he envisages an alternative that in retrospect seems more desirable than his own experience. Despite his fame as a filial son, he sees himself less as a martyr than as a victim: he has lost everything he treasures for an obscure cause. Unlike the canonical narrative of a filial son carrying out his ritual obligations, the story of Filial Guo ends not with an affirmative conclusion, but only with retrospective thoughts that give his experience a final, drastic twist.

Coming at the end of the episode, Guo's remarks incline us to interpret the whole story from a different perspective. If the confrontation with his father contributes, according to my reading, to shaping the image of Guo as a

---

19. Shuihu quanzhuan, p. 484.

filial son, its negative, destructive aspect is not brought to light until the last moment of his confession. The confrontation not only suspends the reunion of father and son but also casts suspicion upon the universal father-son bond that underlies the vision of the ritualized world. On his way home, Guo appears to have lost the certainty that once sustained him, for his final encounter with his father raises a new question that is left unanswered to the end of the story: If his father never recognizes or appreciates his filial piety, is he truly a filial son?

Guo's final confession is an anticlimax: it prevents his ascetic ritual from achieving completeness and coherence. In spite of himself, he comes to embody not so much the vision of a ritualized life as its distortion in the confrontation with reality. To survive the real world, he has to compromise, in word or in action, but compromises inevitably have consequences. As we are informed at the outset, Guo was originally named Wang. Like his father, he changes his family name to avoid persecution. For the same reason, he also disguises his place of origin. If Guo is a filial son rejected by his father, he is now, to make the case even more paradoxical, also a filial son who takes a false family name for himself. In the end, we cannot help wondering: If the father's refusal to recognize him produces an identity crisis, is it not also possible to trace the crisis to Guo's assumption of a new family identity? This is not to say that we should hold Guo responsible for what occurs to him later; rather, it suggests his own complicity in the situation he struggles to make sense of. This filial son bears a false family name; struggles unsuccessfully to balance the conflicting demands of loyalty and filial piety; while trying to carry out his ritual obligations, shows no sign of moral confidence or fulfillment; and in searching for his father, experiences ordeals of every sort and ends up rejected. With Guo's confession as its conclusion, the story verges on collapse. Almost all the elements that have helped to shape his ascetic ritual now turn and contribute, in one way or another, to the ritual's undoing.

Since Guo's reunion with his father deprives the quest of the expected ending that would give it meaning, we realize that Guo has been, from the very beginning, on his way to nowhere. He is a filial son on the wrong journey and in the wrong text, one in which he is doomed to fail. Modern scholars often find the description of his journey incomprehensible in theme and unacceptable in terms of narrative style. In this story, they claim that they encounter not Wu Jingzi "the great novelist" but a mediocre writer or a hack in a hopeless struggle to give a realistic account of a grotesque adventure.

Certainly, Guo's adventure seems out of place in the novel; it is also poorly presented, even in its own terms. But to argue that someone else is therefore responsible for this part of the novel, as some scholars do, is to assert a hypothesis based on false assumptions. Our judgment of Wu Jingzi's individual talents, styles, and intentions does not offer a legitimate and reliable basis for interpretation. It is more appropriate and fruitful to focus instead on the narrative and generic situations that lead to such a peculiar story. In a sense, Wu Jingzi did not invent the narrative by himself. His account of Guo's journey as an adventure is a derivation, as well as a deviation, from the model of the filial son in search of the father prevalent in early Qing literature. In reading the Filial Guo episode, we should examine the author's range of choices and restrictions. We should also explore his sources and agendas, and the potential conflicts between the two.

In the established narrative model, the journey of the filial son seeking his father is staged as a heroic adventure. Yet the adventure unfolds largely at the allegorical level as an ordeal that displays the hero's internal qualities. The detailed description of dangers and hardships is, therefore, organized within a framework of significance and serves specific moral purposes. The hero is essentially safe, despite all the dangers he encounters. His survival, according to the narrator of the story, is due to the protection of the spirits and ultimately to his own lofty virtue, which resonates with Heaven. Omens and dreams are often the media through which the divine message is transmitted, and the hero is literally under the guidance of Heaven on his way to his reunion with his father. In the course of his journey, whatever dramatic shifts and twists he experiences, the filial son has a clear and unchanged vision of what he is doing. He is a hero living with a promise, and his story is its fulfillment.

In contrast with the standard mode of such narratives, whose center of interest resides in a domain of spiritual and psychological values, the account of Filial Guo presents only the surface of his experiences. As I argued above, Wu Jingzi's commitment to the agenda of ascetic ritual does not allow him to penetrate Guo's consciousness and inner world or to add an allegorical dimension to the narrative.[20] But Wu's rejection of the allegorical mode and

---

20. Unlike many other Chinese novels, *Rulin waishi* permits little room for allegorical reading. Although the first chapter sets up a prophecy through Wang Mian's reading of celestial phenomena, the prophecy never fully develops into an allegorical framework for the whole novel. In "The Scorpion in the Scholar's Cap: Ritual, Memory, and Desire in *Rulin waishi*,"

psychological approach does not prevent him from embracing the narrative model of the filial son's adventure; he elaborates all the hardships of the journey to accentuate Guo's determination. The problem is, however, that in the absence of the allegorical framework, the detailed description leaves us with no clues for interpretation.

Although Wu Jingzi's narrator occasionally offers explanations for the miracle of Guo's survival, they lead us to see his survival as the product of pure contingency. As often happens in the stories of the filial son, Filial Guo twice encounters tigers in his adventure. The first time, the tiger decides to bury Guo for a future feast. Then a nameless monster, the true rescuer, conveniently happens by and with little effort knocks off the tiger's head. When it then turns to prey on Guo, the enraged monster accidentally impales itself on the branch of a tree and dies on the spot. In Guo's next encounter with a tiger, the sense of grotesquerie reaches a new height. Guo falls unconscious to the ground but gives a great sneeze as the tiger sniffs at his face. The tiger jumps up in fright. "In a few bounds it reached a mountaintop and fell into a chasm, where it was caught on the spear-sharp icicles and frozen to death" (R. 527; S. 425). Despite its serious tone, the narrative amounts to farce. The sources of the descriptions bring home the sense of peculiarity that infiltrates the narrative: these two incidents are adapted from notes by a Tang and a Qing writer respectively, in the generic category of "records of the strange" (zhiguai).[21] Thus, as peculiar scenes and incidents accumulate, so does our bafflement. In Guo's second encounter with a tiger, we are told: "By the time Guo scrambled to his feet the tiger had disappeared. 'What a narrow escape!' He sighed with relief, shouldered his baggage and went on" (R. 527; S. 425). Guo survives for reasons that neither he nor we understand. Here as elsewhere in the Filial Guo episode, no glimpse is given of Guo's psychological response.

The Filial Guo episode offers a rare case in which textual sources, generic modes, narrative models, and ideological agenda engage in a difficult negotia-

---

Marston Anderson holds that Rulin waishi appears not only to lack an explicit allegorical framework but actively to discourage metaphorical reading: "Although not all passages in the novel that involve dreams and the supernatural conform to this pattern, many must be viewed as intentional parody of the allegorizing tendencies of earlier Chinese fiction" (p. 263). In this sense, an allegorical account of the filial son's journey in search of his father is by nature incompatible with the narrative rhetoric that governs Rulin waishi.

21. See Zhang Zhuo, Chaoye qianzai, juan 2, p. 56. See also Niu Xiu, Gusheng, juan 4, p. 87; and Li Hanqiu, ed., "Rulin waishi" yanjiu ziliao, pp. 190–91.

tion but never merge into a coherent design. The peculiarity of the story results from the tension among its narrative mode, sources, and thematic agenda, and ultimately from its dubious role within the novel's thematic and narrative structure. On the one hand, the story of Filial Guo, following immediately after the Taibo ceremony, is an effort to extend the vision of ceremony into the domain of daily life. On the other hand, the narrative of Guo's experience, in its concrete form, creates a complex situation that neither completely negates nor completely fulfills the ritualistic quest; rather, it imbues it with ambiguities, frustrations, and absurdity. In the end, the story of Filial Guo illustrates both the need to reinforce the ascetic ritual and the difficulty, if not the impossibility, of narrating that reinforcement. Emphasizing the absolute commitment to ritual obligations through action, the ascetic ritual seems to resist representation through narrative, but it does not escape Wu Jingzi's scrutiny; instead, Wu situated it within a mundane context to reveal its potential problems, which would otherwise not be immediately visible. Filial Guo's final confession makes us pause before we move on to the next page of the novel for explication.

The representation of Guo's journey in search of his father initiates a series of frustrated attempts to give concrete expression to the vision of ascetic ritual in Chapters 38 through 55. These episodes and their complexity are the subjects of the next chapter.

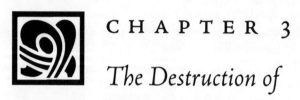

CHAPTER 3

The Destruction of the Taibo Temple: Ascetic Ritual in Crisis

"It is proverbially easier," said T. S. Eliot, "to destroy than to construct; and, as a corollary of this proverb, it is easier for readers to apprehend the destructive than the constructive side of an author's thought."[1] For Wu Jingzi, the question is, however, whether the new structure he has constructed can withstand his own scrutiny without cracking and crumbling. The most visible symbol of this new structure is the Taibo temple, a magnificent artifact transcending the mundane world. From within the temple arises a vision of a ritualized world just as magnificent and just as much an artifact—a perfect performance of a ceremony copied from ritual manuals. But when reenacted outside this ideal temple later in the novel, the ritual is carried either too far or not far enough, and more often than not with unexpected twists and ironies.

Nowhere else are these twists and ironies better represented than in the accounts of the Yu brothers, members of the local gentry fighting a doomed battle against the customs of Wuhe county, and of Wang Yuhui, a compiler of Confucian ritual manuals, who attempts to practice in his own life what he preaches. The episode of the Yu brothers in Chapters 44 and 45 illustrates the absolute extreme of ascetic ritual. In order to raise enough money to give their deceased father a decent funeral, the elder Yu accepts bribes, and his younger brother covers for him. In an exaggerated tone rarely heard

---

1. T. S. Eliot, "The Humanism of Irving Babbitt," p. 277.

in the novel, the narrator gives them praise of the highest order: "As regards both character and learning, the Yu brothers had rarely been equaled since antiquity" (R. 600; S. 488). Commenting on this episode, C. T. Hsia writes: "Only a Confucian fanatic prizing filial piety to the exclusion of all other virtues could approve."[2] This, I suggest, is perhaps what the ascetic ritual is all about. But the episode of bribery is not rendered without a touch of ambivalence and ambiguity. At the beginning of Chapter 46, the elder Yu tells Du Shaoqing in detail about the lawsuit following the bribery incident. "Du Shaoqing sighs deeply" but gives no sign of the approval Yu expects. This ambiguity points to the enigmatic core of the narrative.

The story of Wang Yuhui in Chapter 48 is characterized by the richness of its irony and suggestiveness. Metaphorically, it is a journey from ritual texts to ritual activity, in which Wang is engaged in an imprudent effort to translate his manuals into an occasion of extraordinary conduct. It is also fitting to read it as a narrative journey from the Jiexiao shrine (the shrine of chaste and filial women) to the Taibo temple, for soon after the ceremony dedicated to his daughter in the shrine, Wang Yuhui travels to Nanjing and thence to the temple. The story of Filial Guo begins with the approval of Yu's circle; the story of Wang Yuhui ends with his visit to the Taibo temple for endorsement. The temple becomes, therefore, a point of either departure or return. But whereas Guo struggles with frustration and disillusionment, Wang's journey conjures up an antithesis of the Jiexiao shrine and Taibo temple: despite his nostalgic longing for the fading vision of the Taibo ceremony, his own experience in the shrine has its counterpart in real life, in a highly problematic, if not entirely negative, mirror version.

From Jiexiao Shrine to Taibo Temple

The Wang Yuhui episode begins at the moment of crisis. In Chapter 48 of *Rulin waishi*, we are told that, as a licentiate, Wang has devoted himself to compiling Confucian ritual texts. With almost no financial resources, he lives an ascetic life, leaving his family in wretched poverty. But for all his poverty, he is able to maintain his spirits by drawing moral support from his fellow literati. At the beginning of Chapter 48, he is given an opportunity to introduce his compilation project and wins applause from Yu Youda, a tutor of the Huizhou Prefectural College and one of Yu Yude's former students:

---

2. C. T. Hsia, *The Classic Chinese Novel*, p. 240.

"Such a book should be recommended by the government for general study and circulated throughout the country" (R. 647–48; S. 531). Yu Youda does not speak only for himself; his praise indicates the likely response of his circle. When Wang Yuhui later decides to go to Nanjing, Yu and his brother advise him to take his newly completed ritual manuals. "What a pity Dr. Yu [Yude] isn't there," says Yu Youda, "since you're going to Nanjing! If he were there and saw your books, his praise would make all the printers rush to get them" (R. 651; S. 531). The brothers then write him letters of introduction to Du Shaoqing and Zhuang Shaoguang in Nanjing, because "their words carry weight" (R. 651; S. 531).

Throughout the story, the narrator aligns Wang Yuhui with Yu Yude's circle both in what he writes and in what he does. On hearing of his son-in-law's death, Wang sees a chance to act and advises his daughter to take a course he believes is morally correct: to honor her deceased husband, she should starve herself to death. Under Wang's guidance, this moral drama is carried out in the fashion that he has repeatedly seen in historical texts: after her tragic death she is officially ennobled as a "chaste woman," and her tablet is installed in the Jiexiao shrine.

Just as Wang's writing project echoes the program of the Taibo ceremony, his encouragement of his daughter's suicide confirms Yu Yude's praise of chaste women. In Chapter 36, we are told that Yu Yude agreed to write an inscription on the tablet of a chaste woman. Although no story is told about that person, the idealized role is held up for Wang's daughter to fulfill. Yet the story of chaste women would not be complete without ceremony. To Wang Yuhui, his daughter's suicide provides an occasion for putting his ritual manuals into practice: a grand ceremony in the Jiexiao shrine is dedicated to her, with participants from the elite class of the region.

How Wang perceives this event can be seen from his frequent retelling of the story about his daughter and himself, for example, in this conversation with a friend's son: "Nephew, when your mother was widowed and a neighbor's house caught fire, because she prayed to Heaven a wind sprang up that blew out the flames. Everyone knows that story proving her chastity. Now my third daughter too is renowned for similar conduct that shows her chastity" (R. 654; S. 534). In recounting his daughter's story, Wang projects himself into an imagined world in which his daughter is a magical figure with supernatural powers beyond the comprehension of everyday experience. Fantastic as it is, his conviction of a moral miracle remains rooted in reality.

For in Wang's philosophy anyone who devotes him- or herself to extreme acts of moral heroism, martyrdom, and self-sacrifice can work miracles. His friend's wife did it, and now his daughter has done it as well.

When Wang is encouraging his daughter to commit suicide, he says, "Your name will be recorded in history. Why should I try to dissuade you?" In his philosophy, nothing is more important to an individual than the chance to accomplish extraordinary deeds and secure a position in history. Thus, on hearing the news of his daughter's death, he seems to feel a sense of relief rather than of sorrow. With little difficulty he finds a way to console his wife, who has cried herself half to death:

"You're a silly old woman!" he said. "Our third daughter is now an immortal (*xian*). What are you crying for? She made a good death. I only wish I could eventually figure out such a good rubric (*timu*) under which to die." He threw back his head and laughed. "She died well!" he cried. "She died well!" Then, laughing, he left the room. (R. 650; S. 530)

Wang describes his daughter's death in terms that his wife can understand—she is now an immortal. Yet this description can also serve as an index to his concept of the other world, the world of absolute holiness. More important still is the term "rubric," by which Wang means the category under which his daughter's action will be recorded. For him, moral conduct is no more than a theme on which an essay can be composed. His moral principles are based on a simple maxim: Select a rubric for yourself so that others can write you into the sacred texts of history.

Under Wang Yuhui's guidance, his daughter has, as he sees it, died into the received categories of textual history and acquired a life in transcendental form, a life without physical limits. The transition is symbolically expressed in the form of ceremony. The role of ceremony in confirming one's place in the transcendent realm of history is illustrated in Chapter 37: the audience describes Yu Yude, the ritual master, as a divine sage or transcendent being (*shensheng*) who has come back to earth especially for the ceremony. The word *shensheng* can be translated "spirit" or "sage," or as a combination of the two. In either case, it suggests an elevation of a human being to a transcendent level through ceremonial practice. As shown in Chapter 36, which is entitled "A true Confucian is born in Changshu County / A worthy man becomes the master of ceremony in the Taibo temple," Yu Yude himself is created by and for the ritual. Once it is over, he ceases to be the focus of the narrative. Rather than simply disappearing, however, he is equated with Wu

Taibo, whom he has helped commemorate; he himself becomes a sage to be celebrated in an official ceremony in the last chapter of the novel. The function of the ceremony, it seems, is to beget more ceremony, and the people who enact it become those to whom the next ceremony is dedicated. We may argue that a ritual such as the Taibo ceremony not only provides its practitioners with a point of entry into textual history but also constitutes its own history, a cycle of transformation through which sages are continuously produced, celebrated, and commemorated.

Miracle, history, and ritual: these are the issues at stake in Wang Yuhui's moral vision, which is fully revealed in the way he perceives and manages the story of his daughter. In a sense, he is successful in subjecting the narrative to his own vision: the story moves in the direction he expects it to. What we see next is a ceremony carried out in very much the fashion Wang has rehearsed in his own writings: the tablet for his daughter is made, an honorific title is conferred, sacrifices are offered.

The crisis occurs at the end, when Wang is suddenly seized by unexpected sorrow, an emotion entirely absent from his writings on Confucian ritual. "The other scholars urged Wang to join the feast, declaring that, by bringing up such a virtuous daughter, he had added luster to his clan. But by now Wang was beginning to feel quite sick at heart, so he declined to join them" (R. 651; S. 531). Although surrounded by praise, Wang is deeply disturbed when the unfolding moral drama deviates from its conventional script because of his personal reaction. He cannot even stay till the end.

In sorrow and confusion, he makes a trip to Nanjing to meet the organizers of the Taibo ceremony, who, he believes, share his moral conviction. In his baggage he carries letters of introduction from one of Yu Yude's students and the manuscripts of his newly finished ritual manuals, which he hopes to get published with their endorsement. For all his sorrow and pain, he is now well on his way to winning back his shattered moral confidence.

His plan is soon abandoned. As if on the wrong timetable, Wang is always arriving too late. On his way to Nanjing, he stops in Suzhou to visit an old friend who has been an enthusiastic reader of his books. For him this is another chance to gain approval for his writings and his story. But the meeting never happens, because a few days before his arrival his friend passed away. The last scene of this episode is suggestive: in front of the coffin of his deceased friend, Wang offers a sacrifice, together with his manuscripts. This action can well be taken as a gesture of resignation: his ritual manuals are dedicated to his deceased friend, and Wang's hope for approval is permanently suspended. But this gesture could just as well be ironic, for in the end he fails not only to get his books published but even to find a single reader.

Wang arrives in Nanjing only to discover that he has again arrived too late, for all the participants in the Taibo ceremony have dispersed. He visits the Taibo temple, the central site of the novel at which the lines of vision, longing, and memory converge. On the day of the grand ceremony, the temple had been turned into a stage, with thousands of performers and spectators. The ceremony performed there evoked a new moral vision that became a source of inspiration for those who came after. Now, a dozen years later, Wang Yuhui's visit to the Taibo temple is an occasion of frustration rather than enlightenment:

Deng Zhifu [son of Wang Yuhui's friend] gave a few cents of silver to the caretaker, who opened the door and showed them into the hall. After paying their respects here, they went to the buildings at the back. On the ground floor they found the program of the ceremony (*yizhu dan*) and the list of ceremonial staves (*zhishi dan*) that Chi Hengshan had pasted on the wall, and they dusted these off with their sleeves to read them. Then they went upstairs, where they saw eight large cabinets in which the musical instruments and sacrificial implements were locked. Wang wanted to look at them. "The key is in Mr. Chi's house," said the caretaker. There was nothing for it but to come downstairs. (R. 655; S. 535)

Time has been transformed into a barrier that keeps Wang Yuhui away from the ritual world for which he longs. The utensils and musical instruments once used in the ceremony are now inaccessible, locked away in cabinets, and Wang is denied the "key" to open them; the bulletin containing the program for the ceremony remains on the wall, but it is covered with dust and is now almost illegible.

The moment when Wang Yuhui brushes away the dust and reads the ceremonial program deserves attention, for what he reads actually occurred in Chapter 37—the procedures of the Taibo ceremony modeled on the Confucian ritual manuals (*yizhu*). In a similar way, the list of ceremonial staves (*zhishi dan*) was also presented in that chapter, immediately following the paragraph on the Taibo ceremony. By Wang Yuhui's reading of the *yizhu* and *zhishi dan* on the wall of the Taibo temple, *Rulin waishi* seems to disclose the textual sources for, and the generic mode of, Chapter 37.

What makes this moment even more interesting is that Wang Yuhui is not merely a reader; he is himself a compiler of Confucian ritual manuals.

And he is an equally devoted practitioner who is eager to translate into action the texts that he has edited. The irony is that although the ceremony in Chapter 37 is represented as practice, in Chapter 48 it is read retrospectively as a text disengaged from the realm of real life. Indeed, ritual manuals present a written project yet to be materialized. They are two-dimensional, with the information locked in the surface. And they are devoid of any perplexing problems one might encounter in actual ritual practice. However, since Wang Yuhui assumes the roles of both the ritual practitioner and the author of the manuals, he embodies the ironic tension between action and writing and is caught between his own ritual experiences and the text about the Taibo ceremony. To Wang, the irony is personal: despite his hope of dispelling the doubts he has experienced in his moral practice, he finds in the temple nothing but some inaccessible ritual utensils and ritual texts similar to those he himself has been working on. There is an unmistakable coincidence between the text he reads and those he writes, but it does not tell him what has gone wrong in his own practice. To Wang Yuhui, as to us, this is a moment of confirmation, but it leads only to disillusionment: instead of being enlightened, Wang places the *yizhu* in a new context that calls such texts into question.

As we have seen, Wu Jingzi and his friends often engaged in discussing and compiling Confucian ritual manuals, which they deployed as guides for ritual practice and as illustrations of the vision of the Confucian ritualized world. Interestingly enough, all this is recapitulated in *Rulin waishi*, where we encounter the ritual manuals in the material form of the books and ritual programs to be read, displayed, discussed, and carried from one place to another. The novel's use and representation of these manuals show how its narrative of Confucian ritual is embedded in the larger system of signifying practice of the time. But it also reveals *Rulin waishi*'s awareness of and reflection on that embeddedness. At the end of the Wang Yuhui episode, Wu Jingzi created an illuminating moment in which he confronted his own writing of the Confucian ritual through Wang's reading of the program on the wall of the Taibo temple; this ending raises questions about the nature, encoded meanings, and functions of the ritual manual so familiar to contemporary literati readers and so essential to the narrative design of the novel.

The reduction in Chapter 48 of the Taibo ceremony to the status of a written text casts into doubt the dichotomy of ritual and discourse that Wu

Jingzi tried to establish in the early part of the novel. Contrary to what we see in Chapter 37, the ceremony in reality consists of more than prescribed acts; it is prefaced by a story of calculation, coercion, and verbal and mental manipulation. In the conversation with his daughter that leads her to commit suicide, Wang Yuhui tries to control her utterance, to frame it within his moral categories and give it authoritative guidance. To be sure, when his daughter says, "Now my husband has died, will you have to support me too?" she indirectly indicates her decision (R. 649; S. 529). Yet by putting it in the form of a question, she seems to offer her father a choice. The question indicates her hesitation; she needs to be encouraged or discouraged. The weight of the decision falls upon his shoulders. It would take little to prevent his daughter's suicide. Wang need not prove that he is able to support her after her husband's death; he need only indicate his willingness. But he dodges the question, asking in return a question to which he already knows the reply: "Now what do you want to do?" Immediately after his daughter announces the decision he has anticipated, Wang adds, as if afraid that she might regret her decision and change her mind, that it is impossible to stop someone whose mind is made up. Before the curtain comes down, he loudly announces the end of the drama. When he says to his kinsmen, "Since my daughter sincerely wants to die, you should let her have her way," he leaves her no retreat. The situation has been set up by her father. She loses control over the story she has initiated and is compelled to play the role of a "chaste woman." As he duly reminds her, "You know what you must do!" Despite his role as director as well as a key actor in the unfolding drama, Wang nevertheless assumes a modest posture, pretending to do only what is necessary to help his daughter fulfill her wish.

This story of manipulation does not, however, proceed entirely as Wang Yuhui would have liked. Although he "eggs her on" (as his wife puts it) to make the decision he expects, he fails, nevertheless, to subsume his daughter's voice into his own. Their conversation unfolds in a peculiar way: they converse without communicating and reach the same conclusion for completely different reasons. At the moment when the decision is made, Wang reads it as a triumph of moral will, whereas his poor daughter is preoccupied with the financial straits of her father's family. "A poor scholar like you," she says, "can't afford to feed so many daughters!" The gap between the father's and the daughter's presentations of the story suggests different mentalities. Weighing her decision to sacrifice herself for the sake of the family economy, she discloses the socioeconomic and psychological pressures that impinge on what her father sees as purely a moral drama.

It is also noteworthy that the virtues indicated in the Jiexiao shrine, chastity and filial piety, are absent from the daughter's speech. In her conversation with her father and her husband's parents, she never makes her death a sign of loyalty to her deceased husband. Granted, her explanation of it as an attempt to reduce her father's financial burdens could be understood as an act of filial piety. But since her husband's parents have promised that they will take care of her and ruled out the possibility that she must return to her father's home, her suicide seems almost willful. Even if filial piety remains the professed departure point of her story, as her deliberate self-destruction moves on to its final stage, her husband's parents suffer and her own mother is overcome with sorrow. When her mother collapses and has to be carried home, a Qing commentator asked: "Isn't this contrary to filial piety?"[3]

The narrative of the daughter's self-sacrifice drags on without convincing motivation or definite direction. Her own explanation is developed no further after it is given; what remains are her father's comments indicating the consequences of her moral heroism. "Since this is the case," he encourages his daughter, "your name will be recorded in history." His vision of moral drama is enacted, but in this particular context it offers only an inversion of motivation and consequence: the awareness of consequence now becomes the force that drives the daughter's act. It is largely irrelevant whether she supports this interpretation—the vacancy in the center of the narrative needs to be filled.

Rethinking Ascetic Ritual

The story of Wang Yuhui can be better understood when juxtaposed with "A Poem in the Ancient Style for Chaste Woman Wang in Xin'an."[4] The author, Jin Zhaoyan (1718–89+), a close relative of Wu Jingzi, is said to have sponsored publication of the earliest edition of *Rulin waishi*. In this poem, Jin recounted the story of Woman Wang, who starved herself to death for her deceased husband. He Zehan's study shows that Wu Jingzi probably based his narrative of Wang Yuhui on Jin's verse. Wu set the story in

---

3. See Huang Xiaotian's commentary on *Rulin waishi* in Li Hanqiu, ed., *Rulin waishi*, p. 444.

4. Jin Zhaoyan, "Gushi wei Xin'an liefu Wangshi zhuo."

Huizhou, that is, Xin'an prefecture. Like Woman Wang, Wang Yuhui's daughter is the third daughter of the family. Toward the end of the poem, Jin Zhaoyan attributed Woman Wang's moral heroism to her father's education. This is echoed in the praise that Wang Yuhui receives at the end of the ceremony dedicated to his daughter. But whereas Jin's admiration for Woman Wang was unreserved, Wu subtly revised the story to steer it in a different direction.

As is often the case in the narrative of a chaste woman, Jin Zhaoyan began by recounting Woman Wang's pledge to her dying husband, an episode that, interestingly, is missing from the Wang Yuhui story. Despite his praise of this self-sacrifice, Jin described the efforts of the widow's sisters and brothers to change her decision. The elder sisters say:

> Better not torture yourself too much,
> So that the deceased man can feel relief.

The elder brother provides her with an alternative:

> I have just one word for you,
> Remaining a widow (*shoujie*) and sacrificing one's self for a deceased
>   husband (*xunjie*)—
> Both are rooted in the same principle of antiquity.

In *Rulin waishi*, the advice against suicide is offered by the daughter's parents-in-law; this sets up a contrast with what Wang Yuhui, the father, has to say. Jin Zhaoyan represented Woman Wang's father as overwhelmed by sorrow:

> You are determined in your action,
> But how sad that you will leave me, an old man, behind,
> With my heart broken.

Jin deliberately left the father's language ambiguous: it does not dissuade his daughter, but neither does it amount to a persuasion. Wu Jingzi twisted the first sentence slightly and turned the father's speech into an affirmative instruction: "Now that I think this over, I believe that, since my daughter sincerely wants to die for her husband, we should let her have her way. You can't stop someone whose mind is made up." Wu Jingzi edited the father's words in Jin Zhaoyan's poem in a way that removes the sense of ambiguity. His recasting gave the father a more manipulative and determinative role in his daughter's tragedy.

Toward the end of the poem, Jin Zhaoyan wrote:

> I heard that the Prefecture of Xin'an,
> Has produced worthies ever since ancient times,
> The Learning of Principle had been shining for a thousand years.
> Ceremonies were favored in schools.
> Yet they have declined to the extreme in this time of degeneration,
> The Learning of the Way has become empty words.
> Those who ascend the platform elaborate principles,
> Yet in conduct they seldom measure up to their own words.
> How remarkable that we have this lady,
> Who, in a heroic deed, sacrificed her life for the man she served.
> Therefore, I know that this is due to her family education,
> Which had been carried out by her father for many years.

Jin Zhaoyan mentioned Xin'an, Zhu Xi's ancestral home, to highlight the degeneration of contemporary Neo-Confucianism in its place of origin. Like many of his fellow literati of the day, he believed that Neo-Confucianism's high-minded principle (li) had become a matter of verbal interpretation, disconnected from the sphere of action. This is matched by Wu Jingzi's portrayal of Zhu Xi's ritual as compromised by unending negotiation and circumstantial adjustment (quan) in Chapter 4 of Rulin waishi. In his paean to Woman Wang, Jin suggested that only action can achieve the absoluteness that the Neo-Confucians claim for their principle: whereas the Neo-Confucians fail to match their words with deeds, Woman Wang carries out her silent ritual of self-sacrifice.

The commentator in the Woxian caotang edition of Rulin waishi read the story of Wang Yuhui in a similar light. He acknowledged the tendency of Wang's moral asceticism toward extravagance, excess, and single-mindedness, but he praised its heroic spirit. In his view, Wang's persistent attempts to fulfill his moral convictions, regardless of consequences and circumstances, show the courage and determination essential to moral practice.[5] "The way in which he conducts himself indicates that he can hold his position firmly when facing a crisis. Those who can decisively carry out the obligations of the five basic human relationships and thus achieve extraordinary things are definitely not the 'clever people' (guairen) of the world." This commentator deliberately contrasted Wang Yuhui with "clever people," who,

---

5. See Li Hanqiu, ed., "Rulin waishi" huijiao huiping ben, p. 656.

like Wang Hui and the Wang brothers, can always find an easy way out. As we have seen, these characters are presented in a dualistic world of the sacred as mundane. They practice what I have described as narrative ritual and, by this means, represent themselves as noble Confucians adhering to ritual obligations without sacrificing their self-interest. As an antidote to this practice, Wang Yuhui's ascetic ritual is characterized by its conceptualization of virtue as opposed to worldly interests, by its ascetic discipline of self-denial, by its orientation toward action, and by its fanatical urge for transcendence. Like Filial Guo in his attempt to restore the family bond, Wang finds it unnecessary to justify what he considers to be ritual obligations and sees no room for negotiation and compromise. In his view, ritual obligations are self-evident and demand to be fully realized regardless of time and circumstances.

However, the Woxian caotang commentator sees only one aspect of the story. Wu Jingzi may have drawn on Jin Zhaoyan's poem for his narrative of Wang Yuhui, but he took that story to its logical extreme and exposed its dark consequences. In *Rulin waishi* the dichotomy of ascetic and narrative rituals does not necessarily suggest that the former is a better alternative. At its worst, absolute asceticism that needs no justification becomes a legitimate excuse for violence, torture, and a denial of humanity. Self-sacrifice is the point of the Wang Yuhui story, but it is represented in such a way that it seems to be done for its own sake and is incomprehensible in other terms. We may find it difficult to discuss the daughter's perception of the event, for the narrator does not allow her to develop her own voice, and her story often intersects with her father's. But she resembles her father in at least one way: just as fanatical, she seems to have raised herself above the mundane world and sees no need to make her self-sacrifice comprehensible to ordinary humans. This attitude or mentality is best summed up in Wang Yuhui's dismissive comment to his wife: "Matters like these"—their daughter's suicide—"are beyond you" (R. 650; S. 530).

Unlike the Woxian caotang commentator, Wu Jingzi did not admire Wang Yuhui's commitment and devotion. Rather, he told the story in such a way as to show how much damage can be done in the name of absolute values and transcendental truth. It is not merely that Wang Yuhui inflicts suffering on his daughter but also that he himself becomes a victim of the morality play he directs. Before his drama reaches its end, Wang is torn apart by the sorrow that has overwhelmed his wife. As Wang journeys to Nanjing, he fights back tears on seeing a young widow of his daughter's age.

In the narrative of Wang Yuhui's ritual journey, the two moments of emotional eruption unleash the accumulated pathos suppressed by the extreme discipline of ascetic ritual—moments when asceticism takes revenge on itself. The daughter's suicide is perceived in the commemorative ceremony as a heroic deed that boosts the prestige of the Wang family. Thus Wang Yuhui does not stand alone in encouraging his daughter; he has the lineage system behind him. In this sense, Wu Jingzi's critique of ascetic ritualism is closely connected to his representation of the mechanism of the local lineage system. He saw the dangers that could arise when that system ran the community in the name of absolute moral authority and portrayed the consequences of its tyranny over its many powerless members. Here the key to the explication of the Wang Yuhui saga lies in the books he spends his life compiling. Wang is not only a dedicated compiler of Confucian ritual manuals but also an editor of the Village Compact (xiangyue) and Primer (zishu).[6] Together, these three categories of books constitute a coherent Confucian design for local society, including a temple (ceremonial or ancestral hall), school, and the local community led by lineage heads. With these texts as his guides, Wang coaxes his daughter into action, and the ceremony dedicated to her becomes a crucial event that sets the community in motion. Throughout, the local community reproduces the hegemonic discourse and opinions that have pressed the daughter to commit suicide.[7]

---

6. In Chapter 48, Wang Yuhui introduces his zishu and xiangyue as follows: The zishu "is a textbook that takes seven years to study," and the xiangyue "simply supplies additional ceremonies to help civilize the people" (R. 648; S. 528).

7. Underlying Wu Jingzi's narration of the ceremonies held in the Taibo temple (Chapter 37) and the Jiexiao shrine (Chapter 48) are a welter of complex, politically and ideologically charged issues about the local lineage construction that concerned the literati of the time. The ritual Yan Yuan and Li Gong promoted was by no means an individual endeavor; it was deeply rooted in the local community and lineage system. Li Gong proposed to build "public lineage halls (gongci) and have a lineage elder lead the ceremonies presented to the first ancestor of that lineage" (see Li Gong, "Xueli," in Tushu jicheng chubian, vol. 34, juan 4, p. 726. For the debate on this issue, see Chow, The Rise of Confucian Ritualism in Late Imperial China, pp. 107–24). Wu Jingzi's account of the temple dedicated to Wu Taibo, the "first ancestor" of the Wu clan, can be read in this light. As later Confucian ritualists often do, Yan Yuan strongly advocated female chastity and suicide to preserve chastity (see Yan Yuan, "Er liefu zhuan," in Yan Yuan ji, pp. 482–85). In the ritualists' plan for social reform, strengthening the local lineage and promoting female chastity were two interconnected factors seen as contributing to the revival of Confucian ritual. In this regard, Yan Yuan and Li Gong were little different from the Song and Ming Neo-Confucians, whom they openly criticized. In fact, from the Northern Song on, such prominent Neo-Confucians as Cheng Yi (1033–1107), Zhu Xi, and Wang Yangming were extremely active

Rulin waishi does not allow us to read Wang Yuhui's ascetic practice merely as an abortive miracle play or an example of unsuccessful moral heroism; it portrays it as a scheme of deception, coercion, and distortion. The story of Wang Yuhui seems to begin by presenting a possible option for the literati in their search for status and power: since their unrestrained competition for mundane self-interest leads to the destruction of their moral personality, perhaps asceticism provides a remedy. As the story unfolds, however, we see only a variation on the same old pattern of mundane practice. Despite all his professed detachment, Wang's pursuit of symbolic authority through ritualistic practice is seen as a parallel to, if not an extension of, the struggle for political and economic gain.[8] Although symbolic authority may not be convertible immediately to official status and wealth, it promises a long-term reward of a different order. The story of Wang shows just how far a literatus can go in soliciting such a reward.

---

in reviving the local lineage system through rituals, ancestral halls, local schools, and village or lineage compacts. An advocate of heavenly principle (*tianli*) over human desires (*renyu*), Cheng Yi is known for, among other things, his statement that a widow dying of hunger is a matter of little significance, but her loss of chastity is a serious matter. As Katherine Carlitz ("The Social Uses of Female Virtue in Late Ming Editions of *Lienü zhuan*") and other scholars point out, the cult of chaste women in Huizhou is inseparable from the dominant tradition of the local lineages. In the Wang Yuhui episode, Wu Jingzi exposed two interconnected aspects of the cult of female chastity by showing how Wang, the representative of his clan, advocated the cult to gain prestige for his clan and used ritual to legitimize the violence he inflicted upon his powerless daughter. In the mid-eighteenth century, when construction of local lineage systems remained the dominant trend of literati endeavors, Wu's criticisms of its unstated consequences were perhaps echoed only by his younger contemporary Dai Zhen.

8. The concept of "symbolic capital" or "cultural capital" is developed in Pierre Bourdieu's theory of cultural production. If in the economic field people engage in competition for control of economic capital, in the cultural field, Bourdieu submits, the competition often concerns the authority inherent in recognition, consecration, and prestige. "'Symbolic capital' is to be understood as economic or political capital that is disavowed, misrecognized and thereby recognized, hence legitimate, a 'credit' which, under certain conditions, and always in the long run, guarantees 'economic' profits" (Bourdieu, *The Field of Cultural Production*, p. 75). Judith A. Berling, in her reading of *The Romance of the Three Teachings* (*Sanjiao kaimi guizheng yanyi*), a Ming didactic novel, observes that humanity (*ren*) and righteousness (*yi*) are treated as moral capital, earned and saved like money. "Moral capital (accumulated merit) is just as important as a legacy for one's descendants as land or money. In fact, the successful long-term management of property depends on the management of moral capital; the two cannot be separated." She further traces the view of moral capital to the development of Ming morality books (*shanshu*) and ledgers of merit and demerit (*gongguo ge*). See Berling, "Religion and Popular Culture." See also Sakai, *Chūgoku zensho no kenkyū*; and de Bary, "Individualism and Humanitarianism in Late Ming Thought," p. 176.

Here Wang Yuhui's statement to his daughter, ensuring that she will not renege on her decision to commit suicide, is noteworthy: "You know what you must do." The verb for "to do" (*zuo*) used in this sentence implies deliberate action. Huang Xiaotian, a late Qing commentator, remarked: "*Zuo* is terribly false. How could a chaste lady be created by design?" "Nothing, if deliberately done, can be sincere. Wang Yuhui intended to win the fame of the chaste (*jie*) and the righteous (*yi*), and therefore ordered his daughter to sacrifice herself. How could he be considered sincere?"[9]

In the Taibo ceremony, Wu Jingzi depicted a ritual that involves no conscious effort or deliberation on the part of its participants. That is, indeed, what ritual is all about: formulaic patterns of behavior internalized by practitioners through repetition and then spontaneously enacted on appropriate occasions. But in describing ritual performances in a specific social setting, as in the Wang Yuhui incident, Wu Jingzi allowed the exiled consciousness to return and haunt the practitioners. He never portrayed Wang Yuhui as acting naturally or spontaneously; Wang's ethics left no room for sincerity. To ensure that official historians record your name, you have to deliberately compose (*zuo*) your own essay through action, modeling yourself on those whose names have been recorded under the various rubrics (*timu*) of official history. Wang's comments on his daughter's suicide, "I only wish I could eventually figure out such a good rubric (*timu*) under which to die" (R. 650; S. 530), underscore his insincerity. Wang does not need to make such a wish, since he has already made her death his own rubric. In the course of the entire narrative, her name is never given. As is often the case in historical texts and local gazetteers, she is introduced merely as his daughter.

If the ceremony for the daughter is deliberate and deceptive, its enactment turns out to be rewarding for Wang, who is surrounded by the important figures of the county "declaring that by bringing up such a virtuous daughter he had added luster to his clan" (R. 651; S. 531). Such praise seems to be made for the official histories; the official biographies of chaste women often conclude with similar wording. In the end, Wang Yuhui, an impoverished licentiate with no official title, is able to acquire a position for himself and his clan in textual history through his manipulation of symbolic resources that, not unlike sociopolitical and economic resources, become

---

9. See Li Hanqiu, ed., *Rulin waishi*, 1986, pp. 444, 449.

themselves important capital for acquisition, accumulation, and competition. The way in which the symbolic capital is acquired presents an even more gruesome irony: the daughter sacrifices her life, and the father garners the reward.

Reading Wang Yuhui's ceremony as a drama of maneuvering and manipulation helps to reveal the hidden aspect of the Taibo ceremony. It raises the question of whether that Taibo ceremony in Chapter 37 is similarly self-serving. What is certain is that by dedicating it to the ancient sage, Yu Yude and his fellow literati somehow make themselves Wu Taibo's present-day counterparts, and his temple a monument to themselves. As Chi Hengshan says before recommending Yu Yude: "Since we are going to dedicate the ceremony to a great sage, the master of the ceremony should be a sage himself, to be worthy of Taibo" (R. 487; S. 395). Such a statement can naturally be extended to Chi himself and to his friends, who initiate and design the ceremony. The Taibo ceremony turns out to be the celebrants' self-celebration—one that implicitly demands official recognition. This is reflected in the last chapter of the novel, in which Yu Yude and his fellow literati are posthumously honored by the authorities with the titles of metropolitan graduates and Hanlin scholars and then commemorated in an official ceremony that is ironically drowned out by the din of official announcements, praise, and prayers. These two ceremonies—the Taibo ceremony and the official ceremony—sum up the paradox faced by the literati: those who escape from the center of political power make themselves famous, and consequently they are granted the official titles they seem to hold in contempt.

Since honors may be long in coming, some people try to hasten the process, as Xiao Yunxian does in Chapter 40. A frustrated general removed from his command, Xiao despairs of getting his name recorded in official history and so passed down to future generations. However, using his contacts with eminent literati, he is able to create a history of his own. He has the highlights of his career painted on a handscroll with a detailed written account attached to each picture. The margin is left vacant for famous scholars such as Yu Yude to inscribe their poems, because "their works"—to quote Yu Youda's remarks to Xiao Yunxian—"will confer immortality on your loyal deeds and rescue them from oblivion" (R. 553; S. 445). To ensure his role in history, Xiao mobilizes all the symbolic resources available to him, from written texts to ceremonies, two of which are performed in Chapter 40. After he leads a ceremony dedicated to the God of Agriculture:

To show their appreciation of Xiao's goodness, the people built a temple to the God of Agriculture outside the city, with a shrine to the god in the center, and next to it a long-life tablet for Xiao Yunxian. An artist was also found to paint Xiao in his gauze cap and official robes on horseback, with Mu Nai [Xiao's bodyguard] holding his reins and carrying a red banner to encourage the peasants. On the first and fifteenth of every month, all the men and women of the district would come to burn incense, light candles, and do reverence here. (R. 547; S. 439)

This scene illustrates the mechanism of recognition that functions through ceremony. Although there is an undeniable distinction between public celebration and official recognition, the message about ceremony is unmistakable. It is both a promise and a fulfillment of that promise: those who perform one ceremony will themselves be celebrated in the next.

The Taibo ceremony and Xiao Yunxian's ritual have no serious consequences. In this sense, they differ from Wang Yuhui's ritual. But like the Wang Yuhui incident, they confront us with a profound dilemma in Confucian practice and hence in the representation of the literati practitioners: far from changing society in the intended fashion, literati ritual turns out to be at best a means of accumulating symbolic capital. Fully justified, it opens up another field of equally intense competition. Its worst consequence is played out in the episode of Wang Yuhui: his sublime vision of ascetic ritualism is realized as his poor daughter is sacrificed in the temple dedicated to her.

Ritual and Symbolic Power

Wang Yuhui's ritual ordeal is foreshadowed by Merchant Fang's ceremonial festival in Chapter 47 of *Rulin waishi*. Unlike the Wang Yuhui incident, which concerns the literati's abuse of Confucian ritual and the patriarchal lineage system, this story evinces Wu Jingzi's anxiety over the emergence of merchants displaying their power and demanding public recognition in the symbolic realm. It explores the symbolic dimension of Confucian ritual that appeals to anyone willing to assert his status, and it shows how easily Confucian ritual can be harnessed to any purpose. The Taibo ceremony is supposedly detached from the mundane world, but the ceremonies following it are either carried to the tragic extreme of asceticism or reduced to the farcical parade of mundane power in ceremonial form. The contrasting episodes of Wang Yuhui and Merchant Fang are mutually illuminating.

When it is time for the elite families of Wuhe county to perform the dedication ceremonies to their female ancestors honored by the authorities as chaste women, Yu Huaxuan and the Yu brothers, members of the local gentry, find it difficult to call together the members of their lineage. On the day of the ceremony, their kinsmen opt to participate in a ceremony dedicated to the grandmother of Merchant Fang, one of the richest and the most powerful figures in their town, which they see as a rare opportunity to pay tribute to the merchant. Feeling no moral qualms, they urge Yu Huaxuan and the Yu brothers to join them. Outraged and helpless, Yu Huaxuan and the Yu brothers decide to conduct the ceremony on their own. They have several peasants carry their great-aunts' shrines to the ceremonial hall, where they prepare the sacrifice. But they are soon interrupted by the procession escorting the shrine of Merchant Fang's grandmother:

Presently gonging and drumming filled the street. Two yellow umbrellas and eight flags appeared, as well as four groups of horsemen bearing placards inscribed with golden characters: "The Minister of Ceremony," "The Hanlin," "The Provincial Director of Education," and "The Number One Graduate." These had been lent by the families of Yu Huaxuan and the Yu brothers. As the procession drew near, gongs and trumpets sounded, incense was burned, and the crowd thronged around Mrs. Fang's shrine, which was carried by eight big-footed maids. The sixth Mr. Fang, in a gauze cap and a round collar, followed respectfully behind. After him came two groups: the gentry (*xiangshen*) and the licentiates (*xiucai*). The gentry included the second, third, fifth, and seventh Peng brothers. Then came the metropolitan and provincial graduates (*jinshi* and *juren*), senior licentiates (*gongsheng*), and college students (*jiansheng*) of the two Yu families—sixty to seventy in all. In gauze caps and round collars, they followed respectfully behind the Pengs. In their wake came another sixty to seventy licentiates from the two Yu families, in scholars' caps and gowns, who scuttled hastily after them. The last of the local gentry, second Tang, held a notebook in which he was doing accounts. The last of the licentiates, third Tang, also carried a notebook, keeping accounts. After all, the two Yu families had a family tradition of scholarly education and a proper manner. When they reached their ancestral temple and saw their own aunts' shrines, seven or eight of them actually came over to bow! Then they all surged after Mrs. Fang's shrine into the temple. Behind them were the magistrate, principal of local schools, vice magistrate, and sergeant, who came with the retinue to play music and set up the shrine. The magistrate, the principal of local schools, the vice magistrate, and the sergeant each sacrificed in turn. Then the local gentry and scholars sacrificed, and last of all the Fang family sacrificed. When this was over, they all rushed noisily out and mounted the Pavilion of Honoring the Classics for the feast. (R. 641–42; S. 523–24)

This is local society on parade in a comedy, a combination of incompatible elements. All the prestigious figures are present, arranged in an order that represents the hierarchy of the town. Merchant Fang, as host of the ceremony, occupies the central position and makes the parade his own show. In the procession, Fang appears in official dress, behind placards that bear official titles that do not belong to him. The clothes and placards are more than decoration; they are a declaration of his fantasies, of how he wishes to see himself rather than how he is. Through pomp and ceremony, he tries to overcome the gap between fantasy and reality. Indeed, wealth signals status and demands symbolic expression and recognition.

Following Merchant Fang are the local gentry, all dressed in official garb and arranged according to rank: first the gentlemen from the Peng family, the most prestigious family of the town; then those from the families of Yu Huaxuan and the Yu brothers, ranging from the metropolitan and provincial graduates to senior licentiates and college students. The group of licentiates, holders of the lowest degree, come immediately after the gentry; in their scholars' caps and gowns, they appear somewhat uneasy.[10] As they scuttle along, they see their own aunts' shrines in front of the ceremonial hall. In an ironic tone the narrator states: "After all, the two Yu families had a family tradition of scholarly education and a proper manner. When they reached their ancestral temple and saw their own aunts' shrines, seven or eight of them actually came over to bow!" Using the adverb *jingran* (actually) to convey his sense of surprise, Wu Jingzi's narrator adds another ironic twist to the scene of the ceremonial proceeding. This small, momentary concession to decency only underscores the dominance of mercantile values.

The procession ends with all the local officials, from the magistrate down to the sergeant. Taken together, they form the administrative body that conducts the public affairs of the town. Their presence in the parade is an official recognition of the merchant as an important public figure. As soon as the parade is over, the ceremony begins. The sequence of the procession is reversed: the ceremony begins with the officials and ends with the Fang family, and the literati are again placed in the middle.

---

10. Wu Jingzi drew a clear line between the *xiangshen* and the *xiucai*, and portrayed the latter as a special social group between the gentry and the commoner. For Wu Jingzi's view of social stratification in the Ming, see Ho, *Ladder of Success in Imperial China*, pp. 28–41. See also "Appendix: The Examination System and Official Ranks Referred to in This Novel," in Yang Hsien-yi and Gladys Yang, *The Scholars*, pp. 603–7.

As a public spectacle, the ceremony illustrates the structure of the dominant class, with the literati positioned according to a kind of compromise. It is an occasion in which power, status, and wealth join together to form a single social code. Through the accumulation of wealth, merchants emerge into the realm of power, and they see ceremony as a legitimate medium through which to translate their wealth into prestige. And the ceremony itself is depicted as a morally degraded farce:

The sixth Mr. Fang seemed uncomfortable after such a long ceremony. He replaced his gauze cap and round collar with a headcloth and ordinary gown, then wandered up and down the balconies. Soon a flower seller named Quan came along, and with her big feet climbed the pavilion stairway. "I came to see the old lady enshrined!" she chuckled. The sixth Mr. Fang fairly beamed. He stood beside her, leaning against the railing, watching the flags and musicians, pointing out this and that and explaining things to her one by one. The flower woman kept one hand on the railing and with the other undid her clothes to search for lice, which she popped in her mouth one after another. (R. 642; S. 524)

This brief episode takes us to the core of the farce that the novel evokes: a reversal of the norms of etiquette and a juxtaposition of high and low, sacred and profane. Thus we finally have scandal, debasement, and obscenity as a culmination of the farcical ceremony itself. Merchant Fang's explanation of the ceremony and the flower lady's chewing of her lice are juxtaposed in two parallel sentences and generate a carnivalistic contrast. A similar contrast is also implicit in the staging of this scene in front of the Pavilion of Honoring the Classics (Zunjing ge).

In Chapter 37, the literati conceive of ceremony as an ethical force to counter the corruption of the official and unofficial worlds. But in this scene, it is the symptom of that corruption. Not only does it fail to transform society, it is itself transformed and caught up in the logic of the mundane affairs it resists. The merchant's invasion of the sphere of symbolic power discloses the hidden aspect of the ideal vision of ceremony, for the competition for control of symbolic authority is now described as a parallel to the struggle for political and economic interest. To see this, we need only compare the parade scene with the account of the ceremony in honor of Wang Yuhui and his daughter.

Buying incense and three sacrificial offerings, he [Yu Youda, the tutor at the prefectural college at Huizhou] went to pay his respects before her coffin. This done, he returned to the *yamen*, and ordered his clerk to draw up a petition requesting the authorities to honor this devoted widow. His younger brother helped to draft the petition, which was dispatched that same night. Then Yu Youzhong [Yu Youda's brother] took offerings and sacrifices before the coffin. When the college students saw their tutor show the dead woman such respect, a great many of them also went to sacrifice. And two months later the authorities decreed that a shrine should be made and placed in the temple, and an archway erected before her home. On the day that she was enshrined, Mr. Yu invited the magistrate to accompany the retinue that escorted the virtuous widow into the temple. All the local gentry, in official robes, joined the procession on foot. Having entered the temple and set the shrine in its place, the magistrate, college tutors, and Yu each sacrificed. Then the gentry, scholars, and relatives sacrificed; and last of all the two families sacrificed. The ceremony lasted all day, and they feasted afterwards in the Hall of Manifest Propriety (Minglun tang). The other scholars urged Wang to join the feast, declaring that by bringing up such a virtuous daughter he had added luster to his clan. (R. 651; S. 531)

On the day of the ceremony, Wang Yuhui, like Merchant Fang, makes himself the focus of public attention. The two ceremonies are similar in several respects: both are dedicated to chaste women; they are enacted in the local communities and involve local officials and gentry families; they follow similar procedures; and they are represented in a similar way, despite the differences in the tone of the narrative. But the role of Merchant Fang is performed by Wang Yuhui, an obscure scholar of the local community. If Fang pursues prestige and status, things a merchant, according to Wu Jingzi's narrator, does not deserve, Wang acquires fame legitimately by turning his daughter's death into his own symbolic capital. In both cases, symbolic capital is authorized through ceremony.

There is, therefore, a parallel between those who fight by all means for official status or economic profit and those who care more about symbolic or moral authority. Occasionally they cross the boundaries of their respective fields and encounter each other, as symbolic authority is converted to status and economic profit or vice versa. If the novel makes "fame" one of the primary targets of its social criticism, the criticism is all-encompassing. By rewarding those who disavow interest for that very disinterestedness, the novel designs a fatal paradox for its characters.

We should not overdramatize the paradox, of course. There remains a distinction between those who court fame and those who try to escape it and fail. Even among the former, our ethics of reading may also remind us of the difference between those who deserve fame and those who do not. But the crisis I am discussing occurs primarily at the institutional level rather than that of experience. Despite their efforts to distance themselves from the center of power, the literati can never be independent of the political culture or symbolic system of which they form a part. An individual who engages in moral practice may be innocent in motivation or unaware of the possible rewards, or he may even try, successfully or not, to conceal from himself and others what is at stake in his practice. However, irony is inescapable because it has been built into the existing system, within which his actions are constantly exposed to alternative "contextualizing" perspectives; he may himself be perceived as an actor in the game of gaining fame by attempting to escape profit. As second thoughts pollute an innocent mind, so does the gaze from an alternative perspective. In this changed landscape of literati culture, those who have no sense of self-irony themselves become the object of irony.

From Collapsed Temple to Imagined Marketplace: A Redemption of Elite Culture?

Chapter 55, the next-to-last chapter of *Rulin waishi*, begins with a survey of literati life in Nanjing, when the memory of the Taibo ceremony has faded with time:

By the twenty-third year of the Wanli period [1595], all the well-known scholars had disappeared from Nanjing. Of Dr. Yu's generation, some were old, some had died, some had gone far away, and some had closed their doors and paid no attention to affairs outside. Pleasure haunts and taverns were no longer frequented by men of talent, and honest men no longer occupied themselves with ceremony and letters. As far as scholarship was concerned, all who passed the examinations were considered brilliant and all who failed fools. And as for liberality, the rich indulged in ostentatious gestures while the poor were forced to seem shabby. You might have the genius of Li Bai and Du Fu and the moral worth of Yan Hui and Zeng Shen, but no one would ask your advice. So at coming of age ceremonies, marriages, funerals, or sacrifices in big families and in the halls of the local gentry, nothing was discussed but promotions, transfers, and recalls in the official world. And all impecunious scholars did was try by various tricks to find favor with the examiners. (R. 739; S. 593)

As a locus of ritual activity, Nanjing in Chapters 33 to 37 is a pure land in comparison with other locations. However, by the time the novel returns there in Chapter 55, forty years have elapsed. Not only have those who organized the ceremony left or passed away, but the Taibo temple itself has collapsed. As the temple falls apart, Confucian ritual loses its center and sense of solidarity. In this chapter, Wu Jingzi's narrator focuses on the marketplace, portraying four eccentric characters who are actually literati in disguise inhabiting the low, peripheral space of the market. Driven by a utopian impulse, his narration of their lives and struggles represents an attempt by innocent, noble, and pure-hearted commoners to recover the literati's cultural ideals.

These four people are the embodiment of elite culture: they are fascinated, respectively, by music, chess, calligraphy, and painting (*qin qi shu hua*), the four basic arts of literati taste and cultivation. Without home or livelihood, Ji Xia'nian stays in Buddhist temples. Although he has no formal education, he somehow becomes a superb calligrapher. Wang Tai, from a family of market gardeners, is a chess player. Although his family property declines after his father's death and he has to sell kindling in the market to support himself, he amuses himself by playing chess. We are told that he has no other purpose; he loves the game of chess for its own sake. Originally from a rich family, Gai Kuan once owned a pawnshop. Partly due to his mismanagement and partly due to his fascination with painting, his pawnshop goes bankrupt, and he ends up owning a tea house. Still in his dilapidated house, he creates tasteful surroundings for his daily life:

He would get up early to light the fire, and when he had fanned it into a blaze would put on a kettle to heat, then sit behind his counter to read or paint. In a vase on the counter he kept a few blooms of whichever flowers were in season, and next to this was a pile of old books. He had sold all his other possessions, but could not bear to part with these precious volumes. (R. 744; S. 598)

A willingness to transform one's surroundings through cultural activity is demonstrated in the episode of Jing Yuan. A tailor, Jing Yuan also designs his own lifestyle. He loves poetry and calligraphy and is particularly good at music. During his spare time, he occasionally visits a friend, a gardener in the western section of Nanjing. In his friend's garden, after drinking tea infused with fine water, Jing Yuan comments:

"The ancients longed for a Peach Blossom Spring where they could escape from the world. I don't think any Peach Blossom Spring is needed. To live quietly and contentedly in a green plot in the city as you do, uncle, is as good as being an immortal!" (R. 748; S. 601)

Instead of hiding in mountains as a recluse, Jing Yuan sees the city as a true escape from the world. But the city does not serve as an ideal refuge until he creates in it a garden for cultivating aesthetic taste and sensibility. At the request of his friend, Jing Yuan carries his zither into the garden, and he plays a melody that only the two of them can understand and appreciate.

The account of these four townsfolk may have little appeal for students of Chinese literature, because it verges on a list of clichés about the literati recluse. However, we have to ask: Why did Wu Jingzi render these four characters as commoners instead of literati, and why did he close his novel with an escape from, rather than a return to, the world of the literati?

This story evokes a paradox by suggesting that it is precisely because these men are not literati that they are able to appreciate the true values of literati culture. They practice an art or pursue learning because they love it, and they love it for its own sake instead of the social values attached to it. In other words, they do not acquire aesthetic culture as literati usually do, as a step to personal glory or as a way of accumulating cultural or symbolic capital. It is an end in itself.

Naïve as it may sound, the story of these four townsmen proposes an alternative to the dilemma of the literati culture. Its meaning is revealed in the contrast it establishes with the representation of the literati throughout the novel. Jing Yuan's conversation with his friends is a good example.

"Since you want to be a refined person," said his friends and acquaintances, "why do you stick to your 'honorable' profession? Why not mix with some college students?" "I am not trying to be a refined person," replied Jing Yuan. "I just happen to like these things; that's why I take them up from time to time. As for my humble trade, it was handed down to me by my ancestors. Could it be said that I disgrace my studies by tailoring? Those college scholars don't look at things the way we do. They would never be friends with us. As it is, I make six or seven cents a day, and when I've eaten my fill, if I want to strum my zither or do some writing, there's nobody to stop me. I don't want to be rich or noble, or to make up to any man. Isn't it pleasant to be one's own master like this?" When his friends heard him talk this way, they began to treat him coldly. (R. 747; S. 600)

Jing Yuan's friends attribute his fascination with poetry, calligraphy, music, and books to a desire to be known as a person of refined taste (*yaren*). They conclude that he will never achieve this purpose until he quits his humble profession as a tailor. In response, Jing Yuan begins by saying, "I'm not trying to be a refined person." Here again the verb *zuo* is used. By using it to describe Jing Yuan's fascination with art and learning, his friends suggest a calculated effort at social climbing. But Wu Jingzi's narrator does not portray Jing Yuan as just another self-acclaimed man of culture, or *mingshi*: his cultural practice, as Jin himself states, is for his own entertainment and cultivation.

Jing Yuan's statement recaptures a formula of Neo-Confucianism: learning for the sake of one's own self. Nevertheless, if put in the mouth of a literati character, this statement would sound hopelessly ironical, for the exposure of intellectual pretension and hypocrisy has been built into the narrative pattern of the novel. But the tailor Jing Yuan's sincerity is guaranteed precisely by his low position in the marketplace, his removal from the ladder of social mobility and hence from the elite world. If, as I have said, Jing Yuan is a literatus disguised as a townsman, the disguise becomes essential. Throughout the novel, Wu Jingzi repeatedly exposed the literati's high-sounding statements to irony; he now needed a low-status character to restore the genuineness of those ideals.

As always, literati claim to be refined people (*yaren*) in opposition to the vulgarity of the world. Their claim is, however, often mere empty rhetoric or, even worse, elaborate, unabashed self-advertisement. In a gathering of literati in Chapter 29, a self-described poet suggests that when enjoying such an occasion, they must write poetry. Du Shenqing, himself a poet, wryly replies, "I know this has long been the practice in poetry societies, sir. But in my humble opinion it is so refined as to be vulgar (*ya de zheyang su*), and we would do better just to chat" (R. 400; S. 321). For Du Shenqing, the only way to show his refined taste is to distinguish himself from those who claim to be refined. Interestingly, his response is restated by Jing Yuan in Chapter 55 and given new meaning and vitality. Unlike Du Shenqing, whose rejection of the conventional claim to refinement remains part of the game of intellectual pretension, Jing Yuan testifies to his sincerity by remaining in his humble profession. He means what he says, and he ends the game not by words but by action.

The narrative of the four townsmen harks back to the introductory chapter of *Rulin waishi* on Wang Mian. Wang Mian is also a self-taught artist and a man of learning. Whereas the four townsmen inhabit the marketplace, Wang Mian lives in a village and later in the mountains as a recluse. He acquires no formal education and has no family background that would make him the kind of literatus seen often in the main part of the novel. It is noteworthy that *Rulin waishi*, which mainly concerns literati lives, begins and ends with the characters who are from the nonelite world and have no affiliations with the elite-official community (in the case of Wang Mian, he refuses to serve in the government). In Chapter 46, as Yu Yude bids farewell to Du Shaoqing, he promises to retire soon from service and provide his family with a livelihood from a modest farm; he also wants to teach his son medicine so that he can support himself. Earlier in Chapter 36 we are told that Yu Yude himself practices geomancy and fortunetelling for a living. These episodes about Yu Yude recapitulate an important orientation of Yan Yuan's life.[11] In the specific context of *Rulin waishi*, they echo the Wang Mian story in the introductory chapter and loom large in Chapter 55. But Wang Mian's reclusion does not necessarily separate him from the mundane world he despises. Instead, Wang's self-cultivation often gains him official attention. On several occasions, officials seek him out and offer him an appointment. His story is, therefore, composed of a series of escapes. Anticipating the string of official offers in Chapters 31 through 36, Wang Mian goes to extraordinary lengths to escape and to maintain the purity and integrity of his own world. This story highlights the often-unmentioned subtext behind the literati's narrative of self-cultivation: for all their stated unconsciousness of possible reward, those engaged in high-minded self-cultivation, almost without exception, receive official recognition and are consequently drawn into the political system. In the account of Wang Mian and the four townsmen, low-status outsiders not only come to embody the literati cultural ideal but become its indispensable guardians, who keep it from contamination and rescue it from irony.

The effort to restore authenticity to literati culture reflects a larger trend in Ming-Qing literature and intellectual thought. Despite differences in emphasis, this trend goes back to the Wang Yangming school, especially to such radicals as Wang Gen (1483–1540) and He Xinyin (1517–79) of the Taizhou school. Like them, Li Zhi (1527–1602) and the Yuan brothers, who held views akin to those of the Taizhou school, often juxtaposed the literati with people of low status, whom they endowed with the virtues they thought the literati had lost. These common folk are sincere, since they do not need pretensions for what they do. In contrast with the literati, whose language is inflated with ethical rhetoric, they always mean what they say

---

11. See Chen Meilin's comments on the scene in Chapter 46 of the novel in *Xinpi "Rulin waishi,"* p. 505. Stephen Roddy remarks: "Insignificant though this fleeting episode may appear, it looms large as the final statement of one of the few untainted figures in the book. Dr. Yu leaves the novel saying in effect that he is renouncing all that identifies him as a member of the literati" (*Literati Identity and Its Fictional Representations in Late Imperial China*, p. 2).

and say what they mean. They are less sophisticated and calculating than the literati, and their decisions are often guided by instinct. Since human nature is good, they are more likely to be virtuous than the literati, whose inborn virtues are ruined by the deleterious influence of the official institutions they serve. In a letter to Geng Dingxiang (1524–96), a fellow literatus, Li Zhi, known for his criticisms of literati hypocrisy, revealed the driving force behind the creation of this image of noble, simple men:

Observing your conduct does not make me believe that you differ a great deal from others. We are doing exactly the same thing. This applies to Your Excellency, myself, and everybody else. From morning to evening, ever since we gained knowledge, we all attend to farming to obtain food, buy land to preserve rice seeds, and construct houses to live in comfort. We study so that we can pass the civil service examination to become officials so that we can have prestige and honor, and investigate geomancy so that we can pass our family blessing on to our offspring. When managing our various daily affairs, we consider only ourselves and our own families, leaving others completely out of our minds. But when you open your mouth to talk about general principles, you say that I think only of myself, whereas you are concerned with others; I am selfish, while you want to benefit others. You claim that you sympathize with your neighbor to the east who suffers hunger and also that you think about your neighbor to the west who suffers unbearable cold. You comment that those who are willing to teach people follow the way of Confucius and Mencius, while those who decline to meet you are selfish. You admit that this person, despite his flaws, has good intentions toward others and that person, although well-mannered, always poisons people's minds with Buddhism. Judging by this, you always preach what you do not practice, and your conduct has nothing to do with what you claim. Why is there such a great gap between your words and your deeds? Do you really believe that this is Confucius's teaching? Considering your conduct in this manner, I would rather think highly of the little men in the fields and marketplace (*shijing xiaofu*), who speak only of what they actually do. Hustlers talk about business, and farmhands talk about farming. Their voices are truly the voices of virtue, lively with interest, and never tiring and boring to listeners.[12]

Li Zhi was extremely concerned about the permanent discrepancy between actions and words in Confucian lives, a discrepancy that is also prominent in Wu Jingzi's critique of the literati in *Rulin waishi*. When literati manipulate

---

12. Li Zhi, *Fenshu, juan* 1, p. 30; trans. from Ray Huang, *1587*, pp. 198–99.

words to claim virtues they do not possess, they also suffer a loss of the fundamental virtue they would otherwise have—to use Li Zhi's term, the "child-mind," the original mind of one's very first thinking, free of all falseness and thus entirely genuine. Innocent and natural, the child-mind, however, can hardly survive the thoughts—considerations of gain or loss, honor or disgrace, and all kinds of moral judgments—learned from others. But as shown clearly in this passage, the image of little men in the fields and marketplace does not reflect Li Zhi's primitivism or a utopian dream about an innocent, pure-hearted world of "natural" men, free from the contamination of human society; rather, it is a pessimistic critique of corrupt literati culture incapable of self-renewal.

In Ming and Qing fiction, low characters are often used to give a concrete body to the child-mind, with the literati as their antithesis. *Idle Talk Under the Bean Arbor* (*Doupeng xianhua*), published after the middle of the seventeenth century, includes a story about a child beggar who shows extraordinary filial piety in his service to his blind mother. In the opening passage of the story, the narrator rephrases Li Zhi's theory:

Nowadays, the world has somehow become out of balance, and people have hidden intentions. Those who are clever and smart study books of history, but the learning that occupies their minds somehow becomes the source of falsehood and pretension. When they are put in official positions of high rank, the original thinking of their child-mind is completely corrupted. They always articulate high-sounding words, beyond the expectations of the ghosts and spirits of heaven and earth. But what they do is absolutely discordant with the principles of human relationships. Only those base persons (*cunbi zhi fu*) who do not even read books have their feet planted on firm ground and their hearts in accord with heaven.[13]

In this story about filial piety, the low character is not outside the socially approved value system. He stands in contrast to the literati not for what he claims to be (in fact, he never makes any claim) but for what he does. The literati are men of virtue in words who assert morals they never practice. By contrast, the low character is a man of virtue in action, and his commitment to moral practice is motivated by intuition and natural response rather than calculation of possible effects. In a similar vein, a story (Chapter 7) in *Alarm Bell on a Still Night* (*Qingye zhong*), published probably in 1645, suggests an effort to provide a natural basis for the virtue of filial piety. A child who mur-

---

13. Aina Jushi, *Doupeng xianhua*, p. 48.

ders his father's concubine for abusing his mother is described as acting on his immediate impulse.

People always laugh at someone for being childish, since children do not read books and know little of the ways of the world, and they speak and act in a way different from that of adults. . . . When they do something, they do not know whether it is right or wrong and whether it can be done or cannot be done, nor do they even know the law of the land that is obvious to everyone. People usually regard this as their weak point, but for me it is precisely their strong point. Once they become versed in books as well as the ways of the world, they try to evade dangers and move toward benefits. Also, they know the distinction between self and others, and thus can hardly drive ahead without scruple.[14]

The emphasis on spontaneity and immediacy of moral action can also be found in *The Account of Marriage to Awaken the World* (*Xingshi yinyuan zhuan*), an early Qing novel. In Chapter 52, a high official asks local officials to recommend filial sons, obedient grandsons, righteous husbands, and chaste wives. These role models must be found among people of low status with no formal education.[15] People from rich and noble families should not be considered, for they have obtained all they want except the fame of being role models. With the power of their families, they will win fame anyway. And it is often acquired at the expense of true virtue.

It is, however, impossible to restore the original mind of one's first thinking through differentiation and negation. What we see in Chapter 55 of *Rulin waishi* is an effort to project innocence, which is absent from literati lives, onto the men of the marketplace. Whether the simple, noble townsmen are convincing characters or not, this chapter attests to the limits of reform within the literati world. Unlike the above examples, the account of the four townsmen does not focus on family ethics or concern the issue of literacy and education. On the surface, it also seems to have little to do with ritual. But even before Chapter 55, what is called Confucian ritual, after a series of frustrated efforts to restore its vigor, has lost its drive to transform the world and its all-encompassing vision. The collective practice of ceremony has ebbed and given way to individual efforts to embody its values, fragmented as they are, in the concreteness of daily experience. A closer reading of Chapter 55 shows how the seemingly unrelated narratives of the four

---

14. *Qingye zhong*, in Lu Gong, ed., *Ming Qing pinghua xiaoshuo xuan* (Shanghai: Gudian wenxue, 1958), 1: 96.

15. Xizhou Sheng, *Xingshi yinyuan zhuan*, p. 760.

men's everyday praxis converge on the issues essential to the representation of Confucian rituals in *Rulin waishi*.

The Wang Yuhui episode sums up the problems in ritual practice, to which Chapter 55 responds. As I argue above, Wang Yuhui's ascetic ritual is itself a corrective response to the "situational ethics" of narrative ritual, but in actual practice it is carried to the other extreme to become fully justified, institutionalized violence inflicted on individuals and families. In Wang Yuhui's sublime vision, ascetic ritual is composed of heroic motifs of self-sacrifice and discipline; his absolute loyalty to ritual imperatives deprives him of a sense of humanity and blinds him to the reality of everyday complexity.

The problem with this vision of ritualism is twofold. First, ascetic ritual's denial of humanity creates a legitimacy crisis; its claim to absolute values yields only traumatic consequences and does not guarantee a triumph over human sentiments and emotions. Wang Yuhui is struck by this sense of crisis when his suppressed pathos erupts during the ongoing ceremony of serenity and formality. Second, although the ascetic ritual incorporates a vision of moral autonomy removed from mundane affairs, it is nevertheless portrayed as a calculated effort to claim symbolic capital. The parallel between Wang Yuhui's and Merchant Fang's ceremonies undermines the transcendence the ascetic ritual claims for itself. Wang Yuhui's deliberation and lack of sincerity further expose its artificiality.

In the end, Wu Jingzi left two questions unanswered: How can one connect ritual to humanity and the everyday without compromising its vision of ritualistic life as absolutely autonomous? How does one prevent ritual practitioners from claiming symbolic power and inject a sense of spontaneity and genuineness into ritual, which has become an all too oppressive form of tyranny?

Chapter 55's parallels with the Wang Yuhui episode are manifest in its account of Jing Yuan's visit to the Taibo temple. Although the story of the four townsmen cannot cope with all the problems of Confucian ritual, it risks its own narrative credibility in achieving what is lacking in Wang Yuhui's ritualistic experiences. The four townsfolk are free from the ethical bonds of family, lineage, and rural communities, just as they are disconnected from the official realm. Their parents are either dead or left unmentioned. They themselves are either unmarried or widowed. And they are locked into the peripheral place of the market, with minimum interaction with the world beyond. Ethical obligations are no longer the concern of their stories. However, Wu Jingzi did not forsake the Confucian theme of ritual. Instead, he adopted a new approach to it and set out to restore the imagined homogeneity between the worlds of ritual and everyday life through devotion to the literati arts.

As noted above, Chapter 55 begins with the four literati arts of music, chess, calligraphy, and painting, since they represent ritual for individuals in the same way that ancient ritual constitutes part of the Six Arts. Small wonder that Yan Yuan and other Confucian ritualists often compare ritual practice to the training people receive in playing the *qin* and other music instruments: it requires a lifetime commitment if one hopes to reach the state of spontaneity in performance, in which "one's heart forgets about one's hands and one's hands no longer feel the strings."[16] Wu Jingzi did much in Chapter 55 to convey the sense of immediacy in the performance of the amateur calligraphers and musicians. In his introduction of Ji Xia'nian, the self-taught calligrapher, he conjured up a personality of natural spontaneity:

His calligraphy was superb. He would not study ancient writing, though, but created a style of his own and wrote as his brush dictated. . . . He wrote only if he happened to be in the mood. If he was not in the mood, then no matter whether you were prince, duke, general, or minister, or what silver you heaped on him, he would not even look at you. (R. 739–40; S. 594)

By envisioning a "natural" state of artistic practice, Wu managed to impart a late Ming romantic impulse to his narrative of everyday ritual experience, thereby connecting ritual to nature and counterbalancing institutionalized practice with individual spontaneity and sensibility.

Although it is far removed from the official world and Confucian rural communities, the marketplace is by no means a congenial place for the spirit of detachment and literati aesthetics. As indicated in the account of Gai Kuan, who is cheated of his property by his shop assistants, the marketplace stimulates avarice. Earlier in the novel, the market is exposed to pollution by mercantile values, and the townsmen who fight for economic profit are presented as the counterparts of civil officials and literati struggling for either political power or symbolic authority.

In Chapter 55 of the novel, the marketplace is, however, recast. As exemplified in the scene in the garden, there is an effort to create in the city a

---

16. Yan Yuan, "Cunxue bian," in *Yan Yuan ji*, p. 79.

substitute for nature. In this fantastic realm appear the major characters of the story, the literati recluses, whose guise as townsmen saves them the troubles that have plagued their counterparts in the mundane world of reality. As C. T. Hsia has noted, the account of the four townsmen in Chapter 55 gives compelling expression to the Confucian notion: "When ritual (*li*) is lost, one seeks it in uncultivated places (*li shi er qiuzhu ye*)."[17] If the construction of the Taibo temple is itself an escape from the official world into the world of the literati, the further withdrawal from that world into the marketplace is the last resort for restoring the values treasured by the literati. This last retreat is individual, aesthetic, and imagined; it is bound by necessity but portrayed as pure possibility—a promise that remains largely unfulfilled.

---

17. C. T. Hsia, foreword to the paperback edition of the English translation of *Rulin waishi*, n.p. For Confucius's remarks, see Ban Gu, "Yiwen zhi," vol. 5, *juan* 30, p. 1746.

PART I

Conclusion

One of the central concerns in my interpretation of *Rulin waishi* is the issue of ritual or *li*. This approach has enabled me to illuminate the structure of the novel and explain its development from one section to the next in a dynamic, albeit problematic, process of searching and self-questioning. *Rulin waishi* follows a long trajectory, from attacking official literati culture to reflecting on its alternatives and from a parodic account of the dualistic, narrative Confucian *li* to a critical exposure of ascetic ritual. It is conservative in the sense that it tries not to deviate from Confucianism even in coping with such problems of Confucian practice as hypocrisy, the discrepancy between words and deeds, and the unrestrained competition for control and distribution of economic and sociopolitical resources. But in developing a new vision of ascetic Confucian ritualism, it seems to swing to the opposite extreme: by emphasizing ritual obligation to the exclusion of sociopolitical duty, it creates fanatical protagonists like Filial Guo and Wang Yuhui, who are so committed to what they believe to be their sacred vocation that they see no consequences to their own behavior. Their ascetic ritual therefore either remains unrealized or is realized differently from the way they hoped, and their stories end in frustration, disillusionment, and irreparable ambivalence. By depicting the dark side of ascetic practice, the novel explores the limits of the choices available under Confucianism and, ultimately, the fundamental complexity and irony of the human drama.

The penultimate chapter of the novel, Chapter 55, makes a last effort to recuperate the vision of the Confucian ascetic ritual—an effort that unfolds on the level of imagination and allegory. It tells a fable about literati disguised as townsmen in order to save their own values and ideals, but the disguise is more than a disguise—it is essential. Although in Confucius's time *li* was not supposed to extend to commoners, the novel makes it clear that *li* needs low-status outsiders to ensure its genuineness. Throughout the novel, *li* undergoes a series of significant shifts, from the collective (Chapter 37) to the individual (Chapters 38 through 55), from the ethical to the aesthetic, and finally from practice to pure imagination. As the final site for *li*, the marketplace is merely a less magnificent version of the Taibo temple, one that is constructed both in fiction and as fiction.

The originality of *Rulin waishi* lies not in its critique of Confucian ritual in general. In fact, the novel represents different sorts of ritualistic practice under the rubric of Confucianism. In developing the vision of ascetic ritualism, it provides a critical response to what Wu Jingzi saw as the immanent problems of Confucian discourse, but in so doing, it also tests the limits of Confucianism. The construction of such a ritualized world requires a separate space and a bold conceptualization of Confucian asceticism. The center is located within the local community composed of individual literati and families, as opposed to the court, the center of the official world; it is also symbolized by the temple dedicated to Wu Taibo, a Confucian sage who acted on his private ethics by yielding the throne to his younger brother. At the conceptual level, this ascetic ritualism brings the Confucian claim of family ethics to its logical extreme and turns it into an absolute obligation to be fulfilled at the expense of all other social obligations. Out of such conviction comes extreme behavior, as we see in the narrative of Filial Guo, Wang Yuhui, and the Yu brothers.

The stories of these ascetic heroes suggest that their extremism is necessary to counter narrative ritual, which has slipped into pure verbal articulation or "empty talk." Criticism of empty talk and the discrepancies of discourse and practice is a commonplace in early Qing intellectual discourse. But Wu Jingzi did more than represent these phenomena as such: his in-depth narrative discloses the mechanism that turns practice into discourse and replaces or disguises deeds with words in Confucian lives; it also shows how the dualistic *li* of the Confucian symbolic system shapes the literati's behavior and highlights its internal tension as the cause of its own disintegration.

Although his stories about literati hypocrisy and deception illuminate individual motivations and calculations, Wu Jingzi placed more blame on the system than on its agents. As is made clear in the introductory chapter of the novel, the civil service examinations exemplify the logic underlying the dualistic system of *li*. As testified to again and again in the rest of the novel, this dualistic system encourages verbal negotiation between ritual and sociopolitical obligations; it fuels competition for the control of symbolic authority and mundane power, as well as the exchange between the two. In the end, Wu Jingzi's critique of ascetic ritual is matched by his distrust of narrative ritual.

Despite all the longings and memories surrounding the Taibo temple, Chapter 55 of *Rulin waishi* confirms that the novel will not end with a simple affirmation. With exquisite sophistication, it instead manages to qualify or call into question the vision of the ritualized world that it embodies. If in the temple Wang Yuhui finds himself tragically abandoned, in Chapter 55 the Taibo temple itself is abandoned. When Gai Kuan and an old neighbor visit the temple, he finds only its remains:

The main hall of the Taibo temple with the front half of the roof caving in. Five or six kids were playing ball in front of the double gates, one of which had fallen to the ground. Going in, they came upon three or four old country women, who were plucking shepherd's purse in the temple courtyard. The latticework in the front had disappeared, and the five buildings at the back were completely stripped—not even a floor plank was left. After walking around, Gai sighed. "To think that so famous a place should have fallen into such ruins!" "In those days," said his neighbor, "Mr. Chi bought many utensils, all of the antique kind, and kept them in large cabinets on the ground floor of this building. Now even those cabinets are gone!" (R. 746; S. 599–600)

This scene reminds us of what Wang Yuhui once saw in the same temple. Searching for an answer to his questions, Wang encountered the *yizhu* on the wall that gave no answers, only an echo of his own writings. Standing before the ritual utensils locked in their cabinets, he found that this sacred temple, impressive as it was, felt empty. But he did not realize that this ideal temple was only a step away from collapse. Two dozen years later, it is in ruins. Now people hardly come to it, or else they come for irrelevant reasons. Country women pick vegetables in the courtyard, and children turn the open land in front into a noisy playground. In the context of the mundane world, the sacred temple has collapsed, and the efforts to protect it from the contamination of alien eyes and clamor have failed. This disturbing scene, placed at the end of the novel, suggests a final, retrospective comment on the novel itself as an unsuccessful effort to create a Confucian ritualized world: the temple was constructed in order to be destroyed and suffered the same fate as the ritual program posted on its wall.

PART II

Beyond Official History

Rulin waishi offers critical reflections on a wide range of problems in mid-eighteenth intellectual discourse and practice. But it does so from a historical perspective—it is set in the Ming dynasty. In the preface to the 1803 edition of *Rulin waishi*, Xianzhai Laoren (Old man of the Leisure Studio) linked the novel to Sima Qian's (145–86? BCE) *Shiji* (Records of the grand historian) and Ban Gu's (32–92) *Hanshu* (History of the Han dynasty) and elaborated its significance in terms of the goals and functions of historiography:[1]

> Fiction (*baiguan*) is one of the branches of historiography. Those who are good at reading fiction can advance to reading history. Therefore works of fiction, like history, must praise virtue and condemn evil (*shan shan e e*) so that the reader will be moved to emulate the good examples and take warning from the evil ones, and so that social customs and human hearts will in all likelihood be maintained without being corrupted.[2]

The concept of *shan shan e e* appears in the last chapter of *Shiji*.[3] In this conception, the historian's primary task is to pass judgment on historical figures

---

1. In a similar vein, the commentator in the Woxian caotang edition remarked of Chapter 1 of *Rulin waishi*: "The author [of the novel] employed the talent of a Sima Qian or a Ban Gu in writing fiction" (Li Hanqiu, ed., *"Rulin waishi" huijiao huiping ben*, p. 16).

2. Ibid., p. 763. For David Rolston's English translation of Xianzhai Laoren's preface to the novel, see Rolston, ed., *How to Read the Chinese Novel*, pp. 249–51.

3. See Sima Qian, *Shiji*, juan 130, p. 3297. A similar phrase appears in the *Zuozhuan* (Zuo commentary); see Duke Cheng, 19th year.

and past events for future generations, that is to say, to "praise or blame" (*baobian*) and "approve or disapprove" (*yuduo*), or more specifically, to present positive and negative models of behavior. Despite the different readings Qing dynasty commentators offered of *Rulin waishi*, they were inclined to emphasize its moral and narrative authority in accordance with this model of historiography. The Qixingtang edition commentator regarded Wu Jingzi's conclusion of the list of characters in the final chapter with Guo Tiebi (Iron Pen Guo) as implicit praise of the author himself (*zuozhe zizan*), who, as a historian, was inscribing a permanent, immutable judgment of his characters with a sharp, penetrating pen.[4] In similar fashion, the commentator of the Woxian caotang edition likened the way Wu Jingzi ended the novel with an autobiographical *ci* poem to Sima Qian's closing of the *Shiji* with the "grand historian's own statement," a personal expression of his mission, his ambitions, and his specific understanding of history.[5]

But *Rulin waishi* either does not achieve the level of a history or else goes well beyond it, for *waishi* literally means "outer history" or "history from the outside." Xianzhai Laoren regarded *waishi* as no different from *yeshi* or *baiguan*, that is, as informal or unofficial history, as it was commonly defined during the Ming and Qing periods. So far as *Rulin waishi* is concerned, *waishi* signals its generic category as a vernacular novel.[6] Nevertheless, few novelists of the Ming and Qing periods followed Wu Jingzi and called their work a *waishi*.[7] Xianzhai Laoren argued that, in the case of *Rulin waishi*,

---

4. See Li Hanqiu, ed., *"Rulin waishi" huijiao huiping ben*, p. 760.

5. Ibid., p. 763. In his study of the Wu Liang Ci carvings of the Han dynasty, Wu Hung writes: "The last scene in the series of pictures on the Wu Liang Ci walls, which appears at the lower left corner of the east wall, represents a country official paying respect to an ox-drawn carriage belonging to a retired gentleman. Most scholars agree that the retired gentleman is Wu Liang himself." He regards this pictorial signature of Wu Liang as echoing the historians' statements made at the end of *Shiji* and *Hanshu*. See Wu Hung, *The Wu Liang Shrine*, pp. 213–14, 217.

6. For studies of the relationship between the vernacular novel and historiography, see Plaks, "Towards a Critical Theory of Chinese Narrative," in idem, ed., *Chinese Narrative*, pp. 309–53; and Rolston, *Traditional Chinese Fiction and Fiction Commentary*, pp. 131–65. For further discussion of the terms *yeshi*, *baiguan* (or *baishi*), and *xiaoshuo* in English scholarship, see Rolston, *Traditional Chinese Fiction and Fiction Commentary*, pp. 131–34; and Roddy, *Literati Identity and Its Fictional Representations in Late Imperial China*, pp. 109–11.

7. The term *waishi* was applied to a variety of genres and texts in premodern times, primarily the vernacular novel, such as *Nüxian waishi* by Lü Xiong. Some collections of classical tales also bear this title. In general, genres and texts composed by private authors rather than

naming itself might well be an assertion. Wu Jingzi's use of the term, according to him, demonstrated his willingness to distance his novel from *zhengshi*—orthodox or official history: "The novel is called '*waishi*' because it is not meant to be listed among the *zhengshi.*"[8] Accordingly, I shall translate *waishi* either as "unofficial history" or as "outer history," depending on the context.

Since Wu Jingzi insisted on defining his novel by its differences from *zhengshi*, to understand it we must first examine the concept and practice of *zhengshi*. A brief survey of official historiography shows that the term *zhengshi* dates to the Liang dynasty of the sixth century CE, and the texts included under this rubric are not always of the same kind. In most cases, *zhengshi* designates a dynastic history sponsored by the imperial court and modeled upon *Shiji*, although Sima Qian's work covers a much longer period and crosses dynastic boundaries.[9] Like the authorities of the previous dynasties, the Manchu court of the Qing assumed the task of writing the history of the preceding dynasty, the Ming, as soon as its first emperor was enthroned in 1644. Despite occasional lapses of pace and intensity, the project was carried out with a sense of urgency, largely because of the eagerness of the Manchu court to legitimize its newly acquired authority and prevent Ming loyalists from writing and circulating their own histories of the Ming. The concerted effort of officials and scholars, the *Ming shi* (Ming history) was finally completed in 1735 and printed four years later. Its publication initiated the Qing court's attempts to redefine the concept of *zhengshi*. As the *Siku quanshu* (Complete library of the four treasures), a state bibliographical project, was being compiled, the Qianlong emperor declared that only the *Twenty-four Histories*, from *Shiji* to *Mingshi*, were entitled to be called *zhengshi*. From the perspective of the Qing court, at least, the list of official histories had been completed once and for all.[10]

---

by officially appointed compilers that drew on informal sources or deviated from historical veracity are found under the rubric *waishi*.

8. Xianzhai Laoren seems to have drawn a line between *shi* (historiography) and *zhengshi* (official historiography): he emphasized that *Rulin waishi* is close to *shi* in that it "praises virtue and condemns evil" (*shan shan e e*), but that it does not seek to be listed among the *zhengshi*.

9. For the use of the term *zhengshi* before the eighteenth century, see "Jingji zhi" in *Suishu* and *Jiu Tangshu*. For the official definition of *zhengshi* in the Qing dynasty, see *juan* 45 and 46 of *Siku quanshu zongmu*, 1: 397–417. In this account, it is the Qianlong emperor who issued an imperial edict to define *zhengshi* and to restrict the term to mean the *Twenty-four histories*.

10. *Siku quanshu zongmu*, 1: 397.

What this meant to the literati of the time deserves further inquiry and assessment, yet its impact on the contemporary practice of historiography was immediately apparent. As historians have noted, the completion of the *Ming History*, together with other sociopolitical and intellectual changes, con-tributed to a sharp decline in private scholars' interest in writing about Ming history during the mid- and late eighteenth century.[11] Unlike most scholars, who diverted their energies from recent history, Wu Jingzi spent some twenty years working on *Rulin waishi*. It is difficult to determine exactly when he began writing his novel, but we know from Xianzhai Laoren that by the time the preface was composed the novel had acquired its title.[12] It may not be pure coincidence that the preface is dated the second month of 1736, a few months after the completion of the *Ming History*.

What did it mean to compose a *waishi* during a period when the *zhengshi* were declared to have been completed once and for all? Is *waishi* meant to en-compass what is excluded from the *zhengshi* or to revise what they include? Does it suggest a narrative undertaken from a peripheral perspective and thus refusing to confirm the central narrative of the *zhengshi*? These ques-tions are compounded by the fact that *Rulin* in *Rulin waishi*, literally, "the for-est of Confucian scholars," is derived from a section of *Shiji*, "Biographies of the Forest of Confucian Scholars" ("Rulin liezhuan"), which consists of en-tries on scholars noted for their study of the Confucian classics. Following *Shiji* as model, almost all the dynastic histories contain a "Rulin liezhuan," al-though the definitions of *Rulin* vary.[13] The following questions arise: Should

---

11. See Qiao Zhizhong, *Qingchao guanfang shixue yanjiu*, pp. 222–26; and Huang Aiping, "Mingshi zuanxiu yu Qingchu shixue."

12. Exactly when Wu Jingzi began composing *Rulin waishi* remains a matter of speculation. For further discussion of this debate, see the Appendix. For now it suffices to say that we have no reason to rule out the possibility that Wu Jingzi did not begin until 1736, when Xianzhai Laoren, a friend of Wu (if he was not Wu himself), composed the preface to the novel. Scholars have not reached a consensus as to the identity of Xianzhai Laoren. Since the Woxian caotang commentary on *Rulin waishi* refers to the *Yanlan xiaopu*, which was printed in 1785 (see Li Hanqiu, ed., "*Rulin waishi*" *huijiao huiping ben*, p. 16), some critics argue that the date attached to the Xianzhai Laoren preface is unreliable. But there is no evidence to show that Xianzhai Laoren was necessarily responsible for the Woxian caotang commentary or that the preface and the commentary were composed by the same person.

13. During the compilation of the *Ming History* in the second half of the seventeenth cen-tury, historians held a heated debate on the nature of "Rulin liezhuan." The central issue was whether they should take the *Song History* (*Songshi*) as their model and include a section enti-tled "Biographies of the Neo-Confucians" ("Daoxue zhuan") and assign other scholars whose

Rulin waishi be regarded as a counterpart or as an extension of the "Rulin liezhuan" in the *zhengshi*? And what enables *Rulin waishi* to define itself as a *waishi*, a history beyond the *zhengshi*?

There are some ready answers. One may argue that under the rubric of *Rulin*, Wu Jingzi covers a much broader range of literati characters than found in the "Rulin liezhuan." In fact, few characters depicted in Wu's novel can be regarded as "Confucian scholars" in the conventional sense of the term, as it is used in the *zhengshi*. The novel includes candidates for the civil service examinations, but since they are negative examples of what Confucian scholars ought not to be, the term "Confucian scholars" has to be taken ironically. In contrast to the biographies of Confucian scholars found in *zhengshi*, who are noted for their contributions to the preservation, transmission, and exegesis of the Confucian classics, *Rulin waishi* offers a chronicle of the literati's utter failure to live up to their expected roles and the inevitable effects of that failure on society at large.

We may also try to elucidate the novel's characterization as a *waishi* by examining its relationship to the compilation of the *Ming History*. In terms of temporal coverage, *Rulin waishi* deals with almost the entire dynasty and refers frequently to historical figures and events. In a sense, it presents itself not merely as a *waishi* of the *Rulin* but also as a *waishi* of the Ming, in which Wu Jingzi offers a different account of, or comments on, the same historical incidents found in the official *Ming History*.[14] For instance, in an apparent effort to rebut the *Ming History*'s biography of Wang Mian, Wu Jingzi concluded the introductory chapter of *Rulin waishi* by claiming that Wang Mian died as a recluse: "Curiously enough, writers and scholars nowadays refer to Wang Mian as the advisor [of Zhu Yuanzhang, the founding emperor of the Ming], though actually he never served as an official for a single day, as I have tried to make clear" (R. 16; S. 14).[15] Wu Jingzi's insistence on Wang

---

work was not as "pure" but who contributed to the exegesis of the Confucian classics to the "Rulin zhuan." See Qiao Zhizhong, *Qingchao guanfang shixue yanjiu*, pp. 85–86.

14. For further discussion of this issue, see Roddy, *Literati Identity and Its Fictional Representations in Late Imperial China*, pp. 109–29.

15. The biography of Wang Mian in the official *Ming History* ends by claiming that Wang Mian served as an advisor for Zhu Yuanzhang (see *Mingshi*, p. 7311). This version is based on Song Lian's biography of Wang Mian, which was composed in the early Ming period. Zhu Yizun (1629–1709), an early Qing scholar who served on the editorial board of the *Mingshi*, rejected this account. In his biography of Wang Mian, he portrayed Wang as a recluse who never compromised his personal integrity; Zhu Yizun hoped that the board

Mian's unofficial identity can be taken metaphorically as well: a recluse, prophet, and unwavering critic of official institutions, Wang Mian comes to symbolize *Rulin waishi*'s individual, nonofficial status. Moreover, by correcting the *zhengshi* version of the Wang Mian biography, Wu Jingzi found a most compelling way to stress *Rulin waishi*'s unofficial nature.

In its subversion of the *Ming History*'s account of historical characters and incidents, *Rulin waishi* recalls *Nüxian waishi*. Set in the early Ming period, *Nüxian waishi* deals with one of the crucial events in the Ming, the Yongle usurpation, in which the Prince of Yan (Zhu Di) overthrew the Jianwen emperor and declared himself emperor. Rather than following the official narrative in legitimizing the usurpation, Lü Xiong provided a counterfactual account of how it might have been put right and the legitimacy of the Ming court restored. In this imaginary account, the Jianwen emperor survives the Prince of Yan's pursuit, and the prince himself is constantly challenged both politically and militarily. Interweaving the supernatural into the realm of the human and combining memory with fantasy, Lü Xiong insisted on using the reign title of the Jianwen emperor throughout the novel, thus erasing the Yongle era from the Ming chronology. In this way, *Nüxian waishi* created its own history of the Ming as an alternative to the official account. Interestingly enough, since the official *Ming History* was still under way, this alternative and counterfactual *waishi* was widely circulated among the leading intellectuals of the time, that is, the generation before Wu Jingzi,[16] and its adversarial stance against *zhengshi* may well be reflected in *Rulin waishi*, despite the differences between the two novels in many other respects.[17]

---

would accept his own version instead: "Since Song Wenxian [Lian]'s biography appeared, people have regarded Wang Mian as an advisor [of Zhu Yuanzhang]. But did he ever serve in this post even for one day? Having read Xu Xian's *Baishi jizhuan*, I concluded that Wang probably did not change his mind before he died" (see Li Hanqiu, ed., *"Rulin waishi" yanjiu ziliao*, pp. 166–67). In the introductory chapter of *Rulin waishi*, Wu Jingzi followed Zhu Yizun's version and challenged the *Ming History* account. For further comparison of the existing Wang Mian biographies, see Roddy, *Literati Identity and Its Fictional Representations in Late Imperial China*, pp. 113–18.

16. For the collective commentary on the novel, see Lü Xiong, *Nüxian waishi*.

17. *Rulin waishi* offers conflicting views of the Yongle usurpation, the central event in *Nüxian waishi*, but it never endorses any of them. In Chapter 9, we are told that Yang Zhizhong condemns the Yongle emperor for the Ming's failure to live up to Confucian standards. But in Chapter 29, Du Shenqing claims that the opposite is true: "If Yongle had not stirred up this dynasty, but left the government in the hands of that weakling Jianwen, the empire would now be as weak as in the time of the Six Dynasties" (R, 402; S. 323).

Not unlike *Nüxian waishi*, *Rulin waishi* diagnoses the defining faults of the Ming as the cause of its ultimate downfall. In Chapter 33, Chi Hengshan attributes the degeneration of society to the founding Ming emperor's negligence of "rites and music," thereby justifying the urgent need for the Taibo ceremony. It can be argued that *Rulin waishi*, in a way, presents an ahistorical attempt to redress the literati's failure to restore the Confucian ritual and its consequences.[18] Stephen Roddy rightly states that by setting the ritual reform movement in the Jiajing period, a time of relative stability in the Ming dynasty, and concluding his novel in the Wanli regime, a time of incipient decline, Wu Jingzi offered his own critical comments on the history of the Ming.[19] But this inquiry about the forces that led to the Ming's demise might also suggest Wu's view of his own time. Projecting his fictional alter ego into the Jiajing reign, Wu Jingzi seemed to foresee the coming of the Wanli period, when the destined decline becomes reality. Indeed, the official institutions (including the civil service examination system, with the *bagu* examination essays) of the Ming remained in operation. Song Neo-Confucian discourse was elevated to the status of state philosophy. The pattern of the past persisted, and the future was only too predictable. It is thus obvious that *Rulin waishi* does not merely challenge the veracity of the *Ming History*'s account of a specific incident or historical figure but suggests a different perspective on the past and reality.

What is more important, however, is *Rulin waishi*'s critical reflection on *zhengshi*'s authoritative mode of narrative and normative functions. In fact, the subject of history comes to the fore in my study of *Rulin waishi* because it is closely connected to the operation of the orthodox Confucian symbolic order. As shown in Part I, the Confucian dualistic *li* is, by nature, narrative or discursive; it draws on the words and deeds of the sages of sacrosanct antiquity as its source of significance. Official historical narrative thus played an essential role in elucidating the Confucian norm through concrete configurations and examples and by providing access to the valorized past—the ultimate repertory of value and significance. Confucians regard their own lives as a journey to-

---

18. Several eighteenth-century literati novels, including *The Humble Words of an Old Rustic* (*Yesou puyan*), which, like *Rulin waishi*, is set in Ming times, suggest a similar effort to redress the Ming's faults while addressing contemporary issues. See Martin Huang, *Literati and Self-Re/Presentation*, pp. 75–108. For other studies of *Yesou puyan*'s relationship with the official *Ming History*, see Qian Jingfang, "*Yesou puyan* kao"; and Wang Qiongling, "*Yesou puyan*" *yanjiu*, pp. 56–70.

19. Roddy, *Literati Identity and Its Fictional Representations in Late Imperial China*, pp. 111–13.

ward joining the sages of the past, and their entry into the textual world of historical narrative serves as the final recognition of what life has to offer—immortality. But in order to have their life stories included in history, they first have to re-enact the stories of history in their own lives; their own subjection to history will, in the end, confirm them as its subject. Historical biographies represent both the individuals of the past and the exemplars of human behavior for all men and women, regardless of time and place. Accordingly, reading historical biographies requires emulation in practice: the reader not only defines himself through the lens of history but also selects an appropriate type of biography as the model for his own life. It is only through practice that he is able to ensure the continuity of the narrative past into the present and so engage the normative in the construction of reality.

History so defined requires an ordering of events and personas in narrative form. It absorbs a series of incidents into its preconceived narrative patterns and structures so as to illuminate the moral and cosmic order. The genre of historical chronicle (*biannianti*) renders individual events in a teleological sequence, and its representation of history testifies to the significance of an atemporal moral and cosmic mechanism.[20] As an essential form of official historiography, historical biography (*jizhuanti*) proceeds from the idea that history can be illustrated by the examples of individuals. In collective biographies those individuals are usually grouped into such established categories as "good officials," "harsh officials," "Confucian scholars," "chaste women," and "men of loyalty and righteousness." They are regarded both as people living at a particular historical moment and as the embodiment of certain universal principles and human qualities. Their images are predetermined and disclosed mainly in a single defined direction. Events and sayings are selected from their lives under prescribed rubrics. In most cases, especially in relatively long biographies, these incidents are arranged chronologically, with those that occur in youth as explanations for later actions. With birth as its point of departure, exemplary biography treats a life as a temporally unfolding manifestation of inner virtue or character, and avoids all the ambiguities, contradictions, and crosscurrents that might obscure its narrative orientation.[21] In such a format, "character itself does not grow, does not

---

20. For a further elaboration of this point, see Anthony Yu, *Rereading the Stone*, pp. 42–43; and David Der-wei Wang, "Fictional History / Historical Fiction," pp. 65–66.

21. It would be dangerous to generalize about historical texts that are retrospectively labeled as *zhengshi*. Between the *Shiji* and the dynastic histories that follow its model there are

change," to borrow M. K. Bakhtin's comments on one type of ancient Greek biography; "it is merely filled in: at the beginning it is incomplete, imperfectly disclosed, fragmentary; it becomes full and well rounded only at the end. Consequently, the process of disclosing character does not lead to a real change or 'becoming' in historical reality, but rather solely to a fulfillment, that is, to a filling-in of that form sketched at the very outset."[22] In this sense, historical biographies are ahistorical. To fulfill its putative functions in the reproduction of the Confucian norms, Confucian historiography must manage to contain flowing, transitory time by assimilating it into the preconceived and highly regulated narrative modes.

Since the Confucian dualistic order of *li* is constructed through narrative discourse, it is no surprise that in scrutinizing the dualistic *li* Wu Jingzi questioned the narrative of official history. As shown above, the first half of *Rulin waishi* deals with, among other things, the problems of literati discourse and self-representation. Although the literati characters are well versed in Confucian rhetoric, they use it merely as a legitimate instrument for social mobility and political gain, and their claim to be Confucian spokesmen turns out to be part of their social drama of impersonation and yields nothing but sham and deception. In *Rulin waishi*'s account, the proliferation of Confucian rhetoric contributes not to the duplication or reproduction of the Confucian norms in sociopolitical life but to its own deflation. As part of the repository of Confucian discourse, the narrative mode and recurrent motifs of *zhengshi* lend themselves to ironic rendering.

Wu Jingzi was not alone in disparaging the Confucian narrative discourse embodied in *zhengshi* and other forms. In his own way, he recapitulated the tenor of ritualism and evidential studies of the time. Self-proclaimed Confucian fundamentalists, ritualists claimed direct access to moral propriety through their practice of ancient rituals. They dismissed the Neo-Confucian exegeses of the Confucian classics and their construction of the Confucian genealogy as heterodox—a misleading route by which to pursue the truth.

---

evident differences in narrative schemes. Although the biographies of *Shiji* are often laden with conflicting views that preclude any simple conclusions, that is not true of the official historiography of later periods, which adopts a rigid tone of authoritative narrative.

22. Here I have borrowed Bakhtin's comments on the Plutarchian biographical type (*The Dialogic Imagination*, pp. 141–42). For a systematic survey of the way Ming and Qing fiction commentators use the model of biographical narrative in their approach to the vernacular novels of the time, see Rolston, ed., *Traditional Chinese Fiction and Fiction Commentary*, pp. 131–65.

However, it was the philologists of the early and mid-Qing period who took concrete steps toward undermining the textual, discursive ground upon which Neo-Confucianism rests. Well equipped with the tools of etymology, phonology, and historical linguistics, they developed a historical approach in their studies of the ancient texts. They explored the meanings obscured and distorted by later interpreters and revealed the circumstances under which the texts were compiled, shaped, transmitted, and interpreted. Instead of taking these writings as given, they traced their complex textual history of errors, corruption, fraud, and forgery and thus cast doubt on their integrity and authenticity.

The best example of early and mid-Qing textual criticism of the Confucian classics can be found in the evidential studies of the *Book of Documents* (*Shangshu*), a collection of the official documents of antiquity, which had long been regarded as one of the Confucian classics. As Song Neo-Confucians elaborated their concept of *li* or moral principle, they drew heavily on the section about "the mind of man (*renxin*) and mind of way (*Daoxin*)" in the "Dayu mo" chapter of the Old Text *Documents*. But Yan Ruoju, based on solid evidential research, showed that this section was adopted from a passage in *Xunzi* that was in turn quoted from the *Daojing* (Classic of the Way). In other words, it was a forgery, produced much later than its assumed date of composition. Yan was so vigorous in questioning the authenticity of the Old Text *Documents* that he spared none of the twenty-five Old Text chapters from his scrutiny.[23] Small surprise that his research provoked immediate controversies among the scholars of the day, but Yan also found allies in such scholars as Hui Dong (1697–1758), who had raised similar questions about the Old Text *Documents* before reading Yan's work. The eighteenth-century scholarship on *The Documents* advanced the pursuit of objectivity and the cause of skepticism in academic research. In the following century, when the Confucians of the New Text school, such as Zhuang Cunyu (1719–88), Liao Ping (1852–1932), and Kang Youwei (1858–1927), tried to come up with a radical vision of Confucianism in coping with the crisis of their time, they resorted to the evidential study of the Old Text *Documents* and used it as a weapon against the Confucian orthodoxy.[24]

Elman is correct in arguing that the New Text scholars' political challenge to the Old Text orthodoxy was, in a way, the logical extension of

---

23. Yan Ruoju, *Shangshu guwen shuzheng, juan* 2, pp. 47–48.
24. Elman, *From Philosophy to Philology*, pp. 207–12.

eighteenth-century philological study to political issues, since "Kang You-wei's radical Confucian response to the influx of Western ideas in the late nineteenth century would not have taken the form that it did had not the Old Text versions of the Classics been partially discredited."[25] However, we do not have to wait till the nineteenth century to see the implications of the evidential study. In the eighteenth century, philologists duly facilitated the cause of ritualism by undercutting the Neo-Confucian norms based on the unexamined, questionable versions of the Confucian texts. The ritualists were bold in moralizing. In response to the crisis of the late Ming, they demanded an immediate return to the ancient rituals and institutions as a way of revitalizing classic Confucianism, which they believed had long been neglected. But in envisioning this alternative Confucian practice, they had to repudiate Neo-Confucian discourse. And evidential scholars did this through their relentless textual studies and historical research. Whatever their intentions might have been, they often ended up casting doubt on what had formerly been unquestionable. As a result, the ancient Confucian texts, in the form in which they were handed down from the past, could no longer be taken for granted as the infallible source of timeless moral truth. Instead, they were subject to ferocious historical examination and textual analysis.

It would be wrong to reduce *Rulin waishi* to the objectives of ritualism and evidential study of the time, but in writing the novel Wu Jingzi found his own way to engage these issues. He shared with the ritualists a strong moralizing zeal, and in his novel we see an unmistakable urge to repudiate inflated Confucian rhetoric. Instead of questioning the textual authenticity of the Confucian classics, however, Wu Jingzi exposed the falsity and the lack of sincerity in the literati's speeches, writings, and self-representation. And more often than any of his contemporaries, he emphasized the deepening discrepancy between word and deed in the elite's sociopolitical lives, as well as the inadequacy of Confucian narrative discourse to make sense of the actual experience.

In *Rulin waishi*, the narrative mode of official history does not serve as the organizational framework; instead, it is itself represented in the novel and becomes an object of scrutiny. *Rulin waishi* is remarkably adept in navigating a new horizon of worldly experience that defies this inherited mode and the expectations that accompany it. Under the rubric *waishi*, Wu Jingzi provided what might be called a secular history, in which he introduced a temporal

---

25. Ibid., pp. 22–26; quotation at p. 25.

tenor to his own representation of history.[26] More specifically, he brought the erosions of time to bear on his account of the deterioration of literati mores and ethos, and his narrative takes on the attributes of the secular time it presents. Like the flux of worldly affairs, this secular narrative defies closure, permits no conclusive judgments, and resists reduction to the preconceived structures of historical narrative. Instead of being undertaken from the central, fixed viewpoint of the *zhengshi*, it generates shifting perspectives for examining the role-types its characters assume or claim and exposes the narrative mechanics that make their stories possible in the *zhengshi*.

----

26. Here Zhang Xuecheng (1738–1801) and his elaborations of the Confucian classics and history in *Wenshi tongyi* (The complementary meaning of literature and history) are relevant. Despite his reservations about the contemporary trend to philological evidential studies, Zhang best summed up the revolutionary result of evidential discourse in his famous declaration "The Six Classics are all histories." Although this statement can be traced to earlier thinkers such as Li Zhi and Wang Shizhen, it acquired new meaning and significance by capturing the historical orientation that dominated eighteenth-century studies of the Confucian classics. More specifically, by establishing an equation between the Classics and histories, Zhang, not unlike many contemporary evidential scholars, was able to restore a sense of time to the Classics. In this account, the sages of the antiquity did not deliberately compose the Classics as such. What later came to be called the Classics preserved no more than the "traces" (*ji*) of ancient institutions and practices; they were only gradually separated from history, the generic tradition to which they belonged, and acquired the status of Classics. For instance, Zhang argued that the thriving of private learning contributed to the formation of the Classics, and there were, in fact, no Classics until after the exegeses (*zhuan*) of the ancient texts had become a popular practice. He went as far as to claim that most of the Classics, as they were passed down to the later generations, were originally exegeses themselves, and they were recognized as Classics only after the original Classics had been lost. By delineating this complex process through which the Classics were shaped and transformed, Zhang developed what Wang Hui describes as "the archeology of the Classics" (*jingxue kaoguxue*). He challenged his contemporaries to seriously consider time and historical change in their own conceptualizations of Confucian norms, knowledge systems, and history. For more on Zhang Xuecheng, see chap. 5 in Wang Hui's forthcoming *Zhongguo xiandai sixiang de xingqi*.

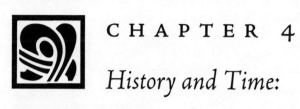

CHAPTER 4

History and Time: Zhengshi As Represented in Rulin waishi

As noted in the Introduction to this part, Wu Jingzi often refused to follow the conventional model of biographical narrative. On the few occasions when he resorted to that model, he seemed interested more in exposing its problems than in using it to make sense of his characters. In Chapters 15 and 16, for example, he introduced Kuang Chaoren as a filial son, but as the story progresses, the filial son outgrows his initial role and degenerates into its antithesis. Wu represented Kuang as engaged in an unfinished process of becoming: he took Kuang past the point where the biography of a filial son normally ends, subjected him to the corrosive influences of time, and allowed his mundane pursuits to reshape his character and destiny. In the end, Wu's portrait of Kuang illustrates the limits of biographical narrative in comprehending a man's transformation and degeneration—it marks the end of the exemplary biography.

Beyond the Exemplary Biography

In a novel known for its fragmentary episodes and its rapid shifts from one character to another, the story of Kuang Chaoren (literally, "Extraordinary Kuang" or "The Kuang Who Surpasses Others") is an exception: running from Chapters 15 through 20, it is the longest treatment of an individual character in the novel. Introduced as a filial son in Chapters 15 and 16, Kuang is blessed with a series of successes in the civil service examinations, and at the end of the passage he is on his way to court to take up an official appointment. But the closer he comes to success, the further he deviates from the image of a filial son, a Confucian icon from the official biographies. In contrast to the standard biography of filial son, which concludes with the son's receiving a reward from the authorities, the main story about Kuang does not begin until after he is acknowledged as a filial son.

As indicated in the headnote to Chapter 16, "A filial son waits upon his father in Big Willow Village. / A good magistrate encourages a poor scholar in Yueqing County," that chapter begins with an account of Kuang faithfully attending his ailing father, despite adversities, including a fire that destroys his parents' house. The second half of the chapter describes the county magistrate's chance discovery of Kuang; the magistrate not only encourages Kuang to take the civil service examinations but also reports the youth's filial conduct to the examiner. The story of Kuang's success begins on the night the county magistrate happens to pass through the village.

> One night he had read till nearly midnight, and was declaiming a *bagu* examination essay with great gusto when he heard gongs sound outside the window and saw a sedan chair pass, surrounded by torches and followed by outriders. He knew this must be the county magistrate, but he went on reading aloud while the party passed. Now the magistrate decided to spend the night in the village office; he marveled to himself: "How remarkable to find a man studying so hard late at night in a little country place like this! I wonder whether he is a successful candidate or a student? Why not send for the headman to find out?" He forthwith sent for Mr. Pan and asked him, "Who is it that studies at night in that house near the monastery, south of the village?" The headman knew that this was where the Kuang family lived. "Their house was burned down," he explained, "so they rented a place there. The man studying is Old Kuang's second son, Kuang Chaoren, who reads every night till well after midnight. He is not a scholar, though, nor even a student, but simply a small tradesman." The magistrate was impressed. "Here is my card," he said. "Take it to Mr. Kuang tomorrow, and tell him I shall not ask to see him now; but the preliminary test is near and he should register for it. If he can write essays, I'll do what I can for him." (R. 231–32; S. 185–86)

This is apparently a simple story about a good magistrate discovering a filial son. But a closer inspection reveals something different. The scene in which Kuang Chaoren reads aloud the *bagu* examination essays beside the bed of his invalid father is ironically anticipated by the advice that Ma Chunshang, an editor of such essays, gives him in Chapter 15:

If you take my advice, after you reach home you should consider passing the official examinations as the most important way of pleasing your parents.... If you are brilliant enough to pass the examinations, you immediately reflect credit upon your whole family. That is why the *Classic of Filial Piety* tells us that to reflect credit on your family and to spread your fame shows the greatest piety. At the same time, of course, you do very well for yourself. As the proverb says: There are golden mansions in study; there are bushels of rice and beautiful women. And what is study today if not our anthologies of *bagu* essays? So when you go back to look after your parents, you must consider study for the examinations of prime importance. Even if your business does badly and you cannot give your father and mother all they want, that need not worry you. Writing compositions is the main thing. For when your father lies ill in bed with nothing to eat and hears you declaiming the *bagu* essays, no doubt about it but his heart will rejoice, his sadness will disappear, and his pain will pass away. This is what Zengzi meant when he spoke of pleasing the parents. (R. 219–20; S. 176)[1]

Ma Chunshang's advice puts the Kuang Chaoren episode in an entirely new light; it predisposes us to read the rest of the story from Ma's perspective and question Kuang's motivation and apparent innocence. At his first appearance in Chapter 15, Kuang, then an innocent village boy, is reading the anthology of *bagu* examination essays compiled by Ma Chunshang; on the night when he attracts the magistrate's attention, he is following Ma's advice and declaiming the *bagu* essays. As the narrative proceeds, Kuang reads himself deeply into Ma's books, only to emerge from them with his personality and mentality transformed.

A close reading of this scene evokes a sense of irony: on hearing the sound of gongs outside, Kuang "knew this must be the county magistrate, but he went on reading aloud while the party passed." Ostensibly concentrating on his reading, he is nevertheless aware that he may be overheard by an important personage. By using the expression *ziranshi* (this must be), the narrator presents this as Kuang's speculation rather than his own judgment. Kuang may read the essay as loudly as before, but his purpose in doing so becomes suspect.

The irony becomes all the more apparent when we realize that the scene is derived from an anecdote about obscure young scholars currying favor with Xu Qianxue, an official of the Kangxi era (1662–1722), who was known for discovering and promoting unknown talents:

---

1. Zengzi, a disciple of Confucius, was known for his filial piety.

All the young men who sought to advance their careers rented rooms near the lane in which he [Xu Qianxue] was living. They did not start declaiming poems and essays until early morning, when Xu set out to the court for the morning session, so that they could be sure he would hear their reciting. After several days of this behavior, Xu would definitely seek them out; if they had special talents, he would spread good opinions about them and recommend them. As a result, rents for the houses near the lane were twice as high as those for other houses.[2]

The discovery of "unknown talents" turns out to be a conspiracy of consent between these young opportunists and Xu Qianxue, who made his name by rewarding and promoting them. For the landlords, it is an opportunity for higher profits. Although none of the participants is as naïve as he pretends, it is their pretended innocence that makes the game possible. Wu Jingzi did not copy this anecdote or narrate the story of Kuang and the county magistrate sarcastically, but his rendering of Kuang's brief pause during his recitation creates a moment of doubt in the reader. As in the anecdote of Xu Qianxue, the point is fame and the opportunity to win it.

Wu Jingzi, in his ironic portrayals of his characters' hypocrisy, ignorance, and narrow-mindedness, made frequent use of anecdotes and jokes from both written and oral sources. According to Zhao Yi (1727–1814), the anecdote about Xu Qianxue had circulated among scholars of previous generations before he wrote it down in Yanpu zaji. Other examples of passages in Rulin waishi based on anecdotes are the one about Fan Jin, an imperial examiner, who has never heard of Su Shi, a famous literatus of the Song dynasty (in Chapter 7); and the one about Yan Dayu (Yan Zhihe, who bought for himself the rank of jiansheng—imperial college student), in the last moments of his life, "stretching out two fingers and refusing to breathe his last" because he is worried that "there are two wicks in the lamp—that is a waste of oil" (in Chapters 5 and 6).[3]

---

2. Zhao Yi, Yanpu zaji. See Li Hanqiu, ed., "Rulin waishi" yanjiu ziliao, p. 180.

3. Students of Rulin waishi have collected all the available sources for the jokes and anecdotes in the novel. The Yan Dayu episode apparently derives from an anecdote about an avaricious Yangzhou merchant. When Ruan Kuisheng recorded it in his Chayu kehua (juan 15, p. 465), evidently after Wu Jingzi's death, he explained that he had first heard it from Wu Shanting (Wu Lang), Wu Jingzi's son. What is interesting about this account is that Wu Shanting claimed to have witnessed the incident. There are two possible explanations: either Wu Jingzi heard the story from his son and then integrated it into his own narrative of Yan Dayu, or the son related a story his father had written and claimed that it was based on his own eyewitness account.

It is hard to generalize about the rhetorical effect that Wu Jingzi achieved by working those borrowed jokes and anecdotes into his novel. In most cases they are introduced with a sense of proportion and detachment; irony is generated by the characters' words and deeds or by the discrepancies between the two, rather than by the narrator's witty comments. Only occasionally are the jokes blown out of proportion and developed into farcical scenes with a note of burlesque and buffoonery. Yet it is not difficult to understand their functions in the thematic and narrative design of *Rulin waishi.* Anecdotes and jokes are fragmentary; they are not constrained by specific context, nor are they subordinated to the larger design of plot. It is hard to stretch them into a longer and more coherent narrative or to build an exemplary biographical narrative upon them; instead, anecdote "introduces an opening into the teleological, and therefore, timeless, narrative of beginning, middle, and end";[4] it opens up the possibility of alternative interpretations of historical and biographical narratives. The anecdote about Xu Qianxue allows an ironic glimpse of what is happening backstage that ruins the effects of the moral drama that dominates the historical and biographical imagination. In similar fashion, Wu Jingzi's rendering of the Kuang Chaoren episode generates a moment of hesitation that disrupts the otherwise seemingly unproblematic narrative of how a filial son is "discovered" by the authorities.

Immediately after Kuang's success in the civil service examination is an episode involving Kuangda, Kuang Chaoren's older brother. In its own way, this passage subjects the story of Filial Kuang to an alternative but no less damaging reading. Even before Kuang Chaoren has realized what he can do with his newly acquired fame, Kuangda has taken full advantage of his position as the brother of an officially recognized filial son. In an incident in Chapter 17, Kuangda becomes involved in a quarrel with a fellow villager over a stand in the marketplace. As the quarrel explodes into a fight, he threatens to drag his rival to court: "'The Magistrate is a friend of my brother's!' he shouted. 'Think I'm afraid of you? Let's go to the yamen'" (R. 236; S. 188). Kuangda never shows any understanding or appreciation of his brother's virtue. He is, in a way, a "bad" reader of his brother's story, for all he sees in it are fame, power, and connections that he can use to his own advantage. What he has to say of his brother tells us about himself—a shame-

---

4. See Joel Fineman, "The History of the Anecdote," p. 61. Fineman uses the term "the history of the anecdote" in characterizing the new historicism and the problems it raises.

less scoundrel who perceives things through the lens of his own self-interest. However, for all the distortions of the lens, he does see in his brother's story the benefits that come with official recognition.

The significance of introducing Kuangda's view is especially evident when we compare it with the usual narrative paradigm of the biography of the filial son. The official biography often ends with the son's being rewarded by the authorities as a matter of justice. But the concept of justice as practiced in the real world is inseparable from the distribution and redistribution of political, economical, and symbolic resources. At stake in any official recognition are status, prestige, and political affiliation. Unlike the official historians, who eschew subjects that might distract them from their coherent stories about Confucian piety, Wu Jingzi created a low character who has no place in official history and is not obliged to see his brother as an exemplary character. In Kuangda's eyes, his brother is someone with enough political pull to cow his fellow villagers. This is one case, I shall argue, in which Wu Jingzi demonstrated that *Rulin waishi* is truly an outer history: he defined a viewpoint beyond the *zhengshi* from which to scrutinize its exemplary biographies and showed that their apparent unity and coherence are achieved by repression and exclusion.

Granted, Kuangda is merely making an assertion, but it constitutes part of the discourse that dictates his brother's behavior. A character who adapts to his immediate environment, Kuang Chaoren is so often contingent on public perception and expectation that he tends to merge into the image projected on him from without. In Chapter 20, when Kuang Chaoren visits his in-laws' home as a candidate for an official post, he speaks to Kuangda in the language that his brother himself has used: "When you go back you must tell the villagers to address you as 'Sir' (*laoye*). We'll have to live in style and keep up appearances" (R. 277; S. 204). Kuang Chaoren's concern with titles and forms of address echoes the moment in Chapter 3 when Butcher Hu addresses Fan Jin, his son-in-law, as "Sir" (*laoye*), immediately after the latter passes the provincial examination. Earlier in the same chapter, Butcher Hu makes a similar speech on the reverence that a gentleman deserves when celebrating Fan Jin's success in the county examinations, which qualifies Fan for the title of gentleman (*xianggong*). In creating a network of correspondences and echoes among his characters, Wu Jingzi liberated the filial son character from the rigid, self-contained form of the exemplary biography, placed him in a larger community of popular opinions and mundane affiliations, and highlighted their enormous influence on his character and orientation.

The only permanent trait we discern in Kuang Chaoren is his constant adjustment to whatever circles he happens to associate with. As he moves from one place to another, his character undergoes drastic alterations, each new personality seeming to have little memory of the old. Such multifaceted complexity and mutability are hardly conceivable in the framework of the traditional biographical narrative. One may well argue that the changes Kuang Chaoren undergoes fulfill a narrative function rather than exemplifying discrete phases in the history of an individual. The need for such a character is evident in Wu Jingzi's representation of a Hangzhou literati world split by factionalism. Kuang is the only character in this world with access to a variety of literati and nonliterati circles, and his constant shuttling between them helps to establish the connections and contrasts among the individuals within them.

But Kuang is no mere device in the larger design of the novel; he is a fully fledged character. Wu Jingzi's use of Kuang as a narrative instrument in the Hangzhou story does not necessarily deprive him of the sense of concreteness essential to his characterization. Granted, in most parts of the Hangzhou story Kuang remains a silent observer. When speaking, he weighs his words with care and says only what he believes appropriate, lest he embarrass himself. Dealing with unfamiliar people in a new place, he needs the guidance, patronage, and authority that his own impoverished personality and experience can hardly provide. The key to understanding Kuang's metamorphosis lies in his relation to and interaction with the characters of the Hangzhou circles; he goes from observing them to identifying entirely with them in word and action. This is a story about imitation, impersonation, and the role of the social relationship in the making of an individual's character.

One literatus whom Kuang Chaoren encounters in his first visit to Hangzhou is Ma Chunshang, from whom he learns the distorted view of filial piety that sets the Kuang Chaoren story apart from the exemplary biography of the filial son. As an editor of *bagu* essays and a candidate for the examinations, Ma Chunshang is an example of how a man's entire life and imagination can be dominated by the examination system. In Chapter 15, he gives Qu Gongsun a lecture about the history of Confucians in terms of the civil service examinations (*juye*). He sees the Confucian sages' exemplary lives as consisting of single-minded devotion to their official careers; Confu-

cius's moralistic discourse and the Neo-Confucians' high-minded philosophy become mere instruments to gain official rank. About the civil examination system in his time, he says: "Even Confucius, if he were alive today,
would be studying *bagu* essays and preparing for the examinations instead of
saying, 'Make few false statements and do little you may regret.' Why? If he
had kept talking like that every day, then who would give him an official position?" (R. 190; S. 151). This utilitarian version of Confucian history reflects
the mentality of the *bagu* essayists and civil officials, which affects their behavior and helps to shape the world in which they live. Tendentious as it
may be, Ma's narrative of Confucian history does capture the aspects that
Confucians have either excluded from their historical narrative or disguised
with moralistic rhetoric.

The Ma Chunshang episode indicates the consequences of his preoccupation with the *bagu* composition by allowing a glimpse of the internal tensions of his character—the conflicts between his narrow-mindedness and
his generosity, and the inconsistencies in his explicit statements, thoughts,
and suppressed impulses. In the well-known scene of Ma Chunshang's visit
to West Lake in Chapter 14, the narrator highlights an ironic contrast between what Ma sees and what he refuses to see or pretends not to have
seen: lacking any interest in the scenic places, Ma is frequently lured away
by the taverns along the lakeshore that offer wine and meat he can ill afford. Similarly, the account of his tour of the lake shows through his eyes
the images of women on a pilgrimage—their facial features, hairstyles, and
sensational dresses—but tells us that he "strides past with lowered head,
not casting so much as a glance at all these beauties" (R. 205; S. 162).[5]
Like Zhou Jin and Fan Jin as portrayed in previous chapters, Ma is another distorted soul under the yoke of official institutions and the examination culture.

As an infectious character, Ma Chunshang plays a crucial role in forming
Kuang Chaoren's mentality. In a sense, it is Ma who introduces Kuang to
the scene and provides him with the guidance he needs for his own story.
Ma Chunshang's advice flatly contradicts the deathbed admonitions of
Kuang's father, a simple villager: "Fame and fortune are external things, after
all; it's goodness that really counts. You have been a good son and a loyal
brother when it wasn't easy, and I don't want you to change and start think-

---

5. For an insightful reading of this episode, see Yue Hengjun, "Ma Chunshang zai Xihu."

ing yourself high and mighty now that things are going more smoothly for you" (R. 239; S. 191). The father's fear that success will ruin his son's character is presented as a prediction: Kuang Chaoren will act out the vision that Ma Chunshang has projected for him and become exactly what his father hoped he would not be.

The second time Kuang Chaoren travels to Hangzhou, he encounters another circle of literati—self-described men of culture, or *mingshi*, who are interested merely in such "refined affairs" (*yashi*) as writing poetry. He immediately realizes that despite their self-proclaimed detachment from official affairs, they are no less enthusiastic about seeking fame (*ming*) than the *bagu* essayists are about seeking profits (*li*). For all their contempt for the essayists, they never miss a chance to brag about their connections with degree-holders and high-ranking officials. Poetry, as they admit, is an effective means of making these connections. As it turns out, the men of culture and the *bagu* essayists have more in common than either is willing to acknowledge. Hiding their worldly desires under the guise of culture, the self-styled poets exhibit a pretension and hypocrisy comparable to that of *bagu* essayists like Wang De and Wang Ren, who disguise their mundane agenda with moralistic rhetoric.

The Kuang Chaoren story sums up the intriguing relationship between the essayists and the poets that is central to Wu Jingzi's portrayal of the literati in *Rulin waishi*. To a literatus, the *bagu* essay and poetry are irreconcilable genres. The *bagu* essay offers a model of writing characterized by Zhou Dunyi (1017–73), a Neo-Confucian scholar, as the conveyance of the Dao (*wen yi zai dao*). But in *Rulin waishi* and much other contemporary literati writing, it is described as having degenerated because of its utilitarian functions in promoting career advancement. However, Wu Jingzi was not inclined toward poetry as the better option; in his account poetry is too compromised and affords no space for the freedom of individual taste, aesthetic imagination, and genuine feeling. As noted above, it had become so conventionalized and so deeply implicated in worldly affairs that Du Shenqing, a poet and a cultured man, has to distinguish himself from his fellow poets by ridiculing their suggestion to compose poetry at the social gatherings they attend as "so refined as to be vulgar" (R. 400; S. 321).

In Chapters 10 and 11, Wu Jingzi suggested an even worse vision: a combination of the *bagu* essay and poetry. In a comic tone, he portrayed a marriage between Qu Gongsun, who joins his fellow poets in belittling the *bagu* essay, and Miss Lu, who has been trained by her father to write the *bagu* essay and who considers all writings unrelated to the examinations trifling and pointless. The marriage, which is frustrating to both of them, is meant to embody, in Theodore Huters's words, a "claustrophobic binary opposition" between two incompatible modes of writing and existence.[6] However, the Kuang episode suggests that the two modes are never truly divorced from each other. In fact, those self-proclaimed poets can barely distinguish poetry from essays in idiom, grammar, and style, and their poems, much to Kuang's astonishment, are replete with so many function words such as "moreover" (*qiefu*) and "it was once said" (*changwei*) cribbed from *bagu* essays and exegeses of the Confucian classics that even Kuang, a novice poet, "feels that his own effort is in no way inferior to theirs" (R. 255; S. 208). Likewise, Qu's essays, composed at the request of his father-in-law, "were full of words and phrases pillaged from poems, a line here resembling Qu Yuan's *Lisao* and a line there reminiscent of the early philosophers" (R. 157–58; S. 125). Kuang Chaoren's association with the poets and *bagu* essayists suggests the dreadful scenario that occurs when both are combined in one person—a scenario Kuang comes to embody.

The narrative of Kuang's third trip to Hangzhou in Chapter 20 leads to his self-representation: a petty-minded status seeker equipped with the capacities of a liar, braggart, and hypocrite, Kuang begins to demonstrate what he has just learned from his mentors and patrons—both the essayists and the poets. Looking forward to an official appointment, Kuang has no interest in meeting with Jing Lanjiang, one of the poets, or with Jiang, a yamen clerk, for they recall his own past, which he now wants to leave behind him. In the restaurant, he starts the conversation by bragging about the prestige his official appointment will bring him—a deliberate strategy to secure a psychological advantage over Jing, who has neither an official title nor a degree. The irony is that when adding concrete details to his story, Kuang sounds just like Jing Lanjiang flaunting his associations with all the important figures of the region. Jing is introduced in Chapter 17 as a braggart who

---

6. Theodore Huters, "The Shattered Mirror," pp. 278–81. Huters notes that Wu Jingzi's critique of both modes seems to have left him no space to define his own writing: "The self-consciousness Wu gained through describing the impasse that writers face provided a crucial critical space. It is by its very nature aporetic, since he portrayed a literary arena in which there was no place for the very platform he was writing from" (p. 281).

initiates Kuang into the practice of boasting about himself. What Jing says is either self-defeating exaggeration or pure fiction undercut by the information we glean from other sources. So, too, is Kuang's account of his imagined glory, for if judged by common sense it is absurd, and it is left unconfirmed by Wu Jingzi's narrator. In *Rulin waishi* an unconfirmed self-representation is immediately suspect.

Kuang Chaoren not only outdoes Jing Lanjiang in boasting but also shrewdly cites official duties in his own defense. When Jing chastises him for not paying a visit to a former patron, Pansan, who is in jail, Kuang responds:

"It's a pity he's in this fix!" said Kuang, "I would have gone to the jail to see him, but my position has changed. As a servant of the throne I have to abide by the law; and to call on him in such a place would show no respect for the law." "You are not a local official," countered Jing, "and you would only be visiting a friend. What harm can there be in that?" "Gentlemen," said Kuang, "I shouldn't say this, but to friends it doesn't matter. In view of what our friend Pan has done, if I had been in office here I would have had to arrest him. If I were to go to the prison to call on him, it would look as if I disapproved of the sentence. This is not the way of a loyal subject." (R. 279; S. 225–26)

Kuang's use of official rhetoric invites an ironical reading, for the previous chapter shows the degree to which he was involved in the crimes with which Pansan is charged; it was Kuang's fear of being implicated in the criminal case that drove him from Hangzhou in the first place. Here as elsewhere in *Rulin waishi*, official rhetoric is undermined by the speaker's motives. In Chapter 6, Yan Dawei (Yan Gongsheng or senior licentiate Yan) uses the civil service examinations as an excuse for missing the funeral rites for his brother: "As the ancient saying put it, 'Public business comes before private affairs. The state comes before the family.' Our examinations are a great affair of state, and since we were busy on state business, even if we had to neglect our own family members we need feel no compunction" (R. 86; S. 65–65). His eloquent self-justification reveals not merely the incompatibility of private virtue and an official career but the potential contradictions in the official promotion of Confucian family piety. This becomes even more evident in the Kuang Chaoren episode. His pretext of official duty as self-defense turns out to be a moment of betrayal. The exemplary narrative of the filial son from which his initial image derived has broken down: Kuang has chosen official rhetoric over private virtue and betrayed what he is supposed to stand for.

Woven through the Kuang Chaoren episode is the theme of books, reading, writing, and editing. Kuang is initially a diligent reader and an obedient student, yet after successfully following Ma Chunshang's advice, he begins to sneer at those less successful, including Ma himself. Commenting on Ma's *bagu* essays, he says, "Although he understands the rules, he lacks genius, and therefore his books don't sell too well" (R. 280; S. 223), which is an ironic inversion of Ma's remarks on Kuang's *bagu* composition during their first meeting.[7] On his way to the capital city to take an official appointment, Kuang no longer needs Ma's books as guides. Instead, he begins to claim the role of author for himself, creating not merely *bagu* anthologies but also the stories about their popularity, as well as the imagined glory of his own success. In the last scene of the episode, Kuang brags to the other travelers: "To tell you the truth, gentlemen, scholars of the five northern provinces respect my name so highly that they often light incense and tapers to me on their desk, calling me 'Master Kuang of sacred memory' (*xianru*)" (R. 280; S. 227). In "telling the truth" about his success, Kuang projects himself into a scenario often seen in conventional biographies of distinguished scholars, not realizing that, as one traveler inconveniently points out, "Only the dead are described as 'of sacred memory.'"

Kuang is also a master of forgery. Of the things he does for Pansan, two mark a new stage in his self-invention: in exchange for money, he forges official seals and letters and takes the civil service examinations in someone else's place. Such acts of forgery and impersonation go beyond any preconceived narrative form and create a permanent distance between his name and identity, as well as between what he says and what he does. To avoid embarrassment over his wife's humble background, Kuang hides his marital status; later he marries the daughter of his superior, an official in charge of the examinations, and cites *The Lute* (*Pipa ji*) to himself in justification: "There is an opera about Cai the Number One Scholar (Cai Zhuangyuan) who had two wives; and it was considered a great romance. What can it matter?" (R. 275–76; S. 223). The textual precedent Kuang cites is appropriate but not for the reason he gives. *The Lute* is not a romance, as Kuang claims; instead, it is

---

7. Ma Chunshang comments on Kuang Chaoren's essay in Chapter 15: "Your essay shows talent, but you are not sufficiently familiar with the method of reasoning" (R. 218; S. 175).

a story of bigamy and betrayal, and Cai is a problematic character unworthy of imitation. But this matters little to Kuang: in creating his own romance, he has the liberty to choose models for himself and interpret them as he pleases. He is no longer loyal to any specific text or any preordained role. His self-representation eludes the control of any established narrative form, particularly the exemplary biography of the filial son.

Secular Time, Secular History

How did Wu Jingzi describe the metamorphosis of Kuang and explain the different stages of his personal history as well as their interrelationships? Commenting on this episode, C. T. Hsia writes: "The story of Kuang Chaoren is extremely interesting, but it is told in such a way that we are never allowed a glimpse of his mental condition as things happen to him. For many readers it will remain puzzling that a filial son of apparent moral integrity could have degenerated so fast."[8] Puzzled by the same question, some commentators try to detect the seed of Kuang's degradation in the narrative of his early life in hopes of grasping a sense of continuity beneath the story. Yet in so doing, they seem to reaffirm the generic logic of the biographical narrative, which Wu Jingzi refused to follow. We are brought back to the central issue of this chapter: How did Wu Jingzi construct his history, both collective and individual, and explain its driving forces and its tendency to degeneration?

The answer lies, I suggest, in Wu Jingzi's treatment of time. He breaks with the biographical tradition of using timeless character types to mirror unchanging moral verities. In the story of Kuang Chaoren, he summoned the filial son from the pages of *zhengshi* only to show him transformed beyond recognition. The Kuang episode confirms the status of the filial son as a product of narrative construction separate from temporal transformation, which few, if any, pre-existing narratives had managed to capture. An exile from historical biography, Kuang drifts along, allowing his current pursuits to define his mentality and guide his destiny. In emphasizing the importance of the temporal dimension in human experience, Wu Jingzi did not, however, necessarily regard Kuang's past as the cause of his present actions. Instead, he portrayed him as living permanently in the present, with little

---

8. C. T. Hsia, *The Classic Chinese Novel*, p. 229.

memory of his own past, let alone his origins. Rootless and restless, he is driven by the temporal flux.

Although the Kuang Chaoren episode is the longest narrative in the book about an individual character, it nevertheless follows the general pattern that governs the greater part of the novel. As the story unfolds, the narrator keeps shifting his focus from one character to another; rather than representing a life in its entirety or from its very beginning, he catches only one or two of its passing moments. The character's past is left in the background or simply omitted, as is his future; the present moment is neither located nor understood in its relationship to the past and future. A life without beginning or end can hardly be presented in the conventional form of biography: Wu Jingzi's narrative of a specific character often begins *in medias res* and ends not with a sense of closure but with unresolved questions about the past and future.

In analyzing *Rulin waishi*'s narrative rhetoric, Marston Anderson focuses on its affinity for metonymy, for it is "through the series of syntagmatic linkages governed by the trope of metonymy that the text establishes its temporal dynamic."[9] For the purposes of this study, it is more important to understand the novel's rendering of time in its account of what might be called secular history. Wu Jingzi perceived the world of mundane experience temporally, as an unfolding sequence of incidents, related or unrelated, driven by worldly desires and official institutions. This sequence, once set in motion, develops into an irreversible current with tremendous momentum. It is no wonder that Wu Jingzi offered a chronicle of frivolous incidents with no "historical significance" in the conventional sense of the term.[10] Despite the constant, rapid shifts from one character to another, there is no real sense of discontinuity in the narrative, for the literati characters, although distinct

---

9. Anderson, "The Scorpion in the Scholar's Cap," p. 268. In the same article, Anderson argues: "In broader rhetorical terms, we may say that the text [of the novel] favors *metonymy*, or relations of contiguity, over *metaphor*, or relations of resemblance" (p. 263). As Anderson acknowledges (pp. 263, 421), his use of the terms *metonymy* and *metaphor* as two basic forces organizing the operation of language and narrative structure is indebted to Roman Jakobson, Peter Brooks, and Paul de Man.

10. For the same reason, Wu Jingzi's use of the historical chronicle does not necessarily affirm the narrative and interpretive patterns of the official chronologies. For further studies of Chinese chronicles, see van der Loon, "The Ancient Chinese Chronicles and the Growth of Historical Ideals"; and Yang Lien-sheng, "The Organization of Chinese Official Historiography."

from one another, are somehow absorbed into the same whirlpool of mundane affairs.[11]

The temporal dynamics of secular activity is best manifested in Wu's account of his characters' constant travel. The section of the novel from Chapters 2 through 30 is peopled by anxious and restless literati characters on their way somewhere else. Unlike the legendary heroes of *The Water Margin*, who live their wandering lives outside society, they engage in journeys to worldly destinations to take the civil service examinations, to assume official posts, to establish official connections, or to take advantage of connections already established. Everyone knows his destination, yet is blindly preoccupied with worldly affairs and thus deprived of a true sense of direction.

Throughout *Rulin waishi*, the rapid shifting from one character to another is accompanied by an equally rapid movement in space. The narrator follows his characters through private and public places. Everything they experience—the noise; the commotion; the disputes; the chattering and scribbling; the gossiping, rumor, and scandal—inflames desire, enhances vanity, and motivates them in their competition for worldly gain. There seems to be no pause for breath and no permanent place of rest. Chance encounters on the road bring in new characters—travelers with an equal sense of urgency and discontent—and subject them, one after another, to the same insanity and absurdity, induced by accelerated competition and its attendant humiliation.

From this perspective, time is not external to the characters; instead, it is assimilated into their lives. To trace their movement, we may cite Georg Lukács's words from *Theory of the Novel*: "Characters having no apparent meaning appear, establish relations with one another, break them off, disappear again without any meaning having been revealed."[12] It is made clear in the introductory chapter of *Rulin waishi* that the flux of secular time has no permanent meaning. As spokesman for Wu Jingzi, Wang Mian makes a critical

---

11. For more discussion of the episodic structure of *Rulin waishi*, see Part III. Here I wish to emphasize the temporal sequence as one of the novel's constitutive principles. It is helpful to recall Georg Lukács's argument that only the novel, by which he means, of course, the Western novel, includes real time among its constitutive principles (*The Theory of the Novel*, p. 121). I do not mean to suggest that *Rulin waishi*'s treatment of time resembles that of the novels Lukács refers to. Yet the following point seems not totally irrelevant: "The unrestricted, uninterrupted flow of time is the unifying principle of the homogeneity that rubs the sharp edges off each heterogeneous fragment and establishes a relationship—albeit an irrational and inexpressible one—between them" (p. 125).

12. Ibid.

statement about the history recounted in the rest of the novel: since the civil service examination requires that candidates compose *bagu* essays in accordance with the officially sanctioned interpretation of the Confucian classics, literati will neglect altogether the values of *wen*, good conduct, and conscientious judgment as to when to serve the authorities and when to retire (*wen xing chu chu*), qualities that would otherwise endow them with a sense of gravity to anchor their rootless lives. What we see in the novel is, therefore, a ceaseless pursuit of such worldly ambitions as career, fame, riches, and rank (*gong ming fu gui*). That pursuit in turn becomes the driving force that motivates and transforms everyone involved.

In his account of worldly pursuits Wu Jingzi does not permit his characters to rise above the mundane flux or construct meaning for their restless lives. Even poetry loses its power to enchant or enlighten; it reveals no higher truth about life, and it fails even to temporarily liberate its practitioners from secular time. Hopelessly degraded at the hands of self-described poets, it becomes instead a badge of social distinction or a tool for political networking; the four "eccentric townsfolk" portrayed in Chapter 55 of the novel have to seek other media for lyrical detachment. And that chapter offers not a restored poetic inspiration or lyrical transcendence but a nostalgic lyricism tinged with an elegiac tone.[13]

Past, Present, and Retrospective Comments

In its narrative of secular history, *Rulin waishi* does not quite achieve a sense of completion. Unlike *zhengshi*, which valorizes the world of the past, secular history is constructed in the sphere of possible contact with the developing, incomplete, and therefore constantly re-evaluated present.

Rulin waishi uses incidents recounted in the past tense in two ways. First, Wu Jingzi adopted the Ming dynasty chronology as the framework of his

---

13. *Rulin waishi* never regards poetry as the ultimate escape from the world of mundane affairs or as a promising alternative mode of writing for characters such as the *bagu* essayists. Wu Jingzi's avoidance of poetry in *Rulin waishi* is, therefore, a matter of deliberate choice. Although from time to time we are told that the characters compose poems on specific occasions, never once does the narrator present those poems in their entirety. Nor does he use poetry as a distinct form of narratorial discourse. Except for the two poems placed at the beginning and the end of the novel, verse is conspicuously absent in *Rulin waishi* in comparison with other Chinese novels. It is noteworthy that *Rulin waishi* was the first Chinese novel not to use poetry in forming its narrative.

novel and carefully wove his fictional characters and incidents into historical events.[14] Second, and perhaps more important, he placed the events of
the earlier part of the novel in the past tense by referring to them, whenever he could, in the recollections of the newcomers. But in *Rulin waishi,* no
business is ever finished. Instead of fading into the permanent, silent past,
the characters depicted earlier re-emerge, often not in person but as a topic
of conversation for those who appear later.[15] These conversations fulfill a
variety of functions: some bring us up to date about the doings and whereabouts of the characters; some refer to what they did before; still others offer different accounts and interpretations of events previously represented.
In the first two cases, the narrator returns again and again to those characters, reminding us that their stories are far from complete. This often has
the effect of unsettling rather than reaffirming the episodes recounted earlier. From these fragmentary oral accounts, we glean the later developments
of previously introduced characters, but they are often fraught with unexpected turns and twists and therefore can hardly be inferred from the previous episodes.[16] In fact, a mere reference to these new developments de-

---

14. One such example is that the fictional characters often refer to the famous *hou qizi* (the
Later Seven Masters) of the Ming dynasty. In Chapter 30 a character claims that he used to
compose poetry with these scholars while he served in the prince's palace in the capital. In response, Du Shenqing claims that two of them (Li Panlong and Wang Shizhen) are his uncles.
When the topic of conversation shifts to Zong Chen, another member of the *hou qizi,* he says,
"Senior Secretary Zong was my father's classmate (both of whom obtained the official degress
in the same year)."

15. Some characters do return, playing minor roles or roles of reduced importance in later
sections of the novel. For instance, Ma Er (Ma Chunshang) reappears in Chapters 33 and 34,
Wang Hui in Chapter 38, and Iron-Armed Zhang (Zhang Tiebi) in Chapters 31, 32, and 37.
But in the last two cases, Wang and Zhang change their names and disguise their own past.
Since the novel covers a long period of time, the generational transition provides a method for
creating contrasts between father and son. Compared with the father, the son is often portrayed in a negative light, testifying to the general trend of degeneration the novelist delineates
throughout. The most striking example is Bao Tingxi, Bao Wenqing's adopted son, whose
behavior bears no resemblance to his father's.

16. One such example is the story of Xun Mei. He is first mentioned in Chapter 2 by
Wang Hui, who dreams of passing the palace examination at the same time as Xun (Xun
Mei is then merely a seven-year-old student). In Chapter 7 Xun Mei does pass the examination but leaves for home to mourn for his mother before receiving an official post. In Chapter
22 we learn that he has been promoted to salt commissioner. But a conversation between two
officers in Chapter 29 reveals an unexpected twist to his story: he has been arrested because of
a scandal. Wang Hui is introduced in Chapter 2 as an arrogant provincial graduate, but what

prives the accounts of these characters of a sense of completion, suggesting that they are small fragments of an ongoing and largely untold story. In the third case, the same character is often described in conflicting comments; there is no prospect of a consensus, and accounts of the same incident vary according to the teller. Each story may be modified by other characters' retellings, which may be just as prejudiced and erroneous and which, with almost no exceptions, are left unconfirmed by the narrator.[17] Sometimes the narrator directs our attention to the circumstantial motivations for the constant retelling, conflicting comments, and possible fabrications. Sometimes he seems interested merely in showing how easily memory is corrupted by time, which leaves those who come later with no guarantee of a reliable version of the past. In both cases, he retrieves the past from memory and opens it up to development, controversy, and distortion.

There are precedents in Qing literature for *Rulin waishi*'s retrospective comments on the same episode from multiple perspectives, for example, *The Palace of the Eternal Life* (*Changsheng dian*). Written by Hong Sheng in 1688, the play presents the tragic love story of Emperor Xuanzong and Yang Yuhuan, the Prized Consort, and their ultimate reunion in an imagined world of eternal happiness. In the second half of the play, Hong Sheng kept returning to the central events of the story: the collapse of the empire and the death of Yang Yuhuan. However, he represented them differently each time he referred to them. The different representations of the past provoke contrasting responses. Most telling is the scene of "Looking at the Stockings" in Act 36. The owner of a wine shop increases her business by exhibiting a pair of stockings left behind by Yang before her forced suicide. The customers see different things in the stockings: a trace of transient beauty and romantic sensation, a testament to the unworldly Taoist's purity, and a witness to the emperor's indulgence and the sufferings of the

---

happens to him later is revealed mainly in other characters' conversations. In his final appearance, in Chapter 38, he is disguised as a monk. Not only does the story of Wang Hui stretch out too long and become too fragmented, it is so full of such unexpected twists that readers can easily lose track.

17. For instance, Ma Chunshang is subjected to continuous comment in Chapters 18, 20, 49, and 52, long after the focus of the narrative has shifted elsewhere. Even before his first appearance in Chapter 31, Du Shaoqing has been referred to in two clashing evaluations, and in Chapters 33 and 34 he is exposed to more controversy.

commoners. In this scene, Hong Sheng illuminated the ironic disparity between the tragic nature of the event and the various reactions it arouses, from commercial interests to a voyeurism mixed with nostalgic sentimentalism. In the same ironic vein, he also showed the degree to which people's reactions to the same event are colored by their predispositions and experience. In Act 38 when Li Guinian, a musician in Emperor Xunzong's orchestra, presents to the public the story of Emperor Xunzong and Yang Yuhuan, there is, unsurprisingly, no consensus as to its meaning. One man sees Yang as evil, another regards her as a romantic heroine, and a third does not even care who she was: he comes just to enjoy the storytelling, and the authenticity of the account is irrelevant.[18] Hong Sheng did not try to reconcile these conflicting views of the same event. In fact, partial or prejudiced as they may be, all are evoked by Li Guinian's storytelling and singing, and none can be dismissed as entirely groundless. As a narrator within the play, Li Guinian not only sums up the major themes and motifs of the first half but also provides us with an occasion for reviewing or rereading the play itself. By staging the internal audience's clashing responses to Li's story, Hong Sheng seems also to have anticipated the audience's or readers' interpretations of his own dramatic rendering.

Like *The Palace of the Eternal Life, Rulin waishi* is interested not in constructing a single narrative of its characters and events but in offering as wide a range of accounts and comments on them as possible. Wu Jingzi did not make the radical epistemological claim that the past is absolutely unknowable, inscrutable, and unintelligible; rather, he showed how the past is shaped and reshaped as it is evoked by different characters in retrospective accounts. His novel represents "history" as a domain of discourse, a field of claims and counterclaims and a contact zone between an unsettled past and a controversial present.

One example of this is an incident in Chapter 54 of the novel. Ding Yanzhi, a lover of poetry whose name echoes the classical definition of poetry—"to express one's abiding aims"—purchases an anthology of the poems said to have been composed at a party described in Chapter 12. But the anthology includes poems attributed to characters, such as Jing Lanjiang, Zhao Xuezhai, and Kuang Chaoren, who did not attend the party, as well as others, such as

---

18. For critical interpretation of these two scenes, see Owen, "Salvaging Poetry."

Ma Chunshang, who have never composed poetry and are known for their abhorrence of it. Although the poets and the *bagu* essayists consciously place themselves in opposite camps, the differences between them become obscured in the anthology. Ding Yanzhi, sharing the anthology with others, enters into a debate about its authenticity. With Chen Munan's mediation, the debate is eventually settled. But Chen's involvement raises new problems: trying to dispel the confusion, he "corrects" the story recounted in Chapter 13 by disclosing what he believes actually occurred to Quan Wuyong, who was present at the party. This leaves us with no stable ground for judgment.[19]

We see in Chapter 54 of *Rulin waishi* not merely the possible misperception, misinformation, and corruption of memory on the part of those who come after but also how what is represented in the novel as "reality" becomes mutable through the passage of secular time. This is especially true when characters choose to play roles or deliberately create fictions about themselves through plagiarism, forgery, and impersonation. In Chapter 13, Qu Gongsun tries to arrange to have his name placed on the cover of a *bagu* anthology compiled by Ma Chunshang. When Ma rephrases Qu's request, he uses the words *zhan fengmian*, literally, "to occupy a position on the cover"— the cover becomes a battleground on which the literati compete with one another in making false claims of authorship. This is not the first time that Qu Gongsun has done so. In Chapter 8, we are told that he added his name as editor to the cover of a selection of Gao Qi's poetry after learning that the copy he has is the only existing one.

Another story of forgery and impersonation, presented in Chapters 21 through 23, is even more dramatic. This time the impostor is Niu Pulang, a young man who steals the late Commoner Niu's (Niu Buyi) manuscripts from a Buddhist monk. For Niu Pulang, reading the manuscript results in the same sudden enlightenment that Kuang Chaoren had in an earlier chapter: "Apparently a man who can write poems doesn't have to pass the examinations in order to make friends with great officials" (R. 288; S. 233). The thought then occurs to him:

This man's name is Niu and so is mine; and he has only written a pen name, Commoner Niu, on these volumes without putting down his real name. Why shouldn't I

---

19. In response to a question about the scandal involving Quan Wuyong that is rendered in Chapter 13, Chen explains, much to our surprise, that Quan was framed by his rivals and was later officially rehabilitated.

add my name to his? I will have two seals made and stamp these books with them; then these poems will become mine and from now on I shall call myself Commoner Niu. (R. 288; S. 233)

In the following part of the story, Niu Pulang, now claiming to be Niu Buyi, puts on the square cap (*fangjin*) of the literatus to signal his new identity.[20]

It is only fitting that such an account is followed by an episode in Chapter 24 about actors whose profession is impersonation: Actor Qian, for instance, is shown wearing the dramatic costumes meant for a gentleman of the Hanlin Academy on everyday occasions, thereby blurring the lines of demarcation between acting and reality. We are then told that Old Man Huang, a former actor, still dresses up in theatrical costumes. When a man teases him by remarking, "Look at this gentleman, Mr. Qian! Why compare him to a retired prefect? Even ministers and vice ministers couldn't look more grand," Huang, without realizing that the man is poking fun at him, "beams with pleasure" (R. 337–38; S. 273). Impersonation without a sense of irony: this is the drama that takes place not on stage but in the sociopolitical world, whose role system is contingent on authority, arbitrary rules, and pretense.

Indeed, *Rulin waishi* often represents sociopolitical life through such dramatic devices as sudden turns and discoveries. Success in the civil service examination constitutes the climax for the literati's self-fashioning and at the same time gives it official sanction. It grants a new status and identity that can be embraced as "reality." In the episode of Fan Jin in Chapter 3, this sudden, violent change creates the moment of psychological breakdown. A frustrated candidate for more than twenty years, he is so overwhelmed by the news of his success that he temporarily loses his mind. Upon recovering consciousness, Fan finds himself being treated with the respect he has never even dreamed of. And this public perception turns him into someone beyond his own recognition. An intellectually impoverished character, he has no internal resources with which to maintain the continuity of his self-identity. His view of self is subject entirely to the arbitrary rules of the examination system, whose credibility is questioned throughout the novel.

---

20. According to Ming regulations, only those who had acquired the *xiucai* and higher degrees could wear the square cap.

In the story of Niu Pulang's impersonation, this sociopolitical drama takes a slightly different twist. It ends with his winning a case brought against him by Niu Buyi's wife: the judge decides that Niu Pulang is Niu Buyi, and the wife must go somewhere else to search for her husband who, according to the judge, happens to share the name. Niu Pulang may well assert any identity he wishes for himself, but in this episode it is only through a peculiar legal procedure that his false self-representation is officially recognized as his true identity.

This is not the end of the Niu Pulang story. Along with many other characters, Niu Pulang is mentioned in Chapter 56, the last chapter of the novel, long after his death. Like Kuang Chaoren, who has undergone just as dramatic a process of self-invention, he is posthumously granted the titles of palace graduate and Hanlin scholar and then commemorated as a neglected man of virtue in a sacrifice organized by the Ministry of Rites. A history so conceived is full of errors, ironies, and unexpected twists. So long as Niu and Kuang are playing the impersonation game, any effort to bring their stories to closure will appear arbitrary, and any final judgment on them will be only tentative.

To better understand *Rulin waishi*'s rendering of time, we should not only read the novel but also probe into its composition. *Rulin waishi* took shape gradually over the course of almost twenty years and thus emerged from a sprawling and yet vigorous process of growing, repositioning, and self-questioning. More important, although Wu Jingzi set his narrative within a preconceived historical time frame, he was often driven by something akin to a journalist's interest in the unfolding of the contemporary events. As shown above, his accounts of many characters are distinctly open-ended. And this unresolved narrative is, I argue, to some extent dependent on the ongoing drama of its empirical sources. Indeed, *Rulin waishi* is known, among other things, for its deep roots in contemporary literati experiences. As a novelist, Wu Jingzi consistently and methodically followed the lives of his acquaintances through narrative; even a few years before his death, he was still updating the most recent changes in his accounts of such characters as Ma Chunshang.[21] In so doing, he succeeded in incorporating temporal dynamics into his narrative and thus gave his work a remarkable sense of becoming

---

21. For more on this topic, see the Appendix.

rarely seen in the Chinese novel. Indeed, no novel before *Rulin waishi* had ever been so conceived and composed, and few subsequent works, if any, achieved its degree of narrative dynamism. In this regard, *Rulin waishi* is truly revolutionary. Its deep engagement in temporal change allows it a new perspective on reality and poses a challenge to preconceived, static narrative paradigms and absolute claims to eternal moral truth.

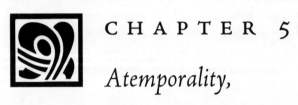

CHAPTER 5

Atemporality, Closure, and Ascetic Ritual

Rulin waishi recapitulates the corrosive force of secular time in its account of the deterioration of literati mores, especially in Chapters 2 through 30. But as it moves to construct the ascetic ritual in Chapters 31 through 37, it adopts a different strategy for dealing with time. To protect this pure vision of the ritualized world from contamination and corruption, Wu Jingzi elevated it above time and locked it into a separate narrative space. But the ascetic ritual has to be practiced, and ritual practice requires its devotees to transform the mundane world according to its vision. This brings the ascetic ritual into confrontation with the flux of secular time, from which it has withdrawn; it must now struggle between its absolute imperatives and the erosive force of ever-passing time and between its utopian impulse and its implementation in ever-changing reality. In representing the ascetic ritual, Wu Jingzi also confronted a narrative dilemma: to assert its transcendence, he had to revitalize the authoritative narrative whose credibility he called into question. Hence the inescapable conflict between different modes of narrative within *Rulin waishi*.

Ascetic Ritual and Time

For the literati characters introduced in Chapters 30 through 36, the temple dedicated to Wu Taibo is a place where they are able to relate to one another and create for themselves a center, a community, and a home, in which they eventually find tranquility. It provides them with a solid structure to grasp against the temporal flux of worldly affairs; they stay in the temple overnight, fasting and purifying themselves, and the ceremony conducted there further insulates them from the noise and restlessness of the outside world. Wu Jingzi's representation of the ceremony is a static, psychologically neutralizing, and almost self-erasing narrative: as the ritual gets under way, all sense of time is suspended, with the practitioners transported into a utopia of timeless harmony and perfect order. The narrative also seems to lose its forward movement, and all it does is to repeat formulaic language patterns.

However, temporal dynamics have been built so deeply into the narrative that to get rid of them is to run the risk of dispensing with narrative altogether. In his reading of Xunzi's discourse on Confucian ritual, Marston Anderson argues, "The successful performance of the rites may be understood to involve a mastering of time." Carrying this over to *Rulin waishi*'s account of the Taibo ceremony, he notes that the Taibo passage suggests a perfect consonance between the text of the ritual and its contemporary performance. "This unity of word and action," he comments, "creates a privileged temporal precinct, in which the participants, freed of disturbing timebound emotions, may give themselves fully to the present tense of the ritual."[1] This is, indeed, a magical moment of suspension, a moment when time-driven narrative comes to an end.

In order to separate the ritualized world from the transitory and morally corrupt present, Wu Jingzi created an internal boundary of temporal discontinuity. Besides representing the ceremony in the formulaic fashion of Confucian ritual manuals, in the account of Yu Yude in Chapter 36 he adopted the standard form of biography and constructed an uninterrupted, closed time sequence that prevents alien views. Yu is the only character other than Wang Mian who is accorded a coherent and consistent exemplary biography. Interrupting the time sequence of the narrative, the biography of Yu begins with a flashback to his miraculous birth, which is itself an elaboration of the myth of Confucius's birth, with all the auspicious omens.[2] Yu thus inhabits a

---

1. Anderson, "The Scorpion in the Scholar's Cap," p. 270.

2. We are told that Yu is born in a town called Unicorn Sash (Linfu). The unicorn is a symbol of benevolence and a metaphor for the man of supreme virtue and talent. In the myth of Confucius's birth, a unicorn appeared to Confucius's mother, Zheng Zai, in a dream as a messenger from Heaven. She understood the meaning of this divine miracle and tied a sash around the unicorn's horn. The sash itself became a witness to Confucius's fate: when a farmer caught the unicorn with the sash on its horn many years later, Confucius knew his life

ritualized world closed to all but those of his own kind, those who are created for and by the ceremony. His interaction with the outside world is reduced to a minimum.

But Yu Yude is not completely relegated to a space outside time. Once he steps out of the privileged bounds of biography, he is confronted by the unsettling, controversial present and subjected to alternative perspectives. In Chapter 37, Wu Shu, one of Yu's students, characterizes two anecdotes about his teacher as "strange" and "laughable" (kexiao and haoxiao). This ironic remark is immediately rebutted by Du Shaoqing, who believes the incidents show Yu's virtue is so lofty that it is beyond the comprehension of common folk, but the importance of Wu Shu's remarks lie in the suggestion of the very possibility of seeing Yu from another angle. Immediately following Yu's biography and the account of the Taibo ceremony, Wu's comment illuminates the contrasts between the ritualistic, biographical world and the world of mundane reality, and between the ways time is treated in each. Indeed, whereas the performance of ritual involves a temporary suspension of time, biographical narrative provides the characters with an exemption from change, development, and alternative views. By contrast, secular narrative is bound to the flow of constant mutation and shifts of viewpoint.

The illusory and transitory nature of the ritualized world is immediately apparent as the narrator resumes his normal pace in his account of worldly affairs outside the temple. Designed to absorb the ceremony practitioners into the timeless vision of a ritualized world, the Taibo temple itself cannot stand the erosion of the secular time and eventually falls apart. In his rendering of the ultimate fall of the temple, Wu Jingzi gave compelling expression to the corrupting power of the temporal flux that no ideology has managed to contain or overcome.

Wu Jingzi's history of literati degeneration begins, however, with a prophetic episode about divine messages, Heaven's will, and the fate of the literati's cultural tradition. Wang Mian announces a divine mission for the literati of the following generations: to maintain the fortunes of culture (wenyun) against the tide of their times.

"Look!" Wang Mian pointed to the stars, saying to his old neighbor, "the Chains have invaded the Scholars. That shows that scholars of this generation will have trouble ahead." As he spoke, a strange wind sprang up. It soughed through the trees

---

was about to end. He held the unicorn in his arms, untied the sash, and wept. See Wang Jia, "Zhou lingwang," in Shiyi ji, juan 3, pp. 62–63.

and made the waterfowl take wing, crying in alarm, while Wang Mian and Old Qin hid their faces in their sleeves for fear. Soon the wind dropped, and when they looked again they saw about a hundred small stars in the sky, all falling toward the southeast horizon. "Heaven has taken pity on the scholars," said Wang Mian. "These stars have been sent down to maintain the fortune of culture. But we shan't live to see it." (R. 15; S. 13)

What is presented here is a variation on the formulaic beginning of many premodern Chinese novels. In *The Story of the Stone* the abandoned stone is reincarnated into the human world to satisfy, in C. T. Hsia's words, its Faustian desire for experience, knowledge, and pleasure, as well as to fulfill its karma.[3] The 108 demonic stars of *Water Margin* are accidentally released from a Pandora's box, and their reincarnation in the human world leads to a series of violent and destructive acts; later we are told that the baleful stars were sent down to carry out a heavenly task, yet their actions are never cleansed of ambiguity.

Beyond the narrative tradition of the novel, Wang Mian's statement about the divine mission of preserving the cultural tradition ultimately derives from the *Analects*:[4] The opening episode in *Rulin waishi* indicates a grand project of Confucian narrative at work.

When under siege in Kuang, the Master said, "With King Wen dead, does culture not reside here in me? If Heaven had intended that this culture should perish, those who died later would not have been able to participate in it. Heaven is not yet about to let this culture perish, so what can the men of Kuang do to me?"

Since Zhou culture "is based on both the models of the ancients and the manifest patterns of the natural order,"[5] Confucius is convinced that the fact that it endured after King Wen's death signals that heaven favors him as its legitimate transmitter. But he does not rule out the possibility that this culture might perish if there is no guarantee of its transmission to the future. What is embodied in the ancient norms can easily be lost or distorted. The cosmic order is by no means self-evident and is often subject to interpretation. Moreover, who can claim the same privilege as Confucius in asserting a role as the carrier of this culture? Who can be so confident that he has been

---

3. C. T. Hsia, essay on *The Story of the Stone*, pp. 262–73.
4. See *Analects*, Book 9. My translation follows Peter Bol's translation in *'This Culture of Ours,'* p. 1.
5. Ibid.

chosen by Heaven to interpret the ancient sages' intentions? And what, after all, does it mean to maintain this culture in the mundane realm of politics and institutions in times when sage and king are no longer perfectly united in one body? To Confucius, the *wen*—what it is, what it does, and how it is transmitted—seems obvious, but in *Rulin waishi*, the mission to save *wen* is doomed from the outset.

Indeed, Wang Mian's divine prophecy in the introductory chapter is immediately followed by a "history" that demonstrates how much the mundane world has deviated from the cosmic order. What we learn in this history is the impossibility of restoring natural order to the changing world of mundane praxis, and the irrelevance of Heaven's will, whatever it is and whatever form it takes, to human existence. In fact, the culture is to be destroyed, despite Heaven's intention to save it. Wang Mian's critique of the civil service examination system reinforces the story's sense of irony and complexity with an ominous twist: it is the authorities' efforts to institutionalize the studies of the Confucian classics that contribute to the distortion, and ultimately to the destruction, of that culture.

Nor can the norms of antiquity be translated into the social practice of the present time without conflict and distortion. Between the ideas and the institutionalized praxis of the past and the world of reality there is time—an ungraspable, invisible phenomenon that erodes the ground for any claims of homogeneity between the two and frustrates human struggles against its power. No examples illustrate the failure of such struggles better than the episodes of the literati's collective practice of the Taibo ceremony in *Rulin waishi*. Despite their urge to overcome the historical distance between past and present and to achieve an identification with the models of the Confucian sages, these characters are bound to a world that is fatally subject to temporal and historical limitations. They reside in the same world as the characters of the first thirty chapters. At the symbolic level, those characters, too, bear the identity of celestial beings—the scholar-stars (*wenqu xing*). But their symbolic bond with Heaven is mentioned merely as a joking matter;[6] it reminds us of

---

6. For instance, in Chapter 3 of the novel, when Fan Jin loses his mind upon hearing the news of his success in the provincial examination, someone suggests that Butcher Hu, his father-in-law, hit him to restore him to sanity, but Hu demurs. "'He may be my son-in-law,' he said, 'but he's a civil official now—one of the stars in heaven. How can you hit one of the stars in heaven? I've heard that whoever hits the stars in heaven will be carried away by the King of Hell, given a hundred strokes with an iron rod, and shut up in the eighteenth hell, never to become a human being again'" (R. 45; S. 35). Immediately after he hits Fan Jin, "his

their privileged status, for which they are not qualified. As members of the literati class, they are supposed to carry the norms of the culture, but their concerns are limited to the immediate advantages of status, power, fame, and economic interest. With no commitment to moral principles, they seem to have abandoned themselves entirely to the passage of time, allowing their lives to be overrun by its currents. Indeed, time will not become the constitutive power in the making of their character and mentality until they themselves are distanced from the ultimate source of meaning and their symbolic bond with the transcendental home is severed once and forever.

The Problem of Final Judgment

In *The Content of the Form*, Hayden White writes, "The demand for closure in the historical story is a demand for moral meaning, a demand that sequences of real events be assessed as to their significance as elements of a moral drama."[7] Carrying this over to Chinese historiography, Anthony Yu argues, "Focused thus upon the exemplary significance of characters and events, history in China assumes the authority of a kind of realized eschatology, to use Christian terminology, because its judgment is thought to be both impartial and virtually irreversible."[8] Written under the sign of history, *Rulin waishi* raises a question about the very possibility of such historical judgment.

As I have argued, *Rulin waishi* resists closure. Throughout the main body of the novel, few characters die, and the exit of a specific character does not provide an occasion for passing a definitive judgment upon him or her. Characters keep alluding to past events in their conversations, not in order to give them closure but to draw them into the ongoing controversy and open them up to future dispute. With no absolute guarantee of the truthfulness of the characters' claims, what we know is not a matter of epistemological possibility but rather of contextual possibility. The episode of Quan Wuyong is apparently closed in Chapter 13, only to be reopened by Chen Munan in Chapter 54. But Chen's version of the story cannot be taken for granted, either. Although he seems to have no reason to lie, his

---

hand began to ache; when he raised his palm, he found to his dismay that he could not bend it." "'It's true then that you mustn't strike the stars in heaven,' he thought. 'Now Buddha does not allow me to get away with it'" (R. 46; S. 36).

7. White, *The Content of the Form*, p. 21.

8. Anthony Yu, *Rereading the Stone*, p. 40.

account of the incident, just like the accounts of all other characters (except for Wang Mian in the introductory chapter), cannot escape the corruptions of perspectivism, the corrosive forces of time, and the uncertainty of memory. As doubt hovers in the air, we find it impossible to take the characters' words at face value. The true closure of the Quan Wuyong case is once again delayed.

Closure or final judgment is, however, required by ascetic ritual, for the ritual embodies norms of value and significance against which to measure the world and history. Closure is also implied in the conventional paradigm of history, historical romance, and other types of the vernacular novel, which as genres are derived from, or related in some fashion to, historiography. For Wu Jingzi, there seems to be no solution except to reinforce the normative authority of the ascetic ritual through a narrative form he often questioned.

Indeed, what Wu Jingzi did in Chapter 56 seems to confirm the formulaic ending of the conventional novel. As is the case with other novels, the concluding chapter is detached from the main story in terms of time and narrative mode. It begins with an imperial edict issued in the forty-third year of the Wanli reign (1615), many years after the deaths of the major characters. In the edict, the Wanli emperor encourages his ministers to recommend men of virtue who are still undiscovered in order to help him govern the state better. In response, a minister suggests that he collect the names of all the men of virtue who passed away without obtaining an official title, mostly due to the restrictions of the civil service examinations, and then to posthumously award them, on the basis of their moral excellence and capacity, the degree of palace graduate (*jinshi*) and the corresponding title of Hanlin scholar. A list of candidates is presented to the emperor; in includes ninety-one names of characters who appear in the preceding chapters of the novel. Fifty-five of them, with Yu Yude heading the list, are finally selected and honored under three hierarchical rubrics. On the same day that the roll of honors is posted in the Ministry of Rites, a government-sponsored ceremony is dedicated to them in the Imperial College. Both the roll of honor and the ceremony give a conclusive recognition to selected heroes of the novel.

The late Qing commentator in the Qixingtang edition wrote that final mention of all the characters is the way for a novelist to close his case.[9] Indeed, most premodern vernacular novels conclude with one or more such

---

9. See Li Hanqiu, ed., *"Rulin waishi" huijiao huiping ben*, pp. 761–62.

lists.[10] Red Inkstone (Zhiyan Zhai) claimed that *The Story of the Stone* ended with a "Final Listing of the Characters with Feeling" (*qingbang*), in which the major characters of the novel are classified and ranked according to the nature and depth of their passions.[11] *The Investiture of the Gods* (*Fengshen yanyi*), *The Journey to the West*, and later, *A Precious Mirror for Judging Flowers* (*Pinhua baojian*) are only a few of the novels that share this feature.

But none of these final evaluations seems to have provoked as much controversy as that in *Rulin waishi*. Jin He (1818–85) was the first reader to question the authenticity of Chapter 56. "Someone, sometime, recklessly added," he wrote in his postscript to the Qunyuzhai edition of *Rulin waishi*, "a *youbang* [posthumous examination roster] *juan*, forming its official proclamations by reassembling parallel sentences taken from Master (Wu Jingzi)'s literary works in the most sloppy, laughable way. It should be deleted so that the novel will be restored to its original form."[12] Despite the lack of supporting evidence, Zhang Wenhu (1808–85), another late Qing commentator on the novel, concurred, as have many modern scholars. This opinion was so influential that almost all editions of the novel published in China up to the early 1980s excluded Chapter 56, as did all English, French, and Japanese translations. Following Jin He's suggestion, the editors of these editions often concluded Chapter 55 with the lyric "Qinyuan chun," which in the Woxian caotang edition (1803), the earliest extant edition of the novel, was found at the end of Chapter 56. The removal of Chapter 56 created many problems for the overall structure of the novel, but the interesting question is what prompted the critics to make such a move. What is at stake in the debate about the ending of the novel?

Although many of the objections brought against Chapter 56 have since been proven baseless, one criticism seems irrefutable: that the final judgments passed on the characters do not do them justice. The inclusion, exclusion, and ranking of the characters in the roster are the focus of the debate. In his 1885 edition-with-commentary of *Rulin waishi*, Zhang Wenhu quoted

---

10. For a more systematic survey of the formulaic ending of the vernacular novel, see Rolston, *Reading and Writing Between the Lines*, pp. 201–8.

11. Odd Tablet, in his comments in chapters 17 and 18 of the novel, indicated that he had read this list in 1762 (Chen Qinghao, ed., *Xinbian "Shitou ji" Zhiyan Zhai pingyu jijiao*, p. 331). Although this list is missing from all existing editions of *The Story of the Stone*, numerous imitations of the novel furnish such a list as a way of evaluating the major characters.

12. See Jin He's "*Rulin waishi ba*," in Li Hanqiu, ed., *"Rulin waishi" huijiao huiping ben*, pp. 764–67.

part of Jin He's postscript and criticized Chapter 56 for including Buddhist monks, boxers, and women under the rubric *Rulin*.[13] He even tentatively attributed the authorship of Chapter 56 to the Woxian caotang commentator, who strongly recommended this chapter and likened it to Sima Qian's postface to *Shiji*. The Qixingtang edition commentator apparently did not share Jin He's conviction, yet he did not hesitate to criticize Chapter 56 for what he saw as an inappropriate mixing of the characters with different moral qualities in the final register. In fact, he replaced the register with his own list of characters, excluding those he despised, such as Kuang Chaoren and Niu Pulang, adding others, and assigning different rankings to still others.[14]

However, it is one thing to argue that the novel is inconsistent in its evaluation of characters, and quite another to hold that the novel was written by more than one author or to attribute a specific section of the novel to someone other than Wu Jingzi. In fact, studies of *Rulin waishi*'s authorship have so far produced no convincing evidence of the involvement of a second author or an editor in the 1803 edition. Even those who dislike or condemn Chapter 56 can hardly deny that it fits the conventional paradigm of the novel and constitutes an integral part of the larger design of *Rulin waishi*. It can be regarded as an echo of the introductory chapter, which is also distanced in time from the main body of the novel. In the introductory chapter Wang Mian's statement about the heavenly mission of maintaining the cultural tradition inaugurates the novel. It conceals within itself an anticipation of the ending, which in turn gives the beginning its meaning and purpose. As Zhao Jingshen has correctly noted, the correspondence between the first and last chapters in *Rulin waishi* is a structural device borrowed from *Water Margin*.[15] Ogawa Tamaki was probably the first to relate the introductory chapter of *Rulin waishi* to its counterpart in *Water Margin*.[16] Following him, Timothy Wong drew a parallel between the overall structure of the two novels. Certainly no one can miss the fact that Chapter 37 of *Rulin waishi* is modeled upon Chapter 71 of *Water Margin*. Both the Taibo temple and the Hall of Loyalty and Righteousness (Zhongyi ting) serve as a locus where almost all the characters come together in grand ceremonies to create the

---

13. Ibid., p. 755.
14. See the *fanli* of the Qixingtang *Zhengding Rulin waishi*, in Li Hanqiu, ed., "*Rulin waishi*" *huijiao huiping ben*, pp. 768–70.
15. Zhao Jingshen, "Tan *Rulin waishi*," 423–30.
16. Ogawa Tamaki, "*Jurin gaishi* no keishiki to naiyō," pp. 184–86.

climaxes of the two novels. Here again, *Rulin waishi* demonstrates structural coherence through the deliberate deployment of the devices of foreshadowing and correspondence. Chapter 36 is a hagiography of Yu Yude, the ritual master in the Taibo ceremony. It corresponds to the exemplary biography of Wang Mian in the introductory chapter. Chapter 37, the Taibo ceremony, is echoed in Chapter 56, in which the ritual participants themselves are commemorated as men of virtue in another ceremony. In Chapter 37 the Taibo ceremony is followed by a list of the literati who organized and participated in it. Like the honorary roster in Chapter 56, this list includes the names of Jin Dongya and others with no greater claim to moral status than Kuang Chaoren and Niu Pulang. If these are not grounds for rejecting Chapter 37, why question the authenticity of Chapter 56?

The controversy regarding the final judgment of the characters in *Rulin waishi* reveals the tension between its innovative narrative and its structural framework, which was adopted from the conventional paradigm. Its ending is an example of reliance on an old scheme that does not function well in its new narrative context. Conferring an absolute judgment on characters who have been previously exposed to multiple perspectives generates nothing but confusion.

This brings us back to the issues previously discussed: the novel's rendering of the past, of memory, of the temporal flux of time, and of the perpetual mutability of history, as well as its constant exposure of its characters to conflicting comments and recollections. All this makes it impossible to say the last word about any character without being controversial or even ironic. Basing his conclusions on the model of historical writings, the Qixingtang edition commentator regarded Wu Jingzi's ending of the roster with Iron Pen Guo (Guo Tiebi) as Wu's means of praising himself. But such self-reference is not without irony, for Iron Pen is by no account as fair, sharp, and critical as his name would indicate. In Chapter 21 Guo is even deceived by Niu Pulang: he cuts a personal seal for "Commoner Niu" that facilitates the latter's scandalous impersonation.

Those who believe the novel should end with Chapter 55 find it difficult to defend such an ending in terms of the conventional narrative paradigm; all they can say is that the novel ends without an ending (*yi bujie zhi jie*),[17] which is to offer not a solution but a paradox. And in this case no solution is possi-

---

17. See Tianmu Shanqiao's (Zhang Wenhu) postscript to *Rulin waishi*, in Li Hanqiu, ed., *"Rulin waishi" huijiao huiping ben*, p. 772.

ble that is not paradoxical. In *Rulin waishi*, the ending exemplifies the problem the novel fails to resolve, the tension between the need for and the impossibility of conclusive claims: the adopted framework requires such a claim, but the main body of the narrative attests to its impossibility. The crumbling temple portrayed in Chapter 55 is a suggestive emblem of the novel as sustained by this old framework: all the attached materials have disintegrated, but the post and lintel system remains to indicate unrealized intentions.

However, this argument should not be taken too far. I am not claiming that *Rulin waishi* completely disavows the possibility of narratorial authority, for after all, Wu Jingzi was able to manipulate our responses to his narrative through various and often subtle devices. The important point is that *Rulin waishi* creates such a complicated narrative situation that any narratorial assertion would sound too naïve, ineffective, and even ironic. Chapter 56, the last chapter of the novel, provides a fitting example.

For modern scholars the problems of Chapter 56 are by no means limited to the misjudgments of the characters; even more perplexing are the novel's apparent thematic contradictions. How can a novel that begins with a severe critique of the civil service examinations end with the imperial awarding of official degrees and titles to its characters? One may cite historical sources for the posthumous examination roster to show that Chapter 56 might not be as absurd as Jin He would have us believe.[18] One could also argue that here *Rulin waishi* is again modeled on the 100-chapter edition of *Water Margin*, which concludes with the conferring of posthumous imperial honors on the bandit heroes.[19] However, neither of these explanations is of much help in dealing with the thematic inconsistencies that critics have discerned in *Rulin waishi*.

He Manzi, in his reading of Chapter 56, detects the ironic tone that permeates the most sophisticated passages of the novel. To him, the opening paragraph of the chapter juxtaposes the narrator's account of the Wanli emperor and the emperor's self-representation to set a tone for the rest of the chapter. The emperor is said not to have held court for years or read any official memorials, but his edict claims that his extraordinary diligence and

---

18. Hong Mai (1123–1202) recorded that in the third year of the Guanghua reign (900 CE) Emperor Zhaozong of the Tang dynasty conferred posthumous imperial honors on men of letters such as Li He and Jia Dao, following Wei Zhuang's suggestion (see *Rongzhai suibi, juan* 7, p. 328). See Fang Rixi, "*Rulin waishi* youbang suoben."

19. Wong, *Wu Ching-tzu*, p. 128.

conscience have left him no time for meals. Although we are told that "every province is plagued by drought or flood, and refugees pack the roads," the emperor, who has completely neglected his duty, wonders why his age has not yet achieved the glories of the Three Dynasties. It follows that the memorial ceremony could be nothing more than an empty political performance, and that the posthumous examination roster is a token gesture. Perhaps more important is the somber irony that this final chapter suggests: even in death, the literati characters cannot escape the civil service examination system that has dominated (and ruined) their lives.[20]

This ironic approach suggests a way of integrating Chapter 56 into the overall design of *Rulin waishi*. But since the chapter is an essential part in the framework of the novel, its ironic stance should not prevent the voices it represents from signifying directly. What we see in the chapter cannot be dealt with merely at the level of representation; in official memorials, elegiac addresses, and ritual prayers we hear the echoes of Wang Mian's (and hence the narrator's) lamentations on the fate of the literati, as well as their critique of the civil service examinations. In fact, in its encounter with the literati (after their death, thus in their absence), the court does make concessions on two major fronts, at least in words. First, in Shan Yangyan's (a pun on "good at remonstration") memorial and Liu Jinxian's ("recommending worthies") panegyric, the two court officials admit the limits, if not the failure, of the oppressive system of the civil service examinations. Within the limited space of two paragraphs they use the term "status" (*zige*) four times: too many men of talent, they claim, failed the examinations and have since been suppressed due to the restrictions of status (*xianzhi yu zige* or *zige kunren*) imposed by the official system. Second, when reflecting upon his possible negligence of duty, the Wanli emperor writes:

In order to advance to the time of prosperity, the first step to take is to recommend and employ men of talent. In the past when Duke Mu of the Qin failed to practice *The Rites of Zhou* (*Zhou li*), a poet criticized him. This was why the poem "Reed" (in the *Book of Odes*) was composed. Nowadays are there not some worthy and wise men who remain in inferior and obscure positions? Otherwise, why has our age not achieved the prosperity of the Three Dynasties? (*R.* 752)

His admission of the court's failure to promote men of virtue to help establish the Confucian rituals and institutions signifies a belated official recogni-

---

20. He Manzi, *Lun "Rulin waishi,"* pp. 75–77.

tion of the literati's practice in the Taibo ceremony in Nanjing.[21] His emphasis on ritual is echoed in the panegyric presented in the ceremony in the Ministry of Rites. Representing the court's attempt to recognize the neglected, marginalized literati and their moral stances, Chapter 56 provides Wu Jingzi with an imagined occasion for negotiating with the court in search of a common ground upon which to settle historical issues. Needless to say, such a negotiation between court and literati cannot avoid conflict and irony. The way in which the court ceremony is represented is an excellent illustration of narrative ritual. What we see in Chapter 56 is not the performance of the ceremony but ritualistic discourse—pure verbal articulation that is entirely absent from the account of the Taibo ceremony in Chapter 37. By the same token, the court officials' critique of the civil service examination system for its reinforcement of the status quo is at best self-defeating. For they propose to reward the neglected, marginalized literati ritualists with official titles and degrees and absorb them into the very examination system that they themselves have explicitly criticized.

The court officials' critique echoes Wu Shu's comments in Chapter 40, in which he attributes Xiao Yunxian's failure to register his name in the *zhengshi* to his low status (*xianyu zige*). Wu Shu's reservations with regard to

---

21. It is noteworthy that the Wanli emperor's mention of Duke Mu of Qin's neglect of the *Rites of Zhou* seems to highlight one of the anecdotes in several versions of Wang Mian's biography. In "The Biography of Wang Mian," Song Lian of the Ming dynasty wrote that Wang Mian "once wrote a book of one *juan* on the model of the *Rites of Zhou*. He carried it with him wherever he went and whatever he did, and never allowed others to read it. In the dead of night he would read it aloud by lamplight, and then with his hands on the book he would sigh: 'If I should live a while longer and by chance meet an enlightened ruler, with this book it would not be difficult to accomplish what Yi Yin and Lü Shang did'" (Song Lian, "Wang Mian zhuan," in Li Hanqiu, ed., "*Rulin waishi*" *yanjiu ziliao*, pp. 164–65). The episode is also related in Huang Zongxi's (1610–95) preface to his *Waiting for the Dawn* (*Mingyi daifang lu*), with the following comments: "He [Wang Mian] died without having had an opportunity to try it out. I have not seen his book and cannot tell whether or not his ideas might have brought peace and order. But since the cycle of disorder has still not come to an end, how could an era of prosperity have been brought about?" (Huang Zongxi, *Mingyi daifang lu*, p. 1; trans. from Wm. Theodore de Bary, *Waiting for the Dawn—A Plan for the Prince: Huang Tsunghsi's "Ming-i tai-fang lu"* [New York: Columbia University Press, 1993], p. 90). Although the episode is found in many versions of Wang Mian's biography (including the one in the *Ming History*), it is omitted from the introductory chapter of *Rulin waishi* despite the novel's focus on Confucian rituals and institutions. But what is missing from this chapter seems to emerge later in the novel and thus contributes to the formation of the larger matrix of discourse on Confucian ritual in *Rulin waishi*.

the *zhengshi* not only reinforce the novel's repudiation of official institutions, especially the civil service examinations, but also highlight its own nature and status as an informal, unofficial, private history.

But why does *Rulin waishi*, which claims a peripheral position for itself, have to make a symbolic move toward the center in Chapter 56? Why does Wu Jingzi have to resort to the authority of the court in the final judgment of his literati characters? His appeal to that authority is further complicated by the fact that in the middle part of the novel (Chapters 31 through 37) Wu conjured up a binary structure of Beijing and Nanjing, the center and the local, and defined the literati community in Nanjing by its rejection of empty rhetoric and its commitment to ritualistic practice. Answering the above questions requires tackling the larger issues at stake in *Rulin waishi*.

In Part I, I show how the ritual project represented in Chapter 37 is subject to the test of time as well as to complex social circumstances. Its critical stance is in the end reduced to the status of a utopia or hope, a token protest raised in the name of independent intellectuals. In other passages, the ascetic ritual degenerates into the antithesis of its goal and becomes only an alternative way of achieving control over mundane and symbolic resources. Instead of providing the novel with an ultimate source of moral authority, it is eventually incorporated into the central, official narrative.

This thematic dilemma is coupled with a narrative one. If Wu Jingzi was eager to replace discourse with ritual, what was his relationship to the narrativity or textuality of his own work? It could well be that Wu conceived of his narrative as a means of casting suspicion on the efficacy of Confucian rhetoric. But unless he considered his own work practice rather than discourse, he must have recognized the contradictions in his account of the ritual. In fact, despite his reservations about discourse, all he offered in its place in Chapter 37 is another type of discourse—a piece of a written program for the Taibo ceremony that Wang Yuhui discovers on the wall of the temple. If *Rulin waishi* makes a strategic move to dismantle the conventional paradigm of novelistic and historical narrative, it is unable to build a true alternative. This is the issue I shall explore in Part IV.

PART II

Conclusion

Rulin waishi ends with the sacrifice and the panegyric dedicated to the deceased literati, dated the year *bingchen* of the Wanli reign (1616). Xianzhai Laoren composed his preface to *Rulin waishi* in a *bingchen* year, two 60-year cycles later, in 1736; the correspondence between the two dates may not be a coincidence. Some scholars argue that 1736 is also the year that Wu Jingzi started to write the novel, and that the date of the preface is of some significance for Wu Jingzi and the novel alike. Equally important to Wu Jingzi is that in 1736 the Qianlong emperor held the *boxue hongci* examination in hopes of winning the support of the literati. Wu sat the primary sessions of this special examination but did not follow through for some reason. We may thus tentatively argue that Wu Jingzi's account of the official posthumous rewards of the literati registers his ambivalence toward the court and official recognition and an unsettled psychological struggle between desire and resignation.

It is fitting to recall once more that Wu Jingzi modeled his literati heroes on his friends and himself and that he based his narrative of the Nanjing literati circle, to a certain extent, on his own observation and experience. During the late 1740s or early 1750s, as he was writing the last part of the novel, he projected his self-representation into the most undesirable part of the past, the years of the ultimate decline of the Ming. At the same time, he imagined a belated, posthumous official recognition of his characters. In the end, the actual time (in which Wu composed his novel) and the imagined time (in which he negotiated between the past and the future or rather, projected the future back into the past) are interwoven into such an intricate whole that no one, not even Wu himself, it would seem, can escape the ultimate irony that is history.

PART III

Narrative and Cultural Transformation

The vernacular novel is a hybrid genre of dubious origin. In its early stages, it was inextricably linked to official historiography. So often did it draw on the *zhengshi* narrative that it became, in a way, that genre's extension and variation in the popular imagination. But folk literature also left an abiding imprint on the novel; its use of the vernacular, the inclusion of folk wisdom, and its popular appeal relegated it to a lower status, as shown by such common appellations as *yeshi*, *baishi*, and *waishi*. So named, *Rulin waishi* stakes a claim to this dubious legacy. It eschews folklore and makes no effort to appeal to the general reading public, but by firmly anchoring the text as a *waishi*, Wu Jingzi secured a vantage point from which to scrutinize texts, motifs, and modes of expression incorporated into the tradition of the vernacular novel from various sources, including historiography. Such scrutiny helps to define *Rulin waishi*'s vernacular narrative as a reflexive medium; it questions the validity of existing modes of representation and forgoes narrative practice that would reproduce a textual model of the valorized past. *Rulin waishi* is thereby located not merely outside official history but also beyond the lineage of the vernacular novel.

To adequately measure *Rulin waishi*'s narrative innovations, we must consider the long, complex process of transformation the vernacular novel underwent after its appearance in print form during the late fifteenth century.[1] The early vernacular novel is characterized by two traits. First, it combines history and fantasy in recounting the cycle of dynasties, military affairs, historical adventures, and religious journeys, with chronology and biography as its main organizing principles. Second, it frames its narrative with a simulated rhetoric of storytelling presumably derived from the oral tradition of urban entertainment and assures a consensus between the narrator and the reader through the illusion of face-to-face verbal communication.[2] Neither the narrator nor the audience is specified or personalized: the narrator, who speaks in the storyteller's anonymous, collective voice, embodies the consciousness of the imagined community, of which his nonspecific reader is also a part.[3]

The literati played a crucial role in the formation of the vernacular novel as a literary form, but their participation also engendered a series of changes. For them, the question was how to accommodate the conventions of this form in addressing their own concerns and consciousness. Literati editors often injected their own sensibilities, tastes, and idiosyncrasies into preexisting texts or oral narratives to produce what have become the received texts of vernacular novels;[4] they also engaged in a negotiation between offi-

---

1. The earliest extant work that can be called a "novel" is *San'guozhi tongsu yanyi* (A popular explication of *The History of the Three Kingdoms*), with two prefaces respectively dated 1494 and 1522. Although it bears significant resemblances to the earlier *pinghua* editions of the same story (published in the fourteenth century), it has more in common with what would later be called *zhanghui xiaoshuo* (fiction in sections and chapters).

2. My account of the vernacular novels does not include the fourteenth-century *pinghua* of Chinese history, for the extant *pinghua* works, with a few exceptions, show no substantial similarities with the *zhanghui xiaoshuo* of the subsequent periods in terms of language style, narrative mode, and structure. For a comprehensive study of the fourteenth-century *pinghua*, see Idema, "Some Remarks and Speculations Concerning P'ing-Hua."

3. The vernacular novel is not alone in this regard; it shares the same mode of narrative with the vernacular story. The formulaic rhetoric of storytelling can be traced to Tang dynasty (618–907) vernacular narrative texts discovered in the Dunhuang caves, especially the genre called *hua* or *huaben*, as, for example, in "Lushan Yuangong hua" and "Han Qinhu huaben." The narrators in these texts adopted storytelling rhetoric, which was elaborated in late Ming vernacular stories—citing common sayings in verse to support their points and posing questions to their audience or from the audience's perspective.

4. Plaks argues that each of the four major novels of the Ming dynasty (*The Romance of the Three Kingdoms*, *The Journey to the West*, *Water Margin*, and *Jin Ping Mei*) "represents not just the most elaborate reworking of the respective narrative traditions, but actually a thoroughgoing process of revision of these materials, one governed primarily by ironic treatment of the prior sources and popular images" (see *The Four Masterworks of the Ming Novel*, 1987, p. x).

cial ideology and popular demands, given the dual origins of the vernacular novel in historiography and folk literature. Closely related to this effort is the tradition of *pingdian* or commentary, which dates to the last decades of the sixteenth century and flourished during the seventeenth century. Jin Shengtan (1608–61), for instance, was known for, among other things, his commentary edition of *Water Margin*. Assuming the dual role of commentator and editor, he projected his own vision of the vernacular novel by radically remolding earlier versions of *Water Margin* (although he credited his changes to the "original" author); he offered an intensive, close reading of the novel by employing methods hitherto applied mainly to elite genres and formal writing. His commentary edition of *Water Margin* subsequently became a model for imitation.[5]

In the last decades of the sixteenth century, the literati began to produce their own novels. Unlike almost all earlier novels, which developed from the repertoire of professional storytellers, *Jin Ping Mei cihua* offered a comprehensive account of Merchant Ximen's household, a private sphere never before rendered in publicly performed literature.[6] Exploring a new territory for literary representation, *Jin Ping Mei cihua* is acutely aware of its divergence from the established form of the vernacular novel. It opens with Wu Song, a larger-than-life hero from *Water Margin*, but places him in a prosaic world of daily chores that is alien and even hostile, thereby beginning a gradual deviation from its sources that will ultimately highlight the contrast with its acknowledged model. Also unlike *Water Margin*, *Jin Ping Mei cihua* is a highly incorporative, quasi-encyclopedic narrative. Packed into it is an extremely broad range of texts and genres, such as jokes, popular songs, comic skits, and short stories, all made available to a wider audience than ever before because of the contemporary boom in commercial publishing. The novelist devised a subtle and often ironic reading of these borrowed texts by appropriating them for a variety of occasions, and thus established this novel not merely as a hybrid genre but also as a highly reflexive form of writing.

After the fall of the Ming in 1644, *Jin Ping Mei cihua* and other major Ming dynasty novels were often reinterpreted and rewritten in the form of sequels (*xushu*), so often that the second half of the seventeenth century can

---

5. For Jin Shengtan's commentary edition of *Shuihu zhuan* (preface dated 1641 and published in 1644), see *Jin Shengtan quanji*, vols. 1 and 2.

6. *Jin Ping Mei cihua* began to be circulated among elite readers in manuscript form around 1595; it was probably first printed in 1617.

be called the age of sequels.[7] Although they differed in style and varied in quality, these sequels had a common mission: they took what they inherited from the earlier novels—subject matter, characters, forms, and narrative schemata—as raw material; re-evaluated and reshaped them; and subjected them to other possible developments. In these works, we see an unfolding process of systematic undermining or iconoclastic "decoding" of the traditional paradigms of the vernacular novel and related genres. Of course, not all the sequels shared this iconoclastic tendency, and even those that did often differed in degree, if not in kind. But this trend does loom large in the vernacular stories of the time as well. The stories by Aina and Li Yu, for instance, often set out to overturn stereotypes, undercut normative values, and debunk historical heroes; they are comic and sometimes blasphemous, and their targets are not confined to those of the vernacular tradition of fiction. In an age of political crises and intellectual divisions, these parodic narratives represented a major rupture in the symbolic world of literary representation.

With unmistakable moralizing zeal, *Rulin waishi* takes the vernacular novel in a new direction, but its parodic edge is reminiscent of the iconoclastic

---

7. For instance, Ding Yaokang, a Ming loyalist, composed *Xu Jing Ping Mei* (A sequel to the *Jin Ping Mei*; preface dated 1660); it was banned by the Qing authorities, but an abridged version soon appeared under the title *Ge lian huaying*. *The Journey to the West* was subject to rewriting in several works. Dong Yue wrote *Xiyou bu* (A supplement to *The Journey to the West*) during the 1640s. Other sequels to *The Journey to the West* written and published during the second half of the seventeenth century and the first decade of the eighteenth century include *Hou Xiyou ji* (commentary by Tianhua caizi). Of the sequels to *Water Margin* composed during the same period, Chen Chen's *Shuihu houzhuan* (1664 edition) is known for its political agenda and artistic achievement. It initiated a sequence of the sequels to *Water Margin*, including *Hou Shuihu zhuan* (preface by Tianhua cang). Historical romance has its own lineage and network of mutual borrowings and correspondences. One such work of the same period was, for instance, called *Hou San'guozhi yanyi* (A sequel to the *Romance of the Three Kingdoms*), and *San'guozhi houzhuan* (or *Xu San'guozhi*) can be dated to the early seventeenth century (preface dated 1609). Not all the sequels produced during this period bear the term *xu* or *hou* in their title; nor is the literary practice of rewriting canonical stories of the past confined to the genre of the novel (*zhanghui xiaoshuo*). Aina Jushi's *Doupeng xianhua* represents a consistent effort to debunk historical personages; see Patrick Hanan, *The Chinese Vernacular Story*, pp. 192–95. For the studies of late Ming and early Qing sequels, see Widmer, *The Margins of Utopia*; Hegel, *The Novel in Seventeenth-Century China*, pp. 141–66; Brandauer, *Tung Yüeh* and "The Significance of a Dog's Tail"; T. A. Hsia, "New Perspectives on Two Ming Novels"; Fu Shiyi, "*Xiyou bu*" *chutan*; Mark Andres, "Ch'an Symbolism in *Hsi-yu pu*"; and Liu Xiaolian, "A Journey of the Mind."

narratives of the seventeenth century. This part investigates the origins of *Rulin waishi*'s art and insights by examining its critical reflection on the ideas, values, motifs, and the narrative schemata of storytelling that constituted the tradition of the vernacular novel. I hope to show that although *Rulin waishi* follows the trends set by its seventeenth-century predecessors, it represents a culmination of their experiments and a form unprecedented in fiction writing.

CHAPTER 6

Rulin waishi,

the Vernacular Novel,

and the Narrator

Rulin waishi's narrative innovations are manifest in, among other ways, its structure. Rather than adopting the conventional plot-oriented structure, the novel is composed of loosely connected and even disjunctive episodes. No major characters are present throughout; the transition from one chapter to the next often introduces a new character, who is on his way somewhere else and will be replaced by those he encounters in the following chapter. This structure has long been a subject of controversy among modern Chinese critics. Shuen-fu Lin has dated criticism of *Rulin waishi*'s lack of a structural framework to the late Qing and early Republican period, when Chinese writers and critics were increasingly exposed to the influence of western fiction and literary concepts. Hu Shi, for instance, wrote in 1922 that *Rulin waishi* "is entirely a series of short stories lumped together. When stories are strung together, a book can become endlessly long. This form is the easiest to learn and is also the most convenient to use. Therefore, this fictional form which is made up of short stories without an overall structure has become the general pattern for recent satirical novels."[1]

---

1. Hu Shi, "Wushi nian lai Zhongguo zhi wenxue," in idem, *Hu Shi gudian wenxue yanjiu lunji*, p. 140. In a critical response to Hu Shi's view, Shuen-fu Lin argues that traditional Chinese cosmology had an impact on various aspects of Chinese culture, including the narrative structure of the vernacular novel: "Instead of arranging events in a linear causal chain, the Chinese view them as forming one vast, interweaving, 'reticular' relationship, or process. Events are no longer described as causally linked: they are simply connected or juxtaposed

Hu Shi's description is not, however, entirely accurate. As noted in Chapter 5, many critics have pointed out that *Rulin waishi* adopts the inherited frame of the vernacular novel as exemplified by *Water Margin*, especially Jin Shengtan's commentary edition. It begins with a standard prologue (*xiezi*), a term borrowed from that version of *Water Margin*.[2] The main body of the novel is set apart in time and space from the incidents recounted in the prologue and reaches its culmination two-thirds of the way through, in Chapter 37. As is often the case in a vernacular novel, the culmination is a ceremony or other public event, involving a formal style of writing (such as prayers, announcements, and occasionally formulaic depictions of the ceremony) and a listing of those who take part. *Rulin waishi* adheres to this model by presenting the Taibo ceremony, the central event of the novel, in the form of the Confucian ritual manual (*yizhu*), although no earlier novels used *yizhu* this way, and following it with a complete list of the participants (*zhishi*). The last chapter presents two lists; the first contains the names of the main characters of the novel, and the second ranks 55 of them according to their virtue and rewards them with the degree of palace graduate (*jinshi*) and official titles—which are again accompanied by such formal writings as imperial edicts and ceremonial prayers.

At a micro-level, *Rulin waishi* also follows the conventions for linking different parts and forming contrasts and correspondences among the characters. One such device is to create a pair of characters in consecutive chapters who share the same personal name (Zhou Jin and Fan Jin in Chapters 2 through 4) or resemble each other in behavior (Kuang Chaoren in Chapters 15 through 20 and Niu Pulang in Chapters 21 through 24; to some extent, Zhou Jin and Fan Jin also fall into this category).[3] Wu Jingzi's use of two Jins (*jin* means "to enter," "to bring in," or "to present") to begin the main part of the novel is reminiscent of the similar function of Wang Jin and Shi Jin in *Water Margin*.[4] The way in which *Rulin waishi* links its characters to one another also has precedents in *Water Margin*. Andrew Plaks has likened

---

side by side as if by coincidence. Thus the temporal sequence of the cause-and-effect relationship is instead spatialized into a dynamic pattern of juxtaposed concrete 'incidents'" ("Ritual and Narrative Structure in *Ju-lin Wai-shih*," p. 250).

2. See Rolston, *Traditional Chinese Fiction and Fiction Commentary*, pp. 246–49, 319.

3. These methods have often been highlighted in traditional commentary on *Rulin waishi*. For modern studies of these devices, see Král, "Several Artistic Methods in the Classic Chinese Novel *Ju-lin wai-shih*."

4. See Rolston, *Traditional Chinese Fiction and Fiction Criticism*, p. 321.

the shifts in narrative focus in the part of that novel retained by Jin Shengtan to the action of a "billiard ball," as one member of the group of the 108 heroes' encounters another of the same group.[5] This technique is carried to an extreme in *Rulin waishi*, where the shifts occur much more rapidly.

However, *Rulin waishi*'s use of the inherited frame and conventional organizing devices of the vernacular novel should not blind us to its structural innovations. For one thing, *Rulin waishi* breaks with the grand narrative of heroic adventures and historical romance and adopts instead an episodic mode as it moves to represent a world of daily experiences caught in endless ironies. More than a century and a half before, *Jin Ping Mei cihua* had developed narrative techniques capable of capturing the patterns and rhythms of the everyday lives of ordinary men and women.[6] However, *Jin Ping Mei cihua* did not adopt the same organizing principles as *Rulin waishi*. Instead of swift shifts of focus both in space and from character to character, as in *Rulin waishi*, it concentrates on Ximen Qing, his wives, and his sworn brothers, with his household in Qinghe as the central stage for their actions.

Although *Rulin waishi* undeniably follows *Water Margin* in its account of the characters' encounters with one another on the road, the differences between the two novels are just as obvious. In its first half, *Water Margin* spends five to ten chapters on each of its major heroes, such as Lu Zhishen, Lin Chong, Wu Song, Song Jiang, and Li Kui, and then brings them together in Liangshan, the geographical and thematic center of the novel. In contrast, most of the characters in *Rulin waishi* make no more than a transitory appearance and, with few exceptions, never return. Nor is the narrative anchored in a specific geographic locus. Nanjing seems to serve as such a center in Chapters 31 through 37, with characters converging in the Taibo temple for the ceremonial occasion, but this center does not hold. As the ritual participants disperse, the temple becomes not a site for action but an

---

5. Plaks, *The Four Masterworks of the Ming Novel*, p. 309.

6. It is perhaps no surprise that the publication of *Jin Ping Mei cihua* was followed by efforts to contain the novel and make it more coherent and less monstrous than it is. The efforts are exemplified in the Chongzhen edition of *Jin Ping Mei*, which streamlines *Jin Ping Mei cihua* by reducing the popular songs and other quoted texts, restructuring the beginning of the novel, and diminishing what its editor sees as digressions. They are also reflected in Zhang Zhupo's (1670–98) comments on the Chongzhen edition of *Jin Ping Mei*, which see the novel as a carefully structured whole, within which everything is interconnected or correspondent to everything else and, therefore, no single stroke of narrative is made arbitrarily. For Zhang's comments, see Huang Lin, ed., *"Jin Ping Mei" ziliao huibian*, p. 68.

illusory object for nostalgic longing and lamentation. Later characters who visit Nanjing find a deserted temple, thriving brothels, and scandalous literati gatherings: the ritual center is hopelessly contaminated and destroyed. This in part explains late Qing novelists' fascination with *Rulin waishi* (as observed by Hu Shi): its episodic structure, which permits a broad coverage of various and often unrelated social circles and locales, fueled their *fin-de-siècle* imagination with the vision of a shattered world that has lost its center of gravity and cohesion.

Such a work can hardly fit within the pre-established frame of the conventional novel. In *Rulin waishi*, this inherited structure seems at odds with the main body of the novel. The internal tension is compounded by the incompatible narrative schemes and the textual sources associated with them: formal writing, an elevated tone, prophecy, an authoritative voice and judgment, and a sense of order and unity clash with narrative perspectivism—a threat to authoritative narrative in whatever form it takes. In *Rulin waishi*, narrative perspectivism is embedded in the episodic scheme. As shown in Chapter 4, Wu Jingzi's incorporation of widely circulated jokes and anecdotes into *Rulin waishi* often creates the illuminating moment that exposes literati hypocrisy and undercuts the unfolding of what would otherwise be Confucian master plots (for example, in the biographies of filial sons).

The vernacular short story, which flourished during the seventeenth century, had just as much influence on the making of *Rulin waishi*. Unlike their European counterparts, the Chinese vernacular novel and short story are, by and large, homogeneous forms with the same origin and narrative model.[7] To explain their development, we must consider their mutual borrowings and influences. Hu Shi is right that *Rulin waishi* is indebted to the short story for its structural scheme, but he sees this in a negative light because the European novel is his normative model. Moreover, he refers to the short story in general and thus fails to specify its development during any specific era and its effects on *Rulin waishi* in particular.

The period from 1620—when Feng Menglong published the first of his three collections of the vernacular *Stories Old and New* (*Gujin xiaoshuo*)—to the 1680s were the culmination of the vernacular story in the late imperial

---

7. In European literature, the novel and the short story are not merely different in kind but also inherently at odds with each other: the novel derives from history and travel records; the short story from the *conte* or anecdote. For more discussion of this issue, see Hanan, *The Chinese Vernacular Story*, p. 22.

era. This period was known both for the quantity and quality of the short stories it produced and for their innovations in exploring a variety of subject matter, forms, and styles; they are more sensitive than the novels and dramas of that period in capturing the rapid changes in the mood and trends of the contemporary culture. Their parody of stereotypes and common assumptions, their ironic voice and tone in accounts of literati inadequacy, hypocrisy, and moral corruption, and their relentless experiments with narrative forms, as well as the prevalence of what might be called novellas and the various ways of linking short episodes to form a longer narrative piece, suggest a new range of possibilities for the vernacular novel, which as a genre was gradually gaining momentum during what was otherwise a period of relative literary inactivity.[8] It was not until the 1650s and 1660s that the vernacular novel reasserted its vitality in the form of the sequel and other forms, which either radically rewrote previous works or opened them to new interpretations;[9] some were obviously driven by the same parodic trend that informed contemporary short stories and thus paved the way for the new kind of novel produced in the following century. However, when *Rulin waishi* appeared in the mid-eighteenth century, the vernacular story as a genre seemed to have run its course.[10] This was when the novel took over and absorbed the energy

---

8. This period produced few novels of great literary merit or influence, but it occupied an important position in the history of fiction criticism, for it was during this period that the annotated and commentary editions of the earlier novels mushroomed, following Jin Shengtan's 1644 edition of *Water Margin*. Although new novels continued to emerge during the first four decades of the seventeenth century, they largely fell into the categories of historical romance and erotic fiction (intertwined with romance—scholar-and-beauty fiction—written in the semi-classical and vernacular languages): the romances are, with few exceptions, conventional and often mediocre, and erotic tales are, in most cases, of little literary value and hardly innovative. The last decades of the Ming witnessed the rise of the vernacular novels concerning the current political and military affairs. These works were often caught between their interest in ongoing, open-ended occurrences and their inherited framework of historical romance; see Chen Dadao, "Mingmo Qingchu shishi xiaoshuo de tese."

9. Dong Yue's *Xiyou bu* (1640s) was perhaps the earliest of this kind of *xushu*; see Liu Fu, "Xiyou bu zuozhe Dong Ruoyu zhuan."

10. The fall of the Ming in 1644 only temporarily interrupted the commercial publication of the vernacular fiction. Several authors (including Li Yu) remained prolific in producing vernacular stories, and commercial publishers were still interested in the collections of short stories during the early decades of the Qing dynasty. However, the creative force that drove the late Ming production of the vernacular story gradually waned. Some short-story collections published during this period were random assemblages of texts from earlier sources, as shown in *Ba duan jin* (Zuiyuelou edition). Commercial publishing seemed to focus more on

of vernacular stories into a more ambitious and all-encompassing form of literary representation.

Critics have long recognized the impact of the vernacular stories of the seventeenth century on *Rulin waishi*'s negative portrayal of the literati and the civil service examination.[11] *Rulin waishi* also shares their ironic vein, despite its differences in emphasis, tone, and narrative style—a subject to which I shall soon return. For now, it is important to point out that these short stories and novellas influenced *Rulin waishi* in many other ways as well. In numerous collections of vernacular fiction of the time, we see a common trend of constituting a single narrative by linking two or more chapters (*hui*);[12] even unrelated, independent stories are often numbered as consecutive chapters, as if they formed a continuous narrative.[13] Sometimes, framing devices are used: the first and last stories of the collection discuss the concepts running throughout the collection;[14] in other cases, the stories are constructed around the same symbol or motif, as, for example, in Li Yu's *The Twelve Towers* (*Shi'er lou*).[15] Putting these episodes or stories together in a single volume does not result, even approximately, in a novel, but it certainly would require little additional effort to make a longer, continuous narrative out of

---

longer narrative forms, such as the historical romance, scholar-and-beauty fiction, and erotic novels and novellas. This trend became conspicuous in the eighteenth century, when fewer new collections of vernacular stories were published, and literati authors seemed to have lost interest in this genre.

11. For instance, *juan* 3 of *Yuanyang zhen* features Bu Heng as a false *mingshi*, whose claims to be talented in both poetry and civil examination essays lead only to humiliations. For more information regarding this subject, see Yenna Wu, *Ameliorative Satire and the Seventeenth-Century Chinese Novel*, pp. 30–32.

12. For instance, *Guzhang jue chen* (preface dated 1631) consists of four stories (under the general rubrics wind, flowers, snow, and moon), each consisting of ten chapters.

13. *Zui xing shi*, an early Qing collection of vernacular stories by Donglu gukuang sheng, has 15 chapters (*hui*); the heading of each chapter is written in a parallel couplet, as normally is the case in a vernacular novel. But the story given in each of these chapters is self-contained and unrelated to those in the previous or the following chapter.

14. *Xihu jiahua* (preface dated 1673) features sixteen independent stories about West Lake in Hangzhou. The first gives an account of Ge Hong, a Taoist recluse of the Jin dynasty, and the last is a story about Shen Zuhong, a Ming dynasty scholar who gave up his career and became a Buddhist. The two chapters carry a heavy dose of discourse on Taoism and Buddhism as a way of elucidating the common theme of the collection.

15. In *Idle Talk Under the Bean Arbor* (*Doupeng xianhua*), a late Ming or early Qing collection by Aina, twelve meetings under the bean arbor form a frame story. Although the twelve stories (*ze*) told in these meetings are disconnected, each of them is a response to the discussions and debates that follow the previous one.

them, whatever it might be called. As shown in *Jin Ping Mei cihua* more than a century and a half before, the vernacular novel kept renewing its creative energy by incorporating all existing narrative devices, motifs, and modes of writing. Emerging after the peak of the vernacular stories, *Rulin waishi* availed itself of all they had to offer. Needless to say, it presents a much more complex structure; contrary to Hu Shi, it is more than a simple accumulation of individual stories. More often than not, however, it does allow individual characters to carry the narrative from one section to the next, and it is thus more susceptible than most earlier novels to the principles by which short stories are organized. Moreover, its ability to combine different narrative tones (such as the ironic and the lyrical), its swift shifts from one character to another, and its way of connecting otherwise unrelated episodes suggest a new sort of dynamics at work.

Another way of measuring *Rulin waishi*'s narrative originality is to examine its departure from what Patrick Hanan describes as the "simulated context of storytelling."[16] In the case of premodern Chinese vernacular fiction, almost all the novelists imitate the voice of the professional storyteller, even though they and their readers are far removed from the entertainment center of the marketplace. Although this simulated rhetoric of face-to-face storytelling is by no means confined to Chinese literature, its prevalence and longevity in Chinese fiction are certainly unparalleled.[17] Obviously, this mode consists of more than inherited narrative devices and formulas; it is closely bound up with the common values, assumptions, and attitudes that are embodied by the storyteller's anonymous, collective voice in addressing the assumed audience, which is equally undifferentiated.

This does not mean that all vernacular fictions that use the simulated rhetoric of storytelling necessarily fall into the category I call "authoritative narrative." The novelists of the Ming and Qing era became increasingly interested in experimenting with the model of storytelling; some of them even went so far as to play with it or diminish the simulated voice of the story-

---

16. Hanan, *The Chinese Vernacular Story*, pp. 20–22.

17. In contrast with Chinese vernacular fiction, which persistently adheres to the model of oral fiction, in European fiction, "the gestures and signals of the storyteller (perpetuated in the English novel well beyond 1857)" and "the coordinates of a face-to-face storytelling institution," according to Fredric Jameson, are effectively disintegrated "by the printed book and even more definitively by the commodification of literature and culture" (*The Political Unconscious*, pp. 154–55). See also Rolston, *Traditional Chinese Fiction and Fiction Commentary*, pp. 231–32.

teller as they delve further into the literati world and explore more delicate human affairs than any authoritative voice can cope with. *Rulin waishi* occupies an important place in this process of narrative innovation, and my reading of the novel in this part begins with a careful elaboration of the significance of its deviation from this simulated mode.

Many critics have agreed that the emergence of *Rulin waishi* in the mid-eighteenth century marked a new stage in the history of the Chinese novel, but what this means has yet to be adequately explained. C. T. Hsia is correct in describing Wu Jingzi as a great innovator of narrative rhetoric. Unlike most previous and contemporary novels, which are still "obliged to adopt the rhetorical conventions of professional storyteller," "*Rulin waishi*," Hsia asserts,

is far less dependent on these conventions. Its author, Wu Jingzi, to be sure, still observes the minimal formal requirements: each of his fifty-five chapters employs an antithetical couplet for its heading and nearly every one begins with the phrase *huashuo* (It is now told) and ends with four lines of verse followed by the formula, "To know what followed, you must listen to the next round of recital." But songs and verse descriptions are conspicuously absent. For the first time in a major vernacular novel, descriptive passages are completely integrated with the narrative text because they are now recorded in colloquial prose. In his avoidance of the standard poetic vocabulary, the author has actually relied on his own observations of persons and places.

In addition to the changes in form, the absence of the traditional narrator is accompanied by an innovation: "the technique of character portrayal":

An earlier novelist usually assumes the role of a puppet-master who introduces his marionettes one by one and tells us who they are and what they are about. Wu Jingzi, however, no longer bluntly guides the reader but places them in a dramatized scene. As the actors in that scene go about their business and talk about sundry matters, they gradually reveal themselves.

Hsia concludes: "For a novelist today, the advantages of indirect dramatic presentation are of course taken for granted, but Wu Jingzi was certainly the first Chinese to make regular, deliberate use of this method."[18]

However, since the characters in *Rulin waishi* are not adequately or explicitly guided by the narrator, the question of narrative authority arises: "Whose words," C. T. Hsia asks, "can be trusted when contradictory reports

---

18. See C. T. Hsia, *The Classic Chinese Novel*, pp. 204, 215, 218.

of a character's behavior are given?"[19] Instead of pursuing an answer to this question, however, Hsia brackets it and suspends the search for an explanation. Timothy Wong notices the ambiguities Hsia and other scholars have encountered in interpreting the novel, but he tends to explain them away technically and historically: "In dramatizing his message, the narrator subtly manipulates the reader, allowing him to make his own discoveries while maintaining the illusion that whatever conclusions he comes to are indeed his own." However, "given the unfamiliarity of most modern readers with the conditions satirized, these conclusions are not always obvious, and conflicting judgments are inevitable." Although he admits all the difficulties of interpreting this novel, he nevertheless asserts: "If *Rulin waishi* is true satire, its moral concern should be clear and well-indicated throughout; it should not need to be salvaged by a great deal of rationalization."[20]

In *Traditional Chinese Fiction and Fiction Commentary*, David Rolston offers two observations on *Rulin waishi* relevant to this issue: first, *Rulin waishi* "represents perhaps the most extreme development of the suppression of the traditional narrator." Second, extant Qing dynasty commentaries on *Rulin waishi* "show that premodern readers did not have the problems with this text that modern readers have had."[21] As I shall show, Rolston's second observation needs to be modified. For now, however, it suffices to point out that premodern commentators on fiction were keenly conscious of their own role as guides for readers. Confessing their own confusion in the reading of a given work would contradict the role they were claiming for themselves. The fact that few of them complained about the ambiguities of Ming-Qing fiction does not necessarily mean that all these works can be adequately understood in terms of the established narrative and interpretive modes. The most important question to be raised here is: Was Wu Jingzi's narrative experiment merely a technical innovation, or did it result in fundamental changes in how the novelist conceives and organizes his narrative, the way he perceives and represents the world, and even the assumptions he makes about the readers? An examination of selected episodes from *Rulin waishi* will help answer these questions.

---

19. Ibid., p. 212.
20. Wong, *Wu Ching-Tzu*, pp. 61–62, 107.
21. Rolston, *Traditional Chinese Fiction and Fiction Commentary*, pp. 312–13.

The Longsan Episode

In Chapter 28, the prior of a monastery, celebrating his official appointment, holds a feast in a Buddhist temple with nearly five dozen official guests from the county and city yamens. This splendid show opens, however, with a scandalous scene of cross-dressing, a reversal of gender roles, and a playful appropriation of language in an inappropriate situation. Longsan, "a swarthy man with brown eyes and a bushy mustache," shows up unexpectedly at the feast in "a paper chaplet, a woman's blue cotton tunic, white skirt and large embroidered slippers," with "two chair-bearers standing in the courtyard . . . waiting for their fare." Yet nothing is said to introduce Longsan or explain his relationship to the prior. The narrator's voice falls silent, leaving the actors to represent themselves.

As soon as the stranger [Longsan] caught sight of the prior, he smiled broadly. "I've come early, husband, to see to everything for you on this happy day," he announced. "Will you pay the chair-bearers for me?" (R. 393; S. 314)

In public Longsan calls the prior "husband" and speaks in the way a legitimate wife would. It is obvious that Longsan does not mean what he says. The conversation is a game of words, a play between what is told and what remains untold, and between the words and their contingent, circumstantial references.

"What is it this time, Longsan?" demanded the prior with a frown. "What a spectacle you're making of yourself!" He made haste to pay the bearers. "Come on now, Longsan!" he urged. "Take off those clothes! Do you want to look a figure of fun?"

"How heartless you are, husband!" responded Longsan reproachfully. "You're an official now, yet you haven't given me the gold chaplet and fine scarlet costume an official's wife should wear, so I've made a paper chaplet for myself. Let people laugh if they like. I'm your wife, aren't I? Why should you tell me to take it off?"

"Longsan! This is no time for joking! Even if you were angry with me for not inviting you today, you should have come in a decent manner. Why dress up like this?"

"How can you say such a thing, husband? A quarrel between husband and wife never lasts overnight. How could I be angry with you?"

"I'll admit I was in the wrong," said the prior. "You had a right to be annoyed when I didn't invite you today. But take off those clothes now and sit down to have a drink. Don't pretend to be a loon."

"I'm the one in the wrong," said Longsan. "A wife should stay in the inner chambers preparing refreshments, peeling fruit, and supervising the preparations. Who ever heard of a woman sitting in the hall? Would not other people say there is no distinction of the inner chamber and the outer chamber in your household?" Thereupon he sailed into the bedroom.

"Longsan!" cried the prior, following him in helplessly. "You won't be able to get away with any of your tricks today! And if the *yamen* officials hear of this, it'll look bad for both of us!"

"Don't worry, husband! It is well put in these words of the ancients: 'Officials can't interfere in family disputes.'" While the prior stamped with rage, Longsan sat himself calmly down and called for the novice. "Tell the tea attendant to bring the mistress tea!" he ordered. (R. 393–94; S. 314–15)

In his dialogue with the prior, Longsan persists in using language appropriate to the wife's role he claims for himself. This becomes the prior's nightmare, for it seems to disclose, although in a distorted way, their secret sexual affair. The prior's desperate effort to silence Longsan only reinforces our suspicions. In the middle of the conversation, Longsan deliberately misinterprets the prior's embarrassment. As if unwilling to upset him, he pronounces that as the prior's wife he should stay within the inner chambers rather than show himself in public. This embarrasses the prior even more. As the narrative continues, more characters participate in the dialogue, but their voices either undercut one another or betray themselves.

"Is that Longsan?" said Jin, who recognized him. "You dog! After swindling dozens of *taels* from me in the capital, how dare you show yourself here in this costume? You're obviously up to your old tricks again, you miserable swindler! Take that chaplet and clothes off him!" he ordered his servant-boy. "Then throw him out!"

At that Longsan lost his head, and removed his chaplet and clothes himself. "I'm just here to wait on you, sir," he said humbly.

"Who wants you waiting on him?" roared Jin. "You were trying to cheat the prior here! Later on I don't mind asking him to give you some money to start a business, but if you make any more trouble now, I'll have you sent straight to the yamen!"

When Longsan, all his bluster gone, had thanked Jin Dongya and slunk off, the prior took his guests downstairs, greeted them again, and begged them to be seated. He could not thank Jin enough! (R. 397; S. 316)

Longsan indeed makes a fool of himself. But those who ridicule him lay themselves open to ridicule. Among the prior's guests, it is Jin Dongya who stops the farce; his voice, charged with righteous indignation, reminds us of the appropriate attitude to take toward a swindler. Yet we may find it difficult to join Jin Dongya in condemning Longsan, since he is himself part of the scandal he explicitly reproaches and his fury is suspect from the very beginning. As Longsan unwittingly reveals, Jin was once trapped in the same situation the prior is in, and probably for the same reason. Longsan's farce conjures up concealed scandals and hidden lives. Longsan in disguise is a master of unmasking. His clowning does not allow us to take anyone's words at face value. The discrepancy between assertion and meaning is part of its logic. The very effort to discredit Longsan is subjected to the same logic it openly renounces.

Throughout the entire scene, the narrator does not offer us a privileged and unified viewpoint from which to approach the dialogue. Characters present themselves in conversation, which unfolds without the mediation of the narrator's voice. When Longsan is introduced, the only thing we learn about him comes from the statement of the novice: "That fellow is here again." The report is made, however, not to us but to the prior, who immediately knows who is meant: "Is it that wretch Longsan?" (R. 393; S. 314). Both the novice and the prior are familiar with "that fellow" or "that wretch." The implication is that Longsan has been a frequent and unwelcome visitor. We do not know the purpose of his past visits, but we are told that this time "he is up to even stranger tricks." These two or three sentences allude to many stories about Longsan, but they are neither explained nor confirmed. From the very beginning readers are denied access to the knowledge or information that both the novice and the prior share.

This would perhaps have struck Qing readers as stranger than it does us, since the narrative conventions familiar to them would have led them to expect more assured if not more authoritative guidance. At the end of the passage quoted above, a Qing commentator wrote:

After Longsan is gone, there must be a few more words about who he is and where he is from. I suppose that the author is so afraid that such an introduction would tarnish his narrative that he skips it. Or perhaps the people present at the scene were as smart as we readers and thus are able to catch the meaning of the story, and so they do not even bother to ask.[22]

Indeed, the commentator is correct that in a conventional novel, if the narrator failed to provide an introduction for a character, he would make up for it by offering some concluding remarks about him either directly or indirectly.

---

22. This comment was made by Zhang Wenhu, a late Qing commentator on *Rulin waishi*. See Li Hanqiu, ed., *"Rulin waishi" huijiao huiping ben*, p. 395.

This comment, however naïve it may sound to modern critics, is valuable in reminding us of Qing readers' expectations of the traditional narrative mode. The absence of the narrator left Qing readers with no absolute assurance of interpretation.

Longsan not only oversteps the role of the narrator in his self-representation but also does so by appropriating "common discourse," which is often expressed in the narrator's voice. To explain this point, I shall explicate what I mean by common discourse and discuss its relationship with the narrator's voice in the simulated mode of storytelling.

The Formation of Common Discourse

By "common discourse," I refer to the popular version of Confucian discourse, which is mixed with or complemented by values and wisdom drawn from other sources. My definition emphasizes not the projection of ruling class ideology on commoners but the construction of common values through oral and written discourse open to all.[23] The discourse so defined is collective in nature. It is both imperative and indicative; it provides a stable structure of values to make sense of the world, and in this sense it also participates in the construction of reality.

In the episode under discussion, common discourse is exemplified in the language that Longsan uses. When describing his commitment to his female role, Longsan resorts to phrases often found in popular editions of Confucian texts. "A wife should stay in the inner chambers, preparing refreshments, peeling fruit, and supervising the preparations," Longsan declares. "Who ever heard of a woman sitting in the hall? Would not other people say there is no distinction of the inner chamber and the outer chamber in your household?" His speech echoes the prescriptions for wives to be found in, for instance, *Etiquette and Ritual* (*Yili*) and *The Analects* (*Lunyu*), and, perhaps more relevant, in such popular Confucian texts as *Required Readings* (*Rensheng*

---

23. Raymond Williams's articulation of the difference between Marxist ideology and Gramsci's hegemony provides a frame of reference for my definition of common discourse: in Gramsci's theory: "What is decisive is not only the conscious system of ideas and beliefs [the expression or projection of ruling class interest known as 'ideology' in conventional Marxist political theory], but the whole lived social process as practically organized by specific and dominant meanings and values" (*Marxism and Literature*, p. 109). On the implications of Gramsci's term "hegemony" for the popular culture of late imperial China, see Johnson, "Communication, Class, and Consciousness in Late Imperial China."

bidu shu) and *Analects for Females* (*Nü lunyu*).[24] A brief examination of these popular texts will tell us more about the common discourse and the way it is shaped, transmitted, and transformed.

Because of the spread of print culture and the literati's increasing interest in education, popular editions of Confucian texts came into wide circulation in the Song and afterward.[25] Three primers, *The Trimetrical Classic* (*Sanzi jing*), *The Hundred Names* (*Baijiaxing*), and *The Thousand-Character Classic* (*Qianzi wen*), constituted the Ming and Qing elementary curriculum. A number of variations existed and were complemented by numerous sequels.[26] Many other educational texts were also in circulation. In both verse and prose, they fall into such categories as miscellaneous glossaries (*zazi*), historical anecdotes (*mengqiu*), and collections of ethical maxims, proverbs, and canons of conduct (*gui*). Under the rubric elementary learning (*mengxue*), language textbooks were often combined with morality books (*shanshu*), conduct books, and social handbooks.[27] Along with the development of ele-

---

24. The *Required Readings*, edited by Tang Yixiu of the Qing dynasty, was intended as an instruction book for females. The *Analects for Females*, one of the earliest texts for female education, is attributed to Song Ruozhao of the Tang dynasty. The *Five Traditional Canons* (*Wuzhong yigui*), edited by Chen Hongmou and published in 1740, included both the *Required Readings* and the *Analects for Females* in vol. 6 under the rubric of "The Traditional Rules for the Daughters" (*Jiaonü yigui*). The *Analects for Females* also appeared in the *Four Books for Females* edited by Wang Xiang, a Qing scholar who was known for, among other things, his contribution to the development of "elementary learning" (*mengxue*). For the wife's role in entertaining guests, see Section 10, "Entertaining Guests" ("Daike") of *Analects for Females* in Chen Hongmou, *Wuzhong yigui*, vol. 6, *juan* 2: 9b. See also the *Required Readings* in Chen Hongmou, *Wuzhong yigui*, vol. 6, *juan* 3: 17a.

25. Of all the Song scholars who participated in editing the primers for children and the illiterate in general, Zhu Xi was the most eminent. He not only defined a new Confucian curriculum but also edited a textbook entitled *Elementary Learning* (*Xiaoxue*). *Elementary Learning* includes primarily the speeches of ancient sages, complemented by ethical maxims, historical anecdotes, and poems. For a discussion of Zhu Xi's new Confucian education project, see de Bary, "Chu Hsi's Aims as an Educator."

26. For the texts, including variations and sequels, of these three primers, see Qiao Sang and Song Hong, ed., *Mengxue quanshu*, pp. 1–63. See Zhang Zhigong, *Chuantong yuwen jiaoyu chutan*, for a systematic study of the elementary learning and curriculum in premodern times.

27. What I call "common discourse" is thus a mixture of elements from various sources, including Buddhist concepts of karma and retribution. But these concepts were already absorbed into a set of widely circulated values, and their Buddhist origins had become almost secondary, if not obscure. See Cynthia Brokaw's discussion of the morality books and the ledgers of merit and demerit (*gongguo ge*) in *The Ledgers of Merit and Demerit*. See also Ogawa Yōichi, "Mingdai xiaoshuo yu shanshu."

mentary learning, the second half of the Ming period witnessed the flourishing of publishing enterprises oriented toward popular consumption.[28] It was in this realm of popular cultural production that Confucian discourse became part of a common discourse.

Needless to say, the very process of disseminating Confucian values involved negotiation and compromise. Consensus was reached only when Confucian morality was fused with, or turned into, a consciousness uncritically absorbed as common sense.[29] The composition of the commonsensical Confucian discourse is probably best illustrated in a variety of collections of well-known sayings. In these books, Confucius's words are juxtaposed or mixed with proverbs, ethical maxims, moral or practical advice, and old sayings that convey the sensibilities as well as the wisdom of worldly experience.[30] This is the storehouse of shared cultural attitudes and stereotypes as well as the kind of knowledge that is generally accepted or taken for granted. As a maxim goes, "You will not be well equipped to speak unless you study *The Enlarged Edition of the Comprehensive Collection of Worthies' Words (Zeng Guangxianwen)*; you will not be well equipped to travel unless you study *The Essence of Elementary Learning (Youxue qionglin)*."[31] These texts provided mod-

---

28. As some scholars have noted, publishing culture developed rapidly during the sixteenth and seventeenth centuries. Dorothy Ko describes this development in terms of "the transition from the age of quality printing to that of quantity printing" (*Teachers of the Inner Chambers*, p. 35). See also Ōki Yasushi, "Minmatsu Kōnan ni okeru shuppan bunka no kenkyū"; and Zhang Xiumin, *Zhongguo yinshua shi*, pp. 678–729.

29. Antonio Gramsci's discussion of "common sense" and "good sense" is relevant to the topic in question. The editors' footnote to Gramsci's *Prison Notebooks* provides a concise definition of these terms: "Broadly speaking, 'common sense' means the incoherent set of generally held assumptions and beliefs common to any given society, while 'good sense' means practical empirical common sense in the English sense of the term" (see Gramsci, *Selections from the Prison Notebooks*, p. 323n1). See also Gramsci, *Selections from Cultural Writings*, pp. 189, 417–18.

30. *Children's Words (Xiao'er yu)*, *The Rules for Children (Dizi gui)*, *The Comprehensive Collection of Worthies' Words (Guangxianji)*, and the *Enlarged Edition of the Comprehensive Collection of Worthies' Words (Zeng Guangxianwen)*, to name only a few of the texts widespread during late imperial times.

31. See Qiao Sang and Song Qi, *Mengxue quanshu*, p. 1897. See also *Youxue qionglin*, p. 8. This remark draws an interesting parallel with Confucius's comments on the *Book of Odes* in the *Analects* (Book 16): "Unless you study the *Book of Odes*, you will be ill-equipped to speak." Confucius's assertion can be better understood with reference to the convention of using the *Book of Odes* in oratory during the Spring and Autumn period (770–256 BCE). In Book 13 of the *Analects*, Confucius sees the *Book of Odes* as the model not only for public speech but also for social practice: "The Master said: 'A man may be able to recite the *Book of Odes*; yet if,

els for speaking and resources of knowledge essential not only to moral education but also to worldly affairs. Through the transmission of printed texts, this common discourse was integrated into the concrete, lived social process.

Vernacular fiction played a significant role in shaping and spreading the common discourse. Many proverbial expressions and common sayings included in a variety of social handbooks first appeared in fiction. In other cases, fiction drew on these handbooks. As in *A Sequel to Children's Words* (*Xu xiao'er yu*), a late Ming elementary text, such discourse is self-affirming: "Don't make the people your enemy; don't defy common opinion (*gonglun*)."[32] The authority of one common opinion found in these books—"Better to have the world wrong me than to wrong the world"[33]—is demonstrated, for instance, in *The Romance of the Three Kingdoms*, a Ming dynasty historical romance: Cao Cao, an absolutely evil character, is portrayed as acting on the motto "Better to wrong the world than have it wrong me," the reverse of the common saying.[34] By maintaining the boundaries between good and evil, common discourse provides the normative structure of values for organizing the fictional world.

To understand the mechanics of common discourse in the construction of vernacular fiction, we have to consider the role of the simulated storyteller. As I shall argue, the dominance of common discourse over the narrative

---

when entrusted with governmental responsibility, he does not know how to act, or if, when sent on a mission to any quarter of the kingdom, he cannot give his replies unassisted, however extensive his learning may be, of what practical use is it?'" Confucius expounded his views of the *Book of Odes* in the following passage (*The Analects*, Book 17): "The Master said: 'My children, why do you not study the *Book of Odes*? For the *Book of Odes* will help you to incite people's emotions, to observe, to keep company, to express your grievances. From it you learn the more immediate duty of serving your father, and the remoter one of serving your lord. From it you also become largely acquainted with the names of birds, beasts, plants, and trees.'" If the *Book of Odes*, as Confucius suggested, provides the source of knowledge and language, it had compelling equivalents in later imperial times. The old saying quoted above attests to the importance of popular written materials in shaping common discourse and daily activity.

32. See Qiao Sang and Song Hong, *Mengxue quanshu*, p. 103.

33. See *Guang Xianwen* (Enlarged edition of *The Comprehensive Collection of Worthies' Words*) and *Zeng guang Xianwen* (Re-edited version of the *Comprehensive Collection of Worthies' Words*), in ibid., pp. 137, 177.

34. The episode occurs in Chapter 4 of *The Romance of the Three Kingdoms*. When Chen Gong tries to stop Cao Cao from killing innocent people, Cao Cao retorts: "Better to wrong the world than have it wrong me" (Luo Guanzhong, *San'guo yanyi*, p. 49; trans. from Roberts, *Three Kingdoms*, p. 38).

world of fiction is achieved most visibly through the agent of the conventional narrator—an anonymous speaker of the collective voice.

The Narrator and Common Discourse

In reading such fiction, we can hardly overestimate the significance of the narrator, whose voice permeates the entire structure of the work and gives it a sense of coherence. Modeled on the storyteller, the narrator resorts to an anonymous, collective, and socially approved voice, which exists prior to any specific utterance.[35] Unlike the discourse enacted between the characters, the narrator's utterances consist of highly stylized language in the form of verse, parallel prose, and proverbs, and his adoption of the simulated rhetoric of storytelling provides him an entry into the storehouse of common discourse composed of shared attitudes, values, and cultural assumptions. The narrator is accordingly able to promise if not the victory of virtue over evil at least a morally intelligible universe.

Just as important is the very form of simulated storytelling—the way the narrator projects the image of his assumed audience and manipulates their responses, as well as the sense of authenticity he evokes through simulated face-to-face conversations with that audience. In the voice of the storyteller, the narrator often questions readers (addressing them as *kanguan*—or "you honorable viewers") or himself from their perspective (referring to himself as *shuoshude*—"the speaker of [what is] written"—or *shuohuade*—"the speaker of the tale"). His ability to switch roles with his audience evokes a specific context of imagined dialogue within which they participate in a series of collective exchanges. Rather than imposing his voice from without, the conventional narrator speaks, not for himself, but on behalf of "us," that is, his assumed audience. This is how he gains acquiescence to his version of the story: since he is faceless, undifferentiated, and without individual identity, his assumed audience—members of the imagined community that he represents—must share with him some basic knowledge and assumptions. In other words, in his occasional use of the second-person pronoun in direct speech to his assumed audience, the narrator presupposes that "you" are one of "us" and thus reinforces the solidarity of this imagined community on the basis of shared attitudes, vocabulary, and values. Moreover, by framing his narrative within a simulated conversation with the imaginary recipient, he

---

35. See David Wang, "Storytelling Context in Chinese Fiction."

calls attention to the present tense of storytelling, thereby giving his voice a sense of immediacy and authenticity that enhances its power of persuasion.

If the narrator's willingness to intervene in the world of reality is reflected in simulated dialogues with his assumed audience, it is also implied in his control over the fictional world. Insofar as that world stands for the actual world, the narrator's control over it is a symbolic effort to organize or restructure reality. How does the narrator's voice, which crystallizes the collective consciousness of the imagined community, achieve dominance over the fictional world of a given story?

The mechanics of this inherited mode of narrative that guarantee the narrator's authority are clear. First and most important, the simulated context of storytelling allows only the narrator's voice to signify directly. Enjoying a privileged status, the narratorial discourse exists on a different plane from the characters' discourse, which is represented and therefore secondary; the latter's varying relation to the "truth" must be measured by its degree of approximation to or divergence from the former. As mentioned above, the narrator so conceived is seldom individualized. Indeed, the highly formulaic language used by the narrator prevents us from regarding his narrative as the product of individual, partial observations and judgments. The authority of his voice lies precisely in its capacity to go beyond the level of the individual and personal.

Second, the employment of an omnipotent viewpoint enables the narrator to perceive the world in a way impossible in our daily life. He knows more than could be known by an ordinary individual and presents an unrestricted view of reality that would otherwise be unattainable. However, in order to grasp the unfolding story, we have to accept whatever the narrator offers. With unchallenged authority, he promises a world more definite than the one around us, a world whose secret life is completely visible. If it has not been fully explained, it is at least explicable. In fiction so conceived, the narrator is neither a dispensable device nor an out-of-date decoration; rather, his presence ensures intelligibility.

This mode, however, is not given or immutable. In reality, a novelist faces a wide range of choices as he adapts received conventions in his own work. Speaking in the anonymous, collective, and socially approved voice, he may find himself in tension with the complex social and historical situations he is trying to represent in the fiction. Even when the storyteller commands the narrative, there is much material that cannot be easily subordinated to narratorial discourse. However, rather than dispense with the rhetoric of simulated storytelling altogether, the novelists of the Ming and Qing periods often made their own accommodations with it and adjusted the narrator's voice as necessary. The common discourse is by definition a mixture of Confucian ideas and common sense and is thus open to negotiation and compromise. In describing a complex situation of a delicate nature, an author may assume a double role, claiming for himself the persona of a public speaker but introducing a much more tolerant, sympathetic private voice that allows a great deal of ambiguity and circumstantial judgment.

One such example can be found in the opening section of "The Pearl-Sewn Shirt" ("Jiang Xingge chonghui zhenzhu shan"), one of the stories in Feng Menglong's *Stories Old and New*.[36] The narrator begins by addressing the danger of lust through the storyteller's voice: "The eye is a go-between for passion, the heart is the seat of desire. At the beginning, your heart is in a turmoil; at the end, you have lost your soul." "When you begin to plan and scheme against the code of society," he warns his audience, "you are seeking a moment's selfish gratification at the expense of the lifelong love and respect of others." He feels no need to define or justify the code, which is assumed by society and readily applied: it is something that must be taken for granted. However, rather than imposing his view on his audience, the narrator asks: "How would you feel if your own charming wife or devoted concubine should become the object of someone else's machinations?" This question parallels the well-known Confucian formula "Do not do to others what you would not have them do to you." Yet it is his use of the simulated rhetoric of conversation that enables the narrator to solicit the expected response from his audience. Although he assumes an authoritative voice, the narrator is by no means a rigid ascetic. Endowed with the wisdom of worldly experience, he shows a sensibility to the delicacy of human affairs and often allows certain latitude for misconduct: "You may gain pleasure from some chance encounter with a 'flower by the roadside,' and it may be that no harm will come of it." Later in the story the narrator manages through the combination of subtle narrative devices to win our sympathy for the female character, Wang Sanqiao, who slips into adultery with a traveling merchant. At a certain point, he addresses "members of the audience" and explains that although Wang Sanqiao has been divorced by her husband, she still loves him, and

---

36. Feng Menglong, *Gujin xiaoshuo*, vol. 20, pp. 3–96; trans. from Birch, *Stories from a Ming Collection*, pp. 37–96.

the husband, who has no alternative but to divorce her because of the affair, feels similarly toward her. Oscillating between his public and private voices and different perspectives, the narrator defines for himself a middle ground on which to negotiate between the demands of public morality and individual sensibilities.[37]

However, as often happens in Ming and Qing fiction, what begins as a negotiation may end up becoming a dispute, when two or more voices or perspectives are locked in conflict with little prospect for reconciliation. During the late Ming period, the maturation of simulated rhetoric in vernacular fiction seems to coincide with the wide use of irony.[38] The coexistence of the storyteller's authoritative voice and narrative irony within a single work generates a great tension that vexes interpreters. In some cases the narratorial voice becomes decentralized; in other cases it is compromised, if not undercut. But equally important is that from the late Ming on, the narratorial voice itself underwent modulations. One extreme example is the narrator of *Jin Ping Mei cihua*, who constantly straddles the roles of a rigid, didactic moralist and a wily opportunist and voyeur.[39] This contradiction contributes to the differing interpretations of the novel: those who heed the moralist read a Confucian novel; those aroused by the voyeur, a work of pornography.

Describing the historical transformation of the narrative paradigm of the Chinese novel, David Rolston remarks:

---

37. In "Storytelling Context in Chinese Fiction: A Preliminary Examination of It as a Mode of Narrative Discourse," David Wang uses the term "middle distance" to describe the way an individual writer modulates the relations between his private sensibilities and public sentiment.

38. Andrew Plaks argues that one of the salient features of the *si da qishu* (four masterworks) of Chinese novels (*The Romance of the Three Kingdoms, The Journey to the West, Water Margin,* and *The Plum in the Golden Vase*) is their use of ironic devices. He regards the *Si da qishu* as forming a literary genre built upon ironic revision of narrative materials from the popular tradition (see *The Four Masterworks of the Ming Novel*). I am not totally convinced by Plaks's argument about literati editors' role in generating the ironies to be found in these novels; I think that some of the ironies Plaks identifies might not be embedded within the text itself but caused by the historical and ethical distances between the author's or editor's time and ours. A potential danger for modern critics is that we are inclined to see contradictions in places where they do not exist; or else they exist but fail to constitute irony in the sense of the term as we now understand it. But in general I agree that irony becomes a prevalent characteristic of vernacular narrative in the Ming dynasty, and even more so during the eighteenth century.

39. For further discussion of this issue, see my essay "*Jin Ping Mei cihua* and Late Ming Print Culture."

After reaching maturity in the late Ming, the simulated context of the oral story-teller developed along two lines. One was for marks of the presence of the narrator as storyteller to drop away to a minimum, as in the *Rulin waishi.* The other was to bring the storyteller persona even more into the foreground, dramatizing the story-telling process, as in the opening chapter of *Huayue hen* or the bulk of *Ernü yingxiong zhuan*, or personalizing the narrator and treating the simulated context of the oral storyteller ironically, as occurs in the fiction of Li Yu (including the *Rou putuan*) and parts of the *Honglou meng*.[40]

This second line along which the oral storyteller evolves can, according to Patrick Hanan, be traced to Ling Mengchu (1580–1644). As the editor of *Slapping the Table in Amazement (Pai'an jingqi)*, Ling followed Feng Meng-long's model but was more innovative in showing himself as "an individual narrator, as distinct from the generalized narrator of most previous fic-tion."[41] Li Yu certainly went further than anyone before him in personaliz-ing the narrator and playing with the simulated rhetoric of storytelling.[42] He equated the narrator with the author by giving the former a distinct autho-rial persona found elsewhere in his own writings. And more often than not, he made the commentary on his own fiction an extension or a complemen-tary form of his narratorial discourse. In one place, his commentator asserts, very much in the way Li Yu's narrator does in bragging about the values of his own work: "If anyone tries to tell me there has ever been a better novel than *The Carnal Prayer Mat (Rou putuan)*, I shall spit in his face!"[43] But Li Yu's ironic stance and playful tone often prevent us from taking seriously whatever statements his narrator and commentator make. At the beginning of "A Tower for the Summer Heat" ("Xia yi lou"), the narrator reinforces his authorial persona by citing a humorous remark "that people at the time told me was worth preserving":[44] "Frivolous and lewd behavior must have something serious and proper about it if it is to be perpetuated." He then

---

40. Rolston, *Traditional Chinese Fiction and Fiction Commentary*, p. 232.

41. Hanan, *The Chinese Vernacular Story*, p. 150.

42. See chaps. 8 and 9 of ibid., pp. 165–207; and Hanan, *The Invention of Li Yu*. Hanan ar-gues that Li Yu's comic force arises from his farcical play with the canonical voice of the con-ventional narrator as well as his parody of some cherished myth or stereotype, whereas Aina's fiction marks a decisive break with the basic model and method of vernacular fiction itself.

43. Li Yu, *Rou putuan*, in Chen Qinghao and Wang Qiugui, eds., *Si wu xie huibao*, vol. 15, p. 350; trans. from Hanan, *The Carnal Prayer Mat*, "Introduction," p. xiii.

44. See Li Yu, *Shi'er lou*, pp. 39–55; trans. from Hanan, *A Tower for the Summer Heat*, pp. 5–6.

applies it to sexual activity: "If sexual intercourse was not considered serious and proper in the very beginning, why has it been handed down from ancient times as a permanent part of life? Because out of the frivolity and lewdness of sex come sons to perpetuate the ancestral shrine and continue our lineage." The narrator seems to take pains to endorse the Confucian ethics of ancestral worship and filial piety, which are often found in the voice of the simulated storyteller in vernacular fiction, but he does so in a tricky way that only makes us suspect his declared intention. Interestingly, unlike the conventional narrator, he goes on to apologize for what might be perceived by the audience as a digression: "This is the point to which my talk of lotus blossoms has brought me. I hope the reader will forgive me for rambling on so." He constantly compromises the conventions of fiction writing and reminds the reader to maintain an ironic distance from his own comments, and he seems to have done all he could to undercut the collective discourse the storyteller often represents.[45]

There are far fewer examples of the other line of evolution of the simulated context of storytelling, that is, the tendency toward diminishing, if not abolishing altogether, the mode of oral literature. *Rulin waishi* is unprecedented in representing this trend, although a few earlier works seem to anticipate it in some minor respects.[46] The diminishing of the narrator's privileged viewpoint has had a significant impact on readers' perception of the narrative world of *Rulin waishi* and of its relation to us. In reading the episode of Longsan, for instance, we are no more than casual onlookers, with no extra vision or knowledge with respect to the characters and incidents recounted. We know nothing more about the prior and Longsan than what is

---

45. As David Rolston notes (*Traditional Chinese Fiction and Fiction Commentary*, p. 293), Li Yu often deliberately destroyed the illusion of face-to-face verbal communication with his assumed audience by asking the reader to "rest his eyes" before turning to the next chapter. See, e.g., Li Yu, "Hegui lou" (*Shi'er lou*, pp. 126–46; Hanan, *Tower*, p. 183); and "Fuyun lou" (*Shi'er lou*, pp. 90–116; Hanan, *Tower*, p. 154). In "Xia yi lou," Li Yu demonstrated his metafictional consciousness by commenting on the novelist's deliberate narrative choice: at a critical moment of the story, the slightest delay would be disastrous for the characters, but "the author insists on a delay at this point, so that he can start a new chapter," because "the story will be far more interesting than if it were told all in one piece" (*Shi'er lou*, p. 49; Hanan, *Tower*, p. 26).

46. For instance, *Water Margin* and *A Sequel to Water Margin* (*Shuihu houzhuan*) occasionally adopt what David Rolston (*Traditional Chinese Fiction and Fiction Commentary*, pp. 239–40) calls the "new descriptive mode" in representing natural settings. See also Widmer, *The Margins of Utopia*, p. 158. *Xiyou bu*, another *xushu* of the time, significantly reduces the language of the conventional storyteller.

present in their conversations, which unfold without being framed or even mediated by the narrator's introduction or comments. At the most puzzling moment of the conversation, the characters seem to exchange information that remains inaccessible to us. What remains unknown might be disregarded as something unimportant or irrelevant. Yet its presence in the novel cannot be simply ignored: it marks the limits of our interpretations of the Longsan narrative and the novel in general. Moreover, these imposed limits remind us of the all-too-familiar conditions of our everyday experience. Rather than presenting the world from the viewpoint of an omniscient narrator as most earlier novels do, the narrative of Longsan confronts us with the ambiguities we encounter in real life. Contrary to our expectations of the orderly consolations of narrative order and transparency, we are left alone to deal with the narrative world of the novel, with no sense of certainty.

In the account of the Longsan incident, the disappearance of the omnipotent viewpoint parallels the absence of the common discourse in the voice of the narrator. That is, the common discourse no longer constitutes the narratorial discourse that frames and thereby measures the characters' discourse. However, it does not simply vanish; the characters sometimes mouth it, albeit in fragmented and distorted ways. The dislocation and relocation of the common discourse deprive it of the authority conventionally associated with it; we observe the enactment of common discourse in a series of conversations that bears no resemblance to the standard simulated context of verbal communication in the mode of storytelling.

Let us re-examine the chaos that Longsan provokes. Presenting himself as the wife of the prior, Longsan uses language that prescribes the female's role in family life. This language, as shown above, derived from popular Confucian texts, including conduct books for women. In the Longsan episode, it is combined with proverbs often used by the traditional narrator in stories about family affairs, such as "A quarrel between husband and wife does not last overnight." In response to the prior's threat of possible official intervention, Longsan again quotes common sayings in the way a conventional narrator would: "It is well put in these words of the ancients: 'Officials can't interfere in family disputes.'" Yet unlike the traditional narrator, Longsan tears these phrases from the texts to which they belong to suit his own agenda. At one moment, the frustrated prior is quoted as saying: "Longsan! This is no time for joking! Even if you were angry with me for not inviting you today, you should have come in a decent manner. Why dress up like this?" The verbal exchange between the two takes place at different levels: Longsan disguises himself with legitimate rhetoric; the prior gives his private reading of it to discredit Longsan. The prior's reading may reveal Longsan's motivation, but it may also be a deliberate misreading intended to prevent Longsan from further disclosing their secret relationship.

Longsan's appropriation of the common discourse has serious implications, for the meaning of his words is now predicated on the specific utterance, an event that is particular and contingent. In other words, the legitimate common discourse signifies only through the context within which it is articulated and exchanged. It can no longer be appropriately used, as in a prescribed ideal situation like the standard simulated context of storytelling; it is instead always appropriated or misappropriated, with connotations shaped by the speaker's objectives and circumstantial motivations. It is difficult to restore credibility to the misappropriated words, and Wu Jingzi's narrator can hardly use the language monopolized and abused by his characters without evoking doubt or a sense of irony. In its account of the Longsan episode, therefore, *Rulin waishi* undercuts the common discourse without creating an alternative for it.

Indeed, the Longsan farce alienates us from the familiar voice that is cultivated in a variety of popular Confucian texts as well as in traditional fiction. It prevents us from recognizing, to say nothing of identifying with, the authority conventionally associated with the legitimate common discourse. This change, which is manifested most evidently in Part II of *Rulin waishi*, is related to other moves Wu Jingzi made. He was reluctant to assume the accepted public persona of storyteller in organizing his narrative and even less interested, it would seem, in maintaining the coded gestures and rhetoric of speaking to the imagined community of a broad audience. Since he forsook the privileged voice of the storyteller in most parts of his novel, his narrative relied more on literary and historical allusions and references—knowledge and rhetoric beyond the assumed audience for conventional fiction but befitting his subject matter.

Clearly, the changes in fiction discussed in this chapter must be understood within the context of the development of the literati novel in the eighteenth century. As explained in the Introduction, eighteenth-century literati novels, as exemplified by *Rulin waishi*, were written by individual literati authors for an audience of their confrères, and they all deal, one way or another, with literati concerns, although they do not always contain autobiographical elements. Their emergence signals a fundamental shift in the way the vernacular novel was created, transmitted, and received; it also suggests that novelists had acquired a different manner of communicating with their readers. Small surprise that most of these novels, such as *The Humble Words of an Old Rustic* and *Tracks of an Immortal on the Green Field*, deliberately downplay the gestures of storytelling. The exuberant wit and erudition of *Flowers in the Mirror* leave almost no room for the repertoire of conventional fiction. *The History of the Bookworm* goes even further by adopting classical language; it not only dispenses altogether with the rhetoric of oral literature but incorporates a tremendous amount of literati learning and references not found in the vernacular novel.

Cao Xueqin, a former resident of Nanjing and the author of the *Story of the Stone*, began, soon after Wu Jingzi, to disparage the same narrative paradigm, albeit in his own way. Critics have long been struck by his sophisticated design of multiple beginnings, the ease with which he moves from the myth to history and the human domain within the limited space of the first few chapters, and his innovative use of the rhetoric of storytelling. After complaining about the complexity of the objects he is dealing with in Chapter 6, the narrator turns to his audience and asks, "Faced with so exuberant an abundance of material, what principle should your chronicler adopt to guide him in his selection of incidents to record?"[47] As he ponders the problem "where to begin," the narrator tells us that the problem has suddenly been solved by the appearance of Grannie Liu, who "turned up at the Rong mansion on the very day of which we are about to write." This is a typical example of how Cao Xueqin made use of the familiar rhetoric of oral literature for a new purpose; unlike the conventional storyteller, the narrator draws our attention to the very act of writing, laying bare the devices of narrative choice, deliberation, and manipulation. In Chapter 1, Cao reveals the mysterious origin of the novel—a piece of text inscribed on a divine stone. He summons the stone to defend the text and then lists the names of those who are said to have copied and edited it, including Cao himself. His sophisticated rendering of the identities of the author, scribe, and editor raises narratological issues too complicated for received conventions of fiction. Moreover, whereas Wu Jingzi reduced the role of the omniscient storyteller to the minimum in *Rulin waishi*, Cao Xueqin created multiple internal narrators

---

47. Cao Xueqin, *Honglou meng*, p. 68; trans. from Hawkes, *The Story of the Stone*, vol. 1; p. 150.

such as Jia Yucun (a pun on "false words preserved") and Zhen Shiyin ("true events concealed"), each of whom reveals only the partial or relative truth of the stories recounted. This generates a constant dialogue and negotiation between the real and unreal, and between truth and fiction. In the mid-eighteenth century, Wu and Cao explored different strategies for dealing with the inherited paradigm of vernacular narrative, and their works inaugurated a new phase in the development of the Chinese novel by revolutionizng how the world is perceived and represented.

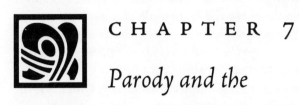

CHAPTER 7

Parody and the
Suspension of History

If in *Rulin waishi* we encounter what we might call a new narrative form, its significance lies precisely in its presupposition of the inherited narrative mode it refuses. The novel's occasional references to earlier texts shows only the inadequacy of their value structure: the reassurance of the conventional narrator is suspended, the characters of previous works are parodied, and canonical plots are placed in changed contexts and subjected to reversal. *Rulin waishi* seems to deliberately disappoint our expectations of vernacular fiction. It demonstrates the incapacity of the old narrative mode to make sense of or construct values from the elements of its own world. An example of this problem occurs early in the novel (Chapters 9, 11, and 12), in the episode in which the Lou brothers, Lou Feng and Lou Zan, two members of the local elite and hopeless romantics, seek out men of virtue, only to open themselves to ridicule.

Old Texts, New Worlds: A Misguided Trip

The Lou brothers are among the characters of *Rulin waishi* out of tune with their own time. Dissatisfied with their prescribed roles in society, they choose instead to live in a textual world inhabited by men of virtue, high-minded recluses, and knights-errant. To them, the present will remain meaningless until they can discover in it the truth of what the texts of the past describe. Their attempt to validate this textual world leads them to search for men of virtue; from books they have learned that real sages always detach themselves from the public and wait quietly for those with the wisdom to recognize and discover them. With these books as their guide, the Lou brothers' search for worthies becomes itself a test of the world that they have constructed from the texts of the past.

One of the major texts that the brothers consult is Sima Qian's *Shiji*, the first general history (*tongshi*), which covers early history through the early Western Han period. One can hardly overestimate the importance of *Shiji* in Chinese historiography, literature, and culture in general: it not only established a model for the official and literati historical narrative in subsequent periods but also constituted the major sources for the popular imagination and conceptualization of history. It is no surprise that the Lou brothers episode takes as its starting point their references to the motifs and rhetoric derived from *Shiji*.

In Chapter 9, the Lou brothers see their chance for action when they discover a man of virtue in Yang Zhizhong, a poor licentiate imprisoned for being unable to repay a debt to a salt merchant. They first hear about Yang Zhizhong from a custodian of their family graves; his recounting of Yang's words catches their interest, for Yang, like themselves, speaks respectfully of antiquity and condemns the present dynasty, which, according to him, has been morally bankrupt since the Yongle usurpation of 1403. They immediately take steps to help Yang Zhizhong get released from jail. Then they stay at home, waiting for him to call on them to express his gratitude. However, "When over a month had passed, the Lou brothers could not help feeling somewhat bewildered. Nevertheless, they called to mind the story of Yue Shifu and were convinced that Licentiate Yang must be a great scholar of the same type. In fact, this only increased their respect for him" (R. 133; S. 103). In this moment of doubt, the brothers take comfort in ancient texts. Their reading of the story of Yue Shifu from *Shiji* leads them to view Yang Zhizhong as his modern-day counterpart and to grow even more convinced of Yang's virtue.[1]

---

1. See Sima Qian, *Shiji*, *juan* 62, p. 2135. The story of Yue Shifu can also be found in the "neipian" of the *Master Yan's Spring and Autumn Annals* (*Yanzi chunqiu*), which was originally attributed to Yan Ying (?–500 BCE) but was probably edited by Han scholars (see Wang Xinzhan, *Yanzi chunqiu jijie*, pp. 63–64). There are some differences between the two versions of the story in the *Shiji* and in the *Yanzi chunqiu*. The novel probably is based on the version in the *Shiji*.

Yue Shifu, a man of virtue, was held in slavery. When Yan Ying encountered Yue on the road, he gave the horse on the left side of his carriage to redeem him and then carried him home. After they arrived, Yan Ying entered Yue's room without saying "Excuse me." After a while, Yue Shifu wished to break off relations with him. Yan Ying was astonished. He straightened his cap and clothes and apologized, saying, "Although I am not perfect, I have saved you from a miserable situation. Why do you want to break off so soon?"

Shifu said, "That is not the point. I have heard it said that a gentleman is treated unjustly by those who do not know him, but treated justly by those who know him. When I was a captive, you did not even know who I was. But you redeemed me with compassion, and that made you my friend. But if a friend treats me without respect, I prefer to stay in jail." Thereupon, Yan Ying invited him into the inner room as an honored guest.

The Lou brothers are skilled enough readers to have caught the message of the Yue Shifu story: in helping a man of virtue, one should not consider oneself a benefactor or expect him to express gratitude. A man of virtue needs friends but not benefactors, and he demands to be treated as an equal, consistently and with due respect. Later, the brothers immerse themselves in *Shiji* rhetoric in their dialogue with each other: "Have you not heard the saying that when Your Grace does good, Your Grace should forget?" (R. 134; S. 105).[2] The function of the rhetorical question is to reaffirm the understanding between the brothers through their common reference to the *Shiji* texts. With the *Shiji* story and rhetoric as their guide, they know what to say and do next: they decide to pay Yang a visit.

The account of the trip is in the mode of the story of Liu Bei's visits to Zhuge Liang, which is first elaborated in *The History of the Three Kingdoms* (*San'guozhi*), an official history composed in the Jin dynasty, and later embellished in *The Romance of the Three Kingdoms*, a Ming dynasty historical romance, which was subsequently adapted into plays and stories and became deeply rooted in the popular imagination of Chinese history.[3] In *The Romance of the Three Kingdoms*, Zhuge Liang, a seer and a scholar of extraordinary wisdom and insight, lives as a recluse in Longzhong. Liu Bei, who represents the legitimate lineage of the Han royal house, makes three visits

---

2. See "Wei gongzi liezhuan" in Sima Qian, *Shiji, juan* 77, p. 2382.

3. Critics have noted that the Lou brothers story is derived from the Liu Bei episode in *San'guo yanyi*. In a study of this story, Roland Altenburger ("Cong huwenxing kan *Rulin waishi de fengci shoufa*") focuses on the issue of intertextuality. See also Chen Wenxin, *Wu Jingzi hua rulin*, p. 51–55.

to Zhuge's thatched hut to solicit advice on political and military strategies. The first two visits achieve nothing, but during the third Liu Bei is granted a chance to meet Zhuge Liang. This long-expected meeting more than repays all of Liu Bei's efforts, for he has finally found the man who is to play an essential role in his future career as emperor of the Shu-Han kingdom.

In Chapter 9 of *Rulin waishi*, the Lou brothers visit Yang Zhizhong's thatched hut three times and, as in the story of Liu Bei, are not able to meet the scholar until the third visit. Again, as in the story of Liu Bei, the first two calls, although fruitless, yield clues to the recluse's character that raise his visitors' expectations. On their way back home, the Lou brothers hear some favorable words spoken about Yang and discover a poem on a sheet of paper signed with the name Yang Zhizhong. But *Rulin waishi* adds an ironic twist to the structural model that it shares with *The Romance of the Three Kingdoms*: the poem may reveal more about Yang Zhizhong than its surface meaning.

The Lou brothers unfolded the white sheet of paper and read the following lines: "I dare not try anything inappropriate, / Because I have studied sòme books. / I have come through bitter frost and blazing heat, / And in no time the spring breeze will visit my thatched hut." Yang's name was signed beneath. The Lou brothers were most impressed. "How remarkable!" they exclaimed. "What an admirable character! But how unlucky we are in all our attempts to meet him!" (R. 138; S. 109)

The brothers greatly admire Yang's moral integrity, to which the poem bears witness. We might well agree with them if we did not know that the poem is abridged from one by a poet of the Yuan dynasty.[4] As is confirmed in the next scene, Yang Zhizhong has a habit of quoting others' lines. But the narrator does not reveal the sources of these quotations. Did he suppose that his ideal reader would be able to identify the true author of the poem? If so, did he mean to suggest that Yang is trying to gain fame by deceiving the public, or that the Lou brothers are not learned enough to tell a real scholar from a fake one, or both? We may pose these questions, but *Rulin waishi* provides no definitive answer. All we see is, in the following chapter, the Lou brothers showing this poem to Mr. Lu, a compiler at the Hanlin Academy, as evidence of Yang Zhizhong's high-mindedness. They take Yang for the author of the poem and read it as his personal statement.

---

4. This poem was written by Lü Sicheng, a prime minister of the Yuan dynasty, when he was a poor and frustrated scholar; see Tao Zhongyi's *Nancun chuogeng lu, juan* 12, in Li Hanqiu, ed., *"Rulin waishi" yanjiu ziliao*, p. 174.

The Lou brothers' quest for Yang Zhizhong is indeed a series of mis-readings on their part and miscommunications between them and Yang Zhizhong. The very idea of the trip comes from a misreading—the Lou brothers misinterpret Yang Zhizhong's failure to respond after being released from jail. We are told at the very beginning that Yang Zhizhong knows nothing of what the Lou brothers have done for him and does not bother to investigate. The brothers' comparison of Yang to Yue Shifu is, therefore, the result of wishful thinking. Cherishing such inflated expectations of Yang Zhizhong, the Lou brothers call on him at his thatched hut. Unlike Liu Bei, who during his first two visits encountered several recluses with elegant bearing and enigmatic speech, however, they meet no one except a half-deaf and half-witted housekeeper, a crone who drops no pearls of disguised wisdom. Here again is miscommunication: upon Yang Zhizhong's return, the old woman tells him that two men called Liu or something have come to see him; the evocation of Liu Bei's last name once again suggests the textual sources of the Lou brothers story. But Yang is not Zhuge Liang, and that name reminds him only of the yamen runner who arrested him when the salt merchant brought suit—a nightmare from which he wishes only to escape. Upon learning that the old housekeeper has invited the visitors to return, Yang Zhizhong reacts with anger and fear; he slaps her face and kicks her. Fearing that the runner will be back, he takes to going out early every morning and wandering about till evening. Thus, when the brothers pay a second visit a few days later, they miss him again.

We have so far seen two different versions of the story. One, presented primarily from the perspective of the Lou brothers, derives from the model of Liu Bei's visit to Zhuge Liang; the other discredits that model. *The Romance of the Three Kingdoms* provides the image of the sage waiting for recognition, and the Lou brothers in *Rulin waishi* are driven to see that image realized in the present. But they are doomed to fail, since they inhabit a novel that does not believe the sages in the way they do. And they go astray in their trip from *The Romance of the Three Kingdoms* to *Rulin waishi*. Adhering to an out-of-date textual guide, they never learn how to decipher the codes of the narrative world in which they figure: they take things and people for what they are not.

In Chapter 10 the brothers have a chance to share their story with Mr. Lu, a compiler at the Hanlin Academy. Contrary to their expectations, every sign in Yang that they have interpreted positively turns out to be negative in the eyes of Mr. Lu.

Presently Mr. Lu asked about the crops that year and whether their native place had recently produced any famous men. Given this opening, Lou Feng mentioned Yang Zhizhong and declared that he could be considered an extremely lofty character. Then, producing the poem, he showed it to the compiler. When Mr. Lu had read it, he looked at them quizzically. "You two gentlemen are a match for all the patrons who ever existed," he said. "Even the Lord of Xinling and the Lord of Chunshen could do no more. But few of these men who appear so brilliant are genuine scholars. In fact, to put it bluntly, if this fellow is really learned, why hasn't he passed the examination? What use is this poem? With your condescension and respect for genius, you must be the best patrons this Mr. Yang has ever encountered in his life; yet he has twice avoided you, as if he were afraid of meeting you. Isn't the reason obvious? If I were you, I would not become too friendly with such people." To this the two brothers made no answer. (R. 142; S. 112)

At the level of the characters' discourse, the brothers' account of Yang Zhizhong has been challenged. Although Mr. Lu's comments are by no means conclusive, they provide an alternative point of view that questions the reliability of the brothers' judgment. Mr. Lu's assessment is, of course, highly subjective: his tone, his language, and the values he applies suggest his personality and social status. In judging Yang's scholarship, he adopts the officially approved standard; to his mind, a true scholar would have passed the civil service examination, as he himself has done. In this fashion he reminds the Lou brothers of his own status; his question also implies contempt for the brothers, both of whom, as related in Chapter 8, have long struggled with the metropolitan examination but never succeeded. Despite his bias and circumstantial motivation, Mr. Lu's general criticism of contemporary scholars throws suspicion on Yang Zhizhong by implying that he might be one of those who try to win undeserved fame. His habit of quoting others' poetry without acknowledgment and his shabby treatment of his maid seems to sustain Lu's opinion, but not for the reasons that Lu gives.

Here again, at the level of the characters' conversation, we encounter the model of Liu Bei visiting Zhuge Liang. The second half of the comments made by Mr. Lu seem to echo the comments about Zhuge Liang made by Guan Yu, a sworn brother of Liu Bei in *The Romance of the Three Kingdoms*. After the two fruitless visits, Guan Yu tries to persuade Liu Bei to give up: "Twice, brother, you have respectfully presented yourself. Such courtesy is indulgence. It seems to me that Kongming [Zhuge Liang] has a false reputation and no real learning. That is why he avoids receiving you. Why are you so captivated by this man?"[5] Similar as they are, Guan Yu's and Mr. Lu's comments assume different roles in shaping the characters commented upon: in *The Romance of the Three Kingdoms*, Guan Yu's criticism of Zhuge Liang is discredited when Liu Bei and Zhuge Liang finally meet and thus contributes, in a negative way, to forming the stable image of Zhuge Liang as a true sage; in *Rulin waishi*, Lu's criticism of Yang Zhizhong provides an alternative interpretation that jeopardizes the Lou brothers' story but remains unconfirmed.

The brothers do not respond to Mr. Lu's comments. Despite his challenge, they silently insist on their own version of the story. But when they meet the man who first recommended Yang to them, they find their version of the story vulnerable not merely to Lu's criticism of Yang but to their own defense of him.

The Lou brothers described their two attempts to call on Yang Zhizhong. "Of course, he couldn't know this," said Zou Jifu. "I have been living in East Village for the last few months, so there was no one to tell Mr. Yang. But he is as honest a fellow as you could find: he would never put on airs and deliberately avoid anyone. He is one of the most friendly people I know, and if he realized that it was you two gentlemen who had called on him, he would travel all night to see you." (R. 159; S. 126)

The story of Yang Zhizhong, even as a positive figure, is recast. In this version he is a man of virtue, but not of the type the Lou brothers expected. In their eyes, he must be an extraordinary man like Yue Shifu, but Yue Shifu would never "travel all night," to use Zou Jifu's words, to pay a visit.

The distance between the Lou brothers and Yang Zhizhong symbolizes the gap between text and reality. The brothers not only read themselves into the texts of the past but also try to read those texts into their own lives. When they set out to discover a present-day Yue Shifu, they test the narratives of which they are a part. Yang Zhizhong, however, is bound to a different world and resists assimilation into the books that they have read. The brothers wander out of *The Romance of the Three Kingdoms* with faith in the intelligible structure of the values embodied in conventional narrative. But in *Rulin waishi* they confront multiple voices that participate in a controversy with no resolution. In the characters' discourse, Yang is either condemned as

---

5. Luo Guanzhong, *San'guo yanyi*, p. 485; trans. from Roberts, *Three Kingdoms*, p. 290.

a swindler or praised as a supremely honest and friendly fellow. He is later described by a nameless townsman in Chapter 12 as "a complete lunatic, gabbling all the time about astronomy, geography and the arts of government" (R. 172; S. 136). There is no longer a unified internal audience representing a standard of public opinion. One person's object of ridicule may be another's sage, and vice versa. More important, none of these versions of the story can claim to be authoritative: there is no longer "the" story guaranteed by the conventional narrator.

Since this dichotomy of text and reality is itself fashioned in the form of a text, it contributes to defining the novel as a new textual world in opposition to the old one. The brothers are caught between these worlds as well as between the canonical texts in which they believe and the novelistic reality in which they figure: they conceptualize people in the light of the canonical texts without knowing that they themselves have been placed in a new text shaped by a different mode of perception and interpretation. However, not merely their mode of perception but also the status of old texts that promise to be continuously fulfilled in new ones are threatened—another contrast between *The Romance of the Three Kingdoms* and *Rulin waishi*.

Like the Lou brothers, Liu Bei in *The Romance of the Three Kingdoms* takes the ancient texts as a guide for his own actions. In Chapter 38, Liu Bei refutes Guan Yu and Zhang Fei, who have tried to stop him, saying, "Long ago Prince Huan of the state of Qi tried five times before he succeeded in seeing the recluse of Dongguo. Getting to see the wise and worthy Kongming may well demand even more of us." He continues, "I suppose you've never heard of King Wen, founder of the Zhou, presenting himself to Jiang Ziya. If King Wen could show a wise man such respect, what excuses your utter discourtesy?"[6] To Liu Bei, the narrative of ancient texts, such as *Shiji*, assumes a double role: it indicates both what things were long ago and what things should be. Following the guidance of the text whose authority has been affirmed, Liu Bei finally, as expected, finds

---

6. Roberts's translation is accurate except for one thing: the recluse of Dongguo does not refer to Guanzhong, the prime minister of the state of Qi. The anecdote of Prince Huan making five visits to the recluse of Dongguo is found in Chapter 36 "Nan (I)" of the *Hanfeizi*, in which the recluse is called Xiaochen Ji; see *Hanfeizi jiaozhu*, p. 507. For King Wen's visit to Jiang Ziya, an honorable worthy, see "Hereditary house of Qi Taigong" (Qi Taigong shijia) in Sima Qian, *Shiji, juan* 32, pp. 1477–78.

Zhuge Liang, who proves to be a true sage. The re-enactment of the ancient texts in *The Romance of the Three Kingdoms* is not a repetition but an active transformation that ensures the consensus of the normative order and reality through the acts of narration and interpretation. In *Rulin waishi*, however, the very sequence of transformation comes to an end. The brothers engage in the same effort as Liu Bei, but they never succeed; instead, they become objects of ridicule.

Who Is Quan Wuyong?

The story of the Lou brothers' search for worthy men does not end with Yang Zhizhong. When the brothers finally meet Yang, he takes over the guiding role in the narrative. Assuming the voice of the conventional narrator, he recommends to the Lou brothers an extraordinary man "unrivaled among our contemporaries."

"I was just saying," resumed Yang Zhizhong, "that since you two gentlemen admire true merit so much, although I am not worthy of your notice, I have a friend living in the hills in Xiaoshan County who is a remarkable genius and a wonderful scholar. One might truly say of him: in retirement he would be a great scholar; and in office he could be the counselor of the kings. Would you like to meet him?"

Marveling, the two brothers asked: "Who is this remarkable man?"

Then, crossing his fingers, Yang told them his friend's name. . . . "A man with my humble capacities is not good enough for gentlemen like you, who admire worth so much," Yang Zhizhong told the Lou brothers. "But I have a friend called Quan Wuyong from Xiaoshan County who lives in the hills. If you invite him here to talk with you, you will see that he has the wisdom of Guan Zhong and Yue Yi, and the learning of Cheng Yi and Zhu Xi, making him unrivaled among our contemporaries." (R. 167–69; S. 132–33)

With its hackneyed phrases, Yang Zhizhong's speech is reminiscent of those of the conventional narrator. In order to revitalize that clichéd characterization and increase its persuasiveness, Yang Zhizhong makes himself a foil for Quan Wuyong, and self-deprecation is the price paid for the voice he adopts from old-style fiction. If Yang tries to live up to the role of the narrator, the Lou brothers are a ready-made audience: they immediately catch the tone, which is both familiar and convincing, and thus no sooner do they hear Yang's recommendation than they send their servant Huancheng to present a letter and gifts to Quan Wuyong. However, on the way Huancheng hears a different story:

"Can it be that fellow?" said the bearded man. "That would be a joke." Then, turning to the youth, he asked, "Don't you know about him? Let me tell you, then. He lives in the mountains and all his ancestors were peasants; but his father made enough money to send him to a country school to study. He studied until he was seventeen or eighteen, when a heartless village teacher did him a bad turn by insisting that he should go in for the examinations. Later on his father died, but this fellow was a good-for-nothing: he could neither till the land nor trade. He just sat at home eating until he had eaten up all his property. He took the examinations for more than thirty years but never even passed the lowest, because he can't talk sense. He used to live in a tutelary temple where he took a few pupils, and every year he prepared for the examinations. In that way he was just able to make ends meet. But then he was unlucky again, for the other year he met the accountant of a Huzhou salt shop in New Market—an old man called Yang— who came to collect bills. This Mr. Yang, who put up in the temple, was a complete lunatic, gabbling all the time about astronomy, geography and the arts of government. When Quan heard him, he became possessed by a devil and lost his senses completely—he stopped taking examinations and became a hermit! But once he became a hermit students stopped going to him; so now he has nothing to live on except what he cheats out of the country people. 'We are such good friends, there should be no difference between us,' he tells them. 'What's yours is mine, and all that's mine is yours.' This is his formula."

"He surely can't deceive many people that way," said the young man.

"Everything he possesses he has tricked out of people," retorted the man with the beard. "Still, since we belong to the same village, I won't say any more." Then he asked Huancheng, "Why did you inquire about this man?"

"For no particular reason," replied Huancheng. "I was just asking." But he was thinking: "Our third and fourth masters are a queer couple. So many high officials and magistrates come to pay their respects, yet they still feel they haven't enough friends and send me all this way, for no reason, to find such a swindler!" (R. 171–72; S. 135–36)

The portrait of Quan Wuyong as a worthy man is abruptly reversed. According to the bearded man, Quan is a good-for-nothing, a fellow who could not even make a living without cheating. However, before the informant's story is fully confirmed, questions about him seem unavoidable: Who is he? Is his voice reliable? We know nothing about him other than his remarks, which have a caustic and cynical tone and suggest more about him than about Quan. Whatever we may say about the bearded man, however, we must agree that he is a sophisticated storyteller; he stops at a point that suggests more stories remain to be told about Quan.

What happens next seems to support this account. After his arrival at the Lou brothers' home, Quan Wuyong has difficulty dealing with Yang Zhizhong's son, a hopeless drunkard who also lives there. Having discovered that this drunkard has taken his money to gamble with, Quan demands an explanation, but the response just repeats his own formula: "Why, uncle, aren't you and I really one? What's yours is mine, and all that's mine is yours. What difference is there?" A Qing commentator considers this to be a moment when the bearded man's judgment of Quan is confirmed, since the drunkard "uses Quan's money in the same way Quan claims he is doing when he uses others' money."[7] In consequence, Quan Wuyong and Yang Zhizhong fall out and do not even speak to each other anymore. As an internal narrator, Yang Zhizhong can no longer control the character he has called forth.

The episode of Quan Wuyong ends in a scandalous scene: in the middle of a feast held in the Lou brothers' house, he is captured and taken away by official runners. The warrants read as follows:

Magistrate Wu of Xiaoshan County reports on a local case of kidnapping. According-ing to the abbess Huiyuan of Lanruo Temple, her pupil, the nun Xinyuan, was seduced and kidnapped by a local vagabond named Quan Wuyong. This felon, before his crime was discovered, ran away to your county; hence we transmit this case to you and request your honorable county to deal with the matter and to send runners to assist our officers to find this culprit, who should then be arrested and brought back to our county for trial. This is urgent! (R. 185; S. 145)

Lou Feng is mortified; Lou Zan is embarrassed. Yang Zhizhong pretends to be an outsider and shifts all the blame onto Quan himself. Quan flushes crimson and desperately protests, but the game is up. As a character in the novel he is "dead." At this point, we are quite sure that the story of Quan Wuyong is simply a parody of the story of ancient recluses—the hero endorsed by the voice of the conventional narrator turns out to be a charlatan who deceives the world to win undeserved credit.

Our confidence remains unchallenged until Chapter 54, by which time Quan is almost forgotten. Chen Munan, an unimportant character, and Monk Chen, an even less important character, are chatting about the past:

---

7. Comment of Zhang Wenhu; see Li Hanqiu, ed., *"Rulin waishi" huijiao huiping ben*, p. 178.

"I heard that Mr. Quan Wuyong got into trouble later," said the monk. "What happened in the end?"

"He was slandered by some licentiates in his college. Later he was cleared of the charge." (R. 730; S. 589)

This piece of conversation is a small digression, a piece of debris falling out of the portrait of Quan Wuyong, which was complete in Chapter 13. But when we try to fit it back in, this final touch apparently disrupts the whole picture. It bothers us. We may even wonder why it is there, since it seems to call into question not merely what we have read, but our way of reading *per se*. As devoted, naïve readers, we have been fooled into accepting an unsubstantiated report of Quan's guilt in much the same way that the Lou brothers accepted Yang Zhizhong's account of Quan's virtue.

Again, as in the story of Yang Zhizhong, the narrator does not show up to confirm or reject what has been said. He steps aside, keeps silent, and abandons his privilege of giving the final word on his character. Readers are left to evaluate the conflicting reports and judgments, with no reliable ground on which to stand.

Yet we do know one thing for sure: Quan Wuyong does not rise to the status of an antihero. The final stroke of the story prevents us from regarding it as a parody of the conventional recluse narrative, a symmetrical inversion of values that might preserve the value system. Quan may be neither a great recluse nor a swindler or kidnapper. As a character, he can only be defined by what he is not; he has fallen into a gray zone of mundane commonalities and contingencies and has thus defied the character types established in the repertoire of conventional fiction.

The Swordsman As Narrator

The third worthy man that the Lou brothers find is Iron-Armed Zhang, a self-proclaimed swordsman, who arrives with Quan Wuyong. Iron-Armed Zhang is not a man waiting for recognition; he is an "active" character, who takes full control of his self-representation and recommends himself to the brothers. Readers know nothing more than what he says about himself, until at last he leaves and fails to return as promised. Adopting the narrative role of the righteous swordsman, Zhang tells us an astounding story about himself, straight out of conventional chivalric fiction.

In Chapter 12, during the feast of welcome for both Quan Wuyong and Iron-Armed Zhang, Zhang introduces himself without being asked:

"I know most of the military arts," announced Iron-Armed Zhang. "I can fight with eighteen different weapons on foot and eighteen different weapons on horseback. I can use the whip, the mace, the ax, the hammer, the sword, the spear, the saber, and the halberd. In fact, I may be said to have mastered all these. But I am unlucky in my temperament, for whenever I see injustice done I must draw my sword to avenge the injured. I cannot resist fighting with the strongest in the empire; and whenever I have money, I give it to the poor. Thus I have ended up without a home, and this is how I come to be in your honorable district." (R. 178; S. 140)

Zhang's self-introduction reproduces all the clichés that a conventional narrator would use in introducing the swordsman.[8] It triggers a stock response from Lou Zan: "This is exactly what one expects of a good fellow!" Once again Lou Zan proves himself an ideal reader of conventional fiction, except for one discrepancy: he permits the character, Zhang, to assume the voice of the narrator in introducing himself. Yet, when Zhang has recourse to the commonplace phrases of the conventional narrator, he takes control of how he will be perceived: he is the director of the drama that he himself acts out.

It does not take long for the drama to reach its climax. One night Zhang drops down from the eaves of the Lou brothers' house and appears in their study, a leather bag in his hands. He offers an account that seems to confirm his self-introduction:

"Please be seated, gentlemen," said Iron-Armed Zhang, "and let me explain. During my life I have had one benefactor and one enemy. I have hated my enemy for ten years without having an opportunity to kill him; but today my chance came and I have his head here. Inside this bag is a bloody human head! But my benefactor is some distance away, and I need five hundred *taels* to repay him for his kindness. Once this debt of honor is paid, my heart will be at rest and I can devote the rest of my life to you who have treated me so well. Believing that only you gentlemen could help me—for no others are so understanding—I made bold to call on you tonight. But if you are unwilling to help, then I must go far away and never see you again." (R. 180–81; S. 142–43)

Zhang's explanation is perfectly designed; it fulfills the expectations for the character type invoked in his self-introduction: always ready to avenge his enemies and repay his friends. Nothing is more important than these two themes in the stories of swordsmen. The Lou brothers are astonished but convinced. This time, however, they are not merely readers of the story; they

---

8. Zhang's speech derives from such earlier stories as "Qiuranke zhuan," a Tang dynasty classical tale about a righteous knight-errant.

are invited to participate in it, and their participation is essential to Zhang's project of acting out the role of the perfect swordsman. Before leaving, Zhang asks the brothers to prepare a feast to celebrate his triumphant return and also the climax of his story, the moment when he will practice the magic art of reducing the human head in the bag to water.

The Lou brothers are left alone to finish the rest of the story Zhang has initiated. They design a human head party, but Zhang never returns. The brothers open the bag themselves, only to find in it not a human head but a pig's! Up to that point, Iron-Armed Zhang has remained in control of his own story, using the standard swordsman narrative, but with this final stroke, he permits it to dissolve into grotesquerie. He has used his game as a way of tricking money out of the brothers, but he has carried it much further than such a practical purpose would require. This, I suppose, has to do with the design of the story: by the trick with the pig's head, the novelist allows Zhang to poke fun at both the readers of the novel and Zhang's internal audience, the Lou brothers, who have faith in the familiar devices of the swordsman story.

To make the situation even worse, during the human head party for the "hero" who never shows up, Quan Wuyong is arrested and taken away. "These two incidents left the Lou brothers rather discouraged. They ordered the gatekeeper, if strangers called, to say that they had returned to the capital. And henceforward they remained behind closed doors, devoting themselves to household affairs" (R. 186; S. 146). This is how the story of the brothers' search for the worthies ends: having experienced repeated disillusions and humiliations, they retreat from the outside world that they fail to comprehend, a world that threatens the stability and reliability of the narrative they have taken to heart.

A careful reading of the Lou brothers story tells us much about the narrative strategies that *Rulin waishi* deploys, especially in Part II. The most distinctive feature of *Rulin waishi* is the parody of the conventional narrator. As shown above, the narrator's voice is often duplicated and subverted at the level of the characters' discourse; it is circumscribed, imbued with individual biases and motivations, transposed into inappropriate contexts, and thus devastatingly discredited. Yang Zhizhong recommends Quan Wuyong in the voice of the authoritative narrator, with all the clichés so familiar to the reader of vernacular fiction, but his recommendation is immediately thrown into question. Iron-Armed Zhang represents himself in the same manner, and his self-representation turns out to be a farcical play on the honor of swordsmen as represented in these stories. The Lou brothers, the faithful audience of Yang Zhizhong and Iron-Armed Zhang, find themselves betrayed again and again.

Not only is the voice of the authoritative narrator disembodied, but the mode through which he perceives the world is also undermined. The Lou brothers are betrayed not merely by other characters, who appropriate the narrator's voice, but ultimately by their own blind adherence to the narrative mode that the narrator represents, be it fiction or history. They read every part of the world they encounter as an index of the world they have read about in books. In their efforts to prove the present truth of conventional narrative, however, they play a more active role than ordinary readers. They cooperate with Iron-Armed Zhang in completing his narrative of the swordsman. In claiming that they recognize a man of virtue in Yang, they themselves assume the role of narrator and tell the story to others in an apparent effort to win their consent. If they fail to convince others of Yang's virtue, so does the authoritative narrator of fiction and history in whom they believe and after whom they have modeled their own judgments.

In this part of *Rulin waishi*, the subject matter and narrative form intersect: the characters' moral corruption and abuse of power lie in their audacious appropriation of the established fictional and historical narrative for their own purposes. The normative order, which is sustained by the canonical texts, may not be destabilized, but it cannot be successfully transformed into the narrative world of *Rulin waishi*; nor can it serve as the ideal model by which to effectively measure that world. The Lou brothers, trying to reinforce that perfect order, are not portrayed as cultural heroes, like Liu Bei in *The Romance of the Three Kingdoms*; on the contrary, they become dupes subject to ridicule.

To a certain extent, the brothers' search for worthies resembles Don Quixote's adventures. With chivalric romances as his written guides, Don Quixote sets out to prove what the books say is true. But the texts do little to help him identify the things he encounters on his journey, and he himself ends up verging on delusion and madness. In *The Order of Things: An Archaeology of the Human Sciences*, Michel Foucault argues: "With all their twists and turns, Don Quixote's adventures form the boundary: they mark the end of the old interplay between resemblance and signs and contain the beginnings of new relations." Foucault asserts that *Don Quixote* is the "first modern work of literature" and "a negative of the Renaissance world," "because in it we see the cruel reason of identities and differences make endless sport of signs and similitudes; because in it language breaks off its old kinship with things and enters into that lonely sovereignty from which it will reappear, in its separate state, only as literature; because it marks the point where resemblance enters an age which is, from the point of view of resemblance, one of madness and imagination."[9] My argument is not that *Rulin waishi* marks the beginning of a new era in the way Foucault believes *Don Quixote* does, but that the Lou brothers narrative presents the end of the practice of translating such old texts as *Shiji* into new ones as authoritative guides for deciphering and constructing both the narrative or symbolic world and the actual world of reality. In this episode, the magic linkages between text and reality, between the past and the present, are broken; the process of transforming the text of the valorized past into the reality of the present is permanently suspended.

---

9. Foucault, *The Order of Things*, pp. 46–49.

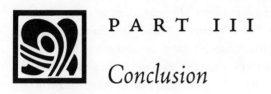

PART III

Conclusion

Wu Jingzi was not the first to disparage the motifs and narrative mode of conventional fiction through metafictional irony. During the late Ming and early Qing periods, such novelists as Dong Yue (1620–86), Li Yu, and Aina were already deft at what we would call "intertextual narrative." Moreover, despite differences in style and subject, their narratives share a salient parodic tenor. The decline of the Ming and the ultimate breakdown of the empire in 1644 raised serious doubts about the validity of Neo-Confucian doctrines, and the mode of *xushu* or sequel that prevailed in the remaining part of the seventeenth century enabled writers of that time to re-evaluate the inherited narrative paradigm and value structures of the vernacular novel. In *A Supplement to "The Journey to the West"* (*Xiyou bu*), Dong Yue recast the image of Monkey by subjecting him to the labyrinth of passion (*qing*), a temptation to which his model in *The Journey to the West* is immune. Dong Yue's allegorical account of Monkey's journey of the mind offers a new angle from which to examine the issues of passion, desire, illusion, and reality so prevalent in late Ming literature.

The boldest debunking of earlier fiction can be found in Li Yu's vernacular fiction, in which the narrator seems to enjoy more than anything else subverting common beliefs, motifs, and stereotypes. Li Yu's comic narrative spares no subject from irony. Remarking on his *Carnal Prayer Mat*, an erotic novel framed by Buddhist rhetoric, the commentator, presumably Li Yu himself, declares: "This is truly a book that mocks everything (*wanshi*)!"[1] The same can be said of his other works. His *Silent Opera* (*Wusheng xi*), an anthology of short stories, includes a parody of "The Oil Seller" ("Maiyou lang du zhan huakui") from one of Feng Menglong's collections: a naïve romantic who adores a singing girl in the same way the oil seller does only ends up cheated and exploited.[2] This character prepares us well for Wu Jingzi's account of Ding Yanzhi in Chapter 54 of *Rulin waishi*—another romantic who invites humiliation by seeking a courtesan who can truly appreciate his poetic talent.

Li Yu did more than parody the established motifs of earlier fiction; he often appropriated the Confucian texts and subjected them to mockery. Elaborating on what books Yuxiang (Jade Scent) should read during the prolonged absence of her husband in *Carnal Prayer Mat*, the narrator goes out of his way to mention such Confucian texts as *The Lives of Virtuous Women* (*Lienü zhuan*) and *The Girls' Classic of Filial Piety* (*Nü xiaojing*), only to blame them for misleading her.[3]

Gentle reader, what kind of books ought she to have read, do you suppose, in order to relieve her distress and boredom? In my humble opinion, no play or novel would have been of any use whatever. Only the books her father taught her to read as a girl, such as *The Lives of Virtuous Women* and *The Girls' Classic of Filial Piety*, would have met her need. If only she had been willing to take them out and read them, they would have relieved her distress and boredom and also quenched her thirst and satisfied her hunger. She might then have been able to endure a real widowhood, to say nothing of the temporary variety. But Jade Scent took a different course and gave undue credence to the "Four Virtues for Girls" and the "Three Obediences for Women," which stipulate: "Before marriage obey your father, after marriage your husband." Accordingly she ignored her father's books and began to read her husband's, taking out his entire stock of obscenity, such as *The Foolish Woman's Story* (*Chipozi zhuan*), *The Unofficial History of the Embroidered Couch* (*Xiuta yeshi*), and *The Life of the Lord of Perfect Satisfaction* (*Ruyijun zhuan*), and going through them carefully and methodically.

The narrator designs a comic paradox in which Confucian teachings are responsible for Jade Scent's decision to read erotic fiction. The Confucian texts

---

1. Li Yu, *Rou pu tuan*, vol. 15, p. 502.

2. See "Ren suji qionggui su piaoyuan," story no. 7, in Li Yu, *Wusheng xi*, pp. 112–25. For Feng Menglong's story, see *Xingshi hengyan*, in Wei Tongxian, ed., *Feng Menglong quanji* (Shanghai: Shanghai guji chubanshe, 1992), vol. 22, pp. 84–192.

3. See Li Yu, *Rou putuan*, vol. 15; p. 312; trans. from Hanan, *The Carnal Prayer Mat*, p. 206.

emphasize men's dominance over women and the wife's obedience to the husband. They do not necessarily ensure, however, that every man is up to his prescribed role as a model superior to women. In Li Yu's narrative the husband advises her to read his collection of erotic fiction, and she is in no position to disobey. It may well be argued that Jade Scent deliberately applies the Confucian teachings to an irrelevant occasion, but what guarantee is there that they can be appropriately followed without distortion or abuse? In this passage, Li Yu exploited the gap between name and reality and between the power structure and the moral hierarchy, the gap in which Confucian discourse is often caught. And the narrator, who recommends a list of Confucian readings, ends up inviting an ironical reading of his own statement.

The playful tone of Li Yu's narrative is perhaps the most telling. Instead of treating Confucian words with reverence and piety, Li Yu removed them from the original context, explored their meanings in all possible ways, and used them in his verbal sport of ridicule and exuberant mockery. Such an attitude pervaded late Ming literature, and the misappropriation of the Confucian rhetoric became the norm of the day. *The Peony Pavilion* (*Mudan ting*), a play by Tang Xianzu (1550–1616), for instance, gives compelling expression to the rhetoric of appropriation: Chunxiang (Fragrance), the maid of Du Li'niang, the heroine of the play, offers her colloquial reading of the lines from the *Book of Odes*; Chen Zuiliang, a tutor turned doctor, takes on the conventional comic role of quack as he quotes from the same book in diagnosing Du Li'niang's illness; and Shi Daogu (Sister Stone), a Taoist nun, systematically misuses the lines from *The Classic of a Thousand Characters* (*Qianzi wen*), a popular primer of the time, in a bawdy account of her sexual experience.[4] *Singing as Whistling* (*Ge dai xiao*), a late Ming drama attributed to Xu Wei (1521–93), follows the same rhetorical pattern; it stages a ribald conversation in the opening scene by drawing on the language of the Four Books (*Sishu*).[5] We have no difficulty tracing Longsan's sport of misquoting legitimate language to late Ming literature.

---

4. See scenes 7, 17, and 18 of Tang Xianzu, *Mudan ting*, pp. 27–34, 83–95; trans. from Birch, *The Peony Pavilion*, pp. 24–29, 79–94. Sister Stone's appropriation of *Qianzi wen* is by no means an isolated case in the literature of the late Ming and the early Qing. *Hui* nine of *Huanxi yuanjia* (vol. 10; pp. 360–65), a collection of the short stories of the time, includes an episode in which the protagonist Zhang Erguan composes a letter of seduction, using the form and vocabulary of *Qianzi wen*.

5. Xu Wei, *Xu Wei ji*, pp. 1135–36. For more discussion of the late Ming mode of misappropriation of Confucian words, see my "*Jin Ping Mei cihua* and Late Ming Print Culture."

Of the early Qing writers, Aina, the author of *Idle Talk Under the Bean Arbor*, was a master at debunking the canonical images of historical personages. One of his stories reverses Sima Qian's representation of Boyi and Shuqi in *Shiji* as two principled loyalists of the Shang dynasty who starved themselves to death rather than serving the new regime. Despite Confucius's admiration of them, Aina portrayed Boyi as a detached loner and Shuqi as an opportunist who shows no confidence in the principle of loyalty at the beginning and ends up rejecting it entirely. However, since, as Aina's narrator suggests, the cosmic forces engage in procreation and destruction without concern for morality, there is no reason to denounce Shuqi either; he simply does what it takes to accommodate the cosmic forces and historical necessity. So conceived, Aina's parody of the Boyi and Shuqi narrative signals the breakdown of faith in the value system essential to the working of the authoritative narrative in both history and fiction.[6]

Wu Jingzi is an heir of these ironists. He carries the parodic trend of the late Ming and early Qing into the mid-eighteenth century, lending it to new intellectual understanding and technical touches. First, *Rulin waishi* manages to present compelling testimony to the end of the grand narrative of history. It does not engage in debunking such historical icons as Boyi and Shuqi; instead, it shows their irrelevance to history as experienced by its characters. In Wu Jingzi's account, the canonical narrative of history is locked into the realm of the absolute past and deprived of its ability to engage and affect the current practices. Wu understood its putative claim over the making of both symbolic and actual reality; the power of his narrative lies precisely in his awareness of the fact that such earlier novels as *The Romance of the Three Kingdoms* continuously confirmed *Shiji* and other early historical texts as the authoritative source for their truth claims. However, in *Rulin waishi*, the Lou brothers, who follow Liu Bei in citing these texts as their guide for action, produce only caricature and parody. What *The Romance* endorses as infallible truth turns out to be the source of errors and fallacies.

Second, since the authoritative narrative of historiography constitutes a major source and paradigm of the vernacular novel, to question its representation of history is to scrutinize the history of representation in both historiography and vernacular fiction. In this sense, *Rulin waishi* is an ambi-

---

6. See Aina Jushi, *Doupeng xianhua*, pp. 185–218.

tious work; it offers a critical reflection on the vernacular novel as a genre by systematically reworking its established narrative modes, motifs, and character types. It can be argued that Wu Jingzi took the tradition of the vernacular novel as the raw material for representation; he allowed his characters to appropriate the role of storyteller in their deceptive self-representation and subjected some recurring narrative motifs and patterns of the earlier novels to an ironic rendering. The tradition of the vernacular novel is composed of multiple sources, and Wu Jingzi summed them up through parody.

Indeed, *Rulin waishi* not only offers an ironic parade of motifs and character types from the historical novels and the stories of swordsmen,[7] but also parodies the scholar-beauty romance in the tales of Chen Munan and Ding Yanzhi in Chapters 53 and 54: Chen deceives and abandons his courtesan lover, and Ding is humiliated by his adored courtesan. In premodern Chinese literature, there is no romance without poetry, but nothing could be more ironic than the moment when Ding Yanzhi pays his respects to Pinniang to discuss poetry:

Upstairs he found Pinniang studying chess moves. He stepped forward and made a deep bow. Wanting to laugh, she offered him a seat and asked him his business.

"I have long heard of your fondness for poetry, madam, and have brought one of my unworthy compositions to ask your opinion of it."

"The rule of our house is not to read poems without first receiving a fee. I'll read your poem, sir, when I've seen your money." Ding fumbled for a long time in his belt, but all he fished out was twenty coppers, which he placed on the rosewood table. Pinniang gave a peal of laughter. "You'd better give your money to the pimp at Feng Family Lane in Yizheng!" she said. "Don't dirty my table with it! Take it back at once to buy a few mouthfuls of food!"

---

7. Although *Rulin waishi* has little in common with the *Water Margin*, it occasionally goes out of its way to depict such characters as the Fourth Mr. Feng (Fengsi), in Chapters 49 through 52, who seem straight out of the *Water Margin*. But Feng is misplaced in the world of *Rulin waishi*: an idiosyncratic loner with no commitment to any public course, he indulges in spontaneous acts of correcting wrongs and mediating disputes. It should not be surprising that Wu Jingzi often creates characters in such a way, as if to test the limits of the existing narrative modes in making sense of them. In Chapter 41, Shen Qiongzhi, a young lady who escapes an arranged marriage and lives independently in Nanjing by selling needlework and poetry, presents an enigma in the eyes of male literati. Wu Shu, for instance, tries to define her identity by ruling out all the possible types, including Hongxian (Red Thread), a swordswoman represented in a classical tale of the Tang dynasty.

Turning red and white by turns in his confusion, Ding hung his head, rolled up the scroll and put it in his gown, then crept downstairs and slunk home. (R. 733; S. 591–92)

Third, unlike Li Yu and other ironists of the seventeenth century, who often indulge in verbal effusiveness, Wu Jingzi was a minimalist; he allowed his characters to run the show and contradict themselves in what they say and do, with little narratorial intervention. Li Yu participated in the same verbal sport of misappropriation and mockery with his characters, and his narrative is permeated by carnivalistic exuberance. Wu Jingzi, by contrast, revealed the scandalous aspect of the literati's sociopolitical drama with ironic detachment. He was not part of the game; his narrative lays bare its hidden patterns and mechanisms rather than identifying with them. As said above, the diminishing of the narrator constitutes part of the larger structural change of narrative conventions, to which Rulin waishi bears witness. From this perspective, what occurs on the level of representation is not unrelated to what is represented in Rulin waishi, for Wu's exposé of the literati's verbal practice—the disjunction and discrepancy between word and deed, the self-interested appropriation of Confucian discourse, and ultimately the dissolution of the Confucian norm—compels him to organize his own narrative in an alternative way.

Indeed, the crisis of the narrative tradition of the vernacular novel is not confined to the collapse of the world of representation; it is "part of the disintegration of an entire universe of social relations of which it was constitutive."[8] A close reading of episodes from Rulin waishi uncovers the patterns that govern both the world of representation and the way it is represented. The narrative world of Rulin waishi, as I see it, offers clues to the very mechanisms that bring the authoritative narrative, whatever forms it takes, to an end; it represents, among other things, the deflation of words, the repudiation of the narratorial voice, and the collapse of the symbolic order—elements that contribute to the decline of the narrative authority of historiography, vernacular fiction, and other related genres.

However, as the Introduction and Parts I and II make clear, Wu Jingzi did not stop with parody. For him, parody was an inevitable step and necessary condition for his search for an alternative vision of the Confucian world.

---

8. My discussion of the crisis of the conventional narrative is related to Pierre Bourdieu's analysis of the crisis of religious language and its performative efficacy; see Bourdieu, *Language and Symbolic Power*, p. 116.

This not only helps to distinguish Wu from the parodists of the seventeenth century but also raises some important questions: How did Wu construct such a vision out of the savaged normative discourse? What were his sources? How did he define his own narrative? And finally, how did he reconcile, if he ever did, his parodic energy and moralistic urges? These are a few of the issues dealt with in Part IV.

PART IV

The Taibo Myth
and Its Dilemma: Redefining
the Literati Novel

Rulin waishi is at its best when disparaging the assumptions and normative functions of the authoritative narrative, but as it moves on to construct an alternative Confucian vision of the world, it raises an inevitable question about its own choice of strategies and sources. What does it create in place of the narrative modes, master texts, and rhetoric that it discredits? How does it embody and sustain its moral imagination? In the middle section of *Rulin waishi*, Wu Jingzi's thematic and narrative deliberations become closely intertwined and mutually complicated, for his rejection of narrative ritual gives rise to a moral vision of ascetic *li* that transcends narrative. It is paradoxical to narrate ascetic ritual, because it is, by definition, opposed to narrative ritual, which relies on narrative discourse to define its meanings. But to do away with narrative is not a realistic solution, for, after all, *Rulin waishi* is itself a novel. In this sense, Wu's representation of ascetic ritual becomes a constant struggle, and his effort to move beyond it betrays a great deal of anxiety about the tension between narrativity and his moral imagination.

As we have seen, in an effort to capture ascetic ritual in action, Wu Jingzi drew on ritual manuals, and this enabled him to highlight the external form of ritual and describe activity in the way it is prescribed. To avoid the pitfall of narrative ritual, Wu also provided a sort of minimum narrative in his account of Filial Guo, which mimics the practice of the ritual—it focuses exclusively on surface and action, with almost no psychological dimension and little dialogue. This part further elucidates the issues at stake in Wu Jingzi's moral imagination by examining his rendering of motifs from the Taibo myth. I shall argue that although *Rulin waishi* is occasionally caught up in the predicament of narrative authority, to which it bears witness and upon which it reflects, the work's self-reflexivity comes to define its quality as a literati novel. As an exemplar of a new medium for cultural criticism, *Rulin waishi* has to rely on constant self-scrutiny to continue functioning.

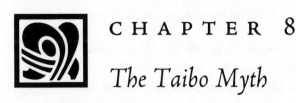

C H A P T E R 8

The Taibo Myth

and the Problem of Narrative

Although the ceremony in Chapter 37 is dedicated to Wu Taibo, and although Yu Yude, who presides at the ceremony, is described as the present-day Wu Taibo, no account of Wu Taibo is provided in the novel. What we see in *Rulin waishi* is a ritual without a myth—pure ritual action with no verbal interpretation of its symbolic meanings or of the significance of Wu Taibo, the symbol of the virtue that the ritual presumably enacts. But the Taibo myth is not irrelevant, and the key to this section of the novel lies in part in its relationship with the myth.

Wu Taibo was the eldest son of King Tai (Danfu), leader of the Zhou clan. According to legend, he yielded the throne to his youngest brother and fled into the Wu region. The authoritative evaluation of him can be traced to Confucius's comment: "Taibo can certainly be called a man of virtue in its supreme form. Although he yielded the throne three times, he did it in such an indirect way that people could not even get around to praising him."[1] Since Wu Taibo "yielded" the throne under various disguises and left no concrete proof of his virtue, Confucius stepped in to assert his sageliness. Despite the lack of a narrative that would substantiate such a claim, Taibo's virtue, once "recognized" by Confucius, must be taken as given. The Taibo myth asserts without narrating; it reinforces a prior judgment about Wu Taibo and becomes part of the naturalized system of Confucian beliefs:

1. *Analects*, Book 8.

"a man of virtue in its supreme form," Wu Taibo comes to embody the ideal of what a Confucian sage is, the paragon against which others must be measured.

In *Rulin waishi*, Chi Hengshan similarly declares in Chapter 33 that "the worthiest man that our Nanjing has ever produced is Wu Taibo." Not unlike the Taibo myth, the novel presupposes the belief necessary to its representation of the Taibo ceremony and takes for granted that Wu Taibo is a Confucian sage. More important, however, is that the account of literati withdrawal from the official world taps into the motif of yielding in the Taibo myth: Taibo is said to have yielded the throne three times, and *Rulin waishi* relates the stories of three major characters (Du Shaoqing, Zhuang Shaoguang, and Yu Yude) turning down recommendations from officials or offers of office. Yu Yude seems especially to resemble Wu Taibo in possessing "hidden virtue" (*yinde*): he does others acts of kindness without publicizing them so that people can hardly find a way to praise him. If Wu Jingzi did not include the Taibo myth in *Rulin waishi*, it is perhaps because he saw no need. After all, he provided accounts of Yu Yude, the present-day Wu Taibo, and other literati ritualists who follow Wu's example. Perhaps more important, the motif of yielding comes to represent the same thing as the mythological claim—a strong urge to go beyond the mundane realm of experience, verification, and controversy and assert the value of yielding on its own terms and by its own standards.

Wu Jingzi shared this mythological urge in projecting his ideal vision of the ritualized world, but his narrative is charged with an equally strong, if not stronger, contradictory drive. In *Rulin waishi*, Wu set up a narrative situation in which no positive assertion can be made without creating controversy or ambiguity. The accounts of Du Shaoqing, Zhuang Shaoguang, and, to a certain extent, Yu Yude are no exceptions. The repeated acts of yielding are contrasted, and none is the perfect choice for the characters. As a result, the virtue of yielding becomes caught in time-bound narrative and subject to shifting perspectives deeply enmeshed in human circumstances and interpersonal relationships.

In his rendering of these ritualists as followers of Wu Taibo, Wu Jingzi seems to have recapitulated the impasse in which the Taibo myth is stuck— the myth is just as controversial, with no prospect of a definitive conclusion. The existence of conflicting versions of the Taibo narrative compels believers in the myth to defend their claim by furnishing narrative details. But in so doing, they remove the myth from the valorized plane of the absolute past and plunge it into an ongoing debate. The Taibo myth and its narrative dilemma offer a starting point for the interpretation of Wu Jingzi's moral imagination.

Taibo Worship: Between Fiction and Action

The worship of Taibo, sanctioned by Confucius's approval, developed largely in the Wu region. We must examine this local phenomenon and its relation with the making of *Rulin waishi*—both Taibo worship as represented in the novel and the role of *Rulin waishi* in reinforcing this cult.

Since Taibo is a symbol of yielding, the core of Taibo worship is the ethic of yielding or noncompetitiveness. Its importance is demonstrated in the way Qing literati diagnosed the social crisis of their own time. In "An Account of Reconstructing Taibo's Tomb as Inscribed on a Stone Stele" ("Chongxiu Taibomu bei"), written in 1818, Qin Ying attributed the problems of contemporary society to the intensified competition among individuals:[2]

In our town [Meili; considered the hometown of Taibo] there is little morality to speak of these days. Public morals steadily deviate ever further from those of ancient times. The virtues of reverence and noncompetitiveness are ignored. . . . Literati forget principle at the sight of profit. Within the same lineage, the noble members bully the base ones, and the younger ones override their elders. Disputes over the most trifling advantage often end in angry curses.

That contemporary society is degenerate and driven by self-interest was a cliché in late imperial times. Qin Ying's comments do not necessarily tell us anything specific about the period he was describing. By citing such a commonplace, Qin Ying reinforced the need for the ethics that he espoused. Noncompetitiveness is seen as a way of redefining social relationships, and Wu Taibo is supposed to have the power to draw people away from competition guided by self-interest. Qin Ying's diagnosis of the disease is tailored to the medicine that he can offer. Within the terms of his prognosis, the cure is meant to be certain. In the local history of Meili, we often encounter wishful narratives on the magic potential of Taibo worship: whereas once people with competing land claims had settled their disputes in court, now

---

2. See Wu Xi, *Taibo Meili zhi* (Gazetteer of Taibo Meili), *juan* 4, pp. 6a–b.

they vie with each other to donate their land to the Taibo temple and tomb reconstruction. The narrative ends with the expected comments: "How deeply this supremely moral man [Wu Taibo] strikes root in the hearts of the people."[3] In their promotion of Taibo worship, the regional elite and officials hope that they can educate the local people and thus, ultimately, to quote Chi Hengshan's words from Chapter 33 of the novel, "improve the mores of the state."

Wu Taibo was celebrated in the Wu region not merely as a sage sanctioned by Confucius but as the founding father of the Wu clan. During the Ming and Qing dynasties, the growing veneration of Wu Taibo was accompanied by an increasing number of temples and ceremonies dedicated to him. Wu Jingzi, who made the Taibo project the central event in *Rulin waishi*, shared this inclination with his contemporary literati. Cheng Jing'er, the father of Cheng Tingzuo, for instance, once suggested commemorating Wu Taibo as a Confucian sage and dedicating a sacrifice to him in Nanjing.[4] Du Zhao, the teacher of Wu Peiyuan, wrote an essay celebrating the reconstruction of a Taibo temple in Meili.[5] Both Cheng Tingzuo and Wu Peiyuan were close friends of Wu Jingzi and served as models for the two major protagonists of his novel, Zhuang Shaoguang and Yu Yude, who preside over the ceremony to Taibo.[6]

To the literati of the Wu region, the recognition of Wu Taibo as ancestor of the Wu clan celebrated the origins of the local culture as well as the identity of a local lineage. Despite the economic and cultural prosperity of the Wu region in late imperial times, scholars from this region still felt obliged to overcome their sense of inferiority about the history of their culture. Its relatively late development in terms of Chinese history made justifying the origins of Wu culture even more urgent. Partly because of its distance from central China, the Wu region had been regarded, in ancient times, as barbarian territory that had still to be integrated into the landscape of civilization as Confucians defined the word. This perception of Wu was not simply imposed by scholars from central China, however; it was embed-

3. Ibid., pp. 12b–13a, 4a.

4. Cheng Jing'er, "Jinling dianshi yi" (On the ceremonies of Jinling), in *Shangyuan xian zhi* (Gazetteer of Shangyuan county), ed. Lan Yingxi, He Mengzhuan, and Cheng Tingzuo in 1751, *juan* 11. Cheng Tingzuo quoted this essay in an article commemorating his father (*Qingxi wenji, juan* 12; quoted in He Zehan, "*Rulin waishi*" renwu benshi kaolüe, p. 60).

5. Du Zhao, "Chongxiu Taibomiao beiji," p. 13b.

6. He Zehan, "*Rulin waishi*" benshi kaolüe, pp. 42–60.

ded in Wu scholars' account of their own history. One scholar wrote that before Taibo arrived, the native people of the Wu region had lived the lives of savages, cutting their hair short, tattooing their bodies, and mingling with animals.[7] To his great disappointment, another Wu scholar discovered that among Confucius's seventy-two disciples only one hailed from the Wu area.[8] The literati of the region struggled constantly to include their region in the Confucian ethical narrative of early history, which had originated and developed in central China.

In Wu Taibo, regional scholars found everything they needed for their project of historical revision. They saw in him a double identity: local and more than local. A member of the Zhou royal family from central China, Wu Taibo established the state of Gouwu and introduced civilization to the region. In so doing, he also acquired his surname, which attested to his local identity. "The worthiest man that our Nanjing has ever produced," declares Chi Hengshan in *Rulin waishi*, "is Wu Taibo." The statement is a reinterpretation of Confucius's praise of Wu Taibo; it relates Wu's sagehood to the role he played in the creation of the state of Gouwu.

Taibo worship appears in an extended version in *Flowers in the Mirror*. Chapters 11 and 12 take place in the Country of Gentlemen, a utopia first mentioned in the *Classic of Mountains and Seas (Shan hai jing)*.[9] According to the *Classic of Mountains and Seas*, the Country of Gentlemen is located somewhere in the east; it becomes well known because its inhabitants are always willing to yield to others and avoid competition. The novel embellishes this account of the Country of Gentlemen and presents it primarily from the perspective of two travelers, Tang Ao and Duo Jiugong, who are from central China, "the Heavenly Kingdom." To them, the inhabitants of the Country of Gentlemen are gracious, respectable, and polite—true gentlemen. Yet they are uncorrupted by the fame they enjoy, for they are so naïve that they do not know why their land is called the Country of Gentlemen or even understand the meaning of the title. This ideal country is set squarely in contrast with the Heavenly Kingdom. In Chapter 11, two civil officials of the Country of Gentlemen launch into a sweeping criticism of the institutions and customs of the Heavenly Kingdom, including its judicial system, which, according to them, tends to encourage self-interested competition. The trav-

---

7. Wu Xi, *Taibo Meili zhi, juan* 4, p. 11a.
8. Cheng Jing'er, "Jingling danshi yi," in He Zehan, *"Rulin waishi" benshi kaolüe*, p. 60.
9. "Hai wai dong jing," in *Shanhai jing, juan* 9, p. 46a–b.

elers cannot agree more, for in their eyes, the Country of Gentlemen stands for the moral vision that has been contaminated and corrupted in their home country.

More important to our purpose is that *Flowers* cites Wu Taibo as a way of exemplifying the vision of this moral community. According to Chapter 12, the inhabitants of this country are none other than the descendants of Wu Taibo. Thus, in the representation of the Country of Gentlemen, we see all the elements of which Taibo worship was formed: the symbol of Wu Taibo, the virtue of noncompetitiveness he embodies, and the civilized land founded by him. But this version of Taibo worship presents the Wu region not as a land to be integrated into the Confucian narrative of the civilization of central China, but as a Confucian utopia against which central China itself is measured and found wanting.

The glorification of Wu Taibo finds sophisticated expression in Wu Jingzi's *Rulin waishi*. In Chapter 37, the worship of Wu Taibo as ancestor of the Wu clan and founding father of Gouwu is reflected in the organization of ceremonial personnel. As Chen Meilin points out, since ancient Gouwu consisted of parts of modern Jiangsu, Zhejiang, and Anhui, the three ritual masters and two ushers are representatives of each region. To achieve this, Wu Jingzi even sacrificed the consistency and integrity of his own narrative. For instance, Ma Chunshang, a character who takes no part in the preparations for the ceremony and demonstrates no particular virtue that would qualify him for a role in it, occupies the position of third master, simply because Ma is the only available character from Zhejiang.[10]

Moreover, we can hardly ignore the fact that Wu Jingzi and his friend Wu Peiyuan, the model for Yu Yude, share a common surname with Wu Taibo. In *Taibo Meili zhi*, Wu Peiyuan is said to be a descendant of Wu Taibo, and his attendance at the Taibo ceremony is described as a ritual obligation toward his remote ancestor.[11] Wu Jingzi also traced his family back to the founding father of the Wu clan.[12] In a poem to Wu Peiyuan, Wu Jingzi acknowledged their common ancestry. This sense of ancestral worship

---

10. Chen Meilin, *Xinpi "Rulin waishi,"* p. 409. Wu Jingzi's local sense is also illuminated in Chapter 46: at a farewell party for Yu Yude, the host claims that all the literati attendants are from "the area of five hundred square li," which roughly refers to the size of ancient Gouwu.

11. Wu Xi, *Taibo Meili zhi, juan* 4, p. 10b.

12. Wu Jingzi, "Yi jia fu" (A *fu* on moving my family away from my hometown), in *Chongyin wenmu shanfang ji*, p. 24. See also Chen Meilin, *Wu Jingzi yanjiu*, p. 140; and idem, *Wu Jingzi pingzhuan*, p. 291.

permeates *Rulin waishi*. Yu Yude's surname derives from Yu Zhong (Zhongyong), a younger brother of Wu Taibo, who fled with him to the Wu area and later succeeded him. According to historical records, Wu Taibo had no male offspring. The origin of the Wu clan was, therefore, traced back to Yu Zhong.[13]

It has been argued that Wu's representation of the Taibo ceremony is based on an actual ceremony. In a story that surfaced more than a century after his death, Wu Jingzi was even recognized as the main organizer of the ceremony, an assertion that bolstered the idea that Du Shaoqing represented none other than Wu Jingzi himself, but this claim remains hypothetical unless it can be proved by sources other than the novel itself.[14] The Temple of Ancient Worthies, which dates back to the Song dynasty, was left in disrepair during most of the Qianlong period.[15] In a brief preface to a poem written in 1753, one year before his death, Wu Jingzi gave an account of the rituals that, like the Taibo ceremony in *Rulin waishi*, took place at the foot of Rainflower Mount, but these were dedicated to Cang Jie, the figure credited in legend with creating the trigrams, the prototype of the Chinese writing system. So far no one has found concrete evidence to substantiate the hypothesis. But, despite the lack of evidence, the parallel between Wu Jingzi and Du Shaoqing has acquired a life of its own. Readers try to find counterparts to the story of Du Shaoqing in the life of Wu Jingzi, and if they cannot, they take the story of Du Shaoqing as that of Wu Jingzi.

Since this (auto)biographical approach has led nowhere, let us consider another way of reading the Taibo incident that might move us beyond this dilemma. We do not know to what extent Wu Jingzi's account of Yu Yude's participation in the Taibo ceremony is based on Wu Peiyuan's life story. But we do know that Wu Peiyuan dedicated a sacrifice to Wu Taibo in 1763,

---

13. See "Wu Taibo shijia," in Sima Qian, *Shiji*, juan 31, p. 1446.

14. In a postscript to *Rulin waishi* written in 1869, Jin He, based on a story he presumably heard from his mother, a descendant of one of Wu Jingzi's distant relatives, claimed that the story of Du Shaoqing, an active participant in the Taibo ceremony, was Wu Jingzi's self-representation: "The Master [Wu Jingzi] brought together like-minded fellows and constructed the Temple of Ancient Worthies (Xianxian Ci) at the foot of Rainflower Mount and offered sacrifices to some 230 worthies from Wu Taibo on. The temple was extremely magnificent, and its cost was very high. The Master sold his house in order to complete the construction project" ("*Rulin waishi* ba" in Li Hanqiu, ed., "*Rulin waishi*" *huijiao huiping ben*, pp. 764–65).

15. See Yuan Mei, *Jiangning xinzhi*, juan 10, pp. 6–7.

almost ten years after Wu Jingzi's death. As a native of Meili, allegedly the hometown of the legendary Wu Taibo, Wu Peiyuan considered Taibo his remote ancestor. After retiring from his official post, he returned to Meili and lived there until his death. In 1763, together with the magistrate of Meili, he presided over a project for reconstructing a Taibo temple and participated in a ceremony dedicated to Wu Taibo.[16]

Thus, to say that Wu Jingzi's narrative of the Taibo ceremony is not a biographical account of Wu Peiyuan is not to say that it has nothing to do with him. If it tells us nothing about what Wu Peiyuan did, it may still suggest something he was expected to do. As a novelist, Wu Jingzi drew on Wu Peiyuan for the biography of his fictional counterpart in Chapter 36 only to cast him in a leading role in the fiction of the Taibo ceremony in the following chapter. But fiction influences life. When Wu Peiyuan finally found an occasion to perform the Taibo ceremony, he was acting not merely in the story of his own life but in that of someone else's as well.

The story of Wu Jingzi and Wu Peiyuan does not, however, end here. It continues with Wu Lang, Wu Jingzi's son. When Wu Lang traveled to Meili and paid his respects to Wu Peiyuan a dozen years after his father's death in 1763, he was invited to visit the Taibo temple constructed under the direction of Wu Peiyuan and the county magistrate. In front of that temple Wu Lang composed a poem recording this memorable moment.[17]

Wu Jingzi did not tell his friends what they should do; nor did he need to wait for them to explain the significance of his novel. By making the Taibo ceremony the central event that unified his imagined literati community, Wu Jingzi was looking to fiction as a way of negotiating with his friends as well as with himself. Disillusioned with official institutions, Wu consigned his hopes to Confucian ritual, which he thought might rescue him and his fellow literati from uselessness and oblivion. For his part, negotiation did not necessarily result in action; it amounted instead to narration, to the construction of a plot, and thus to action of a different kind.

---

16. Wu Xi, *Taibo Meili zhi, juan* 4, p. 10b.

17. Wu Lang, "Passing the Temple of Mount Hui, Staying in the Tingsong Convent, and Composing the Poem Together with Mengquan [Wu Peiyuan] and Aitang," in Li Hanqiu, ed., *Wu Jingzi Wu Lang shiwen heji*, p. 233. At the end of the poem is a note by Wu Lang: "Aitang has recently had a Taibo Temple established within the courtyard of the Temple of Mount Hui." See Chen Meilin, *Wu Jingzi pingzhuan*, pp. 290–91; and Li Hanqiu, ed., *"Rulin waishi" huijiao huiping ben*, pp. 56–57.

As I have argued, writing a novel may have been part of Wu's plan to get his friends involved. Not only could he consult his friends for help in designing the fictional ritual, he could also make use of their ritual notes. In *Rulin waishi*, which he wrote during his Nanjing years, he paid tribute to his friends by modeling his fictional heroes on them. As we have seen, Chi Hengshan and Zhuang Shaoguang were based on Fan Shengmo and Cheng Tingzuo, with whom Wu often discussed Confucian ritual and deliberated on projects for the practice of ritual. Wu also created Du Shaoqing, his autobiographical self, although in a more apologetic and less flattering fashion, and arranged for Du to join the circle of literati leaders of the Taibo project. There is no doubt that writing the novel provided Wu with an occasion to review and reorganize his own life through narrative. It also equipped him with the symbolic means by which to reinforce his own bonds with his group and to solidify the group itself.

Wu Jingzi also wrote with his literati friends in mind as part of his intended (and actual) readership. Although we do not know when he began to show his friends the manuscript of his novel, it is clear that before his death he had made himself known, at least within his own circle, as the author of *Rulin waishi*.[18] These readers knew more than anyone else about the sources of the novel, and Wu left enough marks and clues to help them identify its referents.[19] In giving his manuscript to his friends and acquaintances, he therefore knowingly confronted them with their fictional counterparts.

Other facts highlight the significance of this. For one thing, Wu Jingzi did not complete his novel until a few years before his death, and the writing probably occupied about nineteen years. In the second half, the fictional characters depart on travels in an interesting parallel to what their originals did in real life. For instance, in Chapter 48 Du Shaoqing travels to Zhejiang to visit Yu Yude, an incident that is probably based on the trip Wu Jingzi made in 1748 or 1749 to Zhejiang to visit Wu Peiyuan, who had left Nanjing in 1746.[20]

---

18. In a poem written upon Wu's death, Wang Youzeng, one of his friends, wrote, "Facing Mount Zhong every day in his leisure life, he earned himself fame for his *Rulin waishi*" (Li Hanqiu, ed., *"Rulin waishi" yanjiu ziliao*, p. 17).

19. For instance, Yu Yude's name is derived from the same passage of the glossary of the *Classic of Change* (*Yijing*) as Wu Peiyuan's; see He Zehan, *"Rulin waishi" renwu benshi kaolüe*, p. 45.

20. For Wu Jingzi's trip to visit Wu Peiyuan in Zhejiang, see Chen Meilin, *Wu Jingzi pingzhuan*, p. 305. This also helps us date when Chapter 48 was written.

Moreover, by considering the process by which *Rulin waishi* took shape and was circulated, we may comprehend the role of the novel within a complex and varied network of interaction between writer and reader. Not only could his friends respond to the novel with action, which would then feed into the next part of the narrative, but also Wu Jingzi, as writer, could do much more than a biographer usually does: he could exert a certain influence over his friends by casting them in theatrical scenes and assigning them roles yet to be enacted in their own lives. Thus, by writing about the Taibo ceremony and its advocates, he was able to insert his narrative into the world of experience and generated, in his own way, a dialogue between fiction and reality.

Wu Jingzi and his friends were not alone in their efforts to promote Taibo worship. In 1705, during an imperial tour of inspection of the Jiangnan region, the Kangxi emperor wrote a dedication for the tablet of a Taibo temple in Suzhou.[21] In 1737, the Qianlong emperor granted special funds to renovate the tombs and temples of ancient worthies, among them the Taibo temple in Meili.[22] Fourteen years later, in 1751, on his way to visit the Jiangnan region, the Qianlong emperor sent special envoys to offer sacrifices at nearby Taibo temples. Following his grandfather's example, he wrote an inscription, praising Taibo's "supreme act of yielding three times."[23] At that time Wu Jingzi may have been finishing or revising his novel in Nanjing. The emperor's respect for Wu Taibo may not have influenced the design of the novel, but this contemporary event resonates with the last chapter, in which the participants in the Taibo ceremony receive posthumous awards and are commemorated in an imperial ceremony.

The Taibo Myth, Supreme Virtue, and Absolute Truth

Taibo worship is composed of two parts: myth and ritual. As I have mentioned, the ritual is fully present in *Rulin waishi*, but the myth is absent. I shall begin with what is absent and look for something in it that might help us understand what is present in the novel.[24]

---

21. Zhao Erxun, *Qing shi gao*, vol. 3, *juan* 11, p. 410.

22. Qin Ying, "Chongxiu Taibomu bei," in Wu Xi, ed., *Taibo Meili zhi, juan* 4, p. 6a.

23. See Gao Jin, *Nanxun shengdian*, pp. 213, 1098–99.

24. For the debates on the Taibo narrative from the pre-Qing through the Han periods, see also Kitamura, "Go Taibaku jōkoku no shisō shi." Kitamura mainly examines the debates by placing them in the political and intellectual history of the Han dynasty. He asks different questions and covers largely different sets of material.

In praise of Wu Taibo's yielding of the throne three times, Confucius said that he did so in such an indirect way that "people could not even get around to praising him." In other words, in acting, Wu Taibo leaves no visible trace of his inner virtue, and his nobility is not evident enough to assure unanimous admiration. This has to do with two factors: first, Wu Taibo made no public statements about his intentions; we are told that he yielded the throne on other pretexts. Zheng Xuan's (127–200) commentary on the *Analects* gave concrete form to the Taibo myth: Taibo first fled into the Wu area on the pretext of collecting herbs for his ailing father, then stayed there without attending his father's funeral ceremony, and finally accommodated himself to Wu customs by cutting his hair short and tattooing his body, actions that ruled out a return home. In all three yieldings, Wu Taibo did everything possible to disguise the nature of his noble deed; ironically, this turned out to be the only effective way of achieving his goal.

Second, this account of Wu Taibo's noble conduct does expose him to potential criticism. Although Zheng Xuan's account was highly regarded by such Qing scholars as Liu Baonan (1791–1855) for its fairness, it unwittingly provoked a new round of controversy. Fan Ning (339–401), for instance, offered an alternative reading that undermined the moral implications of the story:[25]

When King Tai fell ill, Taibo left on the excuse of plucking herbs. He did not serve his father properly [or in accordance with the ritual codes] during the latter's lifetime. This was the first time Taibo yielded the throne. When King Tai passed away, Taibo did not return, so that Jili had to preside over King Tai's funeral. Thus Taibo also failed to bury his father in accordance with the ritual codes. This was the second time Taibo yielded the throne. Taibo then cut off his hair and tattooed his body to show that he could not be the successor to the throne, so that again Jili had to preside over the sacrifice to King Tai. Thus Taibo finally failed to sacrifice to his father in accordance with the ritual codes. This was the third time Taibo yielded the throne. This was why Zheng Xuan said that three times Taibo fled the throne indirectly.

In the standard version of the Taibo myth, his yielding of the throne to his younger brother is meant to demonstrate his brotherly love, but it is also construed as a sign of his filial piety to his father, because his father favored the younger brother as his successor. But even if brotherly love and filial piety are the main themes of the myth, Wu Taibo can hardly be said to have

---

25. See Huang Kan, *Lunyu yishu*, vol. 18, *juan* 4, p. 23b.

been a perfect brother and son: he left home when his father fell ill and never returned, even upon his father's death. Even if he did return, as in some versions of the story, that would only have raised more questions about his motivations for leaving and his relationship with his brother. Other commentators faulted Wu Taibo for his private decision to forsake the public duties essential to Confucian ethics. As an embodiment of the ethics of yielding, Wu Taibo is far from perfection. Any efforts to represent him as a Confucian paragon fail miserably and, more often than not, end in contradiction.

Confucius's recommendation of Wu Taibo as "the man of virtue in its supreme form" thus begets two questions: How do we justify Wu Taibo's deed if he was caught between conflicting moral demands? If Wu Taibo did disguise his deed with false statements or excuses, how shall we claim access to the truth and "get around to praising him"?

It is possible to endorse Wu Taibo as a filial son. In one version of the Taibo story, his father favors his younger brother and intends to pass the throne to him; Wu Taibo's move to the Wu region can be construed as a filial deed in accord with his father's will. But as I shall discuss below, this version of the story would inevitably compromise Wu Taibo's image as a sage who yielded the throne voluntarily. In Part I, I introduced an alternative reading of the Taibo myth and argued that Wu Taibo's decision to give up his private and public duties can be best justified on the grounds that in so doing he enacts a higher virtue rather than merely fulfilling his sociopolitical obligations. In other words, as "the man of virtue in its supreme form," he embodies a higher order than the mundane.

In the Taibo myth, Wu Taibo is given a title that denies his kingship, for he is called, paradoxically, a "king of yielding" or a "king who yielded the throne" (rangwang). This title is less paradoxical than it seems at first glance, since it may have been derived from the notion of the "sage-king" (sheng wang), the ideal Confucian rulers of legendary antiquity, known not only for their benevolent governance but also for their yielding of the throne to men of virtue. The Chinese term for abdication of the throne is shanrang, which echoes the title of Wu Taibo as rangwang. It is said that Yao, a legendary sovereign of remote antiquity, passed the crown to Shun, a sage of the time, as did Shun to Yu. This form of succession, according to Confucians, was the norm before being replaced by primogeniture and other forms of succession based on descent. The tradition of yielding the throne became emblematic of a golden age when the political system was perfectly integrated into the moral order as prescribed by Confucianism. At stake in this grand narrative is the story of the Confucian sage-kings, who ruled as sages and yielded as kings. Those who succeeded them as kings were portrayed as no less virtuous, for they, like the sage-kings themselves, were chosen precisely because they were sages.

An elaboration of the same subject, the Taibo myth is conceived in a similar manner. Wu Taibo, who yields the throne to his younger brother, seems to have been modeled after the sage-kings; he is posthumously endowed with the title of king. However, another and probably more persuasive way of stating the case would be to say that the Taibo narrative tends to invalidate, rather than reinforce, the *shanrang* prototype of the sage-king narrative. The most obvious evidence for this is the dissolution of that formulaic combination: instead of being a sage-king, Wu Taibo now has to choose between being a sage and being a king.

The Taibo myth creates a peculiar situation in which any effort to make Wu Taibo both sage and king would inevitably result in self-contradiction. That is to say, if the sage-king model did apply, Wu Taibo should become king, because by yielding or declining the throne, he demonstrated a virtue that would qualify him for it. The Taibo narrative so conceived would have been left in irony. Whether intended or not, yielding would have become a necessary step in claiming the throne. What is described as moral conduct would be only a gesture calculated to cater public favor or a strategic move to gain power. The resulting scandal of political conspiracy and power struggle would mar the Taibo myth, which has tried desperately to purge itself of just such actions.

Although both the sage-king story and the Taibo myth employ the *shanrang* prototype, they diverge in the way they treat the subject of politics. The sage-king story sees politics as public service and status as the recognition of virtue. The correlation between virtue and status is twofold: since virtue is measured in terms of status, those who acquire superior political status are the morally superior as well, hence the perfect combination of sage and king. The Taibo myth, in contrast, separates sagehood from politics and places the sage above the king. In so doing, it also seems to have anticipated the problem embedded in the sage-king formulation: moralizing politics leads only to the politicizing, and thus the compromising, of morality, because any claim to virtue becomes an implicit demand for status and power. To be more specific, Wu Taibo, as a sage, has to give up his sociopolitical obligations, for an insistence on fulfilling them might be interpreted by his political rivals as an attempt to seek political authority. And accordingly, his yielding of the throne best represents his commitment to higher virtue through the sacrifice of his mundane interests. Here we see the prototype of the Filial Guo story in Chapters 37 and 38 of *Rulin waishi*.

Although a mythological claim is, by definition, self-contained and self-evident, one may still need narrative to specify and substantiate it. The question is: What kind? In the case of *Rulin waishi*, the authoritative narrative has been savaged; in the larger context of historical discourse of the late imperial era, it becomes increasingly difficult to restore mythological faith and innocence to the accumulated, and accordingly complicated, narrative of what is called history. In fact, Wu Jingzi's focus on ritual practice does not redeem his ideal ritual from the irony of discourse: the Taibo ceremony is retrospectively viewed as a written program still to be carried out, and efforts to translate it into concrete daily praxis are overcome by verbal and mental manipulation. The Taibo myth does not enjoy a better fate. Wu Jingzi alluded to it but did not articulate it in detail. The truth is that by his time there was no longer a single "myth": it had been torn asunder by competing versions of narrative that permitted no consensus on what Taibo does or represents.

The Narrative of the Taibo Myth and Its Paradox

In *Correct Interpretation of the Analects* (*Lunyu zhengyi*), Liu Baonan, an eminent Confucian scholar of the Qing dynasty, paraphrased Zheng Xuan:[26]

Taibo was the eldest son of King Tai of the Zhou dynasty [Zhou Taiwang, that is, Danfu] and had two younger brothers, Zhongyong and Jili. When Taibo saw that Jili was virtuous and had a son who had a noble appearance [he later became King Wen], he intended to have Jili established as successor to the throne; yet he had received no edict from King Tai authorizing it. When King Tai fell ill, Taibo therefore left for Wu and Yue on the excuse of picking herbs for medicine, and he did not return even after King Tai's death. So Jili presided over his father's funeral. This was the first time Taibo yielded the throne. Then when Jili went to recall him in person, he again refused to go to the funeral. This was the second time he yielded. The third time that he yielded the throne was when the funeral was over, and this time he cut off his hair and tattooed his body. Since his virtue of yielding three times was not demonstrated in an explicit way, people could not even find a way to praise him.

---

26. Liu Baonan, *Lunyu zhengyi*, p. 57.

In this account, Wu Taibo favored his younger brother Jili and arranged for Jili to become the successor to the throne. In order to show his sincerity in yielding the throne, Taibo went to the Wu region and never returned. Liu Baonan revised Zheng Xuan's account slightly, however; a small change on his part alters the message of the story. In Zheng Xuan's note, the subject of the second sentence is King Tai instead of Taibo. According to Zheng Xuan, because King Tai intended to establish Jili as his successor, Taibo, King Tai's eldest son and rightful heir, found no alternative but to leave Zhou territory. Put another way, Taibo did not "yield" the throne until he realized that he was out of favor with his father.

None of the extant editions of Zheng Xuan's commentary on the *Analects* that Liu Baonan could possibly have read supports his version.[27] Without indicating the source of his quotation, Liu explained that after making a careful comparison of the different versions of the Taibo story, he concluded that only Zheng's commentary as he quoted it was genuine or fair (*yun*).[28]

Here Liu Baonan's concern is not so much what Taibo actually did as with what he should have done as a sage sanctioned by Confucius. Liu clearly knew that he must keep Taibo away from the taint of any possible power struggle. If Taibo reached his decision only after his father's decision to make Jili his successor placed Taibo in an awkward and dangerous position, his sagehood would be called into question.

However, few of the early historical records can be read to support Liu Baonan's hypothesis. Liu himself must have discovered that he had misquoted Zheng Xuan when comparing the quotation with its partial source in Sima Qian's *Shiji* (the first half of Zheng Xuan's note was based on "Wu Taibo shijia" [Hereditary house of the Wu lineage] of the *Shiji*). But Liu disregards *Shiji*, because Sima Qian's narrative supports the account of an internal power struggle that drove Taibo away.[29] Moreover, Sima Qian shrewdly suggested that Jili was born of a woman who was not the mother

---

27. For more information about the editions of Zheng Xuan's commentary on *The Analects*, see Zheng Jingruo, *Lunyu Zhengshi zhu jishu*, pp. 118, 402.

28. Liu Baonan, *Lunyu zhengyi*, p. 58.

29. According to "Zhou benji" (Basic annals of the Zhou) in the *Shiji*, King Tai had even sent a signal to Taibo and Zhongyong that he was about to pass the throne on to Jili and then to Jili's son Chang: "When Chang, Jili's son, was born, auspicious omens appeared. Gugong [King Tai] said: 'There must be someone who can make our lineage flourish. Isn't he Chang [*chang* means "to flourish"]?' " (See Sima Qian, *Shiji, juan* 4, p. 115).

of Taibo and Zhongyong.[30] Hence, he posited a sinister competition over the succession between two half-brothers.

The *Zuo Commentary* (*Zuozhuan*) begins long after Taibo's time. However, it documents incidents and dialogue that show us how Taibo was perceived in the Spring and Autumn period. In the fifth year of Duke Xi of Lu, Gong Ziqi, a minister of Yu, had a debate with his lord over a specific foreign policy: "The King said: 'The royal family of Jin is from the same lineage as we are. How could they bring harm to us?' [Gong Ziqi] replied: 'Taibo and Yu Zhong [Zhongyong] were both King Tai's sons. However, since Taibo disobeyed [King Tai], he failed to succeed to the throne.'"[31] This passage engendered many hypotheses and counterhypotheses in subsequent periods. Scholars never reached agreement on what prevented Taibo from ascending the throne: one hypothesis is that Taibo refused his father's order to mount an expedition against the Shang; another hypothesis suggests that he failed to act in submission to his father.[32] In these interpretations the image of the Confucian sage is hopelessly compromised by the taint of political struggle. Liu Baonan, like some other Qing scholars, insisted that if Taibo had ever disobeyed his father, it was only when his father issued an order establishing him as successor to the throne.[33] However, no historical record suggests that such an edict was ever made or would have been made, if Taibo had not yielded the throne.[34]

---

30. *Shiji, juan* 31, p. 1445.

31. Liu Wenqi, *Chunqiu Zuoshi zhuan jiuzhu shuzheng*, pp. 272–73.

32. Ibid.

33. Liu Baonan, *Lunyu zhengyi*, p. 58.

34. A final passage that Liu Baonan would have gleaned from the *Zuo Commentary* would have been the following: in the first year of the reign of Duke Min of Lu, Shiwei, a minister of Jin, advised Shen Sheng, the crown prince of Jin, to follow the model of Taibo when there was no possibility of ascending the throne: "You had better run away in order not to be caught and persecuted. Wouldn't it be best for you to be a Wu Taibo? [Although you will lose your kingdom], you can at least obtain a favorable reputation, instead of encountering possible punishment." As Shiwei saw it, Shen Sheng faced the very situation that Taibo had faced, and he had to make a life-or-death choice, as Taibo evidently did. In Shiwei's eyes, Taibo was worldly-wise and astute. He knew how to avoid impending trouble and seek what was good for himself. In contrast to Confucius's paradoxical praise of hiding from praise, Shiwei thought that one could escape political persecution but win fame for yielding the throne. Seen from this perspective, Confucius ironically comes to represent the audience whose praise and applause make the Taibo drama possible in the first place (Liu Wenqi, *Chunqiu Zuoshi zhuan jiuzhu shuzheng*, p. 223).

History insists on poking its ugly face out from behind the mask of the myth. The effort to repress contradictory evidence necessitated the creation of a new narrative that generated even more problems than it was meant to resolve. If speculation about Taibo's motivation for withdrawal had already blurred the aura of the Taibo myth, then a further account of his act of fleeing the throne plunged the myth back into the depths of controversy.

Zheng Xuan left a detailed account of Wu Taibo's three yieldings: Wu Taibo escapes to the Wu region and remains there even after his father's death. But the question that arises is: In what sense can Taibo be viewed as a Confucian paragon if he achieved the virtue of noncompetitiveness at the expense of filial piety? This question seems to have been anticipated by certain scholars. In order to reconcile the conflicting moral requirements, they gave Taibo one more chance to demonstrate his filial piety after he fled by claiming that he did return upon his father's death and attended his father's funeral in person.[35] However, it is almost impossible to rule out an alternative point of view implicit in this revised account: in the eyes of Jili and his ministers, Taibo's return at such a crucial moment would have been a political demonstration and a challenge to Jili's legitimacy. Thus once again the Taibo myth would have been overshadowed by a power struggle that has been repressed but never fully eliminated.

In *Han Ying's Illustrations of the Didactic Application of the Book of Odes* (*Hanshi waizhuan*), Han Ying (around 150 BCE) presented just such a version of the Taibo story, which unwittingly betrays itself:[36]

The superior man seeks gentleness and moderation in benevolence (*ren*); reverence and yielding he seeks in ritual (*li*). If he succeeds, he feels that he has done right, and if he fails, he also feels that he has done right. Thus the superior man in regard to the True Way is like the farmer tilling his fields. Though he gets no great yield from the year's harvest, he will not change. Danfu, namely, King Tai, had sons named Taibo, Zhongyong, and Jili. Jili had a son named Chang. King Tai regarded Chang as worthy and wished Jili to be his successor. Taibo left and went to Wu.

When King Tai was on the point of death he said [to Jili], "When I die, you go and yield your place to your two elder brothers. It may be they will not come, but you will have done the right thing and so you will feel at ease and justified." King Tai died and Jili went to Wu and told his two elder brothers. His elder brothers went back with Jili.

---

35. Wang Chong, *Lunheng*, pp. 1330–31.

36. Han Ying, *Hanshi waizhuan*, vol. 10, juan 10, pp. 3b–4a; trans. from Hightower, *Han Shi Wai Chuan*, p. 323.

All the ministers wished Taibo to put Jili on the throne, but Jili in turn made way for Taibo, who said to Zhongyong, "Now all the ministers wish me to put Jili on the throne, but Jili in turn makes way for me. How shall we settle it?"

Zhongyong said, "If the point is to support one from a low and humble status, it will be all right to put Jili on the throne." In the end Jili ascended the throne and raised King Wen. King Wen actually received the Mandate of Heaven and ruled as true king.

A close reading of this passage yields some disenchanting implications for the Taibo myth: first, when King Tai orders Jili to go and yield the throne to his elder brothers, he does not think that they will accept it, nor does he change his mind and try to pass the throne to either of them. The point is that Jili has to make such a gesture to legitimize his position and to "feel at ease and justified."

Second, contrary to King Tai's expectations, Taibo and Zhongyong return together with Jili. The narration of Taibo's return is somewhat dubious. If Taibo and Zhongyong decline Jili's resignation, they should not return— or else return merely to help Jili establish himself as a legitimate king. This is, however, not the case. It may also be possible, as some scholars have suggested, that Taibo and Zhongyong go back just to attend their father's funeral. However, King Tai's funeral does not figure in this passage and is not offered as an excuse for Taibo's and Zhongyong's return.

Third, soon after they return, they find themselves in an awkward position: "All the ministers wished Taibo to put Jili on the throne." The motion that Jili's ministers propose immediately removes Taibo from the position of potential successor. Taibo finds himself kept away from center stage and becomes instead the audience for an old drama: the ministers insist that the successor ascend the throne, while the successor persists in declining it. The drama does not end until Jili agrees—as expected—to accept the throne.

Finally, upon his return, Taibo does not decline the throne, nor does he want to. Instead of saying "I wish to put Jili on the throne," Taibo says, "All the ministers wish me to put Jili on the throne." The question that Taibo asks is, "What should I do about this?" It is his turn to make a choice, but he actually has no options. With all the ministers on his side, Jili makes the gesture of declining the throne. This empty gesture demands an answering gesture from Taibo, which, once made, is taken literally.

The account of Taibo in the *Hanshi waizhuan* presents a complex situation in which all the actors are to some extent implicated. The elaboration of

Confucian moral codes, set out at the beginning of the passage, is undermined by the account that follows it. The sense of irony becomes so evident
that Liu Baonan found it intolerable:[37]

After King Tai's death, Jili was supposed to ascend the throne. He had no reason to
go to Wu and report to Taibo and Zhongyong, casting aside funeral affairs and
state affairs. If Taibo and Zhongyong had not followed Jili and returned, should Jili
have stayed there with them, or accepted Taibo's and Zhongyong's refusal of the
throne and returned alone? The *Waizhuan*'s account is careless at this point. If
Taibo had hastened home for the funeral of his father, as the eldest son of his father
he would have been the one to be put on the throne. How could those ministers
propose to establish Jili? Moreover, if he returned later on, why at the outset did he
escape into the barbarian area under the pretext of collecting herbs for medicine?

To Liu, Taibo's return marks the end of the Taibo myth, since it leads his
heroes toward a moral dilemma in which none of the available choices can be
fully justified. However, instead of admitting the collapse of the Taibo myth,
Liu insisted that Han Ying's account is careless (*shu*) or, like Wang Chong's
similar account, does not make much sense (*wei da*).

Rejection of the dubious accounts of Taibo as exemplified in the *Hanshi
waizhuan* creates a void, which is filled only by wishful speculation. This
speculation, however, bears the assertive tone of mythological claim. After
quoting some lines from the *Book of Odes*, Liu Baonan commented:[38]

Judging by this, King Ji's [Jili's] reverence toward his elder brothers was surely beyond the reach of ordinary people. Someone who cherished a friendly affection like
Taibo must have been aware of this. He knew that if he yielded the throne after his
father's death, Jili would definitely not accept it. So he left when King Tai was ill
under the pretext of plucking herbs. After King Tai's death, when Jili went to recall
Taibo, he must have urged him repeatedly [to return]. But Taibo definitely refused.
The "Taibo shijia" (Hereditary house of Taibo) records that the barbarians considered him righteous, and so more than one thousand families followed him and established him as their king. Such a situation did not permit Taibo to return home.
Therefore, having no alternative, Jili accepted Taibo's refusal.

This, the orthodox reading of the Taibo story in the Qing dynasty, reveals
the limits of Confucian mythmaking. In contrast to their precursors in the
Eastern Zhou and Han dynasties, who created myths of the ancient sover-

---

37. Liu Baonan, *Lunyu zhengyi*, p. 59.
38. Ibid.

eigns, the Qing literati were obviously at a great disadvantage: they had to wrestle with the accumulated historical records. Historical anecdotes are multifarious, derived from heterogeneous sources, and can never be fully reduced to the coherent, homogeneous framework required for mythmaking. Without alternative sources, the Qing literati were engaged in the impossible mission of constructing a myth from dubious, conflicting accounts. Their narrative, therefore, deploys a desperate exegetical virtuosity in trying to make sense of the conflicting anecdotes about Wu Taibo by imposing on them a virtue they do not possess. It rewrites them and squeezes them into a coherent narrative framework, while admitting its dependence on them as the only source. In fact, the raw material of historical anecdotes could not easily be absorbed; it was often carried in a distorted form in the narrative of the myth as a destructive force that prevented the myth from completing its design.[39]

There are thus two Taibos in two different worlds. For the Taibo of the Taibo myth, the drama is about a world prescribed by the ethics of yielding or noncompetitiveness, in which everyone gives priority to the concerns of others and nothing is more important than the harmonious relationships that sustain communal life. In this account, both Taibo and Jili are granted a chance to demonstrate the virtue of noncompetitiveness. Jili shows reluctance to be put on the throne and repeatedly begs Taibo to return. His rejection by Taibo in turn enhances Taibo's sincerity.

However, the Taibo of the historical anecdotes is concerned primarily with politics, the power struggle, the dilemma of moral choice, and the possibility of surviving political persecution and the life of an exile. He struggles between conflicting obligations and finds no perfect solution. Worse still, he is eventually left in a world governed by a different logic, in which the ethic

---

39. I am thinking particularly of the moment in Zheng Xuan's account when Wu Taibo decides to cut off his hair and tattoo his body in order to show his determination not to return home. If the Qing scholars made this a part of the standard version of the Taibo myth, was there any way to reconcile the Wu Taibo who accommodated himself to barbarian customs with the Wu Taibo who was believed to have brought the civilization of central China to the barbarian region? This small anecdote has several variations, which intersect or overlap with each other. Any Qing scholar who approved the Taibo myth might still have had a hidden memory of a *Zuo Commentary* account, in which Zhongyong, as successor to Wu Taibo, was also censured for having made compromises with barbarian customs. See Liu Wenqi, *Chunqiu Zuoshi zhuan jiuzhu shuzheng,* p. 346.

of noncompetitiveness is a mere decoration that disguises the mechanism of politics and the relations of power.

Obviously, these two Taibos cannot coexist. But without the support of narrative, the mythological claim of Taibo's absolute, supreme virtue tells us nothing but the fact that it is necessary. When people take it seriously and give it the concrete form of narrative, it collapses, turning into the fragments of a story that the mythmakers do not want to hear—a story that suggests a power struggle, political persecution, and the moral dilemmas of individual choice.

A similar and subtler situation can be found in an extended version of the Taibo myth in *The Flowers in the Mirror*. In its account of the Country of Gentlemen, whose inhabitants are known for the virtue of yielding or noncompetitiveness, *The Flowers* describes a scene in a noisy marketplace.

A soldier, with something in his hands, was bargaining with a shopkeeper, saying, "You have such a wonderful product, but you are charging so little for it! How could I accept it without feeling uneasy? Please do me a favor by raising the price so that I can accept it. If you refuse, it must mean that you are not going to do me the favor of doing business with me."

Tang Ao whispered to Duo Jiugong, "In doing business, only the seller sets the price, while the buyer tries to lower it. Now, although the seller has named a price, the buyer hasn't bargained. Instead, he has tried to raise the price. I have never heard such a conversation before. This must be what they mean by 'doing without competition.'" Then they heard the shopkeeper say, "Your presence here is a great compliment to me. How can I not follow your instructions? But I do feel ashamed—I have asked a high price, yet you leave me no room to hide, saying that my price is too low. To be honest, the article has no fixed price; it is not worth the price asked. As the saying goes: 'The price asked is as high as heaven, that offered is as low as earth.' Now you didn't bargain; instead, you tried to make the price even higher. Your nature is so gentle that I am afraid that I must ask you to go shopping elsewhere, for I cannot comply with your wishes."

Tang Ao said, "'The price asked is as high as heaven, the one offered is as low as earth' is a formula used by buyers, and 'The article has no fixed price; it is not quite worth the price asked' is also a phrase used by buyers. But what is interesting is that now they come, surprisingly, from the mouth of the seller." Then they heard the soldier say, "You have charged me so little for this wonderful article, yet you put the blame on the gentleness of my nature. Are you not infringing on the way of forbearance? The business will not be handled fairly unless both sides stop cheating each other. Everyone has his own secret calculations. How could I be fooled by you?"

The conversation lasted a while, with the seller still refusing to charge more. The soldier then lost his patience. He paid what was asked, but took only half of what he paid for, then started to leave. But could the shopkeeper let him go? No, he stopped him, saying, "You have paid too much but taken too little." Along came a pair of old men, who proposed a fair compromise. The dispute was finally settled when the soldier was ordered to take 80 percent of what he had paid for. Tang Ao and Duo Jiugong could not help nodding their approval of this. [40]

This dramatic scene of reversed bargaining serves, it would seem, to illustrate the virtue of communal congeniality, the approved code of private and public conduct in the Country of Gentlemen. But it is by no means a simple affirmation of the Taibo myth. The ethic of yielding is predicated on a world of imperfection, in which most people will take advantage when it is offered to them. Gentlemen (junzi) always need small men (xiaoren) to help them define themselves. In a world in which everyone is a gentleman, conflict is reintroduced. The old game of competition now continues in a reversed form, as the very logic of noncompetitiveness, carried to its extreme, leads to a new form of competition. Although the buyer and seller exchange their roles in bargaining, their way of making their cases remains largely unchanged. When the buyer protests, "Everyone has his own secret calculations. How could I be fooled by you?" he makes the situation even more ambiguous, if not sinister. The ritual of yielding, once motivated by "secret calculations," verges on a parody of itself.

The account of the Country of Gentlemen confronts us again with the problem in the narrative of the Taibo myth. The two gentlemen do yield to each other in the marketplace, but their act of yielding ends up becoming not a rejection but a reversed simulation of the strategy of market negotiation. Similarly, if Wu Taibo yields the throne, that does not necessarily make him a man of virtue, for the face value of the story might be subject to reversal. The most ironic scene in Liu Baonan's version of the myth comes when Wu Taibo and Jili compete in yielding to each other. This scene amounts to nothing more than a hollow performance, since both are under public pressure to show their sincerity in declining the throne. The historical texts testify that Wu Taibo's decision to yield the throne was predicated on a situation over which he had little control. It might well be perceived as part of the political game: a sign of defeat, a strategy for survival, or a gesture that was solicited and then taken literally by his political rivals. Wu Taibo's en-

40. Li Ruzhen, Jinghua yuan, pp. 66–67.

gagement in establishing the state of Gouwu might also be an indication of the continuous confrontation between him and his half-brother, who took his place and became the head of the Zhou clan in central China.

The problem for the defenders of Taibo's virtue is that their favorite story about the king of yielding seems always to have carried within itself a hidden story of competition and contention. As a result, they can never provide a concrete and coherent narrative to justify their approval of Wu Taibo. In fact, representing Wu Taibo as an embodiment of a moral order higher than the existing sociopolitical one demands a closed, autonomous sphere. The rhetoric of exclusion or repression is essential in claiming Taibo's virtue. There is, however, a constant threat of invasion by the mundane world and its own logic of reasoning and narration. Dependent on the historical texts, the Taibo myth finds it impossible to eliminate the alternative narration that views Taibo as a victim of, or the losing party in, a political struggle, and a controversial figure caught between conflicting social and moral demands.

Not unlike the Taibo myth, *Rulin waishi* asserts a ritualized world beyond negotiation and controversy, but instead of taking an absolutist stance, its narrative points in the opposite direction—skepticism and iconoclasm are its main driving forces. In retelling the story of yielding, Wu Jingzi reproduced the conflicts that had wrecked the Taibo narrative and questioned the very possibility of his own mythological claim in *Rulin waishi*.

CHAPTER 9

Moral Imagination and Self-Reflexivity

The Taibo myth, as shown in the preceding chapter, is a bald presentation of the virtue of yielding without a narrative of its own. Once put in concrete narrative form, the myth tells a story that unwittingly undermines its assertion. *Rulin waishi* preserves the moral vision of the myth without rendering it in narrative. Wu Taibo is therefore presented as the symbol of an abstract ideal; an object of longing and memory, he is duly absent from the pages of the novel. Although the Taibo myth itself is omitted, its motifs, however, persist in a number of variations and offer a key to the interpretation of Chapters 31 through 37. Moving toward the construction of a ritualized world, the novel, like the Taibo myth, takes up the motif of withdrawal from the mundane world. As if to echo Wu Taibo's legendary three yieldings, Wu Jingzi represented three withdrawals and declinings of imperial offers and recommendations for special examinations. In place of the legendary hero is Yu Yude, ritual master of the Taibo ceremony and the present-day Wu Taibo. Around Yu, a group of literati-admirers of Wu Taibo re-enact portions of the Taibo myth in their lives. The question that guides this reading of Chapters 31 through 37 is: How does Wu Jingzi cope with the problems that come with the narrative of the Taibo myth as he rewrites it?

Stories of Yielding

Chapters 31 through 37 introduce four major characters one after another: Du Shaoqing, Chi Hengshan, Zhuang Shaoguang, and Yu Yude. These characters organize the Taibo ceremony and represent the literati community it symbolizes. Yu holds the degree of palace graduate and is a tutor in the imperial college, but the other three, like most of the participants in the ceremony, are neither civil officials closely associated with the imperial court nor members of the local elite. In the Taibo temple, they try to define a separate and privileged space for themselves in order to escape troubles like those encountered by Zhuang in the imperial court and Du in his hometown. Accordingly, the ceremony dedicated to Wu Taibo follows neither court ritual nor Confucian family ritual. It celebrates not the existing sociopolitical order and hierarchy but the order of the imagined ritual community. As I discussed in Part I, the narrative in this section of the novel begins with the literati's declining of official offers and their consequent withdrawal from the mundane world. In other words, the novel initiates a new stage of its development by reworking the Taibo myth.

When we first encounter Du Shaoqing, for example, he is in his hometown of Tianchang. Du has only the *xiucai*, licentiate, degree, which would not truly qualify him for membership in the local elite. But as a member of the important Du family, which has produced several generations of provincial and palace graduates, it is only natural that he becomes the focus of attention in local affairs. But what we read here is a story of failure, a story about the problems of playing the role of local gentry.

From the beginning, we are told that Du Shaoqing refuses to play that conventional role: he is tired of being entangled in disputes and daily routines. Nor does he have any interest in passing a higher level of the civil service examinations in order to secure entry into the official world and enhance the prestige of his family in the community. Instead, he assumes the role of the big patron and gives his money away without even demanding any proof of need. His generosity makes him the prey of swindlers, who flock to his household, reminiscent in many ways of the Lou brothers. As if the Lou brothers episode (Chapters 9 to 12) were being re-enacted, Du steps in to resume the drama they left unfinished. Iron-Armed Zhang, the self-proclaimed swordsman who cheated the brothers and then failed to return as promised, now reappears, making himself Du's honored houseguest under a different name and a forged identity. In Chapter 32, the narrator does, indeed, relate the Du story as an extended and competing version of the Lou brothers' "gallant deeds" (haoju).

But Du Shaoqing does not become simply another Lou brother. Unlike the brothers, Du is not completely blind to the role he assumes and the situation he confronts. Nor does he believe, as they did, in the stories the people tell about themselves. At the transitional point from Chapters 2–30 to Chapters 31–37, Du represents another individual waging war against vulgarity, but he loses faith in what he is doing. Local society, like the official world, is deeply embroiled in endless struggles for wealth and prestige, and even Du Shaoqing, who stands up against these powers, is hardly immune to their influence.

In Chapter 31, Du Shenqing, Du Shaoqing's cousin, describes him as someone who "cannot stand talk about officials or rich men" (R. 422; S. 338). Unlike his cousins, Du Shaoqing opens his door only to visitors such as Iron-Armed Zhang. He never invites local officials and wealthy merchants to his house; nor does he allow them to dominate the conversation of his invited guests. But Du Shaoqing himself never stops talking about them. Whenever possible, he makes them his target of verbal assault. And this becomes his way of defining himself. There is obviously nothing he can do, as he realizes, to prevent the rising literati from obtaining prestigious status. But he tries to compensate for his own decline in status by asserting what he sees as family tradition and culture. On that basis, he is able to reverse his relationship with the local officials: he considers himself a teacher but he would not accept the local magistrate as his student, even if the latter insisted (of course, this never happens). When urged by his fellow literati to pay his respects to the local magistrate, who has recently obtained the title of palace graduate, Du Shaoqing responds:

"I must leave it to you, Third Brother, to call on magistrates and pay your respects as a student," replied Du. "Why, in my father's time—to say nothing of my grandfather's and great-grandfather's—heaven knows how many magistrates came here! I'm sorry I passed the district examination, since it means I have to address the local magistrate as my teacher! As for this Magistrate Wang, who crawled out of some dust heap to pass the metropolitan examination—I wouldn't want him as my student! Why should I meet him?" (R. 430; S. 345–46)

Du might achieve a verbal and psychological triumph over the magistrate, but he is unaware that he lives in a novel that does not fully confirm his words. What Du considers his family legacy is inextricably bound with de-grees and official status. Du Shenqing's account of the family history in Chapter 31 reveals that his ancestors, of whom Shaoqing is extremely proud, rose in the world precisely through the civil service examinations. Like Mag-istrate Wang, they were provincial and palace graduates.

The conflict between Du Shaoqing and the local magistrate—between a descendant of palace graduates and a current palace graduate—contributes little to the moral drama that Du Shaoqing would like. Where Du sees him-self as a moral hero battling alone against vulgar customs, others see some-thing else. Mr. Gao, a Hanlin scholar, describes him as a hopeless prodigal and an example of what a literatus should not be. "If you'll allow me to say so," Mr. Gao says to Chi Hengshan, Du Shaoqing's friend, "this Shaoqing is the first complete wastrel his family has produced!" According to Gao, Du Shaoqing himself is the person responsible for the decline of the family leg-acy upon which he himself relies entirely. Du Shenqing does not share Mr. Gao's viewpoint, but he sees Shaoqing as a pretentious person, a self-styled "big shot" (*dalaoguan*), who squanders his family property in exchange for personal fame. And he cares more about his own image than the people he helps. "He likes to be the one and only patron helping anybody," says Du Shenqing. "He doesn't like others to join in" (R. 421–22; S. 337). In advising an acquaintance to go to Du Shaoqing for financial support, he suggests, "Don't tell him, for instance, how good Prefect Xiang was to you. Keep on harping about the fact that he is the only true patron in the world" (R. 422; S. 338). Du Shenqing is trying to divert to Du Shaoqing those who come to him for help, yet at the same time he reinterprets Du Shaoqing's self-representation as a generous patron. It is not pure coincidence that the man whom Du Shenqing advises is the head of a local acting troupe. Before he takes his own part in the drama to benefit himself as well as assist in Du Shaoqing's self-representation, he prepares himself by rehearsing first with Du Shenqing and then with Du Shaoqing's steward. As the drama unfolds in the way that Du Shenqing has predicted, we can only watch at an ironic distance. This is also true of all the other actors in the similar dramas staged in Du Shaoqing's household. Indeed, in the eyes of those well informed about the secrets of Du Shaoqing's self-fashioning, Du is merely an actor in the same play, exchanging his money for fame. His cynical and sometimes eccentric resistance to what he sees as corrupt local customs is another and subtler form of compromise, if not of cooperation. Despite his declared gesture of opposition, he remains an insider whose rebellion is preconditioned by what he opposes.

The story of Du Shaoqing consists of two parts: the first shows it is impossible to revitalize the ethic narrative within the context of his hometown society; the second searches for the world outside or beyond, a world located in Nanjing. As we shall see below, Du's departure from his hometown is immediately followed by his declining an official recommendation for a special examination. Thus, between his hometown and the center of the official world Du finally finds a place for himself.

The moment when Du Shaoqing declines the official recommendation deserves careful examination, for it takes on the motif of withdrawal that governs not merely Du's story but the next several chapters of the novel. With Du, the pretext for withdrawing is illness. When the local official who wants to recommend him comes to pay his respects, Du pretends to be so sick that he cannot even stand up. Critics of *Rulin waishi* have noticed that this incident may derive from Wu Jingzi's own life. In 1735, two years after he moved to Nanjing, he was recommended for the prestigious erudite scholar (*boxue hongci*) examination. It was prefaced by several preliminary local examinations and finally took place in the imperial court in the fall of the following year. Wu took three preliminary examinations, but he turned down a formal recommendation and never made it to the court.[1] Cheng Jinfang (1718–84), Wu's friend, recorded the incident in his biography of Wu without giving reasons for Wu's decision. Other records provide two explanations: he turned down the recommendation because he was sick or he feigned illness in order to avoid taking the examination. Although the former has been proved to be close to the truth, Wu Jingzi adopted the latter in *Rulin waishi* in his account of his fictional alter ego. In so doing, he obviously reinterprets the incident of his own past, disguising it with the excuse that he makes for his character. But at the same time he also allows his character to do what he wishes for himself. Unlike Wu, whose withdrawal from the examination was, by and large, an unhappy incident, Du Shaoqing's decision to withdraw is deliberate.

Du Shaoqing's kneeling before the magistrate also has uncanny biographical references. In 1729, at age 29, Wu Jingzi took a qualifying test for the provincial examination. In a poem by a friend in celebration of his thirti-

---

1. For a comprehensive account of this incident, see Chen Meilin, *Wu Jingzi pingzhuan*, pp. 190–232.

eth birthday, Wu is said to have knelt and begged an examiner to allow him to pass. For Wu, this turned out to be dreadfully humiliating: rather than complying with his petition, the examiner reprimanded him in public.[2] Although this traumatic incident has left no trace in Wu's extant poems and prose, it is represented in his novel in reverse:

He [Du Shaoqing] knelt down, then failed to get up again. The magistrate hastily helped him to his feet, and they sat down. "The court has issued an important decree, and Governor Li asks for your help," said Magistrate Deng. "I had no idea you were so ill. How soon do you think you will be able to travel?"

"I'm afraid my illness may prove incurable, hence what you ask is impossible," replied Du. "I must beg Your Honor to make my apologies for me." He took a petition from his sleeve and gave it to the magistrate, who, in view of the circumstance, did not like to prolong his visit.

"I will take my leave, sir," said Magistrate Deng. "I fear I have tired you. All I can do is send in a report to my superiors and await Governor Li's decision."

"Thank you, Your Honor. Forgive me if I do not see you out." The magistrate bade Du farewell, and left in his sedan-chair. (R. 463–64; S. 373)

Both the nature and the context of the traumatic incident have been changed: kneeling before an official as Wu once did, Du Shaoqing now begs not to be recommended as a candidate for a prestigious official examination. Engaged in a project of rewriting his personal history, Wu Jingzi allows his fictional alter ego to redeem and compensate for his own past.

In the story that follows, Zhuang Shaoguang, Du's fellow literatus, responds to the official recommendation in a different way. He goes to the capital in response to the imperial call, but only to quit. Zhuang's trip from Nanjing to Beijing, which occupies most of Chapters 34 and 35, polarizes the choice between temple and court. Yet even before Zhuang sets out, he realizes that his journey to the capital may inconveniently prevent him from attending the Taibo ceremony; he has to make his decision even before he leaves.

Zhuang's wife then raises a question that every reader would ask: Why does Zhuang have to go to court if he has decided not to take an official post? Zhuang's answer reveals the principle that sustains his decision: "We are not hermits. Since a decree has been issued summoning me to court, it is my duty as a subject to go" (R. 472; S. 380–81). His decision poses an alternative

---

2. See Jin Liangming, "He Wu Qing zuo," pp. 5–6.

to, and an implicit criticism of, Du's choice. It also problematizes the role that Du claims. Indeed, Du distances himself from the community of his clan and refuses to enter the official world. He therefore casts off the roles traditionally associated with literati: he is now neither a member of the local gentry nor a civil official. The only option for Du is to remain alone as a hermit, a role that Zhuang refuses.

However, Zhuang Shaoguang's words soon come back to haunt him. Although he intends to fulfill his public duty, he returns from court having gained nothing except the Yuanwu Lake of Nanjing as an imperial award. This token gesture of imperial favor makes him, ironically, a state-sponsored hermit, whether he likes it or not. In addition to the lake, Zhuang also wins for himself the fame otherwise impossible to obtain. Even on his way home, he is surrounded by admirers: his act of declining public service has made him the center of public attention.

The problems with regard to Zhuang's choice are highlighted in the comments by Dr. Yu Yude in Chapter 36. When the emperor is seeking men of talent, a fellow official encourages Yu to seek a recommendation from the governor:

"This is a great court ceremony," said You. "I am thinking of asking Governor Kang to recommend you, sir."

"I am not good enough for that," replied Dr. Yu with a smile. "And if Governor Kang wishes to recommend someone, the choice is up to him. To ask such a favor is hardly a sign of high moral character!"

"If you don't want an official career, sir, wait till you receive a summons from the emperor. You may be called for an audience or you may not; but by refusing to take office and returning home, you will demonstrate your superiority even more clearly."

"You are wrong there," retorted Yu. "You want me to ask for a recommendation, yet refuse to take office if I am summoned into the emperor's presence. That would show lack of sincerity both in requesting a recommendation and in refusing to become an official. What sort of behavior is that?" (R. 494; S. 400)

Yu Yude's remarks, placed not far from the story of Zhuang Shaoguang, provide an alternative reading of Zhuang's decision. Where Zhuang defends his trip to court in terms of fulfilling his public obligations, Yu sees a lack of sincerity. When the three different reactions to the official recommendations are juxtaposed, both Zhuang's final withdrawal and Du's feigned ill-ness are open to question.[3]

No one is perfect, it would seem, except Yu Yude. And Yu is exceptional in many regards. Although he refuses to seek official recommendation for himself, he does take the civil service examination. Of the members of the Nanjing literati group, Yu is the only one with the title of palace graduate. Soon after obtaining his degree, he is appointed tutor of the Imperial College in Nanjing. The perfection of Yu lies in part, however, in his ability to combine all the incompatibles: he is an official of reclusive style and also a palace graduate, in Du Shaoqing's words, without the airs of a palace graduate (*jinshi qi*). Martin Huang comments:

In the novel Yu Yude is carefully described as someone for whom the distinction be-tween official and commoner is truly meaningless. He seems to have transcended the traditional concern whether one should consciously play the role of a recluse or an official, a concern that troubled Wu Jingzi and many other characters such as Du Shaoqing or even Zhuang Shaoguang in the novel.[4]

In its narrative of Yu Yude, the novel seems to have reached its own extreme of fictionality: by freeing its hero from the dominant sociopolitical forces that condition his public roles, it makes the impossible possible.

While Yu Yude goes beyond the restrictions of his social roles, his fel-low literati struggle with the limits imposed on them. Recognizing those limits brings us once again to the Taibo myth, which is stuck with the con-flicting narrative accounts. Although Wu Taibo yields the throne three times, none of his yieldings is perfect, and Wu himself is constantly subject to alternative evaluations. The same is true of the three characters' reac-tions to official recommendation in *Rulin waishi*. Like Wu Taibo, whose decision to withdraw is made at the price of his public obligations, Du Shaoqing finds himself criticized for being inactive and socially irresponsi-ble. Yet, Zhuang Shaoguang's declining of an official recommendation does not save him the criticism that Wu Taibo suffered, for his act of yielding might be construed as a deliberate strategy to seek personal fame. The story of Yu Yude provides no realistic alternatives, since Yu lives in a world different from that of his fellow literati and is thus free of the agonizing problem of role choice that tears them apart. As we have seen repeatedly,

---

3. See Martin Huang, *Literati and Self-Re/Presentation*, p. 63.
4. Ibid., 64.

Rulin waishi never allows us to come away with a single viewpoint of the choices literati make. It shows us other aspects of the same decision and then juxtaposes that decision with other equally if not more problematic ones, leaving us with no better options.

It would certainly be wrong, nevertheless, if we fail to differentiate the literati who refuse to serve from those who seek success in their official careers. The fact that the novel renders no simple judgment on what is right and wrong does not mean that it sees no difference between them. It is, to be sure, aware of the possible Confucian critique of the literati's decision to withdraw—unless it is done as a sign of despair when the Dao does not prevail. Yet to justify the literati's engagement in politics in terms of fulfilling their public duty, as Confucians usually do, proves more problematic, since it offers literati a legitimate excuse for their own struggle for status and power. As shown in previous parts of the novel, the perception of this problem in Confucian discourse provides the starting point for its criticism of literati culture. But it soon becomes clear that the effort to explore solutions to this problem is not devoid of critical self-reflection.

Here once again we see the parallel between *Rulin waishi* and the Taibo narrative—or more precisely, the novel now stumbles between the Taibo myth and the controversial accounts of Taibo. Not unlike the historical episodes about Wu Taibo, it integrates multiple perspectives into its narrative of Du's and Zhuang's decisions to withdraw. But following the Taibo myth, it never denies its approval of their decisions or presents alternatives. Du gets stuck in his hometown, incapable of inventing scenarios for change; a frustrated Zhuang at court sees no better prospect for himself. As the novel unfolds, their decisions to withdraw become matters of necessity.

But the question remains: Did Wu Jingzi find a way of narrating the ritualistic act of yielding or withdrawal without slipping into the trap of the Taibo myth? Obviously, Wu was unable to describe the noble deeds of yielding and withdrawing without at the same time noticing alternative interpretations. In most cases, he embraces these alternatives in his own narrative. But in the case of Yu Yude, he seems to have evoked all the alternatives only to rule them out as either insubstantial or irrelevant, thereby creating a story of yielding on its own terms. Let us compare two scenes in the narratives of Zhuang Shaoguang and Yu Yude.

On his way back home, Zhuang Shaoguang meets several merchants and literati.

"Though His Majesty wished to make you a minister, you declined all official rank," said the merchants. "What nobility of mind this shows!"

"I understand Mr. Zhuang's scruples," said Xiao Boquan. "With his rare gifts, he wishes to enter upon an official career the orthodox way, and looks down upon appointment by recommendation. He has come back now to wait for the next examination. Since the emperor knows him, he is sure to come first on the list." (R. 484; S. 391)

As outsiders to the literati circle, the merchants first offer a straightforward interpretation of Zhuang's noble deed. But Xiao Boquan, a literatus, immediately dismisses it as too naïve a reading of Zhuang's mind, because, in his words, "I understand Mr. Zhuang's scruples," or literally, "I understand what Mr. Zhuang's intentions (*yisi*) are." In a reading of this scene, Jack Chen comments:

The function of the claim is to establish a secret community of understanding between Zhuang and Xiao: "I know what your intentions are (so we are complicit together in our knowledge of your subterfuge)." The statement functions as a "knowing wink," a recognition of mutually shared information or guilt. What Xiao's claim assumes is that both Xiao and Zhuang proceed from the same premise: to garner fame and advancement in the official realm by a feigned disinterest.[5]

One may well argue that Xiao, in claiming a shared code and mutual understanding with Zhuang, merely tells us about himself, but his claim is not entirely false. For the emperor does know Zhuang, and Zhuang's rejection of the emperor's offer does bring him prestige. Moreover, we can hardly read this scene out of context. The previous section of the novel portrays many literati characters who act on bad faith and seek prestige through a calculated gesture of disinterest. With suspicion hovering in the air, we can hardly rule out the possibility that Zhuang is merely another such character, or "one of us," as in Xiao Boquan's claim. It is, indeed, difficult to distinguish Zhuang from them, if we base our judgment merely on our observation of his external behavior. In the absence of the conventional narrator, no one is in the position to "know," or claim an absolute knowledge of, Zhuang's intention.

As a ritualist, Wu Jingzi refused to enter the murky sphere of intentions, verbal articulations, and interpretations in representing his characters, unless he had no choice. That is the area where what he portrayed as the narrative

---

5. See Jack W. Chen, "Narrative Claims, Local Knowledges." I thank the author for permission to quote from this unpublished paper.

or discursive ritual gets stuck. But did he manage to present ascetic ritual without at the same time exposing it to interpretations? Was he able to invent a kind of narrative that puts an end to perspectivism or, at least, is less threatening to his representation of the ritualistic code—the code of yielding in particular and his imagined ritualized world in general?

In his account of Yu Yude, Wu Jingzi adopted what I shall call the "rhetoric of negation" as a way of reducing, if not excluding, narrative ambiguities. We are told that Yu Yude once saved a poor peasant from suicide by giving him financial support to help bury his deceased father. Then after six years of serving as a private tutor, Yu has a chance to take the provincial examination.

"I am sure you will pass high on the list this year," said Mr. Qi [the host of Yu Yude], when he came to see him off.

"Why do you say that?" asked Dr. Yu.

"You have done so many secret acts of kindness."

"What secret acts of kindness have I done, uncle?"

"Well, for one thing, you put your whole heart into finding that family a burial ground. And then I've heard how you saved that fellow whose father had died. These are all secret acts of kindness."

Dr. Yu smiled. "Good deeds should be done so unobtrusively that none but the doer knows of them," he said. "Since you have heard of those things, uncle, they aren't secret acts of kindness anymore."

"Yes, they are," insisted the old man. "This year you will pass." (R. 493; S. 399)

That Yu helps others without claiming credit for himself is again a reflection of the Taibo myth. Confucius admired Wu precisely because he yielded his right to rule in such way that "people could not even get around to praising him." In other words, it is *yinde*—"secret acts of kindness," or more literally, "hidden virtues"—that make Wu Taibo (and likewise, Yu Yude) "a man of virtue in its supreme form." But how shall one represent *yinde*? If *yinde* means acts of kindness that are done "so unobtrusively that none but the doer knows of them," as Yu claims, then how did Qi learn of Yu's deeds? In the specific context of the Yu Yude narrative, Mr. Qi is not a substitute for the omniscient narrator or God, who knows truths inaccessible to us. Nor does Yu act secretly, as the term *yinde* would require. As we are told, although Yu declines any repayment from the peasant, he does disclose his name to him and tell him where he lives. The best way of describing Yu's *yinde* is perhaps, as Wu Jingzi did here, to let others use this term in describing the deed, and to make Yu deny its appropriateness. Yu's denial does not necessarily disqualify him for Qi's acclaim, but it does have the function of relieving him of the burden of proving himself truly up to the all-too-demanding criteria of *yinde*. It reveals that Yu is probably unaware of, and certainly does not anticipate, such a perception of his own deed: in helping the desperate, suicidal peasant, he merely does what he is supposed to do without conscious striving, as if he were acting in the ritual over which he himself presides.

Wu Jingzi's account of the Yu Yude story presupposes the existence of a homogeneous world of ritual in which everyone knows his place, when to act and when to give way. In order to secure its internal coherence, Wu prevented Yu from seeing the contradictions others do; Yu always acts "naturally," and as shown above, he crosses all the artificial distinctions without necessarily disturbing the harmony of the ritualized world. The ethic of yielding is inherently unstable; it is predicated on a world of imperfection, in which one choice is often made at the cost of other obligations, and thus it is far from perfect. Even in the "purified" form of the Taibo myth, Taibo refuses his proper public role and acts on a private ethical decision. Wu Jingzi's account of Yu Yude, however, tries to contain or stabilize Taibo's private ethic by turning it into an institutionalized act of ritual. And the ritual so conceived reflects a utopian urge to restore homogeneity where it has been savaged by differentiation and irony—an effort to efface all traces of contradiction by presenting deliberate human deeds in terms of natural reaction. In a narrative world fraught with perspectivism, such an effort becomes as contrived as a failed ideology. Envisaging the essence of a ritual life as pure appearance freed from the schema of mundane forces, moral and psychological conflicts, and agonizing ambiguities, Wu Jingzi made a mythological claim that can rarely be realized in any concrete narrative.

Temple, Island, and Stage

In Chapter 37, the Taibo temple, the symbol of the ritualized world, is set in Nanjing, the center of the literati community, as opposed to Beijing, the center of the official world. As I argued above, the ceremony dedicated to Wu Taibo is not predicated on a specific sociopolitical occasion or related to official institutions or organizations; it is deliberately removed from the mundane world. This strategy of decontextualization operates on the narrative level as well. In the same chapter, the adoption of the form of the ritual manual helps to create a self-contained unit of narrative time and space and separates the ritual scene from the context of the novel.

This effort to decontextualize the temple is counterbalanced, however, by just as strong an impulse toward contextualizing it. In the middle of the novel are two other sites, Zhuang Shaoguang's island and Du Shenqing's stage (for the performance contest), each of which makes an interesting parallel with the temple and illuminates certain aspects of it. To interpret the temple, we should see it not merely as it contrasts with the court, but as it resembles the island and the stage. The episodes about the island and the stage reveal the narrative complexity of the novel's rendering of the Taibo ceremony and the ritualized world.

In Chapter 35, Zhuang Shaoguang, who is becoming tired of greeting all the local officials who come to congratulate him on winning imperial favor, decides to move to Yuanwu Lake as an escape.

This was a huge lake, almost as large as the West Lake in Hangzhou. From the wall on its left you could see Cockcrow Temple. Thousands of bushels of water chestnuts, lotus roots, lotus seeds, and caltrops were produced here every year; and there were seventy-two fishing boats, which every morning supplied the whole city with fish. Four of the five big islands in the lake were fitted with libraries; and the one in the middle, with its immense garden and house containing dozens of rooms, became Zhuang's home. In the garden were old trees, their trunks thicker than a man could encircle with his arms; and with plum, peach, pear, plantain, cassia, and chrysanthemums, there were flowers at every season. There was also a grove of tens of thousands of bamboos. Zhuang's house had large windows on every side from which he could enjoy the lakeside scenery, as enchanting as fairyland. A boat was moored at his gate, and to visit any of the other islands he had simply to ferry across; but without this boat, not a soul could reach him. In this garden, then, Zhuang lived. (R. 486; S. 393)

The island where Zhuang lives is described as a garden, a fairyland, a world of nature, which, like the Taibo temple, is far removed from the world. The island and the temple are two of the few sites that warrant such depiction throughout the novel, and the parallels between the two are fascinating: they are both insulated from the contamination of worldly clamor and restlessness. On this island Zhuang enjoys real and imagined freedom from all social restrictions, and no one, it would seem, can interfere: "Without this boat, not a soul could reach him." The narrator's emphasis on Zhuang's inaccessibility anticipates the temple's location beyond the surrounding world: the device of decontextualization is once again put to use. If the literati's withdrawal from the official world sets the stage for their enactment of the ceremony and evokes a utopian vision of a ritualized human community, Zhuang's retreat to the island enables him to go beyond the human world altogether. One of his visitors comments, "You are living like an immortal—how I envy you!" "We are completely cut off from the world here," replies Zhuang. "Although this is not Peach Blossom Spring, it comes very close to it. I hope you will pay us a long visit, for next time you may not be able to find the way" (R. 486; S. 393–94). In the last sentence of this passage, Zhuang alludes to "An Account of Peach Blossom Spring" by Tao Yuanming, in which the visitor gets lost trying to find his way back to the fairyland.

The narrator wastes no time showing how Zhuang enjoys the view of the lake. "How lovely the lake and mountains look!" he says one day with a smile to his wife, as they lean over the balcony to watch the water. "And all this is ours (*zhexie huguang shanse doushi womende le*)! We can enjoy ourselves here every day, unlike Du Shaoqing, who has to take his wife to Qingliang Mountain to see the blossoms!" (R. 486; S. 393). By claiming "all this is ours," Zhuang is not alluding to the recurrent poetic view of landscape in traditional Chinese literature as open to everyone with the aesthetic sensibility to appreciate its beauty.[6] Such a view is reflected in Du Shaoqing's excursion with his wife in Chapter 33, which Zhuang refers to here. Zhuang means literally what he says: he is making an exclusive claim to the territory, and he is the owner, as he duly reminds his wife, of the lake and island.[7]

Zhuang's claim to ownership is, however, ironically set within the network of correspondences and echoes in the novel; it reminds us of the statement that Fan Jin's mother makes in Chapter 3. After Fan Jin passes the

---

6. For instance, in "Song of Xiangyang," Li Bai (701–62) wrote: "Enjoying the pure breeze and the bright moon does not cost me a single penny" (Zhan Ying, *Li Bai quanji jiaozhu huishi jiping*, pp. 973–84). Su Shi (1037–1101) elaborated this point in his well-known "At Red Cliffs (I)" ("Qian Chibi fu"): "Between Heaven and Earth everything has its own owner; if it is not mine, I would not take it, no matter how small it is. Only the pure breeze across the river and the bright moon between the mountains: my ears take the one and make it sound; my eyes encounter the other and turn it into color. I can take them without prohibition and use them without depletion. These come from the inexhaustible storehouse of the Creator that both you and I can enjoy" (Kong Fanli, *Su Shi wenji*, pp. 5–7).

7. For the study of the concept of possessing nature in Tang dynasty poetry, see Owen, *The End of the Chinese "Middle Ages,"* pp. 12–33.

provincial examination, his household is crowded with visitors and overflowing with gifts. Fan Jin's mother, who has not yet fully comprehended her son's sudden success, has the following conversation with her maids as they are busy washing the bowls, cups, and plates:

"You must be very careful," the old lady warned them. "These things don't belong to us, so don't break them."

"How can you say they don't belong to you, madam?" they asked. "They are all yours."

"No, no, these aren't ours," she protested with a smile.

"Oh yes, they are," the maids cried. "Not only these things, but all of us servants and this house belong to you."

When the old lady heard this, she picked up the fine porcelain and the cups and chopsticks inlaid with silver, and examined them carefully one by one. Then she went into a fit of laughter. "All this is mine (*zhe doushi wode le*)!" she crowed. Screaming with laughter she fell backward, choked, and lost consciousness. (R. 49–50; S. 39)

Such farcical scenes and the characters' discourse of possession and ownership fill the first thirty chapters of the novel. In fact, the burning desire to grasp and possess becomes the driving force that motivates characters. In an entirely different context, Zhuang's statement that "all this is ours" recaptures the theme of these conversations, and his mockery of the Dus' tour lends itself to irony.

Zhuang is not exactly accurate in claiming the lake and island, for the emperor grants them to him; he is their ultimate owner, not Zhuang. In fact, by rewarding Zhuang with an imperial estate, the emperor stakes his claim on him as a state-sponsored hermit. Zhuang's sense of autonomy is, therefore, an illusion; it is immediately called into question, as an intruder in the garden precipitates a series of unanticipated events. Before Zhuang can finish his banquet, a servant reports that hundreds of government troops have seized all the boats so that no one can escape from the island and have surrounded the garden. As it turns out, Zhuang's visitor is charged by the authorities with possessing a copy of a forbidden book. The intrusion of the official troops awakens Zhuang from his dream of fairyland; it reminds him of the imperial claim to the garden, as well as his own subordinate relationship to the authorities. In his conversation with the general commanding the troops, Zhuang resumes his normative role in society; he demonstrates his competence and skill in dealing with delicate political affairs, and his personal association with the emperor and court officials makes a great difference. After the troops leave, Zhuang asks his guest to report to the authorities and then mobilizes all his political resources to plead for his release. Although the guest eventually returns to the garden, the image of the garden as an autonomous sphere is shattered, and Zhuang's connections with the outside world are laid bare, despite all his efforts to conceal them.

Zhuang is a key character in the Taibo ceremony, and his experience on the island offers an implicit comment on the literati's striving to create for themselves the vision of a ritualized world—autonomy of a different order. The intrusion of the outside world on his island anticipates what occurs later at the temple in Chapter 55—an even more outrageous intrusion of the mundane into a sacred space, which has by then been reduced to ruin. The episode also shows that despite his declining of the imperial offer Zhuang is still implicated in a relationship with the official world. The same is also true of other celebrants of the Taibo ceremony. If Zhuang tells a fairy tale about his island, he and his literati friends conjure up a similar tale about their ideal temple. The literati who appear in the temple are detached from the center of the official world, and the ritual they practice breaks with the logic of power and status that governs the realm of sociopolitical affairs. But the temple is only temporarily transformed by the ceremony into a ritualized world. And for most of the participants, their self-proclaimed detachment from the outside world is itself performative; it lasts no longer than required by the theatrical presentation.

This leads us to the performative nature of the ceremony. The Taibo temple provides the literati with a stage on which to carry out their ritual in full public view, with moments of theatrical flair. During the performance, the temple is surrounded by hundreds of spectators. Witness the scene as the celebrants leave the temple after the ceremony:

Their path was lined with people who had brought their old folk and children to throng the temple and watch. They were crying out for joy. "What makes you so pleased?" asked Ma Chunshang with a smile. "We are Nanjing-born and Nanjing-bred," they [*zhongren*, literally, "the multitude"] replied, "and some of us are over seventy or eighty. But we have never seen a ceremony like this, or heard music like this before! The old folk said the gentleman who was the master of sacrifice is a divine sage who has come back to the earth; so we all wanted to see him." (R. 510–11; S. 413)

The response is from the crowd, instead of particular individuals; they are absorbed into the collective identity of the audience: "We" are Nanjing-born and Nanjing-bred, and some are already over seventy or eighty. Still, "we" are the young, for "we" are told by "the old folk" that the master of sacrifice is a sage. In this way, "we" voice a collective, uniform response from the entire audience of the ritual performance, which demands an echoing response from us, the readers. There is no theater if there is no audience. In this scene, the temple is transformed into a theater, with the audience cheering in chorus as the actors step off the stage.

The theatricality of this scene becomes even more evident when read against the dramatic performance staged in Chapter 30. Before Zhuang Shaoguang, Chi Hengshan, and Du Shaoqing initiate the Taibo ceremony, Du Shenqing organizes a dramatic performance contest, which anticipates, in some important aspects, the performance of the ceremony. Like the ceremony, the contest is held outside Nanjing's walls. To enhance the theatrical effect, Du Shenqing sets the stage in a pavilion in the middle of the well-known Carefree Lake (Mochou hu).

When the actors had finished their meal, they put on their costumes and makeup. They were all wearing brand-new headdresses and jackets. One by one they crossed the bridge and walked across the pavilion while Du (Shenqing) and Ji (Weixiao), who had paper and brushes concealed in their hands, made notes. Soon the feast was served, and music sounded as the first actor ascended the stage. One acted "The Feast," another "The Drunken Singer," yet others "Borrowing Tea" or "Killing the Tiger." No two scenes were the same. Wang Liuge presented "The Nun Longs for Earthly Pleasures." When night fell hundreds of lamps were lit, high and low, making everything as bright as day. And the melodious singing lingered in the air. Rich *yamen* officials, merchants, and shopkeepers in the city, hearing of the contest, hired fishing boats, fixed up awnings and hung up lanterns, then had themselves rowed to the middle of the lake to watch. When they were pleased, they applauded and cheered. This went on till dawn, by which time the city gates were open and they went home. (R. 416; S. 334)

Along with hundreds of lamps and lanterns, the audience's applause and cheers in response to the performance on the pavilion transform the darkness and silence of the lake into a splendid theatrical scene. This brings to a climax a series of gatherings in earlier chapters, especially the banquet at Oriole Throat Lake at which the Lou brothers serve as the hosts for Yang Zhizhong, Quan Wuyong, Iron-Armed Zhang, and others.[8] In turn, it an-

---

8. The banquet scene, although on a much smaller scale and with less magnificence, is nevertheless rendered with the same touch of theatricality: "The cabin windows on both sides were opened so that they could hear music from the small boats as they drifted toward the

ticipates the Taibo ceremony, an even more magnificent performative event, and predisposes readers to see that scene in a similar light. Indeed, the Taibo ceremony is framed and regularly punctuated by the performance of music and dance. As in dramatic performance, the practice of the ceremony involves fifty musicians and dancing boys; it is orchestrated by Bao Tingxi, the owner of a local troupe, who was also a key organizer of Du Shenqing's contest.

In a more general sense, the presence of the audience turns all the participants in the ceremony into actors, and this is especially true of Yu Yude. The audience throngs to the temple to see him, a divine sage returned to the human world for this specific purpose. Du Shenqing, who organizes the contest, is not himself an actor, but his role as judge and organizer wins him as much fame as Yu Yude. Chapter 30 ends with the narrator's comments: "Since then . . . the fame of the seventeenth Mr. Du [Du Shenqing] has shaken the regions south of Yangzi River (Jiangnan)" (R. 417; S. 335). As a judge of the contest, Du Shenqing has the results posted outside West Water Gate, and that leads to several days of celebration for the prize-winning actors. In similar fashion, the names of all the ritual participants are posted on the wall of the Taibo temple: the last dramatic display, which invites such belated visitors as Wang Yuhui to imagine the irretrievable moment of the performance.

Although seven chapters apart, the two events are juxtaposed in the memory of the latecomers as testimony to the vanished glories of Nanjing's past.[9] However, with its ironic tone, the Du Shenqing episode challenges us

---

lake. And presently a feast was spread and a dozen servants in wide gowns and tall caps poured wine and served the dishes. It goes without saying that the food was rare, the wine and tea were fragrant, and they drank till the moon was up. Then fifty or sixty lanterns were lit on the small boats and were reflected with the moonlight in the water, making it as bright as day. The music sounded even more clearly in the stillness, its strains echoing for miles around, so that watchers on shore stared at the revelers as if they were immortals, and none but envied them. Thus they boated all night" (R. 179; S. 141–42). One of the differences between the theater scene and the banquet scene is that the latter turns the brothers and his guests into objects of observation and their boat into a moving stage drifting in the middle of the lake. Not unlike the actors in the dramatic performance at Carefree Lake, the brothers and their guests put on their own show, with Commoner Niu chanting poems, Iron-Armed Zhang performing his sword dance, and Chen Hefu cracking jokes.

9. See the conversation between Chen Munan and the ninth Mr. Xu in Chapter 53. Both complain about the deterioration of Nanjing culture. But unlike Xu, who believes that even the actors of the day are inferior to those of Du Shenqing's time, Chen blames Du Shenqing

to consider the relationship between ritual and theater. Is the Taibo ceremony as represented by Wu Jingzi merely an alternative form of theatrical performance? Is the ritual nothing more than a theatrical spectacle, a drama of role-playing, a sensational event that has no lasting impact on the real world?

Essential to the theatrical presentation of the ritual is, indeed, the issue of performance. Even Yan Yuan was often confronted by critics who saw ritual practice as a performance by actors. Yan Yuan's response was straightforward: the reason we are in such deplorable straits is

precisely because we are not as good as actors. The actors keep practicing at ordinary times, and thus they are able to act, move their hands and feet as prescribed without making any slips. Literati (shi) read books the whole day long with their hands in their sleeves. They are completely at a loss when the occasion for action comes. How can they be ashamed of performing rituals?

He cited the example of Confucius and his disciples practicing rituals under the apricot tree and concludes: "Since literati have become ashamed of performing rituals, the world has been degenerating day by day." In response to the question, "If you engage in the practice of rituals, what will you do if people consider you as behaving affectedly (naqiang zuoshi)?" Yan Yuan said:

Why should you avoid behaving affectedly? . . . Assume a tone of ritual and propriety, then there will be reverence. Perform the dance of Shao, then there will be harmony. The Confucian scholars of previous times neglected the form of rituals altogether. This is why rituals and music have all been lost.[10]

Yan Yuan seems to have focused entirely on the dichotomy of practice and discourse and concluded that ritual propriety can be demonstrated only in concrete practice. Therefore, although he admitted the analogy between ritual and theatrical performance, he did not explore its dubious implications and consequences. In fact, he never even troubled himself with questions about role-playing and the desire that motivates performance; nor did he discuss potential gaps between form and content and between action and motivation in the practice of ritual.

---

for actors' audacious transgression of their social roles. It is interesting to note, however, that in Chapter 46 the farewell party to Yu Yude involves the prize-winning actors as well as Bao Tingxi.

10. Yan Yuan, Yan Yuan ji, pp. 632, 665.

As I argued above, Wu Jingzi's representation of the Taibo ceremony closely illustrates Yan Yuan's approach to Confucian ritual by focusing exclusively on its external form. However, the juxtaposition with Du Shenqing's contest for actors does expose the ritual participants to all the potential problems of theater—role-playing, impersonation, self-invention, and insincerity—behaviors and traits that figure prominently in *Rulin waishi*.

Wu Jingzi saw actors ironically: except perhaps for Bao Wenqing, all of them are portrayed as professional impostors who transgress the boundaries of gender and social class and, more often than not, confuse theatrical illusion with reality. Wearing the costumes of the theater on public occasions, they pretend to be the dramatic roles they perform onstage and mix with members of the elite class with no qualms of conscience. But their capacity for theatrical performance both on- and offstage seems to capture the core of the literati's lives and mentalities.

Like the actors, literati characters are driven by the desire to acquire a leading role and imagined glory; they manage to recast their identity and change their status through the civil service examinations, impersonation, and dramatic self-representation. Indeed, the candidates for the civil service examinations, in telling stories about their own life, often project themselves into a scenario in which they win personal favor from the emperor and high-ranking officials and, by this means, replace reality with a much more desirable fantasy. And no less frequently do obscure young men make a name for themselves overnight through impersonation and plagiarism.

A master of self-reinvention, Du Shenqing is perhaps the best actor: after having married a concubine in the name of fulfilling his filial duty, he develops a new interest in actors, who are themselves female impersonators. Even though he is a poet, one of the *mingshi* who often define themselves against the vulgar examination candidates, he passes the civil service examinations and becomes the only *mingshi* in the novel with an official degree and title. In the Du Shenqing episode, Wu Jingzi blurred the line dividing the two groups of professional actors—those who perform on the theatrical stage and those who perform on the social and political stage.

It would be far-fetched, however, to take the account of the Taibo ceremony as part of the general trend toward theatricalization in the literati's lives without examining its rhetoric and thematic agenda carefully. In its exclusive focus on the external form of repetitive ritual activity, the passage seems deliberately dry and thus lacks the drama we associate with theatrical performance. On the rhetorical level, Wu Jingzi did, therefore, manage to distinguish the Taibo ceremony from other theatrical and ceremonial observances. To quote Marston Anderson: "It may not be too much to suggest that the passage is intended as the text's rhetorical degree zero: through it the narrator, by draining his style of all contaminating rhetorical flourishes, strives to attain an authenticity of voice corresponding to the psychological state that the ritual ideally produces in its participants." I would argue, however, that Wu Jingzi's deployment of this rhetorical strategy has more to do with his attempt to contain desire and role-playing. The performance of the Taibo ceremony, as Wu portrayed it, has a psychologically neutral effect on the ritual participants; or, rather, it absorbs them into a utopian vision of ritualized performance without evoking their theatrical impulses and desires for role-playing. Here Anderson refers to Xunzi's idea of the mediating power of ritual:

Desire and memory are, in his view, unavoidable natural impulses, which can never be *eradicated* but may be beneficially *displaced* onto the rites themselves. It is thus entirely fitting that in *Rulin waishi* the rites should become the eventual focus for the multifarious desires that propel the plot line of the first half of the novel; through ritual, desire is transformed into a kind of utopianism, or at least a kind of moral reformism.

Through such a transformation, Anderson argues that the Taibo ceremony "has brought not only the celebrants but the entire community into a renewed relationship with the ancient sages."[11]

In response to Anderson's insightful reading of the Taibo episode, I argue, first of all, that in evoking the utopian vision of the ritual world, Wu Jingzi deployed rhetorical devices and conceptual schemes that contribute to the making of a fiction. In place of the literati's self-dramatization and self-invention, he conjured up a collective ritual performance of self-renewal. Instead of dispensing with role-playing, he insisted that everyone perform his proper role in accordance with the ritual codes. Such role-playing is purged of choice, competition, and social mobility and becomes entirely stagnant and repetitive. Whatever theatrical flair remains is subdued. The success of this ritualized drama depends not on its participants' authenticity but on the perfect matching of name and reality through formulaic performance.

---

11. Anderson, "The Scorpion in the Scholar's Cap," pp. 272–73.

However, ultimately this ritualized role-playing is possible only within the imagined ritualized world, because the roles so defined are devoid of specific sociopolitical connotations and thus deprived of the specificity and concreteness that would give them a sense of reality. In other words, it would be impossible to re-enact the ritual in the real world without radically reinterpreting its codes. The fictionality of this ritualized world is reflected in the generic situation of Chapter 37. As shown in Part I of this book, the status of the ritual representation as a piece of writing inserted into the narrative from without is confirmed by Wang Yuhui's reading of the *yizhu* on the wall of the temple: as praxis becomes magic, prescription is translated into description.

The ritual scene's alienation from its immediate context does not render it immune to contextualization. Once the ghost of perspectivism has been evoked, it becomes impossible to control it, even if one tries. It may be difficult to answer the question of what, after all, differentiates Yu Yude, master of the ceremony, from his counterpart, Du Shenqing, in the acting contest. If Du Shenqing constantly shifts his roles in public and private life, so does Yu Yude, who, as I show above, defies all the normative distinctions and becomes both a palace graduate and the modern Wu Taibo. The difference between them may lie in the fact that Yu Yude's virtue is guaranteed by Wu Jingzi's narrator; we are told that in deciding to take the civil service examinations and accept the role of master of the Taibo ceremony, he is devoid of improper motivations and desires. Thus, despite the similarities between his actions and Du Shenqing's, Yu is said to be acting appropriately and avoiding the sinister inconsistencies that Du commits. The danger is that once again, as in narrative ritual, virtue or moral judgment becomes a matter of perception and interpretation.

It is undeniable that Wu Jingzi's adoption of the forms of biography and the ritual manual secures Yu a separate, privileged space for natural actions and genuine feelings, something impossible for other characters. But these forms are not entirely effective in inoculating Yu against irony. Not only does the narrator's occasional resort to the authoritative voice of the storyteller beg the question, but his endorsement of Yu's status as a reincarnated sage in the collective, anonymous voice of the ceremonial audience sounds hopelessly ironical. Even the Taibo ceremony, whose purity is inherent in the canonical form of ritual manuals in which it is represented, is not completely immune to contamination by the theatricality that permeates the dramatic performance in Chapter 30. It is already subjected to scrutiny through the subtle devices of contrast and correspondence before its advocates try to translate—unsuccessfully—its vision into the concrete praxis of the everyday in the ensuing part of the novel.

Cheng Tingzuo, one of Wu Jingzi's close friends in Nanjing, once criticized Wu Jingzi and Fan Shengmo for their fascination with theatricality in their reform of Confucian ritual. In his letters to Fan, Cheng took issue with a mourning ritual that Fan and Wu designed for a certain Tan family in Nanjing. He argued that the ancient mourning rituals had no music. By incorporating music, Fan and Wu had turned a Confucian family ritual into a theatrical performance (*liyuan zhi banyan*) or Buddhist and Daoist ritual (*Seng Dao zhi jing jiao*), which involve music and dramatic spectacle. Cheng Tingzuo also criticized Wu Jingzi's use of his own lyrics, modeled on "Dazhao" (Great summons) of the *Songs of Chu* (*Chuci*), in the mourning ritual for being a "playful approximation" (*yi jin youxi*).[12] Since the Taibo ceremony goes beyond the level of family rituals in both function and presentation, Cheng's criticism does not apply directly to *Rulin waishi*. Yet, given the evident similarities in the representation of dramatic performance and the ceremony in Chapters 30 and 37, Cheng's concern with theatricality may not be entirely irrelevant. Interestingly enough, Zhuang Shaoguang, the character modeled on Cheng Tingzuo, plays an important role in the Taibo ceremony, whose theatricality might have provoked Cheng's disapproval.

To conclude my reading of Wu Jingzi's reflective narrative of the Taibo temple, I will situate it in the Ming and Qing literati's accounts of temple reconstruction projects. Alongside a growing number of appeals on behalf of Taibo worship, we often find seemingly incongruous reports: the Taibo temple was dilapidated from years of neglect, or most of the ancient pines in the courtyard had been cut down and used for firewood by local residents. Likewise, the Taibo tomb had been left untended and had been trampled on by herdsmen who neither knew nor cared who Taibo was.[13] The best example of this kind of record can be found in *Taibo Meili zhi* compiled by Wu Xi in 1898. In it, the history of the Taibo temple and tomb is portrayed as a

---

12. According to Cheng Tingzuo, Wu Jingzi composed a poem on the model of "Dazhao" and then used it in the mourning rituals to recall the soul of the dead. Cheng criticized Wu for both misreading "Dazhao" and deviating from the tradition of Confucian rituals. See Cheng Tingzuo, *Qingxi wenji fubian*, juan 4, pp. 8–12.

13. Wu Xingzhuo in Wu Xi, *Taibo Meili zhi*, juan 4, p. 11b.

constant struggle of reconstruction and preservation. Local literati's accounts of the stone stele dedicated to Taibo, which are quoted verbatim in *Taibo Meili zhi*, always begin with laments over the ruins of the temple and tomb. The laments prompt them to make the effort to rebuild. But once complete, their reconstructed temple and tomb are equally subject to the erosion of time and are reduced again to ruin.

This cycle of reconstruction and destruction occasionally takes on an ironic note between the main text and the annotations in *Taibo Meili zhi*. In one place the text relates the official effort to maintain a restricted area around the Taibo tomb in Meili. But a note by the editors adds, perhaps unintentionally, an ironic twist. Soon after the erection of the stone stele that bore the official prohibitions, the village children invented a new game. They were interested not in the inscription but in the top of the stone stele, which, as they discovered, was hollow inside. They often competed to throw stones at it to entertain themselves with the tinkling sound. Their frequent misses had seriously damaged the official inscription.[14] With its chipped and largely unintelligible inscription, the official stele was a message yet to be delivered.

This small episode recalls the ritual program posted on the wall of the Taibo temple, which is covered by years of dust and is almost illegible to Wang Yuhui in Chapter 48 of *Rulin waishi*. It also reminds us of Chapter 55 of the novel, in which a number of children, ignorant of who Taibo was, play in the open space before the ruins of the Taibo temple, while old ladies forage for wild greens within the courtyard. Like the episode in *Taibo Meili zhi*, these two scenes suggest the futility of maintaining the temple and the tomb in the face of human destruction and the erosions of time.

Through the project of the Taibo temple, Wu Jingzi constructed an event essential to his novel's thematic design, but he was also aware of the fictionality of his own construction of the temple and allowed it to fall apart. Once the temple collapses, the novel, which sees no compelling alternative, comes to an end. The story of *Rulin waishi* turns out, therefore, to be one of frustration, straddling the rise and fall of the Taibo temple. The fate of the temple suggests an allegorical account of the novel itself: what is constructed in fiction is itself a fiction and ultimately dwindles away into nothing.

---

14. See Wu Xi, *Taibo Meili zhi, juan* 4, p. 1b.

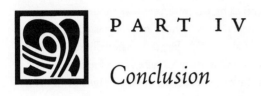

PART IV

Conclusion

Rulin waishi is a literati novel driven by conflicting impulses toward irony and the Confucian moral imagination. How it copes with the tensions between the two has been a primary focus for critics. It has been argued that *Rulin waishi* should be read in terms of satire or the Chinese satirical tradition (*fengci*). And satire is a conservative genre in that "its moral norms," to quote Northrop Frye, "are relatively clear, and it assumes standards against which the grotesque and absurd are measured."[1] Scholars often point out that Chapter 1 of *Rulin waishi* serves to set up precisely such a moral standard against which to measure the absurdity of literati lives portrayed, especially in Part II (Chapters 2 through 30) of the novel.[2] According to them, Part III (Chapters 31 through 37) moves toward the representation of the "positive" characters such as Yu Yude, Zhuang Shaoguang, and Du Shenqing, who are meant to live up to the cultural ideal represented in Chapter 1, and that shift is marked by, among other things, the apparent diminishing, if not absence, of irony. This critical approach suggests that *Rulin waishi* is capable of containing irony and preventing it from destabilizing the novel's value system. It emphasizes *Rulin waishi*'s need for such a system to guide its social criticism; ultimately, Wu Jingzi's moral vision makes his satire possible.

---

1. Frye, *Anatomy of Criticism*, p. 223.
2. This view of *Rulin waishi* has been popular especially among the critics in China. For a similar argument in English, see Wong, *Wu Ching-tzu*.

The questions are, of course: How could Wu Jingzi effectively secure the unambiguous moral vision required by this interpretative model of satire? Could he resort to the normative narrative, whose authority is questioned in Part II of *Rulin waishi*? As shown above, Wu Jingzi occasionally slipped into this mode of narrative in an apparent attempt to renew Confucian norms. His account of Yu Yude takes the canonical form of biography and utilizes the authoritative voice of the conventional narrator to convey the purity of Yu's intention; indeed, Wu Jingzi created an idealized fiction about Yu's virtue by placing him in a homogeneous world of ritual untroubled by differentiation and perspectivism. However, as I have demonstrated, such a narrative approach cannot be taken very far; its effort to decontextualize the Yu Yude narrative does not exclude irony entirely. Moreover, once virtue becomes a matter of representation and interpretation, it is implicated in the crisis of narrative ritual depicted in the previous part of the novel. In other words, Wu Jingzi's occasional recourse to the canonical model of representation ends up reiterating the problems of literati discourse captured in *Rulin waishi*. It verges on self-parody.

A careful reading of Part III of the novel shows that the model of satire is not easily applicable to the interpretation of *Rulin waishi*. For one thing, the moral standard conjured up in Chapter 1 either does not materialize subsequently or becomes obscured or compromised. And the characters, who supposedly adhere to this standard, are often subjected to questioning or trapped in a situation in which none of the available choices is flawless.

Rulin waishi is conceived in the mode of irony. So deeply does irony penetrate the core of its narrative that to endorse a new moral vision Wu Jingzi apparently had no choice other than to diminish his reliance on narrative, if not to dispense with it altogether. In fact, the effort to go beyond narrative is embedded in the very vision of the ascetic ritual Wu manages to create—a moral conviction that transcends narrative discourse and is to be translated into reality through the practice of the ritual. Wu Jingzi asserted Taibo's virtue by assuming a common belief in it and thus shielded it from interpretations and controversies. His representation of the Taibo ceremony replicates the formulaic language of the ritual manual and, like the ritual manual, reduces narrative to a minimum.

However, this approach cannot be taken very far: it either stretches itself too thin to sustain itself or collapses into its own antithesis by generating more verbal elaborations or alternative interpretations. Wu Jingzi reinforced the sagehood of Wu Taibo by not fleshing it out with concrete narrative, but as he rendered the motifs of the Taibo myth in his accounts of Yu Yude, Zhuang Shaoguang, and Du Shaoqing, irony resurfaces, although not as explicitly as we often see in Part II of the novel.

The complexity of Wu's account is further predicated on the conflicts I discern in the narrative of the Taibo myth, which is absent from the pages of the novel. These conflicts are embedded in the tensions between different versions of the myth (one portrays him as a Confucian paragon; another as someone who acts on the private ethics of yielding at the expense of public duties), between the myth and the ritual (the myth asserts the absoluteness of Wu Taibo's virtue, whereas the ritual consists of an attempt to contain the private ethic of yielding by translating it into an institutionalized behavior pattern congenial to the public interaction of the ritualized world), and ultimately, between the mythological claims and the controversial accounts of Taibo (the former defy any concrete narrative; the latter constantly subject Wu Taibo's yielding of the throne to "contextualizing" perspectives and thereby jeopardize the image the myth projects).

Wu Jingzi's narrative in Part III of the novel recapitulates almost all these conflicts: it asserts the literati's withdrawal from the mundane official world but at the same time sees the possibility of interpreting the same action from alternative approaches. And the parallels between the representations of the Taibo temple and Zhuang Shaoguang's island and Du Shenqing's theater further contextualizes the temple, despite its apparent detachment from mundane activities.

True, *Rulin waishi*'s representation of Filial Guo's journey is composed in the minimum narrative style. It eschews his internal world and utterances, but its well-controlled surface is eventually roiled by Guo's repressed emotions and accumulated remorse. The same process is even more evident in the episode of Wang Yuhui, for Wang's ritual leads only to his emotional collapse, which is followed by his repeated retellings of his daughter's story as a miraculous morality play. The effort to equate writing with ritual leads nowhere. Wu Jingzi self-consciously confronted ascetic ritual's limits by subjecting it to the erosion of emotion and words.

In a more general sense, it is Wu Jingzi's narratives of the ritual absolutists' behavior, as shown in the stories of Filial Guo, Wang Yuhui, and the Yu brothers, that help reveal the inconsistencies and even contradictions otherwise difficult to discern in the design of ascetic ritual. The distinction between the absolute ethics of ascetic ritual and the "situational ethics" of narrative ritual sometimes seems more hypothetical than real. Even an as-cetic like Wang Yuhui is portrayed as acting on secret calculations and a de-sire for rewards, and his behavior becomes no less hypocritical than that of *mingshi*, who pursue personal fame under the guise of disinterest. Irony and perspectivism are the inevitable conditions of *Rulin waishi*'s narrativity, and they make no exceptions for the ascetic ritual at stake in Wu Jingzi's moral vision.

Wu Jingzi's representation of ascetic ritual helps to define his fictional narrative as a mode of critical discourse characterized by a relentless exami-nation of its own values and assumptions. I began Part IV of this book by elaborating the potential tension between *Rulin waishi*'s tendencies toward moral imagination and irony, and I shall conclude by saying that the novel is so thoroughly drenched in irony that it does not spare its own moral imagi-nation from scrutiny. Or more precisely, its power of moral imagination lies precisely in its capacity to reflect on its own intellectual sources and narrative choices. It is through such constant self-scrutiny that *Rulin waishi* engages in a full-scale criticism of the cultural tradition in which it is deeply rooted.

In the eighteenth century, the vernacular novel achieved a new sense of intellectual engagement and gravity. As a genre, it offered literati authors a forum in which to address their concerns and participate in ongoing intellec-tual discourse. Rather than purveying the clichés of common discourse as voiced by the conventional narrator of earlier vernacular fiction, several ma-jor novels of the time were intended as contributions to contemporary de-bates: *The Humble Words of an Old Rustic* sets out to revive the authority of Song Neo-Confucianism, *Warning Light at the Crossroads* underscores the importance of the Confucian family regulations,[3] and *Flowers in the Mirror*, completed for the most part in the early part of the nineteenth century, em-braces the horizon of literati learning opened by evidential philological stud-ies. Written for literati readers and circulated among literati circles, these and other novels participate in an imagined community of intellectual dis-course. Their role in the formation of literati consciousness of the time de-serves further investigation.

---

3. In a study of Li Lüyuan's novel *Warning Light at the Crossroads*, Maram Epstein ("Ritual in the Eighteenth-Century Novel *Qilu Deng*") elaborates its interest in ritualism and points out that several manuscript editions of the novel contain a set of household rules that the novelist had compiled. See also Martin Huang, "Xiaoshuo as 'Family Instructions.'"

For the purpose of the present study, it suffices, however, to say that, like *Rulin waishi*, most of these literati novels are characterized by a moralizing zeal and an ironic edge. In *Flowers in the Mirror*, for example, its account of the Country of Gentlemen endorses the lofty virtue of yielding or noncompetitiveness demonstrated by the descendants of Wu Taibo, but this does not prevent it from exposing the pretentiousness and perverseness of that virtue when it is carried to its logical extremes and becomes, paradoxically, a competition to be noncompetitive. In this and other episodes, Li Ruzhen offered a compelling allegorical version of Wu Jingzi's ironic portrayal of literati hypocrisy and perversion. However, Li was so thoroughly saturated in the wisdom of the elite culture that he seems content with dropping witty insights rather than, like Wu Jingzi, exploring the moral dilemmas of literati choices. And Li certainly had little difficulty reconciling his moralizing and parodic tendencies as long as he remained blissfully enchanted with the totality of literati culture, to which his novel gives a refined, witty expression.

Most literati writers of the time still felt at home with their inherited culture, and that is why their sense of irony rarely led to serious self-questioning. Even *The Humble Words*, a Neo-Confucian fantasy, sometimes yields conscious irony, and there are moments when the author, despite his indulgence in moral fallacies, was clearly aware of the fictionality of his own work,[4] but he identified so closely with Wen Suchen, the protagonist—a Confucian superman—that he was utterly incapable of integrating his forays of wit into a consistent pattern of self-reflection, let alone of questioning the values at the core of his own narrative.

Of the literati novels of the eighteenth century, only *The Story of the Stone* is *Rulin waishi*'s true intellectual equal. Despite striking differences in theme and narrative style, it shares with *Rulin waishi* an adversarial stance toward the culture that runs through its own narrative, and it is just as self-reflexive in rendering its account of reality. In a sophisticated manner unprecedented in vernacular fiction, *The Story of the Stone* questions the validity of name and word and frames its own narrative around the dialects of truth and fiction. *Rulin waishi* elaborates on similar issues but sets them in the sociopolitical realm without resorting to allegory: in *Rulin waishi*, the literati's impersonation, plagiarism, empty rhetoric, and deceptive role-playing become the driving forces in shaping their own life and, in many cases, are taken for reality

---

4. For a discussion of this aspect of *Humble Words*, see Huang, *Literati and Self-Re/Presentation*, pp. 109–36.

itself. The question of truth versus fiction leads both novels to reflect on their own meaning and to question the possibility of their own fictional representation. And nowhere else is this better illustrated than in the construction and ultimate dissolution of the ideal temple in *Rulin waishi* and of the utopian garden in *The Story of the Stone*.

Although *Rulin waishi* and *The Story of the Stone* address different subjects, they are equally vigorous not only in exploring literati culture but also in questioning their own choices, and their narratives unfold through a dynamic process of intellectual inquiry and self-negation. *Rulin waishi* is concerned primarily with literati decisions to serve or withdraw; *The Story of the Stone* elaborates on its protagonist Jia Baoyu's refusal to enter the adult world through the civil service examination and government service. Whereas *Rulin waishi* reflects on elite-official mores and seeks alternatives from within the Confucian tradition, *The Story of the Stone* places no hope in Confucianism and searches instead for individual salvation through love, lyrical and theatrical enchantment, and ultimately, Daoist and Buddhist enlightenment. But after exhausting all the available choices, it ends in disillusionment with the literati culture that permeates its own narrative. *Rulin waishi* does not conclude on a more positive note. Its critical inquiry poses more questions than it answers, but its values lie in part in its capacity to question the culture to which it pledges allegiance.

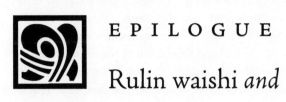

E P I L O G U E

Rulin waishi *and*

Literati Nostalgia for the

Lyrical World

Essential to *Rulin waishi*'s representation of literati degeneration and struggles is the question of how a literatus can live a meaningful life in a time of
disenchantment. More specifically, how can he gain a sense of self-
fulfillment when he is alienated from the traditional sociopolitical roles of
the elite class? How can he create a "home," to which he belongs and from
which he draws meaning and inspiration, when he feels so at odds with the
official world and local society?

Rulin waishi offered Wu Jingzi a critical medium to illuminate the disaf-
fection of the literati; it also constitutes his personal journey in search of a
home. At the end of Chapter 56, the last chapter of *Rulin waishi*, is a song
lyric with a nostalgic, autobiographical voice: "I remember that I left home in
the old days for the love of the Qinhuai River [in Nanjing]. . . ." Wu Jingzi
left Anhui at age thirty-two, because he no longer felt he belonged there, and
settled in Nanjing for the rest of his life. A narrative journey of an intellectual quest under the sign of history, *Rulin waishi* concludes with this compelling personal note, revealing not merely its autobiographical undercurrent
but its competing impulses, from self-exile to a constant search and nostalgic
longing for home.

The longing stems from a sense of alienation: in Wu Jingzi's account, no
literatus succeeds in living a meaningful life as a member of the local gentry,
and the prescribed roles in family, lineage, and local community cease to be
fulfilling. Du Shaoqing, who is weary of his obligations to his lineage and

feels only disgust toward his kinsmen, recapitulates Wu's early trauma of being victimized in a vicious dispute over an inheritance.[1] Estranged from his
own community, Wu Jingzi had to seek a home somewhere else, but where
exactly? If his fictional alter ego finds no satisfaction in playing the role of a
local gentryman, most of his other characters experience even greater disillusionment with their official careers. More often than not, their lifelong slavery to the civil service examinations drains their energy and imagination and
leaves them in a permanent state of mental poverty and moral, if not financial, bankruptcy.

Underlying Wu Jingzi's radical reimagining of li is the motivating force of
the search for home—an attempt to bolster ethical relationships and anchor
an individual life in a time of uncertainty by endowing it with the gravity of
meaning. As did Wu Jingzi himself, Du Shaoqing moves to Nanjing, where
he creates for himself a "family" on the basis not of blood ties but of personal
affinities, shared cultural interests, and a common commitment to the practice of Confucian ritual. Wu's representation of the Nanjing circle is itself an
event; it prepares the novel for the next stage of action and presents, in a
broader sense, an effort to construct a community in a metropolis for literati
who have wandered away from their own local lineages and remain independent from official institutions—an unconventional choice for establishing literati affiliations.

The Taibo ritual in Chapter 37 seals a mutual bond among its participants; its performance creates a moment of suspension in which they raise
themselves above the flux of time and the clamor of the mundane and
thereby achieve unity and harmony, albeit temporarily, among themselves
(the miscellaneous nature of the participants suggests an occasion for reconciliation and regeneration), as well as an identification with the ancient focus
of their worship. Instead of being predicated on a specific sociopolitical
situation, this collective ceremony inside the Taibo temple evokes the vision
of a transcendental home for the literati, who are constantly on the road
with no assured destination.

A strong penchant for moral reasoning drives Wu Jingzi's narrative of the
Confucian ritualized world, but it also leads him into ethical dilemmas. The
ceremonial harmony between the individual and the larger whole can hardly

---

1. At an early age, Wu Jingzi was adopted by his remote uncle Wu Linqi as the heir of the
family fortune and that drew him to the center of domestic dispute. For more information
about this incident in the Wu family, see Chen Meilin, *Wu Jingzi pingzhuan*, pp. 59–89.

replicate a formidably complex and intricate reality. The ritual journeys taken by Filial Guo and Wang Yuhui begin with positive agendas but go astray as they unfold. In these sections of the novel, Wu Jingzi's narrative underscores the problems of ritual practice without offering solutions: attempting to implement the vision of the transcendental home in real life results in the disintegration of that vision and the demoralization, even destruction, of those involved.

Elaborating on the full magnitude of these dilemmas, *Rulin waishi* turns its journey of moral and intellectual inquiries into a merciless scrutiny of its own premises, values, and ethical reasoning. As I argued above, it also offers a critical reflection on almost all existing modes of representation or expression (from the Confucian mythological claim to historiography to vernacular fiction) without sparing its own narrative from an equally rigorous examination. This relentless self-reflexivity—a strong impulse against its own grain—brings no sense of satisfaction and settlement at the conclusion of *Rulin waishi*: a novel so conceived is destined to be homeless.

However, at those points at which his ethical reasoning reached an impasse, Wu Jingzi shifted gears to explore the alternatives offered by lyricism. There is in *Rulin waishi* a subsidiary theme that does not entirely fit within the ethical framework of the novel I have so far delineated: a nostalgic longing for a lyric vision of life. The Epilogue examines this theme and its broader implications for understanding late imperial literati culture.

As I have argued, in the episodes of the four plebeian loners in Chapter 55 of *Rulin waishi*, *li* undergoes a series of fundamental transformations from the collective to the individual, from the ethical to the aesthetic, and from action to meditation and imagination. These changes hark back in part to the classical conceptualization of *li* in *Liji* in terms of "music without sound; ritual without form; and mourning ceremony without mourning clothes [that is, to mourn someone who is not one's kin]."[2] At the heart of Wu Jingzi's final attempt to revitalize *li* lies an elevated lyric vision of human experience that transcends the regulatory form of institutions and thus remains undisturbed by the deterioration of external rules and distinctions. Tapping into the large reservoir of literati culture, Wu acknowledged a personal attachment to its lyric ideal, despite his constant questioning of its ethical tenets and discursive mode. Or more precisely, his elaboration of the

---

2. See chap. 29 of *Liji*, in *Liji zhengyi, juan* 51, p. 1617.

breakdown of the imaginary ritualistic community left lyricism as the only alternative way to envision a harmonic, meaningful totality of life.

It is not always easy to tell where ritualism withdraws and lyricism sets in. The lyric vision of life does recapture the potentially poetic aspects of the Taibo ceremony—homogeneity, self-containment, and the suspension of time. That vision, however, leads to revelations and a sensibility that are conspicuously absent from the all-too-rigid, mechanical, repetitive ritual scene. Toward the end of his narrative journey in *Rulin waishi*, Wu Jingzi sought to reassert the qualities essential to the lyric tradition—genuine feeling, a meditative mood, and a spontaneous yet total foundation in the unity of man and nature—most prominently in his snapshots of the private lives of the four amateur artists in Chapter 55.

Lyric experience is personal and transient, but it penetrated deeply into the literati's collective consciousness because of the omnipresent influence of lyric poetry in their life and their perception and articulation of aesthetic values. It is beyond the scope of this book to probe its cosmological and ontological implications, but clearly this lyric vision epitomizes the literati's cultural ideal in a nonphilosophical way,[3] and its advent in *Rulin waishi* raises three interrelated issues. The first has to do with ethics, for the aesthetic problem, as it is understood in the context of premodern literati culture, is inseparable from human relations and the meaning of the individual life. The questions we must ask are: Was Wu Jingzi proposing what might be called a poetic solution to ethical problems? Does that suggest anything other than a utopian urge—a doomed struggle to conjure up a way of life that has vanished forever, if it ever existed—or a reluctant retreat into the realm of interiority and even fantasy?

A second issue concerns the relationship between the vernacular novel and lyricism. As shown earlier, *Rulin waishi* defines itself as a critical medium through which to reflect on the existing modes of discourse, including its own. Driven by an impulse toward ruthless self-negation, it offers no metaphorical home to which the literati might entrust themselves; nor does it provide them with a source of ultimate meaning and personal comfort in a time of crisis. In fact, the novel is a work about the literati's moral and cultural crises; it perceives reality to be fragmentary and meaningless, and its

---

3. For more on these topics, see Li Zehou, *Mei de licheng*; and Li Zehou and Liu Gangji, *Zhongguo meixue shi*. See also Chen Shih-hsiang, "On Chinese Lyrical Tradition"; Yu-kung Kao, "Chinese Lyric Aesthetics"; and Chang Shu-hsiang, "Shuqing chuantong de benti yishi."

adversarial stance toward the assumptions underlying its own narrative discloses a new critical consciousness coming into play. How can lyricism claim a place within a novel so conceived, if it presupposes a homogeneous vision of the world and solicits empathy, and even identification, with that vision? Indeed, how does the lyric voice function when it is situated among other, conflicting voices? Can lyrical discourse survive within a form that erodes its autonomy and decentralizes, if not engulfs, its lofty vision?

This question has ramifications for a third issue—the style of *Rulin waishi*. When the lyrical consciousness enters the prose narrative of *Rulin waishi*, it does not take the form of monologue or poetry. Whether it is capable of subduing the heterogeneous world of the novel under its cohesive vision, it claims an artistic triumph by penetrating the mood, rhythm, and tone of Wu Jingzi's representation of literati experience and thereby adds a new and different dimension of sensibility to this novel, which is noted primarily for its ironic edge. This point deserves special attention in part because few, if any, subsequent novels in an ironic vein succeed in incorporating a lyric mood and sensibility; in this regard, *Rulin waishi* remains an unrivaled example of artistic experiment and achievement.

In the second half of *Rulin waishi*, we occasionally encounter moments of lyrical flair, as shown in Wu Jingzi's portrayal of Nanjing as the home of the four commoners and Du Shaoqing. Despite his concise, minimalist style, Wu's introduction of Nanjing in Chapter 24 achieves an exuberant poetic tone:

The Qinhuai River, which flows through Nanjing, measures over three miles from the east to the west ford; when its water is high, painted barges carrying flutists and drummers play to and fro on it day and night. Within and without the city stand monasteries and temples with green tiles and crimson roofs. During the Six Dynasties there were 480 temples here, but now there must be at least 4,800! The streets and lanes house 600 or 700 taverns, large and small, and more than 1,000 teahouses. No matter what small alley you enter, you are bound to see at least one house where a lantern is hung to show that tea is sold; and inside the teahouse you will find fresh flowers and crystal-clear rainwater on the boil. These teahouses are always filled. At dusk, bright horn lanterns hang from the taverns on both sides of the road, several thousand lanterns on each main street making the highways as bright as day, so that passersby need not carry lanterns with them. Late at night, when the moon is up, boats playing soft music glide up and down the Qinhuai, enchanting all who hear them with their clear, tender strains. Girls in the houses on both banks roll up their curtains and lean over the railings to listen quietly, dressed in light gauze and with jasmine flowers in their hair. In fact, as soon as the drums sound in the lighted boats, screens are rolled up and windows opened on both sides of the water, and the scent of the ambergris and sandalwood burnt in the houses here floats out to mingle with the moonlight and mist on the water, until you fancy yourself in paradise or fairyland. (R. 334–35; S. 270)

Addressing its anonymous readers in the second person, this passage depicts Nanjing in a personal voice rarely heard throughout the novel: it invites "you" to perceive and experience the city the way it describes. Charged with a poignant sense of personal attachment to the city, this intruding voice is, however, disconnected from any speaking subject. It is intimate, fresh, and bears no resemblance to the storyteller's voice;[4] nor can it be attributed to any of the novel's protagonists, for at this point, no resident of Nanjing has been presented. It is Wu Jingzi, the implied narrator, who is speaking, yet, instead of speaking for himself or in his own capacity (with a concrete physical presence or full-fledged interiority), he evokes the imagery and mood of Nanjing from the inherited lyric repertoire and lays an absolute claim on his literati readers by articulating an anonymous sentiment: his rendering of the spring scene of Nanjing recalls Du Mu's (803–52) poems on Yangzhou, a nearby city, with their gentle spring breezes lingering in Yangzhou's long streets. The moon, which appears at the silent intervals of Wu's narrative, seems to have emerged from the depths of cultural memories of Nanjing as envisioned by Liu Yuxi (772–842) almost one thousand years before.[5]

---

4. It is noteworthy that this passage is devoid of the formulaic language (in the forms of parallel prose and poem) that the simulated storyteller usually uses in depicting scenes, and it is thus impossible to connect its voice to the conventional narrator of the vernacular fiction.

5. In a poem "Parting, II" ("Zengbie") to his beloved courtesan in Yangzhou, Du Mu wrote, "The spring breeze is lingering in the ten-*li* long street of Yangzhou, / raising the curtain before the window, she beams with such splendid beauty that no one can compare" (*Quan Tang shi*, vol. 16, *juan* 523, p. 5988). Wu Jingzi recaptured this posture of raising the window curtain in his scene of Nanjing's nightlife. In Chapter 41 of *Rulin waishi*, the narrator's account of a conversation between Du Shaoqing and Chi Hengshan is followed by a silent scene: "The new crescent moon, having risen from the Qinhuai River, is passing over the bridge." This scene resonates with the last two lines of Liu Yuxi's poem "Fortress on the Rock" ("Shitou cheng"): "By the Huai Water's eastern edge, the moon of olden days, / in the depths of night comes back, passing over the parapets" (*Quan Tang shi*, vol. 11, *juan* 365, p. 4117). For further discussion of Liu Yuxi's poem and the way it shapes the imagery and mood of Nanjing in the literary representation of later generations, see Owen, "Place: Meditation on the Past at Chin-Ling."

So perceived and represented, Nanjing occupies a pivotal position in *Rulin waishi*'s geopolitical and cultural vision. I argued above that Wu Jingzi secured its role as the center for the revival of the Confucian ritual by setting it in a binary contrast with Beijing, the political center of the empire. This dichotomy of temple and court, literati and court officials, is set beside another contrast in which Nanjing embodies literati taste and sensibility in comparison with Hangzhou, crowded with philistines, hypocrites, and shams.[6] At stake in this second dichotomy is the opposition between the poetic and the prosaic.

Inhabited by self-proclaimed poets and best known for the enchanting vistas of West Lake, Hangzhou, as it appears in *Rulin waishi*, seems to have a lot to recommend it as a lyric site. In the novel, however, Hangzhou is a locus for irony—indeed, the Hangzhou episode is a story about the death of poetic consciousness rather than a lyrical paean to men's communion with nature. Wu Jingzi deliberately alienated us from the long poetic tradition about West Lake by forcing us to see the place through the eyes of Ma Chunshang. Culturally impoverished and incapable of aesthetic sensibility, Ma finds nothing appealing as he is carried by the incessant flow of a noisy crowd from one spot to another. This episode recalls the ironic opening statement in "West Lake on the Fifteenth Night of the Seventh Month" ("Xihu qiyue ban") by Zhang Dai (1597–1676?), an essayist of the late Ming and the early Qing: "On the fifteenth night of the seventh month, there was nothing to see at West Lake except the people milling about." Ma, indeed, resembles one of the five types of people Zhang Dai describes as thronging to the lake, who

neither rode nor went into a boat, but after having eaten and drunk their fill, they rushed about in their rowdy dress and sought the crowd at the Celebration Temple or on the Broken Bridge, where it was thickest. . . . They looked at the moon, at those looking at the moon, and also at those not looking at the moon, but actually did not look at anything in particular.[7]

However, even when Ma is removed from the crowd and elevated to the height of a mountain, from which to see the entire lake, the best he can do is

---

6. Whereas Yu Yude personalizes the religious vision of Nanjing as the ritual center, Du Shenqing, who is introduced as the first full-fledged literati character closely associated with Nanjing, illuminates its cultural dimension, with his sense of sophistication, exquisite taste and lifestyle, and irrepressible enthusiasm for theater.

7. Zhang Dai, *Tao'an mengyi, juan* 7, p. 58.

to respond with two sentences from *The Doctrine of the Mean* (*Zhongyong*), a Confucian classic, which he has memorized for the civil service examinations. Soon he once again succumbs to the temptation of food, which beguiles him throughout the tour. Wu Jingzi did not endow Ma with a poetic conscious-ness adequate to turning the lake view into a worthy object or drawing it into a lyrical experience. Without such a consciousness to give it meaning and emotional import, Hangzhou becomes a soulless place; it is abandoned to the indifferent crowd and disintegrates into inessentiality.[8]

Appealing to the sentiments and associations that had already been in-scribed on the image of Nanjing, Wu Jingzi evoked a lyric site to which his literati readers could relate and in which his characters feel most at home. This sense of home registers well in Chapter 33, where we follow Du Shao-qing to his new home near the Qinhuai River:

This was early in the third month, when the houses by the water were beginning to be filled and the sound of a flute could often be heard. Du Shaoqing prepared a feast, and invited four tables of guests. . . . By midday all the guests had arrived, and every window facing the water was opened. The visitors sat where they pleased or leaned over the balcony to watch the water, sipping tea as they chatted, leafing through the books on the tables, or sitting at ease enjoying themselves; each did exactly as he liked. (*R.* 453; *S.* 363–64)

Set free from lineage ties and sociopolitical obligations, Du's house is "open" to nature and thereby assures its residents and visitors a privileged space for genuine feeling and spontaneity. Not all the guests are genuine and sponta-neous, but at Du's party they are assimilated into a different frame of mind and mood and temporarily transformed. Clearly, lyric aesthetics goes be-yond the realm of art and poetry; it permeates all the various aspects of life and gives it a sense of totality: leisure, self-containment, and disinterested-ness constitute a holistic "natural" state of existence, in manifest contrast to the restless, career-oriented life pursued by most literati outside this space. Not surprisingly, commoners far removed from the world of the official elite emerge again as a convenient symbol for this redeeming lyric vision of life. Chapter 29 of *Rulin waishi* encapsulates their mental state in its depiction of a

---

8. It is noteworthy that toward the end of his essay Zhang Dai has to "evacuate" the place in order to assert his lyric subjectivity. It is not until midnight, after all the people have dispersed, that "people like us (*wobei*) move our boats to the shore" to enjoy the scene alone. The lake becomes filled with meaning and poetic vision when it is vacant and open exclusively to "us."

visit by Du Shenqing and his fellow literati friends to Rainflower Mount, a scenic spot in Nanjing:

> They sat there till the sun began to sink in the west, and two dung-carriers set down their empty pails on the hill to rest.
>
> "Brother!" said one, clapping the other on the shoulder. "Now that we've finished business for today, why not go to drink a jugful of the water from Eternal Quiet Fountain, then come back here to watch the sunset?"
>
> "It's true that in a place like Nanjing even cooks and porters demonstrate refined sensibilities for the scenery as found in the Six Dynasties!" Laughed Du Shenqing. (R. 402; S. 323)

The phrase *liuchao yanshui qi* (Six Dynasties' sensibility for the scenery) that Du employs here recalls the history of Nanjing as the center of the Six Dynasties' cultivation of literary taste, aesthetic values, and lifestyle; it also captures the subtle influence of this lyric culture by presenting it as a sensibility or mood filling the air of the place—an invisible essence that one breathes, embraces, and comes to embody. So conceived, nature, just like history, does not exist in the realm beyond consciousness. It permeates the core of lyric subjectivity; the present perception of nature contains echoes from the past, and lived experience becomes aesthetically saturated and shaped. At the center of these heartening passages about Nanjing is a poetic consciousness capable of reconciling men and nature, aesthetics and life, present and past, and thereby incorporate them into a meaningful whole.

In the episode about Du Shaoqing's move to Nanjing, Wu Jingzi made the retreat from the official world and the lineage system the precondition for aesthetic experience, but without further elaborating its social and ethical implications. In forming what might be called a synthetic unity of experience, he presupposed the presence of a subjectively complete world. But how does this poetic consciousness sustain itself if it is so elusive, and so detached and even alienated from concrete sociopolitical relationships? If its lyric vision must be manifested in a specific way of life or state of being, as Wu suggested, can it endure crises when its preferred mode of existence itself is threatened? Moreover, how can Wu claim its authenticity and totality in a prosaic world of representation deeply caught in irony?

These are the issues at stake in late imperial fiction. As Stephen Owen puts it, "The struggle between the need for the poetic and its impossibility lies at the heart of *Honglou meng, Six Accounts of This Life Adrift (Fusheng liuji), Peach Blossom Fan (Taohua shan),* and *The Palace of Lasting Life (Changsheng dian*)." Literati authors, according to him, are always haunted by the question: "How could an activity that epitomized elite culture be genuine in an age when so many manifestations of elite culture came to be potentially regarded with irony?" This question looms even larger in vernacular fiction, in which the increasingly voracious social reality becomes irrepressible. "During the course of the late imperial period," Owen argues, "the demarcation of lyric poetry as a protected space remained constant, but it was increasingly represented as such; that is, it was contextualized." He sees *The Palace of Lasting Life*, a *chuanqi* romance of the early Qing (final version, 1688), as "the last great defense of the poetic and the high style, attempting to redeem them from irony," but "it is both a complex defense and a very uneasy one, deploying its divine machinery to create a literally separate space in which the poetic can exist without contextualizing ironies."[9]

Of the vernacular novels of the eighteenth century, none is more committed to the tradition of lyricism than Cao Xueqin's *Story of the Stone*, but the novel is equally disillusioned with that tradition: it is an allegorical account of "the predicament of Chinese lyricism," to use Xiao Chi's words, "in the face of literary, intellectual, and socio-economic transformations of the late imperial period." On the one hand, the lyrical vision "supplies a mental refuge and source of cheer for the literati more enduring than any political faith,"[10] but on the other hand, in the absence of new ethical and sociopolitical values, it is limited to the realm of art and fiction and will inevitably deteriorate in the face of encroaching reality, which "is forever ready to engulf the poet again after the lyric moment is past."[11] This doomed struggle is epitomized in Jia Baoyu's willful neglect of and ultimate confrontation with the blind forces of society and time, which in the end reduce his privileged utopian garden to ruins.

We do not have to wait until the second half of *The Story of the Stone* to see the gradual erosion of its lyrical ideal, for Jia Baoyu, according to Wai-Yee Li, "fulfills the wonted lyrical ideal of the tradition—spontaneity, intensity, self-containment—while representing the author's unease with that ideal."[12] In this account, the distance between the author and Jia Baoyu becomes the key to the novel's problematic relationship with the lyricism that

---

9. Owen, "Salvaging Poetry," pp. 112, 116.
10. Xiao Chi, *The Chinese Garden as Lyric Enclave*, pp. ix, 19.
11. See Yu-Kung Kao, "Lyric Vision in Chinese Narrative Tradition," p. 230.
12. Wai-Yee Li, *Enchantment and Disenchantment*, p. 202.

runs through its narrative: although Jia is blissfully incapable of irony, the author often renders him in such a way as to invite an ironic reading.

During the Ming and Qing periods, not even poetry necessarily secured a privileged space for lyric experience. Complaints about the failure of poetry grew in direct proportion to the increasing quantity of poems produced. And the effort to "salvage poetry" was accompanied by the sense of irony that pervades poetry and complicates its stylistic profile. Poetic irony and self-mockery can be traced to the mid-Tang period, if not earlier,[13] but they prevailed in late imperial times when the poets often represented their own absorption in lyric experience as a deliberate and ludicrous compulsion.[14] The poetic vision no longer dominated its objects or pretended to be an object unto itself. Its alienation from the outside world constituted the precondition for the existence of poetry.

The seventeenth and eighteenth centuries witnessed the extension of lyricism into the realm of vernacular narrative. That did not, however, result in the formation of a homogeneous discourse in the narrative world; instead, by dramatizing the tension between the lyric mode of expression and the prosaic mode of representation, it often highlighted the transience and fragility of poetic vision. In *Rulin waishi* and *The Story of the Stone*, lyricism is further contested, as Wu Jingzi and Cao Xueqin were caught between their doubts about the late Ming legacy of *qing* (passion), romantic impulse, self-enchantment, and dramatization and their mounting discontent with the rigidity and oppressiveness of the sociopolitical institutions (including the civil

---

13. See Shang Wei, "Prisoner and Creator"; and Owen, "Salvaging Poetry," pp. 112–14, 396n24.

14. Owen's reading of Huang Jingren's (1749–83) "Offhand Compositions: New Year's Eve" best illustrates the problems a poet faces: in the first poem, Huang conjured up a poetic moment of gazing at a single star alone on New Year's Eve, and in the second poem, he returned home only to find himself no less alienated there. Commenting on the lines "Silent I stand on the market bridge, recognized by none, / watching a single star like the moon such a long, long time," Owen writes: "On the one hand, there is no doubting the beauty of the 'poetic image,' whose very form embodies the enclosure of aesthetic attention, the focal point of light that excludes all else, a small thing becoming large by the very intensity of looking. At the same time the experience is mediated by placing the poet in a larger scene, by his seeing himself as he might look to others. Poetic experience is contextualized as such: the poem is not the poetic experience itself; rather, it is 'about' poetic experience, stylized and on the very margin of the ludicrous." In the second poem, laughter becomes audible, when the poet states: "Year after year I waste this eve reciting poems, / by the lamp my children often secretly laugh at me" (Owen, "Salvaging Poetry," pp. 113–14).

service examinations and lineage systems).[15] They saw the need to redeem the lyric vision of life, but they also realized that that vision could no longer be taken as a given. This is where irony comes into play, for it "sees the lost, utopian home of the idea that has become an ideal, and yet at the same time it understands that the ideal is subjectively and psychologically conditioned, because that is its only possible form of existence."[16] Thus, more often than not, lyric vision prevails only momentarily, co-existing with an uneasy conscience and the certainty of defeat. And this also contributes to our understanding of the generic condition of the vernacular novel. At least in the case of *Rulin waishi* and *The Story of the Stone*, the authors' deliberations on the legacy of lyricism reinforced their presentation of the vernacular novel as a new critical medium capable of reflecting on its own choices and the values it has taken to heart.

Wu Jingzi's account of Du Shenqing and Du Shaoqing reveals the range and depth of his reflection on the issue of lyricism. The two Dus are full-fledged characters, with multiple dimensions to their behavior, yet each in his own way personalizes the lyric vision of life. In introducing Du Shenqing, Wu Jingzi drew on the texts and cultural figures of the Six Dynasties; he also invested him with the late Ming fascination with exquisite taste, wayward charm, the ability to create illusion, and whimsical self-indulgence. If there is a poet in *Rulin waishi* who is worthy of the name, it is Du Shenqing, whose insight is best illuminated in an offhand comment on the works of a fellow poet, which is sharp enough to make the latter break into a cold sweat. However, in the banquet scene that follows, Du Shenqing rejects poetry writing as too conventional for the occasion and allows the development of the banquet to be dictated by his own sense of taste and personal whim. His art is to improvise, but its effect is almost magical and reduces the guests to a state of total intoxication and enchantment:

Du Shenqing glanced at Bao Tingxi. "Let me try to entertain you," offered Tingxi, laughing. He fetched a flute from his room, removed the silk wrapper, and sat down

---

15. The literati appear in the scholar-beauty fiction (*caizi jiaren*) of the early Qing period accompanied by a great dose of poetic gesture and sentimentalism. These works deploy poetry as the means for the communication of passion between lovers and kindle the lyrical sparkle by drawing on the repository of standard poetic scenes, motifs, and rhetoric. However, in these works, passion and fantasy are subsumed in the existing social and ethical framework and essentially compromised, if not altogether contained.

16. See Lukács, *The Theory of the Novel*, p. 92.

at the table to play. As the shrill music rang out, a little lad who had come to stand beside him clapped his hands and sang one of the songs of Li Bai. His voice was piercingly sweet and the melody utterly delightful. The three guests set down their cups to listen, leaving Du Shenqing drinking alone. They sat there till the moon came out, lending the peonies an unearthly loveliness and transfiguring a great guelder rose in the garden till it appeared one mass of dazzling snow. (R. 400; S. 320–21)

The high point of the party occurs when the fireworks, which are meant to "sober up" the guests, turn out to be yet another form of magic: "[They] reeled back to their lodgings as if in a dream" (R. 401; S. 320–21).

The art of magic, however, betrays its own weakness: this magic world belongs only to a moment and will soon be overtaken by the banality and triviality of mundane routines, and the unearthly beauty of the peonies and guelder rose in the enchanting moonlight will diminish, if not vanish altogether, with the daylight. Instead of projecting a broad vision and the power to conquer the alien world of reality, Du Shenqing is content to confine his lyric vision to the private sphere and leisure hours, and his delicate, whimsical sensibility is in no way engaged in public life. Even Du's physical fragility seems to acquire a metaphorical dimension; it constitutes part of his deliberate gesture to differentiate himself from the vulgar, but it also symbolizes the flimsiness of the lyrical style he embodies. At his own banquet, Du announces: "I decided to dispense with the usual dishes today, gentlemen. I have nothing to offer you but cherries, bamboo shoots, and Jiangnan herrings to go with your wine while we talk" (R. S. 320). On another occasion when Du joins his friends on an outing, the latter, knowing that he does not like pork, order duck, fish, tripe, minced meat, and wine. "After two cups of wine, they urged Du to eat, and he forced himself to swallow a mouthful of duck, but brought it up again immediately" (R. 401; S. 322). The feast is nothing short of an insult to the delicacy of Du's taste; indeed, even duck proves too strong for his stomach.

The world Rulin waishi portrays is often crude and tasteless; it is rife with ironies and absurdities and resists assimilation into the homogeneous poetic vision that is imposed from without. To insist on this vision invites conflict, if not defeat; to avoid this, the lyric subject has to either withdraw from the world or create a transitory illusion of its own self-sufficiency by taking itself as an object, a choice that verges on self-indulgence and narcissism. In the episode of Du Shenqing's visit to the Rainflower Mount:

They walked to the hill, and in the temples there saw the several stately shrines. Then they climbed to the top of the hill and gazed at the smoke from the thousands of houses in the city, the Yangzi River like a white silk girdle, and the golden glitter of the glazed pagoda. There was a pavilion at the top of the hill, and there Du strolled in the sun for a long time, watching his own shadow, while Zhuge went to have a look at a small tablet in the distance, then came back and sat down. (R. 401–2; S. 322)

In a bizarre twist, Du Shenqing, like Ma Chunshang, does not see the enchanting vista in front of his eyes; yet unlike Ma, he is preoccupied with his own shadow. At the center of this scene is an unquenchable longing that embraces its projected desires as the only true reality. After the disappearance of its vision of the organic, larger whole, lyricism degenerates into narcissism; operating on the much more limited scale of the individual psyche, the narcissistic impulse breaks ties with the outside world, retreating to the sanctuary of the enclosed self.

In a conversation with Ji Weixiao in Chapter 30, Du elaborates on the subject of *qing* (passion or love), essential to late Ming sensibility:

"Weixiao!" he said and heaved a long sigh. "Since the ancients, no man has been able to see through the word *qing*."

"No *qing* is greater than that between the sexes," replied Ji. "Yet you said just now you had no interest in women."

"Is *qing* confined to that between men and women? No, the *qing* of friends is stronger! Just look at the story of the Lord E [who was devoted to a singer from the state of Yue and covered him with an embroidered coverlet]. And in all history I consider Emperor Ai of the Han alone, who wanted to abdicate in favor of [his male lover] Dong Xian, shows the correct understanding of *qing*. Even Yao and Shun were no better than this in all their polite deferring to others. But what a pity that no one is capable of understanding this lofty *qing*!"

"True," rejoined Ji. "Have you never had a lover who truly understands you?"

"If I could live and die with such a man, I would not be grieving and pining away like this! But I haven't been lucky enough to find a true friend, and this is why I so often give way to melancholy!"

"You should look for him among the actors."

"You really know nothing about this, Weixiao! To seek a true friend among actors is like looking for a female lover in the courtesans' quarter. Nothing could be more wrong! Only those who require a spiritual affinity transcending the flesh are the greatest men of all times!"

He struck his knee and sighed.

"But there's no such man in the world. No, Heaven has condemned me, Du Shenqing, for all my gallant spirit and grieving, to pine away alone." With this said, he began to shed tears. (R. 409; S. 327–28)

The search for someone who can truly understand or appreciate him (*zhiji*) seems to lead Du on a journey toward the outside world, apparently in an effort to discover or create the world of the other, which corresponds to his own or at least is more adequate to it than the existing one.[17] This journey, however, never takes him away from himself. The episode about his outing to the Rainflower Mount predisposes us to see the image of his ideal lover as none other than his own shadow, and we are told that Du is interested only in "those who are just like us (*wobei*)," not actors, to say nothing of courtesans. This impression is confirmed when Ji dupes him into a search for such a man, who, according to Ji, "is handsome and elegant, but not in any feminine way." Du's pursuit turns out to be a comic adventure; in the end, he encounters only "a fat priest," who wears "a Taoist's cap and brown robe, has a dark, greasy face, bushy eyebrows, a big nose and thick beard, and looks over fifty" (R. 411; S. 330). Indeed, no one could be further from Du's projected self-image. Reality shows its vulgar face and grimaces at Du; that is enough to shake his world of fantasy and self-absorption.

It would be wrong, however, to assume that Du Shenqing is so committed to a lyric style of life that he would find his entry into the real world poignant and overwhelming. As noted above, his life is carefully compartmentalized; his whimsical indulgences during his hours of leisure do not prevent him from pursuing an official career and becoming successful in the public world. In fact, as Wu Jingzi was quick to show, Du guards his money with the shrewdness of a miser and makes the best of any available opportunities to advance his career. Poet is one of the many roles that Du chooses for himself, and he limits his performance of that role to private, inconsequential moments of his life. This sense of role-playing insulates him from tragic conflicts with the public world; indeed, following the rules of officialdom does not agonize him. In a way, Du represents the entry of the poetic into the realm of the prosaic as an empirical subject in all its refined stylishness and smoothness but also with all its limitations and weaknesses; essen-

---

17. Du Shenqing, in his self-indulgent confession, which sums up the recurring motifs in late Ming literature about love and passion, takes on the image of a lonely, self-pitying woman who pines away in a desperate longing for her absent lover; see Martin Huang, *Desire and Fictional Narrative in Late Imperial China*, pp. 73–79.

tial to his story is a diminished lyric vision incapable of evoking an incorporating, meaning-giving totality from fragmentary, disenchanted reality.

The episode of Du Shaoqing presents an alternative but just as problematic view of the lyric ideal. Wu Jingzi introduces the Dus as two estranged cousins who never meet in Nanjing, despite their common ties to the city. In the narrative of Du Shenqing in Chapters 29 and 30, Wu captured Nanjing's finest scenic spots (ignored by the self-absorbed Du), sophisticated savor, poetic mood, and theatrical flair, but it is apparent that Du Shenqing's connection to Nanjing is superficial and transient: he leaves when he goes to Beijing to take the palace examination. By contrast, Du Shaoqing makes Nanjing his permanent home after declining an official recommendation, and his commitment to the place is telling. The implication of this commitment is revealed in Chapter 33, when Du Shaoqing becomes one of the major figures in Nanjing. There, the destination of his lifetime journey, Du anchors his life with a sense of gravity and self-recognition, and apparently his Nanjing introduces him into a new community of the like-minded and provides mental tranquility by sheltering him from the disturbing commotions raging outside. Unlike his nimble cousin, who is forever ready to accommodate himself to the world he deems so vulgar, Du Shaoqing stands firm in rejecting it altogether, not merely for its vulgarity but for its trivialities, vanities, and lack of meaning. In any event, he proves himself an adamant guardian of the lyric consciousness that sustains his vision of Nanjing as home.

Du Shaoqing's poetic conviction is perhaps best demonstrated in his idiosyncratic reading of the *Book of Odes* in Chapter 34. Commenting on a poem, "The Lady Says: The Cock Has Crowed," which presents a conversation between a couple, Du says:

"The thing is that those scholars who hanker secretly after becoming officials want to cut a fine figure before their wives. Their wives again, who want to become great ladies but can't, find fault with everything and quarrel the whole time with their husbands. Look at this couple, though. They don't have the slightest thought of career, fame, riches, and official rank (*gong ming fu gui*). They play the lyre and drink, completely contented with their lot. This is how true gentlemen of the first three dynasties regulated themselves and their families. But no earlier commentators have pointed this out either." (R. 469; S. 378)

This remark has little to do with the poem; it tells us more about Du's mentality and self-representation. Although making his point in Confucian ethical language, Du elaborates the necessity of a disinterested attitude to aesthetic experience; his condemnatory use of the terms *gong ming fu gui* echoes Wu Jingzi's lamentation in the same words on the vanity of human ambition in the poem opening the novel. Perhaps more important, Du organizes his argument through the rhetoric of negation: instead of recovering the assumed naïveté of the ancients, he can only try to gain access to that disinterested aesthetic experience by understanding it in the negative terms of not thinking or talking about mundane benefits. In so doing, he forces us to read the poem as part of a network of differences and exposes it to the voice of negation or exclusion already present within the supposedly pure *cogito* of lyric consciousness.

What has been negated will not go away, however; its persistence turns Du Shaoqing's poetic vision into something of a second thought—a response to what is already there, whose existence disrupts its presumed autonomy. In other cases, Du is incapable of casting aside the voices that are at odds with his own; all he can do is ignore them or pretend to turn a deaf ear to them. As Du continues, he says of another poem in the *Book of Odes* that it "is simply about a married couple who took a stroll together." Ji Weixiao comments: "No wonder you and your wife enjoyed yourselves so much the other day in Yao Garden. You were keeping up the romantic old tradition of lyre-playing and drinking, and presenting each other with orchids and peonies" (R. 469; S. 378). This episode is related earlier, in Chapter 33. Mr. and Mrs. Du, accompanied by several maids and a cook, make a visit to the garden:

Mrs. Du and Mrs. Yao had not been sitting there long when Du Shaoqing arrived by chair with his golden goblet, which he placed on the table and filled with wine. Then, reveling in the spring warmth and balmy breeze, he carried the goblet to the balustrade and started to do some heavy drinking. Very drunk at last, he took his wife's hand and walked out of the garden, holding the golden goblet and roaring with laughter. So they strolled several hundred yards down the hillside while the other women followed them, chuckling. All who saw were so dazed and amazed that they dared not look up at them. When Du and his wife had mounted their chairs and left, Mrs. Yao and the maids plucked branches of peach blossom and loaded their chairs with these, then were carried home. (R. 454; S. 365)

Du Shaoqing's excursion is marked by flamboyant, theatrical posturing that scandalizes his unwilling audience, but instead of securing the dominance of Du's voice over the scene, the narrator allows us to hear the chuckles of Du's maids, who are either amazed or amused but in no way impressed. Du's studied lack of regard for conventional decorum constitutes his claim for distinction, but the mixture of laughter and chuckles and the unvoiced shock or embarrassment of the unlookers invites only an ironic reading. Claiming a victory over the prosaic world of banality and pettiness, Du is nevertheless aware of the presence of others, and he knows only too well the distance between his self-representation and their view of him: here narrative perspectivism is again in play. In a retrospective comment by Imperial Editor Gao in Chapter 34, this episode is inflated into a magnified caricature:

In less than ten years, he ran through 60,000 or 70,000 taels of silver. Then, with Tianchang too hot to hold him, he moved to Nanjing, where he takes his wife to the taverns to drink every day, and parades with a copper bowl like a beggar! Who could have thought his family would produce such a ne'er-do-well! (R. 467; S. 375)

Gao's retelling of the story cannot be taken literally, but it does present a certain aspect of the truth that Du may find difficult to swallow. What is important to our concerns here is that Du's voice is again interrupted by other voices. In *Rulin waishi*, the rhetoric of negation is always accompanied by narrative perspectivism, which pointedly hampers its effect.

From the very beginning of the novel, an acute awareness of different perceptions is built into the poetic consciousness, and no lyrical discourse is allowed to run in a sweeping flow without interruption. The introductory chapter of the novel presents Wang Mian as a self-taught artist with a lyric vision of life. However, when he models himself on his poetic icon, Qu Yuan, a legendary ancient poet of flamboyant gesture and imagination, by wearing a high hat and loose gown, a band of laughing children tag after him, and we are told that he "did not mind them." In another scene, Wang's meditation on the picturesque view of a lake is cut short by a conversation among three anonymous men, who, emerging from nowhere, prefigure the most repugnant characters to fill the pages of the next 30 chapters. This scene is followed by another episode, in which Wang Mian's paintings of lotus flowers, a symbol of detached purity, win him public attention, from which he cannot wait to flee. In an ominous twist, the product of his aesthetic experience is drawn into the socioeconomic network of transaction, collection, and consumption, becoming a commodity to be sold in exchange not merely for benefits but also for official favor and recognition. His lyric ideal of life is again in danger.

Indeed, Wu Jingzi represented poetic consciousness and discourse as part of private, solitary experience constantly in danger of interruption by menacing outside forces. Retreat is the basic pattern of lyrical existence. Wang Mian, who withdraws from the public world, is said to have no friends except an elderly neighbor, like Gai Kuan and Jing Yuan in Chapter 55. It is with a pessimistic account of their solitary state that *Rulin waishi* begins and ends; it promises no possible transmission of this poetic culture to any outsiders, not to mention future generations. As Wang Mian dies in isolation and obscurity, his lyric ideal, which remains unengaged with the world at large, perishes with him silently, unnoticed.

In a time of crisis when history failed to provide meaningful guidance, Wu Jingzi still relied on the lyric vision for personal solace, but this did not hamper his capacity to expose its intrinsic limits and problems: fragmentary and solitary, it is confined to privileged private spaces and, surely just as important, proves itself fit only for the moments of intensive experience. It is, indeed, incapable of enduring. In a novel so concerned with history and time, there is no way to save lyricism from irony other than to relegate it to the sanctuary of the elegiac memory of the pure past. Chapter 55 of the novel begins with the authorial voice announcing the death and dispersal of the protagonists, including Du Shaoqing, Wu Jingzi's fictional alter ego. Literarily, Wu envisaged his own disappearance into the memory of his imagined characters and of his readers as well. This brings us back to the concluding poem of the novel, with which I began this epilogue, since it conveys Wu Jingzi's personal voice in a retrospective account of his own past and stretches beyond the historical time frame (mainly the Ming dynasty from the Chenghua to the Wanli period) that has governed his novel up to this point. This is one rare moment when Wu broke free from the tyranny of time to assert the authenticity of his lyrical voice, which could not but be elegiac. With secular time as both its subject and its organizing principle, *Rulin waishi* is condemned to a permanent status of homelessness. Its final lyric surge signals an unquenched nostalgic longing for the lost home, a home the novel has placed forever beyond reach.

Appendix

APPENDIX

Texts and Authorship

of Rulin waishi

The Woxian caotang text, the earliest extant edition of *Rulin waishi*, was published in 1803. Interpreters of the novel have long tried to exclude some of its fifty-six chapters as forgeries. For these readers, the ideological frame and narrative design of *Rulin waishi* will not be coherent unless these parts are removed. My study has addressed this issue by illuminating the forces driving *Rulin waishi*'s dynamic process of critical inquiry and self-questioning. I argue that, as it unfolds, this process generates tremendous thematic and narrative tensions (especially in Part IV of the novel, in which Wu Jingzi began to question his own intellectual choices and stances, expand the scope of his narrative, and outrun his sources). Any interpretive scheme has to confront these tensions. I also point out that Chapter 56 constitutes part of the novel's framework, a framework that stands in an uneasy relationship with the innovative narrative scheme that dominates the main part of the novel and defies any definitive conclusions. When modern scholars spot what they deem to be ideological inconsistencies and even contradictions in *Rulin waishi*, they often reveal their own lack of understanding about its narrative dynamics and complexity and thereby fail to support their judgments on the issues of the novel's authorship and editions. This appendix further explores these and other related topics.

Editions of Rulin waishi

Wu Jingzi's authorship of *Rulin waishi* is confirmed in several unrelated contemporary sources and has never been seriously challenged.[1] But whether Wu was responsible for all fifty-six chapters of the Woxian caotang edition of the novel remains the focus of ongoing debate. The scholars who question the credibility of the Woxian caotang edition hypothesize that the original edition of the novel contained either fifty or fifty-five chapters. Proponents of the fifty-chapter hypothesis cite Cheng Jinfang's (1718–84) "Biography of Wu Jingzi" ("Wenmu xiansheng zhuan"), which states that *Rulin waishi* consists of fifty *juan*.[2] The fifty-five-chapter theory dates to a postscript to the (Suzhou) Qunyuzhai edition of the novel by Jin He (1818–85), who was remotely related to Wu Jingzi by marriage and also a descendant of Jin Zhaoyan (1718–89+), a close friend of Wu Jingzi.[3] Jin He claimed that someone had "recklessly" added Chapter 56 to the novel and that in the original version Chapter 55 serves as the last chapter, concluding with Wu Jingzi's autobiographical account of his own past in the lyric song "Qinyuan chun."[4] Modern scholars who read the Woxian edition with doubtful eyes have struggled to determine which five chapters are later additions; Chapter 56 was often considered problematic enough to warrant its exclusion from modern editions of the novel.

Before we examine the early editions of *Rulin waishi*, it is important to remind ourselves that these two hypotheses are not without problems. Cheng Jinfang noted that the novel was still circulating in manuscript form in 1770 or 1771 as he was composing the "Biography of Wu Jingzi." His use of the term *juan* instead of *hui* in referring to the number of chapters may have been meant as a tentative measurement; the two terms, although often

---

1. See Cheng Jinfang, "Huairen shi" and "Wenmu xiansheng zhuan"; and Wang Youzeng, "Shu Wu Zhengjun Minxuan xiansheng *Wenmu shanfang shiji* hou."

2. See Li Hanqiu, ed., *"Rulin waishi" yanjiu ziliao*, pp. 12–13. Scholars have often cited *The Draft Gazetteer of Anhui (Anhui tongzhi gao)* and Ye Mingfeng's (1811–59) *Qiaoxi zaji* to confirm Cheng Jinfeng's fifty-chapter theory (see ibid., pp. 60–64), but these two texts are abridged versions of Cheng's account, and thus, as Timothy Wang points out, "Cheng Jinfang becomes the sole authority for all those who subscribe to the fifty-chapter edition" (*Wu Ching-tzu*, p. 130).

3. Jin He's postscript does not appear in any of the extant (Suzhou) Qunyuzhai editions. For instance, it is missing from the copy at Fudan University.

4. Li Hanqiu, ed., *"Rulin waishi" huijiao huiping ben*, pp. 764–66.

used synonymously, may not necessarily refer to the same thing.[5] This is perhaps especially so in the case of handwritten manuscripts, whose division into *juan* could be more random and less uniform than it would be in printed versions. It is noteworthy that the manuscript copy of the novel owned, and perhaps also commissioned, by Pan Shi'en (1769–1854) included Cheng's biography but omitted the sentence saying that the novel consists of fifty *juan*.[6]

Jin He composed his postscript to *Rulin waishi*, which was based primarily on his mother's oral testimony, in 1869, 115 years after Wu Jingzi's death. Not surprisingly, his credibility has long been in question, and many of his arguments have been either disproved or challenged. For instance, he contended that all the books authored by Wu Jingzi contain an odd number of *juan*, and the same is true of *Rulin waishi* (that is, it is composed of fifty-five chapters). But he is proved wrong both in his reasoning and in his presentation of this "fact."[7] Moreover, his statement that "someone, sometime, recklessly added a *youbang* [posthumous examination register] *juan* [that is, Chapter 56], forming its official proclamations by reassembling the parallel sentences taken from the Master's (Wu Jingzi) literary works in the most sloppy, laughable way" only serves to undermine his own speculation, for he saw the apparent consistency between Chapter 56 and Wu Jingzi's other writings in terms of language style and vocabulary and even regarded the latter as the textual sources of the former. Jin He wrote the postscript to the edition sponsored by Xue Shiyu (that is, Xue Weinong); according to *Guangxu Quanjiao xian zhi* (The gazetteer of Quanjiao, compiled in the Guangxu reign), Jin He gave Wei his own copy of the novel for reprinting.[8] If this account is trustworthy, it shows that Jin's own copy must have consisted of fifty-six chapters, since that is the number of chapters in Wei's edi-

---

5. Liu Ts'un-yan (*Lundun suojian Zhongguo xiaoshuo shumu tiyao*, p. 335) made this argument, suggesting that fifty *juan* may actually contain the fifty-five or more *hui*. In any case, Cheng's use of *juan* seems to make his statement of the number of chapters less definitive than it otherwise would be. One may argue that Jin He, too, used the term *juan* in reference to *Rulin waishi*, but he chose the term perhaps because he was arguing that Wu Jingzi's anthologies of writings always consist of odd numbers of *juan*. Obviously, it would be inappropriate to describe these anthologies in terms of *hui*.

6. Cheng Jinfang's biography was hand-copied by Pan Zuyin, Pan Shi'en's grandson. See Li Hanqiu, ed., *"Rulin waishi" yanjiu ziliao*, pp. 127–28; and Chen Xin, "*Rulin waishi* Qingdai chaoben chutan."

7. See Hu Shi, postscript to *Wu Jingzi nianpu*, in Li Hanqiu, ed., *"Rulin waishi" yanjiu ziliao*, pp. 92–93.

8. See Li Zhongming, "*Rulin waishi* de kanben," p. 532.

tion. Otherwise, Jin would have cited that fact as compelling evidence for the exclusion of Chapter 56.

The earliest known mention of *Rulin waishi* dates to 1749, when the novel was being transmitted in handwritten form.[9] We do not know the range of its circulation, but according to Cheng Jinfang, it had become popular by 1770 or 1771, when "people competed with each other in circulating and transcribing it."[10] In Jin He's account, the earliest printed edition of *Rulin waishi* was sponsored by Jin Zhaoyan during his tenure as an instructor (*jiaoshou*) in Yangzhou prefecture in 1768–79. "From then on," Jin He claimed, "several printed editions came out of the commercial press in Yangzhou." Since Cheng Jinfang made no mention of these printed editions in 1770 or 1771, Jin Zhaoyan's Yangzhou edition, if it did exist, could have appeared only after 1771. There is no other evidence of its existence, however, except a vague mention by Xu Yunlin of the "original Yangzhou edition" (*Yangzhou yuanke*) in an afterword dated 1884 to his collated Conghaozhai edition.[11] We are still not certain what Xu meant by the original Yangzhou edition, which he used in collating his own version. It might designate any earlier printed edition of *Rulin waishi* perhaps published in Yangzhou during the late eighteenth century and the early nineteenth century, including the Woxian caotang edition.[12] Although no direct evidence proves that this edition was printed in Yangzhou, its commentary on the novel demonstrates an intimate knowledge of Yangzhou and thus suggests a strong tie to the place.[13] And

---

9. Cheng Jinfang, "Huairen shi."

10. Cheng Jinfang, "Wenmu xiansheng zhuan," p. 13.

11. See Li Hanqiu, ed., "*Rulin waishi*" huijiao huiping ben, p. 776.

12. Xu Yunlin alleged that he collated his copy with reference to the original Yangzhou edition, which he had borrowed from someone else. He also made it clear that the edition he had was that of (Suzhou) Qunyuzhai, and he agreed with his friend Wang Chengji that Pan Zengwei (i.e., Pan Jiyu, Pan Shi'en's fourth son) had done a poor job of collating the text. In so saying, he seemed to suggest the Pan family had played a role in the publication of the (Suzhou) Qunyuzhai edition, although Wang Chengji discredited this as a rumor in response (see Li Hanqiu, "*Rulin waishi* de banben jiqi yandi," in idem, ed., "*Rulin waishi*" huijiao huiping ben, pp. 4–6; see also his "*Rulin waishi*" yanjiu ziliao, p. 142). Obviously, Xu viewed the Yangzhou edition much more favorably than the (Suzhou) Qunyuzhai edition, without denying that the latter might actually derive from the former; what makes the Suzhou edition inferior in quality is, as he indicated, its lack of solid editing.

13. The 1816 Zhulige edition was published in Qingjiangpu, which is close to Yangzhou, and the fact that it resembles the Woxian caotang edition in both text and format offers another piece of evidence to help pin down the place of publication of the Woxian caotang edi-

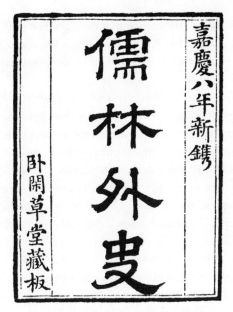

嘉慶八年新鐫

儒林外史

臥閒草堂藏板

Title page of the Woxian caotang edition
of *Rulin waishi* (1803)

what Xu called the original Yangzhou edition does not seem unlike the
Woxian caotang edition, at least in its inclusion of Chapter 56.[14]

As the earliest extant edition of *Rulin waishi*, the Woxian caotang edition
is the most crucial text for our studies of the novel. It takes the form of a
small size "handbook" (*jinxiang ben*), each page (recto or verso) contains nine
columns of text with eighteen characters per column. The cover page features the title *Rulin waishi* in the *lishu* style, with "Newly cut in the eighth
year of the Jiaqing reign" (that is, in 1803) in the upper right-hand corner,
and "the woodblock preserved by the Woxian caotang" in the lower left-
hand corner (see above). A preface by Xianzhai Laoren (Old Man of the

---

tion. For this point, see Li Hanqiu, "*Rulin waishi de banben jiqi yandi*," in idem, ed., "*Rulin waishi*" *huijiao huiping ben*, pp. 2–3.

14. Xu Yunlin does not indicate how many chapters this "original Yangzhou edition" had,
but if it consisted of fifty-five chapters, he would have used this as further evidence for disparaging the Qunyuzhai edition. Perhaps more important, his collated Conghaozhai copy, which
was presumably based on the so-called original Yangzhou edition, does not exclude Chapter
56. In a letter in response to this copy, which is attached to the table of contents, Wang
Chengji wrote: "The last chapter is a snake's tail and should therefore be cut off" (see Li Hanqiu, ed., "*Rulin waishi*" *yanjiu ziliao*, p. 142).

Leisure Studio) is dated the second month of the first year of the Qianlong reign (1736). As discussed in Part II, this date is important for our interpretation of *Rulin waishi* as a critical response to *The History of the Ming*, which had been completed a few months before.

Although no information is available on the identity of Xianzhai Laoren, it has been suggested that he was none other than Wu Jingzi himself, given the practice of the time: novelists often wrote prefaces to and comments on their own works under pen names and pseudonyms. Critics have tried to verify this hypothesis. Some see similarities in the writing style of Wu Jingzi's calligraphical works and Xianzhai Laoren's signature.[15] Others cite Wu Jingzi's frequent use of *xian* (leisure) in his writings to buttress his identification with Xianzhai Laoren.[16] Still others argue that 1736 was a watershed in Wu Jingzi's life, since it was the year he abandoned the idea of pursuing an official career through the civil service examinations. It might not be pure coincidence that in the second month of 1736, when Xianzhai Laoren's preface was presumably written, more than 200 literati (including several of Wu Jingzi's personal friends) gathered in Beijing for a special imperial *boxue hongci* examination (although the examination was postponed to the ninth month of the year). Wu Jingzi took the first three preliminary examinations but did not follow through and thus failed to appear at court.[17] This event is captured in various ways in Wu Jingzi's poems written during this period and later. It also seems to resonate well with Xianzhai Laoren's summary of the novel's theme in terms of a steadfast denunciation of *gong ming fu gui* (career, fame, riches, and official rank). Although this identification of Xianzhai Laoren remains a hypothesis, no evidence has been found to contradict it. I am interested in Xianzhai Laoren's decision to write such a preface in 1736, or to date it to that year, not only because that was a year of great significance for Wu Jingzi but also because at that time Wu either had just begun writing the novel or was at an early stage of composing it.[18] If Xianzhai Laoren was not Wu

---

15. For this argument, see Chen Meilin, "*Rulin waishi* Woxian caotang pingben," in idem, ed., "*Rulin waishi*" cidian, pp. 535–45.

16. See Tan Fengliang, "*Rulin waishi* chuangzuo shijian, guocheng xintan."

17. See Hu Shi, "Wu Jingzi nianpu," in Li Hanqiu, ed., "*Rulin waishi*" yanjiu ziliao, pp. 69–93; see also Chen Meilin, Wu Jingzi pingzhuan, pp. 190–232.

18. Scholars have not reached a consensus on when Wu Jingzi began to write *Rulin waishi*. Lu Xun's speculation that the novel was complete before 1736 has been proved wrong, because many incidents mentioned in the second half of *Rulin waishi* did not occur until the

Jingzi himself, then he must have been someone close enough to Wu to be able to announce the title of the ongoing novel early in its development, if we accept the 1736 dating of the preface.

The Woxian caotang edition contains anonymous chapter comments at the ends of all but six chapters of the novel.[19] No evidence suggests that the commentary and the preface were written by the same author. Since the comment on Chapter 30 refers to *Yanlan xiaopu*, which was first printed in 1785 and mentions an event that occurred in 1782, it seems that we must exclude the possibility that these comments were written by Wu Jingzi.[20] But we have no reason to assume that all the comments came from a single hand at the same time. The inconsistency of these chapter comments is reflected in their variations in length (from one sentence to several paragraphs) and in location (some chapters attract extensive comments; others have none).

Almost all the pre-twentieth century editions of *Rulin waishi* confirm the Woxian caotang edition. The 1816 (Qingjiangpu) Zhulige and Yigutang editions are based on the Woxian caotang edition not only in content but also in page format. Other editions, such as the manuscript edition owned by Pan Shi'en and the Qunyuzhai edition (postscript dated 1869), were produced in Suzhou;[21] although they never explicitly indicate their sources, they differ from the Woxian caotang edition in terms of format but not in the

---

1740s. Hu Shi (see his "Wu Jingzi nianpu," in Li Hanqiu, ed., *"Rulin waishi" yanjiu ziliao*, pp. 69–93) argues that the novel must have been written between 1740 and 1750. He Manzi (*Lun "Rulin waishi"*) insists that first twenty-eight chapters were completed before 1736, and Meng Xingren and Meng Fanjing (*Wu Jingzi pingzhuan*) hold that Wu Jingzi began his novel as early as 1733, soon after he moved to Nanjing, and had completed at least twenty chapters before 1736. Tan Fengliang ("*Rulin waishi* chuangzuo shijian, guocheng xintan") argues that the first twenty-five chapters were written between the fall of 1735 and the second month of 1736, and that Wu Jingzi did not finish revising the novel until 1754.

19. These are Chapters 42–44 and 53–55. For an English translation of the Woxian caotang commentary by Shuen-fu Lin, see Rolston, ed., *How to Read the Chinese Novel*, pp. 252–94.

20. See Li Hanqiu, "*Rulin waishi* de pingdian jiqi yandi," in idem, ed., *"Rulin waishi" huijiao huiping ben*, pp. 16–22.

21. The (Suzhou) Qunyuzhai edition was reprinted many times. Scholars used to call the copies bearing Jin He's postscript the Suzhou shuju edition, and those without it the Qunyuzhai edition. Li Hanqiu points out that the copies preserved at Huadong shifan daxue and Shanghai shifan daxue include Jin He's postscript and at the same time present themselves as printed with movable type by the Qunyuzhai. With or without the postscript, all these editions are almost identical to one another. See Li Hanqiu, "*Rulin waishi* de banben jiqi yandi," in idem, ed., *"Rulin waishi" huijiao huiping ben*, pp. 4–5.

main text.[22] The Suzhou Qunyuzhai edition corrects textual errors in the Woxian caotang edition (but creates new errors at the same time) and served as the basis for the two Shenbao guan editions (the first appeared in 1874 and the second in 1881) and Xu Yunlin's Conghaozhai collated edition (afterword dated 1884).[23]

None of these editions radically alters the text of Rulin waishi, unlike the Qixingtang zengding (supplemented) edition (preface by Xingyuan Tuishi dated 1874). The editor of that edition not only made random changes to the main text of the novel in the name of improving it but also added comments to the six chapters lacking comments in the Woxian caotang edition and filled out the chapter comments that he considered too short.[24] The Zengbu (supplemented and fleshed out) Qixingtang edition, which appeared in 1888, went even further by adding four chapters to elaborate on the peculiar adventures of Shen Qiongzhi, one of the rare female characters in Rulin waishi. These chapters were inserted into the second half of Chapter 43, and occupy the space between there and the second half of Chapter 47 in that edition.[25] The editor of this sixty-chapter edition offered no explanation about his sources and made little effort to hide the traces of his work. At one point, he referred to Lü mudan (Green peony), a Qing dynasty novel first published in 1800, and his additions deviate greatly from Wu Jingzi's novel by elaborating on bawdy scenes and superstitious motifs.

These editions demonstrate only slight textual variations, except for the two Qixingtang editions. Scholars tend to see them as derived, directly or indirectly, from the Woxian caotang text. However, there is no reason to exclude the possibility that some of them might be based on an earlier text (perhaps one of the Yangzhou editions that Jin He mentioned, if his words are trustworthy), from which both they and the Woxian caotang edition

---

22. Through a comparison with the Woxian caotang edition, Li Hanqiu (ibid., pp. 6–9) shows that these two editions follow it with only slight alterations.

23. It is worth mentioning that it is on the (Suzhou) Qunyuzhai edition that Zhang Wenhu (1808?–85), Huang Xiaotian (1795–1867), and other literati of the time based their comments on Rulin waishi. For all but Huang Xiaotian's commentary, see Li Hanqiu, ed., "Rulin waishi" huijiao huiping ben; for Huang Xiaotian's commentary, see Rulin waishi (Hefei: Huangshan shushe, 1986).

24. See Xinyuan Tuishi's preface and "Liyan" in the Qixingtang zengding Rulin waishi in Li Hanqui, ed., "Rulin waishi" huijiao huiping ben, pp. 767–70.

25. For these four chapters, see Appendix II in Li Hanqiu, ed., "Rulin waishi" huijiao huiping ben, pp. 794–824.

were developed. As argued above, the Woxian caotang commentary reveals a close connection to Yangzhou, and that edition of *Rulin waishi* could well be the product of Yangzhou commercial publishers, if not one of the Yangzhou editions Jin He mentioned. Some scholars suggest that Pan Shi'en's manuscript copy might well derive from an earlier handwritten manuscript dating to the time when people competed to copy and circulate *Rulin waishi*, as attested by Cheng Jinfang.[26] Even if this is true, however, Pan's text does not suggest the existence of a different manuscript version of the novel, given its unmistakable similarities to the Woxian caotang text.

This brief survey of the editions of *Rulin waishi* yields no evidence for questioning the credibility of the Woxian caotang text. In fact, we have no legitimate textual ground for the exclusion of any of its parts, if we base our judgment on the existing editions of the novel.

Inconsistencies, Errors, and the Problems of Open-Ended Narrative

Most of the scholars who argue for the exclusion of certain parts of the novel as later additions base their claims on what they see as narrative inconsistencies or errors in these sections, rather than on any textual evidence.[27] For instance, Zhang Peiheng insists that the original edition of the novel consisted of fifty chapters, and he takes it upon himself to exclude text totaling six

---

26. See Li Zhongming, "*Rulin waishi* de kanben," p. 532.

27. Linguistic studies have also contributed to the controversies over the authorship of *Rulin waishi*. Yu Xiaorong ("*Rulin waishi*" *cihui yanjiu*) argues that the first twenty-two chapters of *Rulin waishi* show features of Old Mandarin and the Quanjiao (Wu Jingzi's hometown) dialect, whereas the remainder of the novel shows less influence from the Quanjiao dialect. Basing herself on lexicon analysis of *Rulin waishi*, she suggests that the two parts of the novel may have been written by different authors. Her study sheds new light on the complex nature of the language in *Rulin waishi*, but as Yu notes, the linguistic approach raises many questions regarding its assumptions and methodologies, and efforts to identify the elements of local dialects in premodern vernacular novels have so far yielded more controversy than consensus. In fact, Yu's conclusion does not necessarily challenge Wu Jingzi's authorship of *Rulin waishi*; on the contrary, it neatly fits Wu Jingzi's linguistic profile. As shown above, Wu Jingzi spent almost twenty years in composing *Rulin waishi*. If he used the lexicon of the Quanjiao dialect at the early stage of writing, his exposure to Nanjing Mandarin could easily have gradually influenced the language style in the second half of the novel. Moreover, it seems to me that Yu does not show substantial lexical differences between the two parts of the novel. As she admits, if the last twenty-four chapters were indeed written by a different author, his language background must have been similar to Wu Jingzi's (ibid., pp. 90–91).

chapters in length. These sections include half of Chapter 36, Chapters 38 and 39, the first half of Chapter 40, the section from the end of Chapter 41 through the beginning of Chapter 44, and Chapter 56.[28] Zhang's main justification is that these sections differ from what we would expect from the other chapters in their handling of narrative time and their account of characters' ages. But such discrepancies are by no means unprecedented in premodern Chinese fiction. Indeed, one may well question Zhang's assumption that only forgers make such mistakes by citing similar errors in the early manuscripts of the *Honglou meng* and in the texts of other novels; in these works the same kinds of problems do not generally cause scholars to question their authorship. One can also argue that similar slips can easily be detected in other sections of *Rulin waishi*, although they seem to occur more frequently in the second half of the novel. Instead of attributing these inconsistencies or errors to imagined forgers, I am interested in exploring what they may tell us about the composition of the novel and the process by which it took shape.

Rulin waishi is a novel with an overall design, but it is also a work of becoming, for it sums up Wu Jingzi's intellectual journey during the last twenty years of his life and thus involves a process of growing, repositioning, and self-questioning. I have argued that the novel contains several parts, which vary in terms of thematic concern, narrative style, and tone. These variations are facilitated by the episodic structure the novel assumes. It should also be noted that each part draws on different kinds of sources.[29] Chapters 2 through 25 developed largely from historical sources, jokes, and anecdotes. Chapters 26 through 35 drew on the author's friends and acquaintances (and even the author himself) for the creation of such characters as Yu Yude and Du Shaoqing. Although this trend continues throughout the remainder of the novel, Wu Jingzi gradually expanded his narrative scope by depicting individual adventures and military campaigns from Chapter 36 on (especially in Chapters 37 through 43). It would be improper to question Wu Jingzi's authorship of this section simply because it extends into a new and unfamiliar subject area. In fact, what we see in these episodes is a narrative rendering of the ritualist Yan Yuan's Confucian project of *li yue*

---

28. See Zhang Peiheng, "*Rulin waishi* yuanshu ying wei wushi juan," "*Rulin waishi* yuanmao chutan," and "Zai tan *Rulin waishi* yuanben juanshu."

29. For further elaboration of this point, see Tan Fengliang, "*Rulin waishi* chuangzuo shijian, guocheng xintan."

bing nong (ritual, music, military training, and farming), so essential to the ideological design of the novel. In his not always successful attempt to flesh out this preconceived agenda with concrete narrative, Wu Jingzi stretched his imagination thin, and more often than in earlier parts of the novel, he had to fill in his narrative with material from such incompatible sources as *zhiguai* about fantastic and peculiar matters, and military romance. His narrative of Filial Guo's trip is an awkward mixture of *zhiguai* anecdotes and a *Water Margin*–like account of an individual hero's quest, and his depiction of military campaigns in Chapters 39 and 43 is in the end an inferior version of similar scenes in *Water Margin* and *Romance of the Three Kingdoms*.

Most relevant to my concerns, however, is that Wu's narrative often seems to slip into inconsistencies when the fantastic becomes mixed with the (auto)biographical. These inconsistencies are especially manifest in the increasing tension between the progress of the novel's fictional time and the biographical time of Wu Jingzi's friends and acquaintances.[30] Although he strove to weave the episodes of individual lives into the temporal frame of his work, Wu Jingzi was often guided by the empirical models for his characters. As the novel progresses, inconsistencies and contradictions in narrative time become inevitable.

Wu Jingzi closely followed the movement of his friends and acquaintances in creating such characters as Yu Yude, Xun Mei, Tang Zhentai (Tang Zou), and Ma Er (Ma Chunshang).[31] Wu Peiyuan served as tutor in Shangyuan county (whose administration was based in Nanjing) from 1738 to 1746; one year later he assumed the post of magistrate of Yuyao county in Zhejiang; in the following year, he was transferred to Sui'an county, also in Zhejiang. Chapter 46 of *Rulin waishi* depicts the party held for Yu Yude, his fictional counterpart, before he leaves Nanjing. In Chapter 48, we are told that Du Shaoqing travels to Zhejiang to visit Yu Yude; this incident is based on Wu Jingzi's trip to Zhejiang to pay his respects to Wu Peiyuan in 1748 or 1749. In another instance, several major events in the official career of Lu Jianzeng, the model for Xun Mei in *Rulin waishi*—his appointment to the

---

30. Ibid.

31. In so saying, I do not deny Wu Jingzi's role in the creation of these characters and their status as fictional characters. We can certainly read the episodes about them without reference to their real-life counterparts. But a valid source study should provide information on *Rulin waishi* otherwise impossible to obtain. As mentioned above, He Zehan's "*Rulin waishi*" *renwu benshi kaolüe* pioneered the study of *Rulin waishi*'s sources.

post of salt commissioner of the Liang-Huai area in 1736 and his arrest because of a scandal in 1742—are well captured in the narrative of Xun Mei in Chapters 22 and 29, however briefly. Evidence shows that Tang Zhentai is modeled upon Wu Jingzi's friend Yang Kai and his narrative of Ma Er is often taken from episodes in the life of Feng Cuizhong; in both cases, Wu Jingzi traced the ups and downs of their careers with remarkable consistency.

However, problems arose when Wu Jingzi placed his account of these characters within the temporal frame of the novel. In Chapter 46, Yu Yude bids farewell to Du Shaoqing, saying, "I used to be a poor scholar, but during the six or seven years that I've been in Nanjing I've saved enough to buy a paddy field producing thirty bushels a year" (R. 623; S. 508). Zhang Peiheng cites this speech as an example of possible forgery, for the previous part of the novel indicates that Yu Yude had lived in Nanjing for more than ten years by that point. Although Zhang is correct in pointing out this slip, his conclusion is misleading. I would argue that when Wu Jingzi wrote this passage, he had Wu Peiyuan's life in mind and thus deviated from the fictional time frame he had adopted for this part of the novel. In other words, although his narrative suggests that Yu Yude must have spent more than ten years in Nanjing, the author's rendering of Yu's conversation with Du Shaoqing was dictated by his empirical sources. This, indeed, caused errors, but errors that only Wu Jingzi could have made. As noted above, Wu Peiyuan stayed in Nanjing for less than eight years.

Similar problems occurred when Wu Jingzi related the characters modeled on his acquaintances to other characters portrayed in the previous parts of the novel. In Chapter 44, Tang Zhentai, who is modeled on Yang Kai, pays a visit to his old brother Tang Feng, a retired official. But when Tang Feng first appears in Chapter 4 of the novel, he is already a middle-aged palace graduate, and between Chapter 4 and Chapter 44 there is a time gap of seventy-five years. Wu Jingzi is consistent in his attempts to integrate his characters into a network of affiliations and correspondences. By relating Tang Zhentai to Tang Feng in Chapter 44, he introduced new narrative threads for the following section of the novel, but in this instance, he seems to have forgotten that by then his narrative time has stretched beyond that particular individual's life span.[32]

As I argued in Chapter 4, *Rulin waishi* forms an open-ended narrative by constantly reopening previously recounted incidents to development, con-

---

32. For this point, see Tan Fengliang, "*Rulin waishi* chuangzuo shijian, guocheng xintan."

troversy, and distortion. Here I emphasize its frequent habit of referring to previously introduced characters in latecomers' conversations. Sometimes these conversations serve only to bring us up to date about their doings and whereabouts and indicate that their stories are by no means complete. But Wu's efforts to engage the characters of earlier sections in the conversations of the unfolding narrative sequence sometimes cause temporal errors. The best example of this problem can be seen in the narrative of Ma Chunshang. Ma is introduced in Chapters 13 through 15 as someone over forty. After his participation in the Taibo ceremony in Chapter 37, he fades from the narrative focus of the novel and re-emerges merely as a topic in other characters' conversations. For instance, we are told in Chapter 49 that he is on his way to Beijing because of an official recommendation. However, if we follow the novel carefully, it becomes clear that since Ma's first appearance in Chapter 13 at least fifty years have passed, and it is absurd to imagine someone who is almost 100 years old still looking for an official appointment.

Although Wu Jingzi set his narrative within the historical frame of the Ming dynasty, he is often driven by a journalist's interest in tracing the development of the ongoing events. Indeed, his account of such characters as Yu Yude, Du Shaoqing, Zhuang Shaoguang, Ma Chunshang, Tang Zhentai, and Xun Mei is remarkably open-ended and, to a certain extent, contingent on the unfolding drama of their empirical sources. As mentioned above, Yu Yude leaves Nanjing in Chapter 46, and that incident refers to Wu Peiyuan's life; Wu Jingzi's visit to Yu Yude in 1748 or 1749 is well captured in Du Shaoqing's trip to Zhejiang in Chapter 48. These incidents were by no means preconceived, for they corresponded to ongoing events in Wu Jingzi's life and in the lives of his acquaintances, neither of which Wu could have anticipated when he began writing his novel during the 1730s. The incident of Ma Chunshang traveling to Beijing for an official examination, for instance, is derived from the life of Feng Cuizhong, who obtained the degree of provincial graduate in Shuntian prefecture (Shuntian fu, whose administration was based in Beijing) in 1752.[33] This shows that even two years before his death Wu Jingzi was still updating his representation of Ma Chunshang in accordance with the new developments in Feng Cuizhong's career. Conceived in this way, his narrative is open to infinite potential temporal development and unforeseeable turns and twists.

---

33. See He Zehan, *"Rulin waishi" renwu benshi kaolüe*, pp. 12–14.

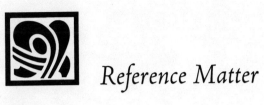 *Reference Matter*

Bibliography

Chinese- and Japanese-Language Works

Aina Jushi 艾衲居士. *Doupeng xianhua* 豆棚閒話. In *Guben xiaoshuo jicheng* 古本小説集成. Shanghai: Shanghai guji chubanshe, 1990.

Altenburger, Roland 安如巒. "Cong huwenxing kan *Rulin waishi* de fengci shoufa" 從互文性看儒林外史的諷刺手法. Paper presented at the International Conference on *Rulin waishi*, Yangzhou, 1996.

Ba duan jin 八段錦. In Hou Zhongyi 侯忠義, ed., *Mingdai xiaoshuo jikan* 明代小説輯刊. Chengdu: Bashu shushe, 1993, vol. 1, pp. 831–907.

Bai Dun 白盾. "Wu Jingzi chuangzuo sixiang chutan" 吳敬梓創作思想初探. In Li Hanqiu, ed., *"Rulin waishi" yanjiu lunwen ji* (q.v.), pp. 331–43.

Ban Gu 班固. "Yiwen zhi" 藝文志. In *Hanshu* 漢書. Beijing: Zhonghua shuju, 1975, pp. 1701–84.

Bieben Erke pai'an jingqi 別本二刻拍案驚奇. Taibei: Tianyi chubanshe, 1986.

Cao Xueqin 曹雪芹. *Honglou meng* 紅樓夢. Beijing: Renmin wenxue chubanshe, 1973.

Chang Shu-hsiang 張淑香. "Shuqing chuantong de benti yishi—cong lilun de yanchu jiedu 'Langtingji xu'" 抒情傳統的本體意識—從理論的演出解讀蘭亭集序. In idem., *Shuqing chuantong de xingsi yu tansuo* 抒情傳統的省思與探索. Taibei: Da'an chubanshe, 1992, pp. 41–62.

Chen Chen 陳忱. *Shuihu houzhuan* 水滸後傳. Shanghai: Shanghai guji chubanshe, 1981.

Chen Dadao 陳大道. "Mingmo Qingchu shishi xiaoshuo de tese" 明末清初時事小説的特色. *Xiaoshuo xiqu yanjiu* 小説戲曲研究 3 (1988): 181–220.

Chen Duxiu 陳獨秀. "*Rulin waishi* xinxu" 儒林外史新敍. In Zhu Yixuan and Liu Yuchen, eds., "*Rulin waishi*" ziliao huibian (q.v.), pp. 454–55.

Chen Hongmou 陳宏謀. *Wuzhong yigui* 五種遺規. *Sibu beiyao* 四部備要. Shanghai: Zhonghua shuju, 1936.

Chen Huijian 陳慧劍. "*Rulin waishi* xu" 儒林外史序. In *Rulin waishi* 儒林外史. Beijing: Remin wenxue chubanshe, 1958.

Chen Meilin 陳美林. *Wu Jingzi pingzhuan* 吳敬梓評傳. Nanjing: Nanjing daxue chubanshe, 1990.

———. *Wu Jingzi yanjiu* 吳敬梓研究. Shanghai: Shanghai guji chubanshe, 1984.

———. *Xinpi "Rulin waishi"* 新批儒林外史. Nanjing: Jiangsu guji chubanshe, 1989.

———. "Yan-Li xueshuo dui Wu Jingzi de yingxiang" 顏李學說對吳敬梓的影響. In idem, *Wu Jingzi yanjiu* (q.v.), pp. 1–14.

Chen Meilin 陳美林, ed., "*Rulin waishi*" cidian 儒林外史辭典. Nanjing: Nanjing daxue chubanshe, 1994.

Chen Qinghao 陳慶浩, ed. *Xinbian Shitou ji Zhiyanzhai pingyu jijiao* 新編石頭記脂硯齋評語輯校. Taibei: Lianjing, 1986.

Chen Qinghao 陳慶浩 and Wang Qiugui 王秋桂, eds., *Si wu xie huibao* 思無邪匯寶. Taibei: Faguo guojia kexueyuan yanjiu zhongxin and Taibei Daying baike, 1995.

Chen Wenxin 陳文新. *Wu Jingzi hua rulin* 吳敬梓話儒林. Taibei: Yatai tushu, 1995.

Chen Xin 陳新. "*Rulin waishi* Qingdai chaoben chutan" 儒林外史清代鈔本初探. *Wenxian* 文獻 12 (1982): 83–87.

Chen Xin 陳新 and Du Weimo 杜維沫. "*Rulin waishi* de wushiliu hui zhenwei bian" 儒林外史的五十六回真偽辨. In "*Rulin waishi*" yanjiu lunwen ji (q.v.), pp. 153–64.

Cheng Jinfang 程晉芳. "Huairen shi" 懷人詩. In Li Hanqiu, ed., "*Rulin waishi*" yanjiu ziliao (q.v.), p. 9.

———. "Mianzhuang xiansheng muzhi ming" 綿莊先生墓誌銘. In Zhu Yixuan and Liu Yuchen, eds., "*Rulin waishi*" ziliao huibian (q.v.), p. 60.

———. "Wenmu xiansheng zhuan" 文木先生傳. In Li Hanqiu, ed., "*Rulin waishi*" yanjiu ziliao (q.v.), pp. 13–14.

Cheng Tingzuo 程廷祚. *Qingxi wenji* 青溪文集 and *Qingxi wenji fubian* 青溪文集附編. Beiping: Beijing daxue, 1936.

———, ed., with Lan Yingxi 藍應襲 and He Mengzhuan 何夢篆. *Shangyuan xian zhi* 上元縣志. 1751 ed.

Ding Fubao 丁福保, ed., *Quan Han San'guo Jin Nanbeichao shi* 全漢三國晉南北朝詩. Beijing: Zhonghua shuju, 1959.

Ding Yaokang 丁耀亢. *Xu Jinpingmei* 續金瓶梅. In *Ding Yaokang quanji* 丁耀亢全集. Zhengzhou: Zhongzhou guji chubanshe, 1999, vol. 2.

Dong Yue 董説. *Xiyou bu* 西游補. Beijing: Wenxue guji kanxingshe, 1955.

Donglu gukuang sheng 東魯古狂生. *Zui xing shi* 醉醒石. Taibei: He Luo tushu chubanshe, 1980.

Fang Rixi 房日晰. "Rulin waishi youbang suoben" 儒林外史幽榜所本. *Guangming ribao* 光明日報, Jan. 1, 1985.

Feng Menglong 馮夢龍. *Gujin xiaoshuo* 古今小説. In Wei Tongxian 魏同賢, ed., *Feng Menglong quanji* 馮夢龍全集. Shanghai: Shanghai guji chubanshe, 1993, vols. 20–21.

Fu Shiyi 傅世怡. "Xiyou bu" chutan 西游補初探. Taibei: Xuesheng shuju, 1986.

Gao Jin 高晉, ed. *Nanxun shengdian* 南巡盛典. Imperial preface dated 1771. Taibei: Wenhai, 1966.

Gao Ming 高明. *Yuanben Pipa ji* 元本琵琶記. Ed. Qian Nanyang 錢南揚. Shanghai: Shanghai guji chubanshe, 1980.

Guben xiaoshou jicheng 古本小説集成. Shanghai: Shanghai guji chubanshe, 1990.

Guzhang jue chen 鼓掌絶塵. In Liu Shide 劉世德, Chen Qinghao 陳慶浩, and Shi Changyu 石昌渝, eds., *Guben xiaoshuo congkan* 古本小説叢刊. Beijing: Zhonghua shuju, 1990, vol. 11.

Hanfeizi jiaozhu 韓非子校注. Nanjing: Jiangsu renmin chubanshe, 1982.

"Han Qinhu huaben" 韓擒虎話 (畫) 本. In Wang Zhongmin et al., *Dunhuang bianwen ji* (q.v.), pp. 196–208.

Han Ying 韓嬰. *Hanshi waizhuan* 韓詩外傳. In Cheng Ying 程榮 (fl. 1592), ed., *Han Wei congshu* 漢魏叢書, vol. 10.

He Manzi 何滿子. Lun "Rulin waishi" 論儒林外史. Rev. ed. Beijing: Remin wenxue chubanshe, 1981.

He Qifang 何其芳. "Wu Jingzi de xiaoshuo *Rulin waishi*" 吳敬梓的小説儒林外史. In Li Hanqiu, ed., *"Rulin waishi" yanjiu lunwen ji* (q.v.), pp. 83–104.

He Zehan 何澤翰. "Rulin waishi" renwu benshi kaolüe 儒林外史人物本事考略. Shanghai: Shanghai guji chubanshe, 1985.

Hong Mai 洪邁. *Rongzhai suibi* 容齋隨筆. Beijing: Zhongguo shijieyu chubanshe, 1995.

Hong Sheng 洪昇. *Changsheng dian* 長生殿. Beijing: Renmin wenxue chubanshe, 1997.

Hu Shi 胡適. *Hu Shi gudian wenxue yanjiu lunji* 胡適古典文學研究論集. Shanghai: Shanghai guji chubanshe, 1988.

———. "Qingxi wenji xu" 青溪文集序. In Cheng Tingzuo, *Qingxi wenji* (q.v.).

Huanxi yuanjia 歡喜冤家. In Chen Qinghao and Wang Qiugui, eds., *Si wu xie huibao* (q.v.), vols. 10 and 11.

Huang Aiping 黃愛平. "*Mingshi* zuanxiu yu Qingchu shixue" 明史纂修與清
初史學. *Qingshi yanjiu* 清史研究 2 (1994): 83-93.

Huang Kan 黃侃. *Lunyu yishu* 論語義疏. In Yan Lingfeng 嚴靈峰, ed., *Wuqiu-
bei zhai Lunyu jicheng* 無求備齋論語集成. Facsimile reproduction. Taibei:
Chengwen shuju, 1966.

Huang Lin 黃霖, ed. "*Jin Ping Mei*" ziliao huibian 金瓶梅資料匯編. Beijing:
Zhonghua shuju, 1987.

Huang Zongxi 黃宗義. *Mingyi daifang lu* 明夷待訪錄. In *Congshu jicheng chubian* 叢書集成初編, vol. 0760.

Jin He 金和. "*Rulin waishi ba*"儒林外史跋. In Li Hanqiu, ed., "*Rulin waishi*" huijiao huiping ben (q.v.), pp. 764-67.

Jin Liangming 金兩銘. "He Wu Qing zuo" 和吳檠作. In Li Hanqiu, ed., "*Rulin
waishi*" yanjiu ziliao (q.v.), pp. 5-6.

Jin Shengtan 金聖嘆. *Jin Shengtan quanji* 金聖嘆全集. Nanjing: Jiangsu guji
chubanshe, 1985.

Jin Zhaoyan 金兆燕. "Gushi wei Xin'an liefu Wangshi zuo" 古詩爲新安烈
婦汪氏作. In idem, *Zongting shicao* 棕亭詩鈔. See He Zehan, "*Rulin waishi*"
renwu benshi kaolüe (q.v.), pp. 97-98.

Jiu Tangshu 舊唐書. Beijing: Zhonghua shuju, 1975.

Kitamura Yoshikazu 北村吉和. "Go Taibaku jōkoku no shisō shi—inpeisetsu o
megutte" 吳泰伯讓國の思想史—隱蔽説をめぐって. *Chūgoku: shakai to
bunka* 中國社會と文化 2 (1987): 223-41.

Kong Fanli 孔凡禮, ed. *Su Shi wenji* 蘇軾文集. Beijing: Zhonghua shuju, 1986.

Kong Shangren 孔尚任. *Taohua shan* 桃花扇. Beijing: Renmin wenxue chubanshe, 1997.

Lanling Xiaoxiaosheng 蘭陵笑笑生. *Jin Ping Mei cihua* 金瓶梅詞話. Hongkong: Taiping shuju, 1982. Reprint of the edition in the Beijing Library.

Li Baichuan 李百川. *Lüye xianzong* 綠野仙蹤. Ed. Li Guoqing 李國慶. Beijing: Zhonghua shuju, 2001.

Li Gong 李塨. *Shugu houji* 恕谷後集. In Yan Yuan 顏元 and Li Gong, *Yan Li
yishu* 顏李遺書. Taibei: Guangwen shuju, 1965.

———. "Yan Xizhai xiansheng nianpu" 顏習齋先生年譜. In Yan Yuan, *Yan
Yuan ji* (q.v.).

———. "Xueli" 學禮. In *Tushu jicheng chubian* 圖書集成初編, vol. 34.

Li Hanqiu 李漢秋. "Rulin waishi Taiboci daji he Rujia sixiang chutan" 儒林外
史泰伯祠大祭和儒家思想初探. *Jianghuai luntan* 江淮論壇 5 (1985):
96-102.

Li Hanqiu 李漢秋, ed. *Rulin waishi* 儒林外史. With Huang Xiaotian 黃小田
commentary. Hefei: Huangshan shushe, 1986.

————. *"Rulin waishi" huijiao huiping ben* 儒林外史會校會評本. Shanghai: Shanghai guji chubanshe, 1984.

————. *"Rulin waishi" jianshang cidian* 儒林外史鑒賞辭典. Beijing: Zhongguo funü chubanshe, 1992.

————. *"Rulin waishi" yanjiu lunwen ji* 儒林外史研究論文集. Beijing: Zhonghua shuju, 1987.

————. *"Rulin waishi" yanjiu ziliao* 儒林外史研究資料. Shanghai: Shanghai guji chubanshe, 1984.

————. *"Rulin waishi" yanjiu zonglan* 儒林外史研究縱覽. Tianjin: Tianjin jiaoyu chubanshe. 1992.

————. *Wu Jingzi Wu Lang shiwen heji* 吳敬梓吳烺詩文合集. Hefei: Huangshan shushe, 1993.

Li Lüyuan 李綠園. *Qilu deng* 歧路燈. Zhengzhou: Zhongzhou shuhuashe, 1980.

Li Ruzhen 李汝珍. *Jinghua yuan* 鏡花緣. Beijing: Zhonghua shuju, 1951.

Li Yu 李漁. *Li Yu quanji* 李漁全集. Hangzhou: Zhejiang guji chubanshe, 1992.

————. *Rou putuan* 肉蒲團. In Chen Qinghao and Wang Qiugui, eds., *Si wu xie huibao* (q.v.), vol. 15.

————. *Shi'er lou* 十二樓. Shanghai: Shanghai guji chubanshe, 1992.

————. *Wusheng xi* 無聲戲. Ed. Ding Xigen 丁錫根. Beijing: Renmin wenxue chubanshe. 1989.

Li Zehou 李澤厚. *Mei de licheng* 美的歷程. Beijing: Wenwu chubanshe, 1981.

Li Zehou 李澤厚 and Liu Gangji 劉綱紀, eds. *Zhongguo meixue shi* 中國美學史. 2 vols. Beijing: Zhongguo shehui kexue chubanshe, 1984, 1987.

Li Zhi 李贄. *Fenshu* 焚書. Beijing: Zhonghua shuju, 1975.

————. *Xu cangshu* 續藏書. Beijing: Zhonghua shuju, 1974.

Li Zhongming 李忠明. *"Rulin waishi de kanben"* 儒林外史的刊本. In Chen Meilin, ed., *"Rulin waishi" cidian* (q.v.).

Liang Qichao 梁啓超. *Zhongguo jin sanbainian xueshu shi* 中國近三百年學術史. Beijing: Beijingshi Zhongguo shudian, 1985.

Liji zhengyi 禮記正義. Annotations by Zheng Xuan 鄭玄 and commentary by Kong Yingda 孔穎達. In Ruan Yuan 阮元, ed., *Shisanjing zhushu* 十三經注疏. Photofacsimile reproduction. Beijing: Zhonghua shuju, 1980, pp. 1221–696.

Ling Mengchu 凌濛初. *Pai'an jingqi* 拍案驚奇. Ed. Shi Changyu 石昌渝. Nanjing: Jiangsu guji chubanshe, 1990.

————. *Erke Pai'an jingqi* 二刻拍案驚奇. Ed. Shi Changyu. Nanjing: Jiangsu guji chubanshe, 1990.

Liu Baonan 劉寶楠. *Lunyu zhengyi* 論語正義. Shanghai: Shangwu yinshuguan, 1993.

Liu Fu 劉復. *"Xiyou bu zuozhe Dong Ruoyu zhuan"* 西游補作者董若雨傳. In Dong Yue, *Xiyou bu* (q.v.).

Liu Ts'un-yan 柳 存 仁. *Lundun suojian Zhongguo xiaoshuo shumu tiyao* 倫 敦 所 見 中 國 小 説 書 目 提 要. Hongkong: Lung Men Bookstore, 1967.

Liu Wenqi 劉 文 淇. *Chunqiu Zuoshi zhuan jiuzhu shuzheng* 春 秋 左 氏 傳 舊 注 疏 證. Beijing: Kexue chubanshe, 1959.

Lü Xiong 呂 熊. *Nüxian waishi* 女 仙 外 史. Tianjin: Baihua wenyi chubanshe, 1985.

Lu Xun 魯 迅. *Zhongguo xiaoshuo shilüe* 中 國 小 説 史 略. Reprinted—Hongkong: Xinyi chubanshe, 1981.

Luo Guanzhong 羅 貫 中. *San'guo yanyi* 三 國 演 義. Shanghai: Shanghai guji chubanshe, 1985.

"Lushan Yuangong hua" 盧 山 遠 公 話. In Wang Zhongmin et al., *Dunhuang bian-wen ji*, pp. 167–95.

Meng Xingren 孟 醒 仁 and Meng Fanjiing 孟 凡 經. *Wu Jingzi ping zhuan* 吳 敬 梓 評 傳. Zhengzhou: Henan Zhongzhou guji chubanshe, 1987.

Mingshi 明 史. Beijing: Zhonghua shuju, 1975.

Niu Xiu 鈕 琇. *Gusheng* 觚 賸. In *Qingdai biji congkan* 清 代 筆 記 叢 刊. Shanghai: Wenming shuju, 1936, *juan* 4.

Ogawa Tamaki 小 村 環 樹. "Jurin gaishi no keishiki to naiyō" 儒 林 外 史 の 形 式 と 内 容. In idem, *Chūgoku shōsetsu shi no kenkyū* 中 國 小 説 史 の 研 究, pp. 181–97. Tokyo: Iwanami shoten, 1968.

Ogawa Yōichi 小 川 陽 一. "Mingdai xiaoshuo yu shanshu" 明 代 小 説 與 善 書. *Hanxue yanjiu* 漢 學 研 究 6.1 (June 1988): 331–40.

Ōki Yashushi 大 木 康. "Minmatsu Kōnan ni okeru shuppan bunka no kenkyū" 明 末 江 南 に お け る 出 版 文 化 の 研 究. *Hiroshima daigaku Bungakubu kiyō* 広 島 大 學 文 學 部 紀 要 50, no. 1 (special issue, Jan. 1991): 1–176.

Qian Jingfang 錢 靜 方. "Yesou puyan kao" 野 叟 曝 言 考. In idem, *Xiaoshuo cong-kao* 小 説 叢 考. Taibei: Cang'an chubanshe, 1979, pp. 162–67.

Qian Xuantong 錢 玄 同. "Rulin waishi xinxu" 儒 林 外 史 新 敍. In Zhu Yixuan and Liu Yuchen, eds., "*Rulin waishi*" *ziliao huibian* (q.v.), pp. 445–53.

Qian Zhongshu 錢 鍾 書. *Tanyi lu* 談 藝 錄. Rev. ed. Beijing: Zhonghua shuju, 1984.

Qiao Sang 喬 桑 and Song Hong 宋 紅, eds. *Mengxue quanshu* 蒙 學 全 書. Changchun: Jilin jiaoyu chubanshe, 1991.

Qiao Zhizhong 喬 治 忠. *Qingchao guanfang shixue yanjiu* 清 朝 官 方 史 學 研 究. Taibei: Wenjin chubanshe, 1984.

Qin Huitian 秦 蕙 田. *Wuli tongkao* 五 禮 通 考. 1880.

Qiu Jun 丘 濬. *Jiali yijie* 家 禮 儀 節. Preface dated 1474. 1618 ed.

Quan Tang shi 全 唐 詩. Beijing: Zhonghua shuju, 1960.

Ran Kuisheng 阮 葵 生. *Chayu kehua* 茶 餘 客 話. Beijing: Zhonghua shuju, 1959.

"*Rulin waishi*" *xuekan* 儒 林 外 史 學 刊. Ed. Zhongguo Rulin waishi xuehui 中 國 儒 林 外 史 學 會. Hefei: Huangshan shushe, 1988.

"Rulin waishi" yanjiu lunwen ji 儒林外史研究論文集. Ed. Anhui sheng ji'nian Wu Jingzi dansheng erbai bashi zhounian weiyuanhui 安徽省紀念吳敬梓誕生二百八十周年委員會. Hefei: Anhui renmin chubanshe, 1982.

Sakai Tadao 酒井忠夫. *Chūgoku zensho no kenkyū* 中國善書の研究. Tokyo: Kokusho kankōkai, 1960.

Shang Wei 商偉. "Yishi, xushu yu *Rulin waishi*" 儀式，敍述與儒林外史. In Chen Pingyuan 陳平原, Wang Der-wei 王德威, and Shang Wei, eds., *Wanming yu wanqing: lishi chuancheng yu wenhua chuangxin* 晚明與晚清：歷史傳承與文化創新. Wuhan: Hubei jiaoyu chubanshe, 2001, pp. 409–22.

Shanhai jing 山海經. *Sibu congkan* 四部叢刊 ed.

Shi dian tou 石點頭. Taibei: He Luo tushu chubanshe, 1970.

Shuihu quanzhuan 水滸全傳. Chengdu: Sichuan wenyi chubanshe, 1986.

"Shuihu zhuan" huipingben 水滸傳會評本. Ed. Chen Xizhong 陳曦鍾. Beijing: Beijing daxue chubanshe, 1981.

Siku quanshu zongmu 四庫全書總目. Beijing: Zhonghua shuju, 1965.

Sima Qian 司馬遷. *Shiji* 史記. Beijing: Zhonghua shuju, 1975.

Song Lian 宋濂. "Wang Mian zhuan" 王冕傳. In Li Hanqiu, ed., *"Rulin waishi" yanjiu ziliao* (q.v.), pp. 164–66.

Tan Fengliang 談鳳梁. "*Rulin waishi* chuangzhuo shijian, guocheng xintan" 儒林外史創作時間, 過程新探. In Li Hanqiu, ed., *"Rulin waishi" yanjiu lunwen ji* (q.v.), pp. 229–47.

Tang Xianzu 湯顯祖. *Mudan ting* 牡丹亭. Beijing: Renmin wenxue chubanshe, 1997.

Tao Zongyi 陶宗儀. *Nancun chuogeng lu* 南村輟耕錄. *Sibu congkan* 四部叢刊 ed. Beijing: Zhonghua shuju, 1937.

Tu Shen 屠紳. *Yinshi* 蟬史. Photolithographic reproduction of 1800 Leike shanfang 磊砢山房 ed. Taibei: Tianyi chubanshe, 1976.

Wang Bijiang 汪辟疆, ed., *Tangren xiaoshuo* 唐人小説. Shanghai: Shanghai gudian wenxue chubanshe, 1955.

Wang Chong 王充. *Lunheng* 論衡. Beijing: Zhonghua shuju, 1979.

Wang Guimin 王貴民. *Shang Zhou zhidu kaoxin* 商周制度考信. Taibei: Wenming shuju, 1989.

Wang Hui 汪暉. *Zhongguo xiandai sixiang de xingqi* 中國現代思想的興起. Beijing: Sanlian shudian, 2003.

Wang Jia 王嘉. *Shiyi ji* 拾遺記. In *Shenyi jing* 神異經, *Zhenzhong ji* 枕中記, *Shiyi ji* 拾遺記. Beijing: Zhonghua shuju, 1991.

Wang Qiongling 王瓊玲. *Qingdai si da caixue xiaoshuo* 清代四大才學小説. Taibei: Taiwan shangwu yinshuguan, 1997.

―――. "*Yesou puyan*" yanjiu 野叟曝言研究. Taibei: Xuehai chubanshe, 1988.

Wang Xinzhan 王心湛, ed. *Yanzi chuanqiu jijie* 晏子春秋集解. Shanghai: Guangyi shuju, 1936.

Wang Youzeng 王又曾. "Shu Wu Zhengjun Minxuan xiansheng *Wenmu shanfang shiji* hou" 書吳徵君敏軒先生文木山房詩集後. In Li Hanqiu, ed., "*Rulin waishi*" *yanjiu ziliao* (q.v.), pp. 16–17.

Wang Zhongmin 王重民 et al. *Dunhuang bianwen ji* 敦煌變文集. Beijing: Renmin wenxue chubanshe, 1984.

Wu Cheng'en 吳承恩. *Xiyou ji* 西游記. Beijing: Renmin wenxue chubanshe, 1997.

Wu Gongchen 吳拱宸 (Huayang sanren 華陽散人). *Yuanyang zhen* 鴛鴦針. In *Guben xiaoshuo jicheng* (q.v.), vol. 45.

Wu Jingzi 吳敬梓. *Chongyin "Wenmu shanfang ji"* 重印文木山房集. Shanghai: Shanghai Yadong dushuguan, 1931.

———. *Rulin waishi* 儒林外史. Woxian caotang 臥閒草堂 ed., 1803. Photolithographic reproduction—Beijing: Renmin wenxue chubanshe, 1975.

Wu Xi 吳熙, ed. *Taibo Meili zhi* 泰伯梅里志. Taibomiao dongyuan cangban 泰伯廟東院藏板. Preface dated 1897.

Wu Zuxiang 吳組緗. "Lun *Rulin waishi* de sixiang yu yishu" 論儒林外史的思想與藝術. In Li Hanqiu, ed., "*Rulin waishi*" *yanjiu lunwen ji* (q.v.), pp. 4–39.

Xia Jingqu 夏敬渠. *Yesou puyan* 野叟曝言. Ed. Huang Ke 黃克. Beijing: Renmin wenxue chubanshe, 1997.

Xiao Chi 蕭馳. *Zhongguo shuqing chuantong* 中國抒情傳統. Taibei: Yunchen wenhua, 1999.

Xihu jiahua 西湖佳話. Shanghai: Shanghai guji chubanshe, 1980.

Xizhou Sheng 西周生. *Xingshi yinyuan zhuan* 醒世姻緣傳. Ed. Huang Suqiu 黃肅秋. Shanghai: Shanghai guji chubanshe, 1985.

Xu Wei 徐渭. *Xu Wei ji* 徐渭集. Beijing: Zhonghua shuju, 1983.

Xu Yikui 徐一夔. *Daming jili* 大明集禮. *Siku quanshu* 四庫全書 ed. Taibei: Shangwu yinshuguan, vol. 649.

Yan Ruoju 閻若璩. *Shangshu guwen shuzheng* 尚書古文疏證. In Wang Xianqian 王先謙, ed., *Huangqing jing jie xubian* 皇清經解續編. Reprinted—Taibei: Fuxing shuju, 1972.

Yan Yuan 顏元. *Yan Yuan ji* 顏元集. Beijing: Zhonghua shuju, 1987.

Yili zhushu 儀禮注疏. Annotations by Zheng Xuan 鄭玄 and commentary by Jia Gongyan 賈公彥. In Ruan Yuan 阮元, ed., *Shisan jing zhushu* 十三經注疏. Photofacscimile reproduction—Beijing: Zhonghua shuju, 1980, pp. 941–1220.

Youxue qionglin 幼學瓊林. Changsha: Yuelu chubanshe, 1986.

Yu Lin 于鱗. *Qingye zhong* 清夜鐘. In Lu Gong 路工, ed., *Ming Qing pinghua xiaoshuo xuan* 明清平話小説選. Shanghai: Gudian wenxue, 1958, pp. 82–120.

Yu Xiaorong 遇 笑 容. "*Rulin waishi*" *cihui yanjiu* 儒 林 外 史 詞 匯 研 究. Beijing: Beijing daxue chubanshe, 2001.

Yuan Mei 袁 枚. *Jiangning xinzhi* 江 寧 新 志. 1748 ed. In Zhongguo kexueyuan tushuguan, ed., *Xijian Zhongguo difangzhi huikan* 稀 見 中 國 地 方 志 匯 刊. Beijing: Zhongguo shudian, 1992, vol. 11.

——. *Suiyuan sanshi zhong* 隨 園 三 十 種. Qiantang Yuanshi kanben 錢 塘 袁 氏 刊 本.

Yue Hengjun 樂 衡 軍. "Ma Chunshang zai Xihu" 馬 純 上 在 西 湖. *Chun wenxue* 純 文 學 4, no. 6 (1970): 35–62.

——. "Shiji de piaobo zhe—*Rulin waishi* qunxiang" 世 紀 的 漂 泊 者—儒 林 外 史 群 像. In Ke Qingming 柯 慶 明 and Lin Mingde 林 明 德, eds., *Zhongguo gudian wenxue yanjiu congkan: xiaoshuo zhibu (3)* 中 國 古 典 文 學 研 究 叢 刊: 小 說 之 部 (三). Taibei: Juliu dushu gongsi, 1970, pp. 175–91.

Zhan Ying 詹 瑛, ed. *Li Bai quanji jiaozhu huishi jiping* 李 白 全 集 校 注 匯 釋 集 評. Tianjin: Baihua wenyi chubanshe, 1996.

Zhang Dai 張 岱. *Tao'an mengyi* 陶 庵 夢 憶. Ed. Zhang Xiaotian. *Congshu jicheng* 叢 書 集 成 ed. Changsha: Shangwu yinshuguan, 1939.

Zhang Guofeng 張 國 風. "*Rulin waishi*" *jiqi shidai* 儒 林 外 史 及 其 時 代. Taibei: Wenjin chubanshe, 1993.

Zhang Peiheng 章 培 恒. "*Rulin waishi* yuanmao chutan" 儒 林 外 史 原 貌 初 探. In idem, *Xianyi ji* 獻 疑 集. Changsha: Yuelu shushe, 1993, pp. 463–80.

——. "*Rulin waishi* yuanshu ying wei wushi juan" 儒 林 外 史 原 書 應 爲 五 十 回. In idem, *Xianyi ji* 獻 疑 集. Changsha: Yuelu shushe, 1993, pp. 446–62.

——. "Zai tan *Rulin waishi* yuanben juanshu" 再 談 儒 林 外 史 原 本 卷 數. In idem, *Xianyi ji* 獻 疑 集. Changsha: Yuelu shushe, 1993, pp. 481–515.

Zhang Xuecheng 章 學 誠. *Wensi tongyi xinbian* 文 史 通 義 新 編. Ed. Cang Xiuliang 倉 修 良. Shanghai: Shanghai guji chubanshe, 1993.

Zhang Xiumin 張 秀 民. *Zhongguo yinshua shi* 中 國 印 刷 史. Shanghai: Shanghai renmin chubanshe, 1989.

Zhang Zhigong 張 志 公. *Chuantong yuwen jiaoyu chutan* 傳 統 語 文 教 育 初 探. Shanghai: Shanghai jiaoyu chubanshe, 1962.

Zhang Zhuo 張 鷟. *Chaoye qianzai* 朝 野 僉 載. In "Puji" 普 集 of *Baoyantang miji* 寶 顏 堂 秘 笈, ed. Chen Jiru 陳 繼 儒. Shanghai: Shangwu shuju, 1936.

Zhao Erxun 趙 爾 巽, ed. *Qing shi gao* 清 史 稿. Beijing: Zhonghua shuju, 1978.

Zhao Jingshen 趙 景 深. "Tan *Rulin waishi*" 談 儒 林 外 史. In idem, *Zhongguo xiaoshuo congkao* 中 國 小 說 叢 考. Ji'nan: Qilu shushe, 1980, pp. 423–30.

Zheng Jingruo 鄭 靜 若. *Lunyu Zhengshi zhu jishu* 論 語 鄭 氏 注 輯 述. Taibei: Xuehai, 1981.

Zhou Ji 周 楫. *Xihu erji* 西 湖 二 集. Hangzhou: Zhejiang renmin chubanshe, 1983.

Zhu Xi 朱 熹. *Wengong jiali* 文 公 家 禮. *Sibu congkan* 四 部 叢 刊, vol. 142. Shanghai: Shangwu yinshuguan, 1937.

———. *Zhuzi daquan* 朱 子 大 全. Shanghai: Zhonghua shuju, 1930.

Zhu Yixuan 朱 一 玄 and Liu Yuchen 劉 毓 忱, eds. *"Rulin waishi" ziliao huibian* 儒 林 外 史 資 料 彙 編. Tianjin: Nankai daxue chubanshe, 1998.

Western-Language Works

Anderson, Marston. "The Scorpion in the Scholar's Cap: Ritual, Memory, and Desire in *Rulin waishi*." In Huters et al., *Culture and State in Chinese History* (q.v.), pp. 259–76.

Andres, Mark. "Ch'an Symbolism in *Hsi-yu pu*: The Enlightenment of Monkey." *Tamkang Review* 20, no. 1 (1989): 37–64.

Bakhtin, Mikhail Mikhailovich. *The Dialogic Imagination*. Austin: University of Texas Press, 1981.

Baxandall, Lee, and Stefan Morawski, eds. *Karl Marx and Frederick Engels on Literature and Art: A Selection of Writings*. New York: International General, 1974.

Bell, Catherine. *Ritual Theory, Ritual Practice*. Oxford: Oxford University Press, 1992.

Berling, Judith A. "Religion and Popular Culture: The Management of Moral Capital in *The Romance of the Three Teachings*." In Johnson et al., *Popular Culture in Late Imperial China* (q.v.), pp. 188–218.

Birch, Cyril, trans. *The Peony Pavilion*. Boston: Cheng & Tsui, 1994.

———. *Stories from a Ming Collection—The Art of the Chinese Story-teller*. New York: Grove Press, 1968.

Bol, Peter. *'This Culture of Ours': Intellectual Traditions in T'ang and Sung China*. Stanford: Stanford University Press, 1992.

Bourdieu, Pierre. *The Field of Cultural Production*. New York: Columbia University Press, 1993.

———. *Language and Symbolic Power*. Cambridge, Mass.: Harvard University Press, 1991.

Brandauer, Frederick. "The Significance of a Dog's Tail: Comments on the *Xu Xiyou ji*." *Journal of the American Oriental Society* 113, no. 3 (1993): 18–22.

———. *Tung Yüeh*. Boston: Twayne, 1978.

Brokaw, Cynthia. *The Ledgers of Merit and Demerit: Social Change and Moral Order in Late Imperial China*. Cambridge, Mass.: Harvard University Press, 1991.

Carlitz, Katherine. "The Social Uses of Female Virtue in Late Ming Editions of *Lienü zhuan*." *Late Imperial China* 12, no. 2 (Dec. 1991): 117–48.

Chen, Jack W. "Narrative Claims, Local Knowledges: Writing the End of History in the *Rulin waishi*." Unpublished paper, 1997.

Chen, Shih-hsiang. "On Chinese Lyrical Tradition." *Tamkang Review* 2–3 (1971–72): 17–24.

Chen, Weigang. "Confucian Marxism: Hegemony, Mass Democracy, and Authoritarianism." Ph.D. diss., Harvard University, 2000.

Chow, Kai-wing. "Purist Hermeneutics and Ritualist Ethics in Mid-Ch'ing Thought." In Richard Smith and D. W. Y. Kwok, eds., *Cosmology, Ontology and Human Efficacy: Essays in Chinese Thought*. Honolulu: University of Hawaii Press, 1993, pp. 170–204.

——. *The Rise of Confucian Ritualism in Late Imperial China: Ethics, Classics, and Lineage Discourse*. Stanford: Stanford University Press, 1994.

Clunas, Craig. *Pictures and Visuality in Early Modern China*. Princeton: Princeton University Press, 1997.

de Bary, Wm. Theodore. "Chu Hsi's Aims as an Educator." In Wm. Theodore de Bary and John W. Chaffee, eds., *Neo-Confucian Education: The Formative Stage*. New York: Columbia University Press, 1989, pp. 186–218.

——. "Individualism and Humanitarianism in Late Ming Thought." In idem, ed., *Self and Society in Ming Thought*. New York: Columbia University Press, 1970, pp. 145–247.

de Bary, Wm. Theodore, and Irene Bloom, eds. *Eastern Canons: Approaches to the Asian Classics*. New York: Columbia University Press, 1990.

——. *Principle and Practicality: Essays in Neo-Confucianism and Practical Learning*. New York: Columbia University Press, 1979.

Ebrey, Patricia Buckley. *Confucianism and Family Rituals in Imperial China: A Social History of Writing About Rites*. Princeton: Princeton University Press, 1991.

Ebrey, Patricia Buckley, trans. *Chu Hsi's Family Rituals: A Twelfth-Century Chinese Manual for the Performance of Cappings, Weddings, Funerals, and Ancestral Rites*. Princeton: Princeton University Press, 1991.

Eliot, T. S. "The Humanism of Irving Babbitt." In *Selected Prose of T. S. Eliot*. New York: Harcourt Brace Jovanovich, 1975, pp. 277–84.

Elman, Benjamin. *Classicism, Politics, and Kinship: The Ch'ang-chou School of New Text Confucianism in Late Imperial China*. Berkeley: University of California Press, 1990.

——. *From Philosophy to Philology: Intellectual and Social Aspects of Change in Late Imperial China*. Cambridge, Mass.: Harvard University Press, 1984.

Epstein, Maram. "Ritual in the Eighteenth-Century Novel *Qilu deng*." Paper presented at the annual meeting of the Association for Asian Studies, 2002.

Fineman, Joel. "The History of the Anecdote: Fiction and Fiction." In H. Aram Veeser, ed., *The New Historicism*. New York: Routledge, 1989, pp. 49–76.

Fingarette, Herbert. *Confucius: The Secular as Sacred*. New York: Harper Torchbooks, 1972.

Foucault, Michel. *The Order of Things: An Archaeology of the Human Sciences*. New York: Vintage, 1973.

Frye, Northrop. *Anatomy of Criticism: Four Essays.* Princeton: Princeton University Press, 1973.

Geertz, Clifford. *The Interpretation of Cultures.* New York: Basic Books, 1973.

Gramsci, Antonio. *Selections from the Prison Notebooks of Antonio Gramsci.* Ed. and trans. Quintin Hoare and Geoffrey N. Smith. New York: International Publishers, 1971.

————. *Selections from Cultural Writings.* Ed. David Forgacs and Geoffrey Nowell-Smith; trans. William Boelhower. Cambridge, Mass.: Harvard University Press, 1985.

Hanan, Patrick. *The Chinese Vernacular Story.* Cambridge, Mass.: Harvard University Press, 1981.

————. *The Invention of Li Yu.* Cambridge, Mass.: Harvard University Press, 1978.

————. "Nature of Ling Meng-ch'u's Fiction." In Plaks, ed., *Chinese Narrative* (q.v.), pp. 85–114.

Hanan, Patrick, trans. *The Carnal Prayer Mat.* New York: Ballantine Books, 1990.

————. *A Tower for the Summer Heat.* New York: Columbia University Press, 1992.

Hawkes, David, and John Minford, trans. *The Story of the Stone.* New York: Penguin, 1973–86.

Hegel, Robert. *The Novel in Seventeenth-Century China.* New York: Columbia University Press, 1981.

————. *Reading Illustrated Fiction in Late Imperial China.* Stanford: Stanford University Press, 1998.

Henderson, John. *The Development and Decline of Chinese Cosmology.* New York: Columbia University Press, 1984.

Hightower, James Robert, trans. *Han Shi Wai Chuan (Hanying's Illustrations of the Didactic Application of the Classic of Songs).* Cambridge, Mass.: Harvard University Press, 1952.

Ho, Ping-ti. *Ladder of Success in Imperial China: Aspects of Social Mobility, 1368–1911.* New York: Columbia University Press, 1962.

————. "The Salt Merchants of Yang-chou: A Study of Commercial Capitalism in Eighteenth-Century China." *Harvard Journal of Asiatic Studies* 17 (1954): 130–68.

Hsia, C. T. *The Classic Chinese Novel: A Critical Introduction.* New York: Columbia University Press, 1968.

————. An essay on *The Story of the Stone (Honglou meng).* In de Bary and Bloom, *Eastern Canons* (q.v.), pp. 262–73.

————. Foreword to the paperback edition of the English translation of *Rulin waishi* by Yang Hsien-yi and Gladys Yang. *The Scholars.* New York: Grosset and Dunlap, 1972.

Hsia, T. A. "New Perspectives on Two Ming Novels: *Hsi You Chi* and *Hsi Yu Pu.*" In Tse-tsung Chow, ed., *Wen-lin: Studies in the Chinese Humanities.* Madison: University of Wisconsin Press, 1968, pp. 229–45.

Huang, Martin. *Desire and Fictional Narrative in Late Imperial China.* Cambridge, Mass.: Harvard University Asia Center, 2001.

————. "The Dilemma of Chinese Lyricism and the Qing Literati Novel." Ph.D. diss., Washington University in St. Louis, 1991.

————. *Literati and Self-Re/Presentation: Autobiographical Sensibility in the Eighteenth-Century Chinese Novel.* Stanford: Stanford University Press, 1995.

————. "*Xiaoshuo* as 'Family Instructions': The Rhetoric of Didacticism in the Eighteenth-Century Chinese Novel *Qilu deng.*" *Tsing Hua Journal of Chinese Studies,* n.s. 30, no. 1 (2000): 67–91.

Huang, Ray. *1587: A Year of No Significance. The Ming Dynasty in Decline.* New Haven: Yale University Press, 1981.

Hummel, Arthur, ed. *Eminent Chinese of the Ch'ing Period.* Washington, D.C.: U.S. Government Printing Office, 1944.

Hunt, Lynn. *Politics, Culture, and Class in the French Revolution.* Berkeley: University of California Press, 1986.

Huters, Theodore. "The Shattered Mirror: Wu Jianren and the Reflection of Strange Events." In idem et al., *Culture and State in Chinese History* (q.v.), pp. 277–99.

Huters, Theodore; R. Bin Wong; and Pauline Yu, eds. *Culture and State in Chinese History.* Stanford: Stanford University Press, 1997.

Idema, Wilt. "Some Remarks and Speculations Concerning P'ing-hua." In idem, *Chinese Vernacular Fiction: The Formative Period.* Leiden: E. J. Brill, 1974, pp. 5–134.

Jameson, Fredric. *The Political Unconscious: Narrative as a Socially Symbolic Act.* Ithaca: Cornell University Press, 1981.

Johnson, David. "Communication, Class, and Consciousness in Late Imperial China." In idem et al., *Popular Culture in Late Imperial China* (q.v.), pp. 34–74.

Johnson, David; Andrew J. Nathan; and Evelyn S. Rawski, eds. *Popular Culture in Late Imperial China.* Berkeley: University of California Press, 1982.

Kao, Yu-kung. "Chinese Lyric Aesthetics." In Alfreda Murck and Wen C. Fong, eds., *Words and Images: Chinese Poetry, Calligraphy, and Painting.* Princeton: Princeton University Press, 1991, pp. 47–90.

————. "Lyric Vision in Chinese Narrative Tradition: A Reading of *Hung-lou Meng* and *Ju-lin Wai-shih.*" In Plaks, *Chinese Narrative* (q.v.), pp. 227–43.

Ko, Dorothy. *Teachers of the Inner Chambers.* Stanford: Stanford University Press, 1994.

Král, O. "Several Artistic Methods in the Classic Chinese Novel *Ju-lin wai-shih.*" *Archiv Orientalni* 32 (1964): 16–43.

Langer, Susanne K. *Philosophy in a New Key.* New York: New American Library, 1951.

Li, Wai-Yee. *Enchantment and Disenchantment: Love and Illusion in Chinese Literature.* Princeton: Princeton University Press, 1993.

Lin, Shuen-fu. "Ritual and Narrative Structure in *Ju-lin wai-shi.*" In Plaks, *Chinese Narrative* (q.v.), pp. 244–65.

Liu Xiaolian. "A Journey of the Mind: The Basic Allegory in the *Hou Xiyou ji.*" *Chinese Literature: Essays, Articles, Reviews* 13 (1991): 35–56.

Lukács, Georg. *The Theory of the Novel.* Cambridge, Mass.: MIT Press, 1971.

Mote, Frederick W. "The Intellectual Climate in Eighteenth-Century China: Glimpses of Beijing, Suzhou, and Yangzhou in the Qianlong period." Special issue: Ju-hsi Chen and Claudia Brown, eds., *Chinese Painting Under the Qianlong Emperor, 1735–1795. Phoebus* 6, no. 1 (1988): 17–55.

Naquin, Susan, and Evelyn S. Rawski. *Chinese Society in the Eighteenth Century.* New Haven: Yale University Press, 1987.

Owen, Stephen. *The End of the Chinese "Middle Ages": Essays in Mid-Tang Literary Culture.* Stanford: Stanford University Press, 1996.

————. "Place: Meditation on the Past at Chin-Ling." *Harvard Journal of Asiatic Studies* 50 (1990): 417–58.

————. "Salvaging Poetry: The 'Poetic' in the Qing." In Huters et al., *Culture and State in Chinese History* (q.v.), pp. 105–28.

Peterson, J. Willard. *Bitter Gourd: Fang I-chih and the Impetus for Intellectual Change.* New Haven: Yale University Press, 1979.

Plaks, Andrew. *The Four Masterworks of the Ming Novel.* Princeton: Princeton University Press, 1987.

————. "Full-length *Hsiao-shuo* and the Western Novel: A Generic Reappraisal." In William Tay, Ying-hsiung Chou, and Heh-hsiang Yuan, eds., *China and the West: Comparative Literature Studies.* Hongkong: Chinese University Press, 1980, pp. 163–76.

Plaks, Andrew, ed. *Chinese Narrative: Critical and Theoretical Essays.* Princeton: Princeton University Press, 1977.

Roberts, Moss, trans. *Three Kingdoms.* Berkeley: University of California Press, 1991.

Roddy, Stephen John. *Literati Identity and Its Fictional Representations in Late Imperial China.* Stanford: Stanford University Press, 1998.

Rolston, David. *Reading and Writing Between the Lines: Traditional Chinese Fiction and Fiction Commentary.* Stanford: Stanford University Press, 1997.

Rolston, David, ed. *How to Read the Chinese Novel.* Princeton: Princeton University Press, 1990.

Ropp, Paul S. *Dissent in Early Modern China—"Ju-lin wai-shi" and Ch'ing Social Criticism.* Ann Arbor: University of Michigan Press, 1981.

Schneider, Lawrence. *Ku Chieh-kang and China's New History.* Berkeley: University of California Press, 1971.

Schwartz, Benjamin. *The World of Thought in Ancient China.* Cambridge, Mass.: Harvard University Press, 1985.

Shang Wei. "Jin Ping Mei and Late Ming Print Culture." In Zeitlin and Liu, *Writing and Materiality in China* (q.v.), pp. 187–238.

————. "Prisoner and Creator: The Self-Image of the Poet in Han Yu and Meng Jiao." *Chinese Literature: Essays, Articles, Reviews* 16 (1994): 19–40.

————. "Ritual, Ritual Manuals, and the Crisis of the Confucian World: An Interpretation of *Rulin waishi.*" *Harvard Journal of Asiatic Studies* 58 (1998): 373–424.

Slupski, Zbigniew. "Three Levels of Composition of the *Rulin waishi.*" *Harvard Journal of Asiatic Studies* 49 (1989): 5–53.

Smith, Joanna Handlin. *Action in Late Ming Thought: The Reorientation of Lu K'un and Other Scholar-Officials.* Berkeley: University of California Press, 1983.

Tambiah, Stanley Jeyaraja. "A Performative Approach to Ritual." In idem, *Culture, Thought, and Social Action: An Anthropological Perspective.* Cambridge, Mass.: Harvard University Press, 1985, pp. 123–68.

Tu, Wei-ming. "Yan Yuan: From Inner Experience to Lived Concreteness." In idem, *Humanity and Self-Cultivation: Essays in Confucian Thought.* Berkeley: Asian Humanities Press, 1979, pp. 186–215.

Turner, Victor. *The Ritual Process: Structure and Anti-Structure.* Ithaca: Cornell University Press, 1969.

van der Loon, P. "The Ancient Chinese Chronicles and the Growth of Historical Ideals." In W. G. Beasley and E. G. Pulleybank, eds., *Historians of China and Japan.* London: Oxford University Press, 1961, pp. 24–30.

Wang, David Der-wei. "Fictional History / Historical Fiction." *Studies in Language and Literature* 1 (1985): 64–76.

————. "Storytelling Context in Chinese Fiction: A Preliminary Examination of It as a Mode of Narrative Discourse." *Tamkang Review* 15 (1985): 133–50.

Watson, James L., and Evelyn S. Rawsky, eds. *Death Ritual in Late Imperial and Modern China.* Berkeley: University of California Press, 1988.

Weber, Max. "Science as a Vocation." In H. H. Gerth and C. Wright Mills, eds., *From Max Weber: Essays in Sociology.* New York: Oxford University Press, 1946, pp. 129–51.

Wei, Cheng-t'ung. "Chu Hsi on the Standard and the Expedient." In Wing-tsit Chan, ed., *Chu Hsi and Neo-Confucianism.* Honolulu: University of Hawaii Press, 1986, pp. 255–72.

White, Hayden. *The Content of the Form: Narrative Discourse and Historical Representation.* Baltimore: John Hopkins University Press, 1987.

Widmer, Ellen. *The Margins of Utopia: "Shui-hu hou-chuan" and the Literature of Ming Loyalism.* Cambridge, Mass.: Harvard University, Council on East Asian Studies, 1987.

Williams, Raymond. *Marxism and Literature.* Oxford: Oxford University Press, 1977.

Wong, Timothy. *Wu Ching-tzu.* Boston: Twayne Publishers, 1987.

Wu Hung. *The Wu Liang Shrine: The Ideology of Early Chinese Pictorial Art.* Stanford: Stanford University Press, 1989.

Wu, Yenna. *Ameliorative Satire and the Seventeenth-Century Chinese Novel: "Xingshi Yinyuan Zhuan"—Marriage as Retribution, Awakening the World.* Lewiston, Me.: Edwin Mellen Press, 1999.

Xiao Chi. *The Chinese Garden as Lyric Enclave: A Generic Study of "The Story of the Stone."* Ann Arbor: University of Michigan Press, 2001.

Yang Hsien-yi and Gladys Yang, trans. *The Scholars.* Beijing: Foreign Language Press, 1957.

Yang Lien-sheng. "The Organization of Chinese Official Historiography: Principles and Methods of the Standard Histories from the T'ang Through the Ming Dynasty." In W. G. Beasley and E. G. Pulleybank, eds., *Historians of China and Japan.* London: Oxford University Press, 1961, pp. 44–59.

Yu, Anthony. *Rereading the Stone: Desire and the Making of Fiction in "Dream of the Red Chamber."* Princeton: Princeton University Press, 1998.

Yu Yingshi. "Some Preliminary Observations on the Rise of Ch'ing Confucian Intellectualism." *Tsing Hua Journal of Chinese Studies* 11 (1975): 105–46.

Zeitlin, Judith T., and Lydia H. Liu, eds. *Writing and Materiality in China: Essays in Honor of Patrick Hanan.* Cambridge, Mass.: Harvard University Asia Center, 2003.

Zito, Angela. *Of Body and Brush: Grand Sacrifice as Text/Performance in Eighteenth-Century China.* Chicago: University of Chicago Press, 1997.

Character List

The entries are ordered syllable by syllable, ignoring word breaks.

Daojing 道經
Daqing huidian 大清會典
Daqing tongli 大清通禮
Daxue 大學
"Dayu mo" 大禹謨
dazan 大贊
"Dazhao" 大招
"Daike" 待客
dai shengxian liyan 代聖賢
　立言
Dai Zhen 戴震
Danfu 亶父
Dao 道
Daotong 道統
Daoxin 道心
Daoxue 道學
Deng Zhifu 鄧質夫
Dizigui 弟子規
Ding Yanzhi 丁言志
Dongguo 東郭
Donghua lu 東華錄
Du Fu 杜甫
Du Li'niang 杜麗娘
Du Mu 杜牧
Du Shaoqing 杜少卿 (杜儀)
Du Shenqing 杜慎卿
Du Zhao 杜詔
Duo Jiugong 多九公

Fan Jin 范進
fanli 凡例
Fan Ning 范甯
Fan Shengmo 樊聖謨 (樊明徵)
fangjin 方巾
fengci 諷刺
Feng Cuizhong 馮粹中
Fengshen yanyi 封神演義
Fengsi 鳳四
fu 賦
Fusheng liuji 浮生六記

"Fuyun lou" 拂雲樓
fuzan 副贊

Gai Guan 蓋寬
gangchang 綱常
Gao Qi 高啓
Ge dai xiao 歌代嘯
Ge Hong 葛洪
Ge lian huaying 隔簾花影
Geng Dingxiang 耿定向
gongci 公祠
gongguo ge 功過格
gonglun 公論
gong ming fu gui 功名富貴
gongsheng 貢生
Gong Ziqi 宮子奇
Gouwu 句吳 (勾吳)
Gugong 古公
Guwen Shangshu 古文尚書
Guan Yu 關羽
Guan Zhong 管仲
guairen 乖人
Guangxian ji 廣賢集
Guangxu Quanjiao xian zhi 光緒全椒
　縣志
gui 規
Guo Tiebi 郭鐵筆
Guo Xiaozi 郭孝子

Hanlin 翰林
Hangzhou 杭州
haoju 豪舉
haoxiao 好笑
"Hegui lou" 鶴歸樓
He Xinyin 何心隱
Hongxian 紅線
hou 後
hou qizi 後七子
hua 話
huaben 話本

huashuo 話説
hui 回
Hui Dong 惠棟
Huixue 徽學
Huizhou 徽州
Huangchao liqi tushi 皇朝禮器圖式
Huancheng 宦成
Huang Jingren 黃景仁
Huang Xiaotian 黃小田

ji 跡
Jili 季歷
Ji Tianyi 季恬逸
Ji Weixiao 季葦蕭
Ji Xia'nian 季遐年
Jiajing 嘉靖
Jia Yucun 賈雨村
jiansheng 監生
Jianwen 建文
Jiangnan 江南
"Jiang Xingge chonghui zhenzhu
    shan" 蔣興哥重會
    珍珠衫
jiangxue 講學
Jiang Ziya 姜子牙
Jiaonü yigui 教女遺規
jiaoshou 教授
jie 節
Jiexiao ci 節孝祠
Ji Cifu 金次福
Jin Dongya 金東崖
Jin He 金和
Jinling 金陵
"Jinling jingwu tu shi" 金陵景物
    圖詩
jinshi 進士
jinshi qi 進士氣
jinxiang ben 巾箱本
Jin Zhaoyan 金兆燕
jing 敬

Jinghe 景和
Jing Ke 荊軻
Jing Lanjiang 景蘭江
"Jinling dianshi yi" 金陵典祀議
"Jingji zhi" 經籍志
jingran 竟然
jingxue kaoguxue 經學考古學
Jing Yuan 荊元
jingzuo 靜坐
juren 舉人
juye 舉業
juan 卷
junzi 君子
jizhuanti 紀傳體

kanguan 看官
Kangxi 康熙
Kang Youwei 康有爲
kaozheng 考證
kexiao 可笑
kexue de gudian xuepai 科學的
    古典學派
kenqie 懇切
Kuang Chaoren 匡超人
Kuangda 匡大

Langxian 浪仙
laoye 老爺
li (profit) 利
li (ritual) 禮
Li Bai 李白
Li Guangdi 李光地
Li Guinian 李龜年
Li Panlong 李攀龍
"Lisao" 離騷
li shi er qiuzhu ye 禮失而求諸野
lishu (ritual book) 禮書
lishu 隸書
Liwen shouchao 禮文手鈔
lixue 理學

li you jing, yi you quan 禮有經，亦有權

li yue bing nong 禮樂兵農

liyuan zhi banyan 梨園之搬演

lizan 禮贊

Liao Ping 廖平

liezhuan 列傳

Linfu 麟紱

Liu Bei 劉備

Liuchao yanshui qi 六朝煙水氣

Liu Jinxian 劉進賢

liuyi 六藝

Liu Yuxi 劉禹錫

Liu Zhu 劉著

Longsan 龍三

Longzhong 隆中

Lou Gongzi 婁公子

Lou Feng 婁琫

Lou Zan 婁瓚

Lu Huashi 盧華士

Lu Jianzeng 盧見曾

Lu Xiangshan 陸象山

Lü Sicheng 呂思誠

Lü mudan 綠牡丹

Ma Chunshang 馬純上 (馬二，馬靜)

Mao Qiling 毛奇齡

mengxue 蒙學

ming 名

Minglun tang 明倫堂

mingshi 名士

Mingtang 明堂

Mochou hu 莫愁湖

Mu Nai 木耐

naqiang zuoshi 拿腔作勢

Nanjing 南京

neipian 內篇

Nie Zheng 聶政

Ninghe 寧和

Niu Buyi 牛布衣

Niu Pulang 牛浦郎

Nü Lunyu 女論語

Nü Xiaojing 女孝經

Pansan 潘三

Pan Shi'en 潘世恩

Pan Zengwei 潘曾瑋 (潘季玉)

Pan Zuyin 潘祖蔭

Pipa ji 琵琶記

Pinhua baojian 品花寶鑒

Pin'niang 聘娘

pingdian 評點

pinghua 平話

"Qi Taigong shijia" 齊太公世家

Qixingtang 齊省堂

Qixingtang zengding *Rulin waishi* 齊省堂增訂儒林外史

"Qian Chibifu" 前赤壁賦

Qian Daxin 錢大昕

Qianlong 乾隆

Qianzi wen 千字文

Qiaoxi zaji 橋西雜記

qiefu 且夫

qin qi shu hua 琴棋書畫

Qin Ying 秦瀛

"Qinyuan chun" 沁園春

qing 情

qingbang 情榜

Qingjiangpu 清江浦

qiufeng 秋風

"Qiuranke zhuan" 虬髯客傳

Qu Gongsun 蘧公孫

Qu Shenfu 蘧駪夫

Qu Yuan 屈原

quan 權
Quanjiao 全椒
Quan Wuyong 權勿用
Qunyuzhai 群玉齋

rang 讓
rangwang 讓王
ren 仁
rendao zhuyi 人道主義
Rensheng bidu shu 人生必讀書
"Ren suji qionggui su piaoyuan" 人宿
　　妓窮鬼訴嫖冤
renxin 人心
renyu 人欲
ru lin dabin 如臨大賓
"Rulin liezhuan" 儒林列傳
Ruyijun zhuan 如意君傳

"San'guozhi" houzhuan 三國志後傳
"San'guozhi" tongsu yanyi 三國志通
　　俗演義
Sanzi jing 三字經
Seng Dao zhi jing jiao 僧道之經醮
Shan shan e e 善善惡惡
shanrang 禪讓
shanshu 善書
Shan Yangyan 單颺言
Shangshu 尚書
Shenbao guan 申報館
Shen Qiongzhi 沈瓊枝
Shensheng 申生
Shen Zuhong 沈祖宏
Shensheng 神聖
shengwang 聖王
shi (history) 史
shi (literatus) 士
Shi Daogu 石道姑
Shijing 詩經
Shi Jing 是鏡
　shijing xiaofu 市井小夫

"Shitou cheng" 石頭城
shixue 實學
shoujie 守節
shu (art) 術
shu (careless) 疏
Shuqi 叔齊
Shun 舜
Shuntian fu 順天府
Shuohuade 說話的
Shuoshude 說書的
Sicun bian 四存編
Siku quanshu 四庫全書
Sishu 四書
Song Lian 宋濂
Song Ruozhao 宋若昭
Suishu 隋書

Taibo ci 泰伯祠
Taimiao 太廟
Taiwang 太王
Taizhou 泰州
Tang Ao 唐敖
Tang Feng 湯奉
Tang Yixiu 唐翼修
Tang Zou 湯奏 (湯鎮臺)
"Taohua yuan" 桃花源
taoli 桃李
Tao Zhenfu 陶甄夫
Tianchang 天長
Tianhua caizi 天花才子
Tianli 天理
Tianmu shanqiao 天目山樵
timu 題目
tongshi 通史
tongxin 童心
tongzan 通贊

waishi 外史
Wanli 萬曆
wanshi 玩世

Wan Sitong 萬斯同

Wang Chengji 王承基

Wang De 王德

"Wang Liben tianya qiufu" 王立本天涯求父

Wang Ren 王仁

Wang Gen 王艮

Wang Hui 王惠

Wang Mingsheng 王鳴盛

Wang Mian 王冕

Wang Shizhen (1526–90) 王世貞

Wang Shizhen (1634–1711) 王士禎

Wang Tai 王太

Wang Xiang 王相

Wang Yangming 王陽明

Wang Youzeng 王又曾

Wang Yuan 王原

Wang Yuhui 王玉輝 (王蘊)

weida 未達

"Wei Gongzi liezhuan" 魏公子列傳

wen 文

wenqu xing 文曲星

Wenxue yianjiu jikan 文學研究集刊

Wen Suchen 文素臣

wen xing chu chu 文行出處

wen yi zai Dao 文以載道

wenyun 文運

wobei 我輩

Woxian caotang 臥閒草堂

Wu Guodui 吳國對

Wuhe 五河

Wu Linqi 吳霖起

Wu Peiyuan 吳培源

Wu Shu 武書

"Xihu qiyue ban" 西湖七月半

xili 習禮

Xizhai 習齋

"Xia yi lou" 夏宜樓

xian 仙

Xianhe 咸和

xianru 先儒

xianyu zige 限於資格

Xianzhai Laoren 閒齋老人

xianzhi yu zige 限制於資格

xianggong 相公

xiangshen 鄉紳

"Xiangyang ge" 襄陽歌

xiangyue 鄉約

Xiao Boquan 蕭柏泉

Xiaochen Ji 小臣稷

Xiao'er yu 小兒語

Xiaoren 小人

xiaoshuo 小説

xiao ti zhong yi 孝悌忠義

Xiaoxue 小學

Xiao Yunxian 蕭雲仙 (蕭采)

xiezi 楔子

Xinling Jun 信陵君

xinxue 心學

Xinyuan Tuishi 惺園退士

Xiong Cilü 熊賜履

Xiucai 秀才

Xiuta yeshi 繡榻野史

Xu "Jinpingmei" 續金瓶梅

Xu Qianxue 徐乾學

xushu 續書

Xu Xian 徐顯

Xu "Xiao'er yu" 續小兒語

Xu Yunlin 徐允臨

Xuzhuan Jurong xian zhi 續纂句容縣志

xueshu 學術

Xue Shiyu 薛時雨 (薛慰農)

xunjie 殉節

Xun Mei 荀玫

Xunzi 荀子

ya de zheyang su 雅的這樣俗
yamen 衙門
yaren 雅人
yashi 雅事
Yan Dawei 嚴大位 (嚴貢生)
Yan Dayu 嚴大育 (嚴監生,
　嚴致和)
Yan Hui 顏回
Yanlan xiaopu 燕蘭小譜
Yanpu zaji 檐曝雜記
Yan Ying 晏嬰
Yang Kai 楊凱
Yang Yuhuan 楊玉環
Yang Zhizhong 楊執中
Yangzhou 揚州
Yangzhou yuanke 揚州原刻
Ye Mingfeng 葉名灃
yeshi 野史
"Yijia fu" 移家賦
yi (meaning) 意
yi (righteousness) 義
yi bujie zhi jie 以不結之結
Yigutang 藝古堂
yi jin youxi 亦近遊戲
yisi 意思
"Yiwen zhi" 藝文志
yizhu 儀注
yizhu dan 儀注單
yinde 陰德
yinzan 引贊
Yongle 永樂
Youbang 幽榜
Yu 禹
Yuduo 予奪
Yu Huaxuan 虞華軒
Yuxiang 玉香
Yu Youda 余有達 (余特)
Yu Youzhong 余有重
　(余持)
Yu Yude 虞育德

Yu Zhong 虞仲
Yue Shifu 越石甫
Yue Yi 樂毅
yun 允

zazi 雜字
zanli 贊禮
ze 則
"Zengbie" 贈別
Zengbu Qixingtang "Rulin waishi"
　增補齊省堂儒林
　外史
Zeng "Guangxianwen" 增廣
　賢文
Zeng Shen 曾參 (曾子)
zhan fengmian 占封面
zhe doushi wode le 這都是
　我的了
zhexie huguang shanse doushi
　womende le 這些湖光山色
　都是我們的了
Zhang Erguan 張二官
Zhang Fei 張飛
zhanghui xiaoshuo 章回小説
Zhang Jingzhai 張靜齋
Zhang Wenhu 張文虎
Zhao Xuezhai 趙雪齋
Zhao Yi 趙翼
Zhen Shiyin 甄士隱
zhengming 正名
zhengshi 正史
zhengtong 正統
zhide 至德
zhiguai 志怪
zhiji 知己
zhijuwen 制舉文
zhiqi 至契
zhishi dan 執事單
zhongren 眾人
Zhongyi ting 忠義廳

Zhongyong 仲雍
Zhongyong 中庸
Zhou Dunyi 周敦頤
Zhou Jin 周進
Zhou Lingwang 周靈王
Zhu Da 朱耷
Zhu Di 朱棣
Zhuge Liang 諸葛亮
Zhulige 注禮閣
Zhu Xi 朱熹
Zhu Yuanzhang 朱元璋
Zhu Yizun 朱彝尊
Zhuzi xue 朱子學
zhuan 傳

Zhuang Shaoguang 莊紹光
(莊尚志)
Zhuang Cunyu 莊存與
zige 資格
zige kunren 資格困人
ziranshi 自然是
zishu 字書
Zong Chen 宗臣
Zou Jifu 鄒吉甫
Zuiyuelou 醉月樓
Zunjing ge 尊經閣
zuo 做
zuozhe zizan 作者自贊

Index

Harvard-Yenching Institute Monograph Series
(titles now in print)